The Vocabulary of Modern French

'Students of the French language will find in this wide-ranging text-book a mass of information and ideas. Teachers will appreciate its useful exercises and bibliographies. And there is food for thought here for all those who wish to improve their understanding of the vagaries and puzzles of the French vocabulary.'

Theodore Zeldin, St Antony's College, Oxford

The Vocabulary of Modern French provides the first comprehensive overview of French vocabulary today: its historical sources, formal organisation and social and stylistic functions.

Topics covered include:
- external influences on the language
- word formation
- semantic change
- style and register
- the relationship between social and lexical change
- attempts at intervention in the development of the language

Each chapter is concluded by notes for further reading, and by suggestions for project work which are designed to increase awareness of specific lexical phenomena and enable the student-reader to use lexicographic databases of all kinds.

The Vocabulary of Modern French is an accessible and fascinating study of the relationship between a nation and its language, as well as providing a key text for all students of modern French.

Hilary Wise is Senior Lecturer in French at Queen Mary and Westfield College, University of London.

York St John

3 8025 00536095 6

The Vocabulary of Modern French

Origins, structure and function

Hilary Wise

LIBRARY, UNIVERSITY COLLEGE
OF RIPON & YORK ST. JOHN
RIPON HG4 2QX

ROUTLEDGE

London and New York

First published 1997
by Routledge
11 New Fetter Lane, London EC4P 4EE

Simultaneously published in the USA and Canada
by Routledge
29 West 35th Street, New York, NY 10001

© 1997 Hilary Wise

Typeset in Times by
J&L Composition Ltd, Filey, North Yorkshire

Printed and bound in Great Britain by
T.J. International Ltd, Padstow, Cornwall

All rights reserved. No part of this book may be reprinted or
reproduced or utilized in any form or by any electronic,
mechanical, or other means, now known or hereafter
invented, including photocopying and recording, or in any
information storage or retrieval system, without permission in
writing from the publishers.

British Library Cataloguing in Publication Data
A catalogue record for this book is available from the British Library

Library of Congress Cataloguing in Publication Data
A catalogue record for this book has been requested

ISBN 0–415–11738–0 (hbk)
    0–415–11739–9 (pbk)

To French friends

Contents

List of figures, maps and tables   x
Preface   xi
List of phonetic symbols and abbreviations   xii

1 Questions and concepts   1
Why study words?   1
What is a word?   2
Grammar versus lexis   3
Words and meaning   3
Is the lexis structured?   4
Do lexical gaps exist?   9
Multiple meaning: polysemy and homonymy   10
The company words keep   12
The origins of words   12
How many words are there in French?   14
Lexical competence   15
The frequency of words   16
Tools of the trade   17
Dictionary entries   18
Dictionaries of the future   21

2 The lexical foundations of French   26
The language of Empire   26
Spoken Latin   26
The Greek element in Latin   31
The Celtic substrate   32
Early Germanic influence   34
History in place names   38
From Latin to French   40

3 *Les racines nobles*: borrowing from Latin and Greek   45
A two-tier lexis?   45
The effects of phonological change   45

Complementarity and rivalry between Latin and French   47
Patterns of borrowing, from Old French to the present day   49
Types and forms of borrowings   51
Internal motivation for borrowing   53
Latin and Greek influence on orthography   54

4 The Romance contribution   59
The Northern dialects   59
Occitan   61
Regional borrowings and niveaux de langue   62
Italian influence   63
Suffixation and assimilation   69
The influence of Spanish, Portuguese and Catalan   71
'Exotic' borrowings in the Romance languages   72

5 English influence: good neighbours or false friends?   79
Contact and exchange   80
Enrichment or redundancy?   86
Borrowings in sheep's clothing: cognates and calques   89
The assimilation of Anglicisms   90
Solutions   95
The outlook   97

6 New words for old: the derivational processes of French   103
Affixation   103
Compound words   120
Current trends in word formation   123

7 Cognitive processes and semantic change   132
The basic issues   132
Metaphor   133
Metonymy   134
Innovation, cliché and dead metaphor   135
Metonymy in everyday language   137
Metaphor, comparison and simile   138
The sources of metaphor   139
Metaphor as conceptual tool   145
Metonymic connections   146
Metonymy and ellipsis   149
Literary imagery   149

8 Lexis in society   157
The structure of semantic fields   158
Centres of expansion   160
The rise and fall of affixes   161
Words and stereotypes   162

Women and words   164
Euphemism, dysphemism and taboo   169

9 Lexis in context   176
Linguistic varieties   176
Linguistic varieties and lexical labels   180
Le français soutenu – *and beyond*   183
Register, sociolect and literary style   186
Occupational styles   189
Advertising – words that sell   195

10 Argot: from criminal slang to *la langue des jeunes*   202
Definitions   202
From argotique *to* familier   203
Argot *and youth culture*   205
The sources of argot   206
Slang and word games   212
Argot, jargon *or* jargot?   214

11 Codification, control and linguistic mythology   220
Establishing the norm   220
The norm and dictionary making   225
Linguistic myths   228
The language and national identity   232
The defence of French   233
The enemy within   237

Bibliography   244
Index   253

Figures, maps and tables

FIGURES

1 The semantic field of *siège*   6
2 Changes in a semantic field   7
3 The relation of hyponymy   9
4 Lexical paradigms associated with the root *sens*   10
5 Larousse *Thésaurus*: organised by conceptual field   20
6 The Celtic languages   32
7 Italian borrowings in French from the thirteenth to the
  nineteenth century   65
8 Gallicisms in English from 1100 to the present   80
9 Anglicisms in French from 1600 to the present   82
10 *Ticket* and related items in English and French   84
11 Borrowings and hyponymy   87
12 Synaesthetic transfer   144
13 Circular on feminisation, *Journal Officiel* 16 March 1986   166
14 Lexical transfer among taboo fields   172

MAPS

1 The Romance languages   27
2 The Gallo-Romance dialects   35
3 Some much-travelled loan words   76

TABLES

1 Class-changing derivational suffixes   107
2 Derivational prefixes   110

Preface

This book aims to give some idea of the variety and complexity of the French lexis, which has over the centuries shown itself to be infinitely and instantly adaptable to the changing needs of its speakers.

The first part of the book describes the most important formative periods, while the two central, pivotal chapters deal with creative lexical processes that have been at work in the language throughout its history. Later chapters look at some of the social and stylistic functions of the lexis, and the book ends with a brief, critical examination of traditional and official attitudes to the language, including attempts that have been made to control and direct it.

The 'Further reading' and project topics supplied at the end of each chapter are designed for serious students of the language; but the non-specialist should also be able to browse comfortably on any topic of special interest, with the help of the subject index. Quotations from early texts have been modernised for greater ease of comprehension.

In the course of preparing such a wide-ranging book, it has been invaluable to have the comments and suggestions of various friends and colleagues. In particular, I would like to thank: Wendy Ayres-Bennett, Marie Caffari, Jenny Cheshire, Tony Gable, Pierre Gounin, Marie-Anne Hintze, Roger Huss, Tony Lodge, Marie-Christine Press, Anne Reymond, Penny Sewell and Neil Smith. Above all, I must thank the many cohorts of students whose curiosity, scepticism and enthusiasm provided the stimulus for this book. Needless to say, any shortcomings are entirely my responsibility.

Hilary Wise
April 1997

The author and publisher also wish to thank the following for permission to reproduce cartoons. Every effort has been made to contact copyright holders and we apologise for any inadvertent omissions.

Page 41: R. Blachon, *Trésors des racines latines*, Jean Bouffartigue & Anne-Marie Delrieu, © Belin, 1981. Page 56: Rene Pétillon, *Lire*,

November 1990. Page 104: Willem, *Libération*, July 1994. Page 123: Du Bouillon, *Le français dans le monde*, no. 243, 1991. Page 142: D. Pessin, *Le Monde*, 1994. Page 167: *Diagonales*, no. 8, supplement to *Le français dans le monde*, no. 220, 1989. Pages 170, 190 & 193: Bruno Léandri, *La Grande Encyclopédie du Dérisoire*, Fluide Glacial, 1996. Page 204: José-Louis Bocquet and Christian Gaudin, *Le Petit Dico Illustré du Docteur Pet*, Editions La Sirène, 1994. Page 214: *Le zonard des étoiles*, Tramber & Jano, Les Humanoïdes Associés. Page 236: Plantu, *Le Monde*, July 1994.

Phonetic symbols and abbreviations

PHONETIC SYMBOLS

b	*b*out	ɲ	si*gn*er	a	*p*atte
d	*d*oute	p	*p*oule	ɑ	*p*âte
f	*f*ou	r	*r*oue	e	*f*ée
g	*g*oût	s	*s*ous	ɛ	*f*ait
ʒ	*j*oue	z	dou*z*e	i	s*i*
dʒ	*j*azz	ʃ	*ch*oux	y	s*u*
j	fo*y*er	t	*t*out	œ	s*œu*r
k	*c*oup	tʃ	ma*tch*	ø	*c*eux
l	*l*oup	v	*v*ous	ə	*l*e
m	*m*ou	w	*ou*i	o	d*os*
n	*n*oue	ɥ	*h*uit	ɔ	d*or*t
ŋ	shoppi*ng*			u	d*ou*x
				ɑ̃	d*an*s
				ɔ̃	b*on*
				ɛ̃	m*ain*
				œ̃	*un*

ABBREVIATIONS

DFC	*Dictionnaire du français contemporain*
GLLF	*Grand Larousse de la langue française*
PLI	*Petit Larousse illustré*
PR	*Petit Robert*
TL	*Thésaurus Larousse*
TLF	*Trésor de la langue française*

Chapter 1

Questions and concepts

WHY STUDY WORDS?

Words are the elements of language most closely associated with the way we conceptualise the world we live in. As our world changes, so do the words that reflect it. It is therefore through the study of vocabulary, or lexis,[1] that we can discover which areas of experience are of particular importance or carry a particular emotional charge for a speech community, at any given point in time. Certain fields may be taboo, and veiled in euphemism; some may suddenly burgeon while others dwindle and fade; whole strata of the lexis may be exclusive to particular social groups, or restricted to use in certain types of discourse. It is up to the lexicologist to detect such concentrations, gaps and shifts, and to draw conclusions which will inevitably be closely linked to the social and cultural history of the speakers concerned.

The lexis of a language is also one of the surest reflections of contact with other cultures. Lying geographically at the heart of western Europe, France has necessarily been subject to migration and conquest, and has been involved in the ebb and flow of political, cultural and religious movements of all kinds, all of which have left their mark on the lexis (see Chapters Two to Five). While most linguistic influences stem from interaction with immediate neighbours, trading links with the wider world and colonial adventures have introduced more 'exotic' words into the language; this small but culturally significant element of the lexis is looked at briefly in Chapter Four. Whatever their origins, once in the language words are subject to complex processes of change and recycling, through which new words are constantly being formed, in response to the changing needs of the community. As these creative processes are responsible for the vast majority of items in the language, Chapters Six and Seven which investigate them may be considered pivotal to the book.

If we are to grasp fully the specificity of French, then in a sense we should know what makes it different from its neighbours. Linguistic research suggests that grammatical differences between languages are essentially superficial; if significant differences do exist, they are primarily lexical. There has been much (sometimes almost mystical) speculation about the correspondence between linguistic differences and different 'world views'. A proper exploration of the subject is beyond the scope of this book, but it is a theme which is touched on at various points, most notably in Chapter Seven.

WHAT IS A WORD?

What constitutes 'a word' would seem to be self-evident, in that in their written form words are separated by spaces, in most languages. These spaces do not of course correspond to pauses in speech, in which there may be few clues as to where words begin and end (see p. 231). Nevertheless, irrespective of phonetic clues or orthographic conventions, words are usually identifiable as freely mobile units, able to occur in a wide variety of environments, and carrying a relatively stable meaning. Some elements traditionally thought of as words are, however, limited in their patterns of distribution – like the pronouns *je*, *se* or *le*, which are closely associated with verbs, and which in some ways behave more like appendages or 'affixes' than like independent words.

Another grey area is that of 'compound' words; *grands-parents* and *bonhomme* are semantically and distributionally single units, although they consist of elements which can themselves function independently as words. In other sequences of adjective + noun, like *petits pois* or *petit-bourgeois*, it is less clear whether we are dealing with a single compound word or a phrase. The much-disputed question of where to draw the line between the two is discussed further in Chapter Six.

Another problem with the term 'word' is that it can be used in two quite different senses. In one sense, *savoir* and *su*, or *aller* and *va*, are different words, in that they differ in form; in another sense they are different forms of the same 'word', in that only one entry in the dictionary is required for each verb, whose basic meaning remains constant, whatever the person or tense involved. In referring to 'word' in this latter, global sense, linguists often prefer to use the term **lexeme** or **lexical item**. Some dictionary entries are phrasal in form, like *avoir peur* or *se rendre compte*, but have the semantic coherence of single lexical items. One might go so far as to argue that idioms like *casser la croûte*, *rouler sa bosse* are also single lexical items, on similar grounds.

Words may be the most obvious meaningful units of a language, but they are not the most fundamental. Many can be analysed into smaller, though less mobile, meaningful elements. *Démontable*, for example, consists of three parts: the prefix *dé-*, the root *-mont-* and the suffix *-able* – all of which are to be found in other words in the language, with much the same meanings. Affixes like *dé-* and *-able* are often given separate entries in dictionaries, in recognition of their lexical status. The way in which these minimal lexical elements (known as **morphemes**) are organised into lexical items is investigated in Chapter Six.

GRAMMAR VERSUS LEXIS

We have already seen that the distinction between *savoir* and *su* is a grammatical rather than a lexical one, and would be discussed in a grammar book, where verbal paradigms are set out, rather than in a dictionary. Certain words may be considered grammatical rather than lexical elements, typically carrying information such as the tense, aspect or person of a verb, or the number or gender of a noun, or indicating relations between different parts of the sentence. Examples would be auxiliary verbs, pronouns, determiners and prepositions. Their incorporation into a dictionary poses something of a problem for the lexicographer, who is generally obliged to provide a good deal of complex grammatical information. (Compare, for example, the adjacent entries of the essentially grammatical *de* and the lexical *dé-*, in the *Petit Robert* or any other monolingual dictionary.)

Some words may have a double function. In *il a une nouvelle voiture*, *avoir* is a lexical item roughly synonymous with *posséder*, while in *il a acheté une voiture* it has the grammatical function of expressing past tense. Similarly, *faire* in *il fait une très bonne soupe* has a lexical function, but a grammatical (specifically, causative) one in *il fait construire une maison*. In some languages, grammatical categories like 'past' or 'causative' may be more clearly grammaticalised, as an affix attached to the verb.

Unlike lexical items, grammatical elements form small, closed subsystems which change only very gradually with time. The lexis of a language, on the other hand, is open-ended, a potentially infinite set of elements in a constant state of flux, subject to more or less conscious manipulation by its speakers. This is perhaps one reason why professional linguists, interested in explaining just how languages work, have tended to focus on the study of grammar. It is a difficult, but conceivable, task to discover how limited subsets of elements combine, according to a finite set of rules and formal constraints. The size and volatility of the lexis, and its apparent lack of structure, make it less amenable to analysis and to the construction of grand, explanatory theories; lexicologists have to be content with investigating bite-sized samples of the lexis, on the basis of which they may hope to make some interesting generalisations about the system as a whole.

WORDS AND MEANING

The term 'meaning' has been used rather freely so far, as if its own meaning is self-evident. But it has been the subject of much debate and numerous interpretations, by both philosophers and linguists. To enter fully into the debate would take us far beyond the scope of this book. The next few pages simply focus on those aspects of meaning which will be relevant to topics raised in subsequent chapters.

For present purposes, one important distinction is that between **denotation** or 'reference', and **connotation**. Many words 'refer to' or designate things or events in the real world (that which is actually being referred to is known as the 'referent'). One could in fact claim that this is one of the prime functions of language. Most speakers will agree on the denotational value, or 'reference' of *taureau*, for example, although they might express it in different ways. The definition of *taureau* given in the *Petit Robert* is: 'mammifère ruminant domestique, mâle de la vache, apte à la reproduction'. However, in addition to referential meaning, words frequently carry secondary associations – in the case of *taureau*, ones of strength and irascibility. The *Petit Robert* makes an additional observation to this effect: 'un animal puissant et irritable'. Such associations or 'connotations' may be widely shared by the speech community, in which case they often give rise to metaphors which become part of the lexical fabric of the language (see Chapter Seven).

It is possible to differentiate the two types of meaning by applying a relatively simple test. If a statement includes elements of referential meaning which are contradictory, it will be bizarre to the point of being un-interpretable. It is therefore very difficult to make sense of '*Ce taureau est femelle*' because part of the referential meaning of *taureau* is 'male'. If however a statement contradicts only the connotations of one its constituent items, the result may be surprising, but make perfectly good sense, as with the sentence '*Ce taureau est très docile*'.

Connotations are often associated with the social context in which a word is habitually used. A noun like *policier* is neutral, in the sense that it can occur in many different kinds of text and discourse. From a denotational point of view, *keuf* is synonymous with it, but, occurring as it does in informal conversation, especially among the young, it carries rather different connotations, implying an attitude of humour, hostility or lack of respect. (Such non-referential distinctions in the lexis are the focus of Chapters Nine and Ten.) Since the two words are essentially synonymous, from a referential point of view, *les keufs* could be substituted for *les policiers* in any sentence, without the risk of producing a nonsensical utterance; at most, the hearer will find it stylistically inappropriate.

IS THE LEXIS STRUCTURED?

We have noted that, compared to the tightly structured grammatical system of a language, the lexis appears to be amorphous and fluid. However, it is far from being a random collection of unrelated items, as dictionaries, with their essentially arbitrary arrangement of words in alphabetical order, might suggest.

The father of European structuralism, Ferdinand de Saussure, asserted that the value of every element in a linguistic system – at the grammatical, phonological or lexical level – is defined by the value of neighbouring elements. A change in one part of the system is therefore bound to have repercussions for adjacent elements. Colour terms, which impose structure on what is actually an unbroken continuum, are often taken to illustrate the interrelatedness of lexical items. In a sense *vert* is defined by the terms *bleu* and *jaune*; if *vert* was not part of the system (and some languages do not have a corresponding term), then the meaning of *bleu*, or *jaune*, or both, would cover that semantic ground. Similarly, in French there are a number of words corresponding approximately to 'wall' in English: *mur*, *muraille* and *paroi*; if *muraille* did not exist, *mur* would have a broader meaning. Conversely, when new items such as borrowings are introduced, they often have the effect of reducing the semantic scope of existing items. Many instances of this will be found in Chapters Four and Five, which discuss some of the external influences on the language.

Semantic fields

To investigate more fully the relations between closely connected items, the notion of 'semantic field' was elaborated in the 1920s and 1930s (see Lyons 1977, vol. 1: 250–61). A field usually corresponds to a generic term in the language, within which the meaning of other lexical items may be subsumed. Some, like *plante*, are very wide-ranging, covering other items like *fleur*, *arbuste*, *cactus*, *arbre*, and so on, which in turn include terms like *chêne*, *aulne*, *peuplier*, etc. It is not only scientific taxonomies in fields like botany and chemistry that lend themselves to such hierarchical arrangements. Terms for human artefacts, and even abstract ideas, can be analysed in this way.

To take a more detailed example, we might look at one part of the broad semantic field covered by *meubles* – that of *siège*, represented in diagrammatic form in Figure 1. What is important is what differentiates the various items in the field. *Banc* and *banquette* differ from *fauteuil*, *chaise*, *tabouret* and *pouf* in that they are seats designed for more than one person. *Banquette* has the further specification in most dictionaries, that it is upholstered. *Fauteuil* and *chaise* differ in that *fauteuil* means a seat with armrests. They are both differentiated from *tabouret* and *pouf*, in that they have backs, where the latter do not. A *chauffeuse* is a low *chaise*, for sitting by the fire, a *bergère* 'wing chair' and a *berceuse* 'rocking chair' are specific types of *fauteuil*, and so on. The interrelatedness of semantic fields is shown by the items *canapé*, *sofa* and *divan*, which can be linked to both *siège* and *lit*, since they are designed for both sitting and lying.

This series of items can also be used to demonstrate the difference between the terms semantic field, lexical field and conceptual field, which

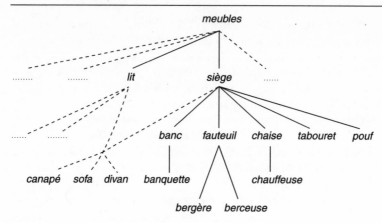

Figure 1 The semantic field of *siège*

are often used somewhat interchangeably. One can imagine a language in which there is a term for all pieces of furniture designed for both sitting and lying, which would therefore include the terms *canapé*, *sofa* and *divan*. It is not difficult to conceptualise, and if such a term were introduced into French, speakers would probably have no problem using it appropriately. Similarly, some languages may not have a term corresponding to *meubles*, but their speakers will nonetheless be able to perceive the difference between pieces of furniture and other household objects, such as pots and pans, soft furnishings, white goods, and so on. In other words, it is quite possible to have a concept without a corresponding lexical item. The very flexibility of our conceptualising processes makes possible rapid transformations in the lexis we use.

If we work from concepts to words, we can think in terms of concepts being mapped onto lexical items. This is useful where no broad cover term exists, corresponding to an entire field; for example, we might wish to investigate the scope of words in English covered by the concept 'positive mental state', 'social hierarchies' or 'four-wheeled vehicles'. In such cases, the notion of **conceptual field** is appropriate. But if we think rather in terms of the semantic ground covered by specific items, all included in the scope of one cover term, then **lexical field** is more appropriate. The term **semantic field** tends to be used in both senses, and of course there are many cases where lexical and conceptual fields coincide.

The much vaguer notion of **associative field** is also used by linguists and psychologists, to refer to words which are psychologically related for a speaker, although the semantic connections between them may be far from obvious.[2]

One way of representing semantic fields, favoured by the early field theorists, is to visualise semantic 'space' as a patchwork of interlocking

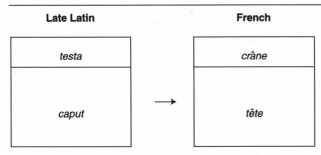

Figure 2 Changes in a semantic field

items. This is particularly useful in highlighting the way in which semantic changes occur within a language. Figure 2, for example, shows how the same conceptual field is divided, in Late Latin and in modern French.

Latin *caput* was the general word for 'head' (gradually changing in form to become *chef*), while *testa* (which became *tête*) was introduced, first as a slang term, and then as an anatomical term to mean 'skull'.

During the Middle Ages, *tête* gradually gained ground at the expense of *chef*, which eventually became relegated to metaphorical uses. *Crâne* was borrowed from Latin (*cranium*) in the fourteenth century, and came to fulfil much the same role as *testa* did in Late Latin. The basic conceptual field is therefore divided up in much the same way, but after considerable reorganisation of the lexical material involved.

Tracking developments in semantic fields is of particular interest if the fields represent key cultural or intellectual concepts. Trier, for example, examined the way in which terms within the conceptual field of 'knowledge' in German were transformed in the course of one century, in the Middle Ages. He showed how lexical changes corresponded to changes both in social structure and in the way in which practical, intellectual and spiritual kinds of knowledge were perceived (see Lyons 1977, vol. 1: 256–7). Similar work was carried out by Matoré (1953: 99–117), who investigated a variety of conceptual fields including that of 'art' and related concepts in French, from the eighteenth to the nineteenth century.

Field theory can also be used to demonstrate the different ways in which two languages structure essentially the same conceptual field. Even English and French, representing closely related cultures, make different distinctions within the same field. If a diagram were to be drawn up for English 'seat', corresponding to Figure 1, we would find that 'armchair' would have to be included under 'chair', and that there is no equivalent for *chauffeuse*.

Semantic components

The notion of 'inclusion', clearly central to semantic field theory, was made more explicit by the analysis of denotational meaning in terms of semantic components or features – an analytic method, known as **componential analysis**, which had been successfully developed in relation to phonological systems (see Kempson 1977: 18–20). Essentially, the meaning of the word can be viewed as a bundle of semantic features, at least one of which serves to distinguish it from the meaning of other words. These features are established by comparing the meanings of lexical items that are semantically very close. As we have seen, the difference between *fauteuil* and *chaise* is the presence or absence of armrests – what we might schematise as +*accoudoirs* and −*accoudoirs*. This same feature proves relevant to the semantic make-up of the series *canapé*, *sofa* and *divan* (see below). *Divan* and *canapé* typically do not have armrests, whereas *sofa* does. On the other hand, *divan* and *canapé* are distinguished by the fact that the meaning of *canapé* includes the feature +*dossier*, while *divan* excludes it.

canapé	sofa	divan
+*dossier*	+*dossier*	−*dossier*
−*accoudoirs*	+*accoudoirs*	−*accoudoirs*

The ultimate, albeit unrealised aim of this type of analysis was to discover the finite set of components which make up the meanings of all the lexical items in the language – the semantic primes, so to speak. While it is clear that some components, such as ±*animé*, or ±*humain*, are shared by many items, and are no doubt universal, as we move down the hierarchies, more and more highly specific components need to be added, with some, like ±*dossier*, distinguishing only a handful of items. The most complex items, like *berceuse*, may have a feature (in this case +*pied courbe*) which possibly occurs nowhere else in the lexis.

One can see that, working downwards through the hierarchy, the semantic components of one item are included in the semantic make-up of the items immediately below it. This relation of inclusion is given the technical name of **hyponymy**: *banc*, *chaise*, *fauteuil*, etc. are all **hyponyms** of *siège*, which is itself a hyponym of *meuble*, and so on. The cover term is known as the **superordinate**; hence *siège* is the superordinate of *fauteuil*, and *banc* the superordinate of *banquette*. Hyponyms of the same superordinate can usefully be termed **co-hyponyms**. It is not uncommon for a term to be used both as a superordinate and a hyponym: *parent* in the sense of 'parent' is a hyponym of parent in the sense of 'relation', together with other terms like *oncle* and *cousin* (see Figure 3).

For present purposes, we do not need to delve more deeply into componential analysis, except to say that it applies more sucessfully to some types of lexical item than others.[3] It is not, for example, particularly well suited to the analysis of items which represent degrees of gradation along a continuum, such as colours. Suffice to say that semantic components and the notion of hyponymy are useful when it comes to looking at fine

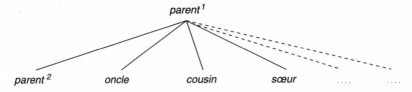

Figure 3 The relation of hyponymy

distinctions of referential meaning, and at the processes of semantic change.

DO LEXICAL GAPS EXIST?

Everyone knows of words which are particularly difficult to translate succinctly – *Schadenfreude* in German, or *mondain* in French. Usually they embody complex social or psychological notions and may require lengthy paraphrases by way of translation. If they are perceived as fulfilling a need they may well be borrowed; hence the French borrowings 'panache' and 'savoir-faire' in English, or the Anglicisms *fairplay* and *stress* in French. But if there is no corresponding word in the language, should we then think of there being a gap in the lexis?

Our brief examination of semantic fields showed that different languages – or rather their speakers – make different choices when it comes to lexicalising experience. For example, French *chaise* and English 'chair' embody slightly different concepts, but it would be a rather negative approach to claim that a superordinate is 'missing' in French, and a hyponym in English. In Figure 1 there are various points in the diagram where lexical items sharing a number of features could be given a superordinate, such as *sofa*, *canapé* and *divan*, and all the other hyponyms of *siège* which share the feature *pour une personne*. Carried to its logical conclusion, the filling of all such 'gaps' would lead to a totally unwieldy proliferation of lexical items. Nevertheless, somewhat chauvinistic arguments are sometimes based on differences of lexical structure, in efforts to claim that one language is 'richer' or 'more precise' than another. Arguments of this kind that have been used in relation to French are examined briefly in Chapter Eleven (pp. 228–32).

The processes of word formation, which are discussed in Chapter Six, have always been the major source of new words for the language. From a single root any number of new words may be derived by the addition of prefixes and suffixes. The root *-sens-*, for example, has given rise to over a score of words, including those given in Figure 4.

Such words form semi-regular series, or **lexical paradigms**. Some processes are particularly productive; at the moment, for example, it is difficult to monitor all the words being created by the addition of *télé-* or *-iser*.

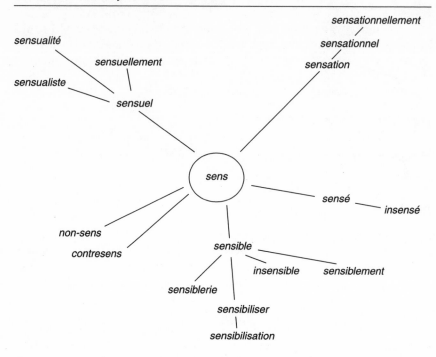

Figure 4 Lexical paradigms associated with the root *sens*

It is usually possible to add the adjectival suffix *-al* or *-el* to a noun ending in *-sion* or *-tion*, as in *passionnel*, or *national*. But no adjective *compassionnel* exists corresponding to *compassion*, no doubt because the adjective *compatissant* 'compassionate' exists. Two adjectives in Figure 4, *insensé* and *insensible*, begin with the very common negative prefix *in-*, but no negative counterpart *insensationnel* exists, alongside *sensationnel*. Should we then say that a gap exists in this particular lexical paradigm? Again, to exploit all the derivational potential of the language would lead to unmanageable redundancy in the lexis.

MULTIPLE MEANING: POLYSEMY AND HOMONYMY

It will be clear from Chapter Seven that the meaning of words is subject to constant change. In particular, words that have been in the language for a long time have often accumulated a range of quite disparate meanings. One lexical item may therefore belong to more than one semantic field, and have quite distinct sets of semantic features; *berceuse*, for example, means 'lullaby' as well as 'rocking chair', and *bergère* means 'shepherdess' as well as 'wing chair'.

The problem in such cases is whether we should think in terms of single lexical items with rather different meanings, or of quite separate lexical items, which just happen to have the same form (which most people would agree to be the case with, say, *botte* meaning 'boot' and *botte* meaning 'sheaf'). The latter can be recognised as **homonyms**, which are generally given quite separate entries in the dictionary.[4]

Banquette means a built-in seat, such as a window-seat or car-seat, as well as a free-standing piece of furniture, but all senses have several semantic features in common, and it seems reasonable in this instance to consider *banquette* a single item, with a range of related meanings – a case of what is known as **polysemy**.

As often happens in matters of linguistic classification, it is not always easy to know where to draw the line between homonymy and polysemy. 'Difference of meaning' is after all a very elastic notion. *Siège*, for example, means both 'seat' and 'siege'. One might well claim that these are two separate words that have nothing in common, semantically. But with a little imagination, one could say that in a siege, an army is encamped, or seated round a town or fortress. This is, in fact, the approximate historical connection between the two senses.

However, since Saussure made the sharp distinction between the synchronic and diachronic study of language, it has been almost an article of faith with linguists not to take facts about the history of a language into account in a synchronic analysis. The vast majority of speakers are after all not aware of the etymologies of the words they use, and a language functions as a system quite independently of the forms which have given rise to it. For example, the fact that *voler* 'to fly' and *voler* 'to steal' can both be traced back to Latin *volare* 'to fly' is irrelevant to their current status, and they can be considered homonyms. Conversely, one might wish to class as one polysemous word *sens* 'sense' and *sens* 'direction', despite the fact that they have different etymologies, on the grounds that they are both connected with human cognitive faculties. In borderline cases, however, like *sens* and *siège*, one suspects that lexicographers are often influenced by etymology to class words with a common etymology as polysemous rather than homonymous, if any current semantic connection can be found.

Additional features distinguishing words which are otherwise identical in form are differences of word class and gender. It is generally assumed that a difference of word class (the verb *savoir*, versus the noun *savoir*), or of gender (*un aide* versus *une aide*) must imply homonymy rather than polysemy. It is certainly more convenient to give them separate entries in a dictionary, but from a semantic and historical point of view such pairs are obviously closely connected. Occasionally a pair of homophones like *dessin* 'drawing', 'design' and *dessein* 'plan' are closely related semantically and etymologically, but since they are differentiated in their spelling they are never considered as classifiable as a single polysemous item.

THE COMPANY WORDS KEEP

So far, words as meaningful units have been considered as forming vertical or paradigmatic hierarchies, connected by the relation of inclusion. But words are also connected syntagmatically, in linear fashion along the horizontal axis. There are certain constraints imposed by the syntax on the relative ordering of nouns, adjectives, verbs, and so on. A determiner like *les* or *ces* will always be followed by an adjective or noun, while an object pronoun like *me* or *se* must be followed by a verb. Certain constraints also operate on the specific choice of lexical item that may be inserted at any given point in the syntagmatic chain. The verb *hocher* can only be followed by *la tête*: as in *il a hoché la tête* 'he nodded', while *hongre* 'gelded' can only modify *cheval*. At the other end of the scale, there is very considerable freedom in the way lexical items are combined; the verbs *naître* and *mourir* can take any subject specified as '+animate' (unless the word is being used metaphorically – an issue discussed in Chapter Seven). *Décéder*, on the other hand, is more limited in its **collocations**, or the words with which it may co-occur; its subject must be '+human'.

A good dictionary entry includes information on such constraints, sometimes known as **selectional restrictions**, either in the definition of the word or, less directly, in the examples it provides. In particular, the collocations of lexicalised metaphorical extensions have to be specified, as they cannot always be deduced from the original meaning; knowing that *blond* refers to hair colour, we can deduce that it may co-occur with *barbe* or *moustache*; but the dictionary must specify that we can also talk about *une bière blonde* 'light ale', 'lager'. Mastery of the lexis of a foreign language includes knowledge of the selectional restrictions which apply to its items – not an easy task since these often fail to correspond across languages. In English 'croak' is the sound made both by crows and by frogs or toads; in French *coasser* is used for the latter, *croasser* for the former.

THE ORIGINS OF WORDS

While synchronic linguistics only really developed in the Western world this century, interest in the origin of languages, and of individual words, goes back much further (see Robins 1967). The term **etymology** is used to refer to the history of the form and meaning of individual words, and also to the field of study as a whole. An **etymon** is the word or root which we can consider to be in some sense the original ancestor of a word – or more frequently, of a whole set of words. Such are the effects of both semantic and phonological change that words with the same etymon as their root morpheme may have very little in common today, in form or meaning.

One might guess for example that *hôte* and *hôtel* are related, but the connections with *hôpital, hospitalité* and *otage* are less clear, although they are all derived from the Latin *hospes ~ hospitis*, meaning both 'guest' and 'host'. Even more disparate is the etymological 'family' deriving from Latin *causa* 'cause', which includes *chose, accuser, causer* 'cause' and *causer* 'chat'.

The vast majority of French words are of Latin origin. The fact that so many etymologically related words vary greatly in form is partly due to the tradition of borrowing extensively from the parent language. (The reasons for this tradition and its linguistic effects are discussed in Chapters Three and Six.) Words have also entered French from other Romance languages (that is, languages which are also descended from Latin), in which they have undergone a separate phonological and semantic development, hence adding to the formal and semantic variety of Latin-based words in French. For example, *œuvre, ouvrage, ouvrable* and *ouvrier* can all be traced in a direct line to the Latin root etymon *opus ~ operis* 'work', as it developed on French territory, while *opéra* was borrowed from Italian in the seventeenth century, and a whole range of words, including *opération, opérable* and *opuscule*, were borrowed from Latin, or created from the Latin root, from the medieval period onwards.

Although the origins of most French words are specified confidently in the larger monolingual dictionaries, the notion of 'origin' is not unproblematic. Thanks to the work of historical linguists from the late eighteenth century onwards, we know a great deal, not only about the Romance family but also about the development of the wider Indo-European family, to which Latin belongs. Latin, Greek and Sanskrit are the oldest Indo-European languages for which we have written evidence, but we can partially reconstruct a common ancestor, Proto-Indo-European, spoken at least three thousand years BC in the vicinity of southern Russia. Further than that, we cannot go. One can often reconstruct an etymon underlying known Greek and Latin words, and words from other Indo-European families, like Celtic and Germanic. We know, for example, that the Proto-Indo-European root meaning 'die' must have been pronounced something like *mer- – ancestor to modern English 'murder' and French *mourir*, amongst others.[5]

So when we are trying to pinpoint the origins of a word, how far back in time should we go? As far as French is concerned, the Latin spoken in Gaul early in the Christian era is usually given as the starting point, or, in the case of learned borrowings, the written, classical form of the language (see Chapters Two and Three). On this basis *bon* (< *bonus* 'good') and *beau* (< *bellus* 'pretty') are assigned different etymons. However, if earlier forms were to be taken into account, one would have to recognise a shared etymon, since *bellus* was originally a diminutive form of *bonus*. Similarly, *ivre* (< *ebrius*) and *sobre* (< *sobrius*) are also ultimately related, since *sobrius* derived from a forerunner of *ebrius*.

Many learned borrowings were made from Classical Greek roots, in the creation of much scientific and medical terminology in French, and naturally enough it is the Greek etymon that is given as the origin of such words in a dictionary. But since Latin and Greek are related, as we have indicated, it is sometimes possible to posit an earlier etymon, common to both Latin and Greek. If we were taking a 'shallow' interpretation to the notion of origin, we would give *soleil* (< Latin *soliculum*) and *hélium* (< Greek *helios*) quite separate etymologies. But if we probe deeper into the past, we can assign to them a common ancestor, which was pronounced something like **sawol*. Similarly, most dictionaries give one etymological origin to the words *serf*, *servir*, *sergent* and *concierge*, and another to *garder*, *garer*, *garnir* and *guérir*; and yet both strands can ultimately be traced to the Indo-European root **swer*, meaning 'to take care'.

In dictionaries it is the usual practice to give the most immediate source of a borrowing. The origin of *opéra* is therefore generally given as Italian, rather than Latin. There is however a certain amount of variation and indeed arbitrariness in the approach of different lexicographers. For example, although the *Petit Robert* gives *opéra* as coming from Italian, on the 'first stop' basis, the nineteenth-century borrowing from English, *rail*, is traced two steps further back in the past, to Old French *reille* and thence to Latin *regula*. Dictionaries also tend to give fuller etymological histories of much-travelled 'exotic' words, such as *pyjama*, coming into French from Hindi via English, or *douane*, which was borrowed first from Persian into Arabic, and from Arabic into Italian, at which point it came into contact with French (see Chapter Four).

HOW MANY WORDS ARE THERE IN FRENCH?

To ask how many words there are in a language seems to be a reasonable question, and estimates have certainly been made. However, given the built-in capacity of the lexis for innovation, by the kinds of processes mentioned earlier, it is impossible to know just how many different words are in current use. The question also presupposes that we know the answers to several others:

• How should 'French' be defined? As any variety of the language, spoken anywhere in the world, or as the accepted standard language of metropolitan France?
• Should one include words that were commonly used in the past, but that are now largely confined to written texts?
• How frequently does a foreign word have to be used for it to be considered part of the language?

We must remember too the technical problems mentioned earlier, of defining the notion of 'word', and of distinguishing between homonymy and polysemy.

It would take several volumes to try and answer these questions, without reaching any very definite conclusions. Perhaps we should look instead at the words that are to be found in current dictionaries, bearing in mind that these are far from being exhaustive inventories of the modern lexis.

The largest dictionary (as opposed to encyclopedic work) is the recent *Trésor de la langue française*, containing over 100,000 lexical items; it was based on a huge corpus of predominantly literary texts, so that many technical and slang terms are excluded. Moreover, it was the policy of the editors to exclude most words that occurred less than 100 times in the corpus (see 'Tools of the trade', below). Dictionaries are clearly artificial constructs, the inventories of many different speakers – or rather writers – and in the course of their compilation conscious choices are operated by the lexicographer.

It has been suggested (Müller 1985: 124) that there may in fact be well in excess of half a million words in the language altogether – but here we are entering into the realms of speculation.

Another approach to quantifying the lexis is to ask how many words an individual speaker might know or use.

LEXICAL COMPETENCE

The Chomskyan notion of the linguistic 'competence' of the individual has been successfully applied at the grammatical level. It assumes a largely unconscious knowledge of a finite set of rules and structural principles, which enable a speaker to produce a potentially infinite set of sentences, and to recognise well-formed sentences produced by others using the same set of rules and principles. Can such a notion of linguistic competence be extended to account for knowledge of the lexis? It could perhaps be applied to the rules of word production, referred to above. For example, a speaker coming across the word *démontable* for the first time will recognise it as a well-formed French word (unlike, say, *abledémonte*), and will even be able to make a reasonable guess at its meaning. New words are constantly being produced according to these rules, although only a small number actually survive and take root in the language. However, not all words are 'transparent' in this way; most have to be learnt as unanalysable units.

The lexis is also different from the grammatical system in that lexical knowledge is quite variable from speaker to speaker. (It is unlikely that a policeman with a keen interest in angling and DIY will have the same personal lexicon as a computer programmer who goes rock-climbing and bird-watching in her spare time.) Moreover, in the course of our lifetime, our lexical knowledge is likely to change significantly, which is not the case with grammatical competence. Nor is there any parallel in grammar with the phenomenon of 'half-knowing' the form or meaning of a lexical item. We may know that a word is mildly insulting, or connected with open-heart surgery, but feel unable to use it accurately ourselves. In the case of polysemous words we may be aware of some but not all of their meanings.

Knowledge of items which, unlike *démontable*, are not rule-based, is perhaps better captured by something closer to the Saussurean dichotomy of *langue* versus *parole*, which is more social in character. *Langue* is the common pool of linguistic knowledge upon which all may draw, but which no individual masters in its entirety. *Parole* is the use the individual makes of *langue*. As Saussure says in his *Cours de linguistique générale* (1949: 30): 'La langue n'est complète dans aucun [cerveau], elle n'existe parfaitement que dans la masse'; and (p. 31): 'Elle [la langue] est la partie sociale du langage, extérieure à l'individu...'.

There is no reliable way of capturing the *parole* of an individual (see Miller, 1991, 134–8), still less the *langue* of the entire community, with regard to the lexis. At most, we can analyse the lexis contained in an author's published works, thanks to optical readers allied to powerful computers. However, the comparison of large numbers of such corpora may at least help to reveal the elements of the lexis in common use at any point in time.

THE FREQUENCY OF WORDS

From the 1940s and 1950s, when computers started to be used for analysing large amounts of linguistic data, various databases were established, primarily to investigate the frequency with which different lexical items occurred (see Müller 1985: 114–33). Gougenheim *et al.*'s study (1964), based on the transcription of thousands of spoken utterances, suggested that in spoken mode at least the active vocabulary of an average speaker is something like 8,000 words.[6] In the written mode, analysis of one edition of *Le Monde* in 1972 gave 4,800 different items, while the *Dictionnaire des fréquences* (1971), based on a huge literary corpus which was the forerunner of that used for the *Trésor de la langue française*, revealed about 70,000.

It was no surprise to discover that in all types of discourse – spoken, journalistic and literary – grammatical words were by far the most frequent; the thirty 'top' items were all words like pronouns, determiners, prepositions, auxiliary verbs, conjunctions and the like. Then came lexical items with very broad meanings like *mettre, aller, autre, petit, grand...* Any one text or utterance consists of many occurrences of this kind of word, plus a far wider range of much less frequently occurring words. To be more specific, in the corpus of the *Dictionnaire des fréquences*, a mere 907 words each occurred more than 7,000 times, accounting for about 90 per cent of the total corpus, and 5,800 words occurred between 7,000 and 500 times (about 8 per cent of the corpus). This means that the vast majority of the 70,000 items in the corpus were extremely rare, with 21,000 occurring only once. A similar pattern, albeit on a reduced scale, emerged from the Gougenheim study.[7]

If a chronological perspective is brought to bear on such data, some interesting facts emerge about the historical formation of the modern lexis. Müller (1985: 60–4), using the corpus of *Le Monde*, suggests that as many as 40 per cent of the words commonly used in contemporary French were already in the language by the fourteenth century, with only about 4 per cent being twentieth-century borrowings or creations. The most deeply embedded of all seem to be the grammatical elements. As Müller says (p. 62): 'Plus un mot est fréquent, plus il est ancien' – casting doubt on the widely held belief that the modern lexis has been subject to profound transformations.

What emerges then, for the lexis as a whole and probably for the lexical competence of the individual, both synchronically and diachronically, is a kind of cosmological image of a lexis which consists of a dense, stable core, surrounded by layers of progressively more rarefied, volatile material.

TOOLS OF THE TRADE

Since the first monolingual dictionaries were produced in the seventeenth century as part of the overall process of codification of the language (see Chapter Eleven), the readership has broadened progressively. No longer designed solely for the cultivated reader seeking to adhere to the approved norm, many dictionaries now aim to reflect current spoken usage, and to provide lexical inventories of specialist technical fields of all kinds.

The eighteenth century saw the birth of the encyclopedia, a close cousin to the dictionary. But where the dictionary provides essentially linguistic information, which should enable the reader to use a term appropriately in everyday situations, encyclopedias give less information about the lexical item and more about its referent. For example, the *Dictionnaire du français contemporain (DFC)* defines *sel* as 'substance incolore, cristallisée, soluble dans l'eau, d'un goût piquant qui sert à l'assaisonnement et à la conservation des aliments', and adds metaphors and set phrases in which it occurs, such as 'mettre son grain de sel' 'to put one's oar in'; the dictionary– encyclopedia, the *Petit Larousse illustré (PLI)*, gives the same basic definition as the *DFC*, but omits the metaphorical and idiomatic uses; it also explains the difference between rock salt and sea salt and mentions some industrial as well as culinary uses.

In addition, encyclopedias give information about people and places, whose names cannot be thought of as forming part of any structured linguistic system. Photographs, maps and diagrams help to convey the kind of information given in encyclopedias, but are rarely felt to be necessary in dictionaries.

Monolingual dictionaries range in size from the *Micro-Robert* (35,000 words) to the nine-volume *Grand Robert* (80,000 words), and largest of all, the recently completed *Trésor de la langue française* (100,000 words). Most publishers in this field – Robert, Larousse and Hachette being the best-known – produce a substantial single-volume dictionary containing 50–60,000 words. Their editorial policy differs to some extent. For example, the *Petit Larousse* (about 45,000 words), updated every few years, contains many technical expressions and words from informal registers, but fewer literary or archaic items than the *Petit Robert*. The most traditional and normative dictionary remains that of the French Academy; its most recent edition, currently being republished, contains about 45,000 words, as it is very cautious about accepting neologisms, borrowings and technical words (see Chapter Eleven).

The last twenty to thirty years have seen a veritable explosion of specialist works: dictionaries of acronyms, slang, homeopathy, sport, mythology, genetics, agriculture and many more. These range from short selective glossaries to comprehensive works, some of which are more like specialist encyclopedias than dictionaries.

DICTIONARY ENTRIES

The difference between a multi-volume dictionary like the *Grand Robert* and its slimmed-down version the *Petit Robert (PR)* is not only, or even mainly, the number of words they contain (80,000 and 60,000 respectively), but the amount of information and illustrative material provided in each entry. The minimal information about a word required of any monolingual dictionary is, besides the written form, its pronunciation (if this cannot be derived from the spelling), a semantic definition, and essential grammatical information (such as gender, if the word is a noun, and in the case of a verb, any prepositions that follow it).

The semantic definition is in essence a specification of the superordinate term, and of the word's own distinguishing semantic components; *chaise* is therefore defined as 'siège à dossier et sans bras' in the *PR*. A good dictionary avoids as far as possible providing definitions which are circular in an immediate sense, that is, which send the reader to another entry, which promptly refers him back to the first.[8]

Layout, typography and numbering are all used to bring out major and minor semantic differences – most especially that between polysemy and homonymy. On the other hand, space is at a premium in the smaller dictionaries, and this may lead to semantically unrelated items being classed under one headword; for example, *pomme de terre* is found under the entry for *pomme* in the *PLI*, although they have little in common, semantically. Practical commercial considerations must sometimes override theoretical niceties.

If a word has a very restricted collocational range, occurring only with certain other items, then the latter are included, even in pocket dictionaries. For example, the adjective *saur* only occurs in the expression *hareng saur* (meaning 'smoked herring' or 'kipper'). Larger dictionaries give space to established similes like *soûl comme un cochon, bête comme un âne*, in which items are linked in a fixed syntactic pattern. Such expressions, one step removed from a compound word, are generally referred to as 'idioms' (in French, *locutions*).

Larger dictionaries also often provide near synonyms; these may be either co-hyponyms (such as the items *bâtiment, hôtel, logement...* given as part of the entry for the headword *maison* in the *PR*), or words differing from the headword in their connotations rather than in their referential meaning (the entry for *livre*, for example, includes *bouquin*, its colloquial equivalent). Some also provide **antonyms**, or words which represent 'opposites' in a gradable or non-gradable sense, like *chaud* in the entry for *froid*, or *vivant* in the entry for *mort*.

Illustrations, often from literary sources, serve a double purpose. They help to convey some of the connotations and metaphorical extensions which are attached to an item, and they provide examples of habitual collocations, if these have not already been made explicit in the entry.

The minimal etymological information provided by the larger dictionaries is the word's origin, and usually the date at which it was first attested in a written text in French (a very approximate indication of when the word first came to be widely used). The multi-volume dictionaries usually give much more detail on past forms and uses of the word, with examples from texts at different periods. Some dictionaries in fact specialise in this kind of information, like the Robert *Dictionnaire historique de la langue française*, in which the form and meaning of the word today are of secondary importance. Etymological dictionaries, like Picoche's *Dictionnaire étymologique du français*, focus exclusively on the ultimate origins of words, drawing together under one heading words whose common ancestor often lies far back in pre-history.

The importance of the derivational processes of the language, in both diachronic and synchronic terms, is acknowledged by the inclusion, in the larger dictionaries, of inventories of the most productive affixes, and of Latin and Greek morphemes which are heavily used in the production of technical terminology. Growing interest in this field has given rise to the production of the *Robert méthodique* (1990), which lists lexical morphemes – roots, prefixes and suffixes – as well as words, with indications of how these elements combine. The *DFC* and the Larousse *Lexis* also group together words according to their root morpheme, although this principle is not strictly adhered to. (*Déplaire*, for example, is classified under *plaire* in the *DFC*, but *démonter* is given an entry quite separate from *monter*.) This approach is useful in familiarising the reader with the processes of word formation favoured in French, but it often takes a little longer to actually locate a word.

Useful adjuncts to traditional dictionaries are works which organise lexical material on a conceptual basis, in terms of broad semantic or even associative fields. These are known as *dictionnaires analogiques* in French, and are organised alphabetically, but the main items listed represent broad concepts; within these entries related words are given: hyponyms, co-hyponyms, and words which are collocationally related. In Maquet's *Dictionnaire analogique*, for example, under *désert* are grouped words like *jungle*, *savanes*, *maquis*, *steppes*, and in a separate subsection *solitude*, *éloigné*, *vide*, and so on. No attempt is made to differentiate the meanings of the items within a given field, but such works are obviously of great help if you are seeking an alternative expression, or a word which is on the tip of your tongue. They also enable the reader to see at a glance which semantic fields are particularly well endowed in the language.

The Larousse *Thésaurus* represents a more structured work of this kind, since it organises all the entries into a conceptual network. From very broad headings, like *L'Homme* and *La Société*, it passes to narrower fields like *Le Corps* or *La Vie collective*, down to headwords under which are listed numbers of closely associated words (see Figure 5).

Dictionaries of synonyms, like that by Bailly, take words which differ

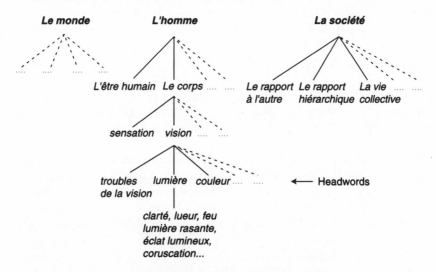

Figure 5 Larousse *Thésaurus*: organised by conceptual field

minimally in terms of their reference or their connotations, and make these differences explicit. For instance, Bailly tells us that *une mer* implies a smaller body of water than *un océan*, that *fiévreux* is an everyday term, compared to the more technical *fébrile*, and that the verb *éplucher* involves the removal of all kinds of external layers, of fruit, vegetable or nuts, whereas *peler* is used only of soft outer skins.

DICTIONARIES OF THE FUTURE

In addition to these traditional sources of lexical information, the reader now has access to computerised dictionaries and databases, either on CD-ROM or directly, on-line to databases which are constantly being updated. The *Robert électronique* on CD-ROM, for example, contains essentially the same entries as the *Grand Robert*, but enables the reader to move around very rapidly, passing from a brief to a detailed entry, or to an associated entry like a synonym or antonym, and to assemble and compare large amounts of information, such as all words ending in the same suffix. The substantial number (160,000) of illustrative quotations accessible on the *Robert électronique* also constitute an important database, which can be used not only for literary purposes but also to investigate recurring collocations (see Project 4 of Chapter Eight). As far as on-line databases are concerned, *FRANTEXT* constitutes the largest collection of mainly literary texts. It lends itself to historical, lexicological and literary research of all kinds. In some cases findings may serve to confirm the researcher's intuitions; in others, quite unexpected patterns may emerge.[9]

New technology is having an even more revolutionary effect on our notion of what constitutes an encyclopedia, since CD-ROMs can now incorporate computer graphics, audio and film clips and music. (Larousse and Hachette have been pioneers in the field, with their 'multimedia' encyclopedic works.)

Lexicography is clearly being revolutionised by modern technology. Access to the databases behind the modern dictionary means that the reader is no longer reliant on the lexicographer's own choice of illustrative material. The use of corpora that are constantly being updated will also enable dictionaries to provide a genuine reflection of current written usage, at least. When technical advances allow us to undertake the automatic analysis of speech as well as texts, new dimensions will be added to our statistical knowledge of the lexis, shedding more light on the *parole* of the individual, and on the *langue* as a whole.

Undoubtedly, the contemporary lexis is very much larger than that of the language in its earliest, formative period, owing to the variety of functions it has been called upon to perform. The next few chapters show just how successive strata of lexical material have been laid down, starting with the bedrock of spoken Latin.

NOTES

1 **Vocabulary** is a word non-specialists are familiar with, but it has the disadvantage of being ambiguous, since it is often associated with specific fields – the vocabulary of space exploration, archery, hairdressing, etc. **Lexis**, meaning the totality of words in the language, has the advantage of being formally related to other useful words like **lexical** and **lexicalisation**. The term **lexicon** is used in various ways: as a rather old-fashioned term for dictionary; technically, by generative linguists, to mean that component of a theoretical model which deals with lexical material rather than grammatical or phonological rules; and as the individual's personal repertoire of words.

2 Psychological tests are used, requiring rapid verbal responses to specific words, with the aim of revealing a speaker's subconscious preoccupations. Although some responses may be highly personal, they tend to follow certain patterns. The stimulus of an adjective like 'big' may trigger its antonym or opposite, 'small', or a noun with which it is conceptually associated, such as 'elephant', or a word with which it occurs in a set phrase or cliché, like 'bad', in 'big bad wolf', and so on. The examination of associative fields may tell us something about the way in which words are stored in the mind (see Aitchison 1987: 73–5).

  The notion may also be relevant to linguistic change, in that occasionally the form of a word may be influenced by that of a neighbour within the same associative field. It is thought, for example, that *écrire* (< Latin *scribere*), which would have become *écrivre* if it had followed its regular pattern of phonological development, became *écrire* under the influence of *dire* and *lire*, within the same broad field. The common remodelling of *infarctus* 'heart attack' to *infractus* is probably due to the influence of *fracture*, another 'medical' word implying sudden trauma.

3 Apart from technical problems relating to the existence of more than one possible superordinate (as is the case with the group *canapé, sofa, divan*), there is that of deciding just what the distinguishing feature(s) should be on some occasions. For instance, do *tabouret* and *pouf* share the features *−dossier*, *−accoudoirs*, but differ in the feature *±pieds*? Or is it more appropriate to focus on the material involved in their manufacture – say, *±étoffe*? Or should *pouf* in fact share no features with *tabouret*, but be classifed as a hyponym of *coussin*? It will also have been noted that many of the components are themselves not semantically simple. The theoretical issues and practical problems of analysis are considerable...

4 The term **homophone** is often used to refer to words with the same pronunciation but different written forms (like *sang* and *cent*), while homonyms are identical in both written and spoken form – that is, homonyms are necessarily **homographs**. Homographs are not necessarily homophonous (for example *couvent* from the present tense of the verb *couver*, and *couvent* meaning 'convent'). **Homophone** is also used in a rather wider sense, to refer to words pronounced in the same way, whatever their spelling. This can be useful, if one wishes to refer to a whole series of words like *vers* 'verse', *vers* 'towards', *verre* 'glass', *ver* 'worm', *vert* 'green', in which there is a mixture of both homonyms and homophones in the narrow sense.

5 In historical linguistics, reconstructed forms which are not actually attested in texts are indicated by an asterisk.

6 Gougenheim's corpus formed the basis of the *Dictionnaire du français fondamental*, consisting of about 3,500 items, representing the absolute 'core' of the lexis – what might be considered essential for the foreign learner.

7 Zipf carried out seminal work (e.g. 1945) on statistical regularities in language. He established various statistical 'laws', demonstrating, for example, that within a given corpus there is a constant mathematical relationship between the rank order of a word and its frequency, and that there is an inverse relationship between the length of a word and its frequency.

8 As Picoche (1977) points out, ultimate circularity is inevitable, since dictionaries use words to define words. What should be avoided is the kind of circularity observed by Muller (1993) in the 1935 edition of the dictionary of the French Academy, in the entries for *injure, insulte, outrage* and *offense,* which are all defined in terms of one another. To put it somewhat technically, neither superordinates nor adequate distinguishing semantic components are given in their entries.

9 For example, one might discover that some words enjoyed a vogue for a relatively short period of time, or that certain collocations of items, like *guerre froide,* reached a peak in texts around a particular period, and declined sharply at a later date. In the literary sphere, it had always been known that Corneille used a very narrow lexical range in his plays (fewer than 5,000 words, compared to 15,000 in Shakespeare), but it required computer technology to show how his repertoire in fact grew progressively more restrained in his later works (see Muller 1993). Conversely, it has been possible to show how the literary vocabulary of Racine broadened with time. In addition to word counts it is of course possible to look at habitual collocations and carry out syntactic analyses, to discover the structures which predominate in certain types of text, or in the works of specific authors.

PROJECTS

(One or two substantial monolingual dictionaries and a thesaurus or *dictionnaire des synonymes* will be needed.)

1 What differences of denotation or connotation distinguish the following pairs of words?

presqu'île / péninsule
seconder / aider
mijoter / bouillotter
sottises / conneries
lancer / jeter
mariage / noces

2 Propose semantic definitions for the following:

appartement, moineau, flâner, chandail

To which lexical items is it necessary to compare them, to arrive at a satisfactory definition? Check your definitions against those given in a monolingual dictionary.

3 Examine the semantic definitions for the following sets of words, and suggest how they might be organised in terms of their semantic components. If necessary, express the relationships between them in diagrammatic form.

ficelle, corde, cordon, câble
soupe, potage, bouillon, velouté

4 Check the origins of the following sets of historically related words, using a

monolingual dictionary that has etymological information, or an etymological or historical dictionary (e.g. Picoche 1994 or Rey 1993). Which might be considered borrowings, and which come from spoken Latin?

appuyer, pied, pieuvre, podium, piège
achever, chavirer, chef, capital, caprice
wagon, véhicule, voie, voiture
boisson, poison, abreuver, symposium

5 Investigate the habitual collocations associated with the following items:

vagir, corsé, aquilin, margoter, riche, vert

Discuss differences in the restrictions which operate on approximately equivalent items in English.

FURTHER READING

Aitchison, J. 1987 *Words in the Mind*, Oxford, Blackwell; for some discussion of how we learn, store and retrieve words from our mental lexicon.

FRANTEXT; a computerised database used for the *TLF*, available to the public, consisting of the works of 500 authors; produced and administered by the *Institut national de la langue française*.

Gorcy, G. 1989 'Le TLF: un grand chêne isolé', in *Lexiques* – special issue of *Le français dans le monde*, August–September; gives the background to the production of the *TLF*, in the context of modern French lexicography. *Lexiques* includes a wide range of papers on different aspects of the history, production, variety and pedagogical uses of dictionaries.

Gougenheim, G., Mechéa, R., Rivenc, P. and Sauvageot, A. 1964 *L'Élaboration du français fondamental*, Paris, Didier

Kempson, R. 1977 *Semantic Theory*, Cambridge, Cambridge University Press; Chapter 6 deals specifically with the question of word meaning.

Lehrer, A. 1974 *Semantic Fields and Lexical Structure*, Amsterdam/London, North Holland Publishing; an appraisal of the usefulness of semantic field theory, includes some interesting analysis of French (and other) cooking terms.

Lyons, J. 1977 *Semantics* (2 vols), Cambridge, Cambridge University Press; a comprehensive and detailed introduction to all aspects of meaning, at the levels of word and sentence.

Matoré, G. 1953 *La Méthode en lexicologie*, Paris, Didier

Miller, G.A. 1991 *The Science of Words*, New York, Scientific American Library; Chapters 7 and 9 summarise the evidence we have for the way in which the brain processes lexical information; Chapter 7 also discusses the problems associated with quantifying the number of words in a language, or in the lexicon of an individual.

Muller, C. 1993 *Langue française: débats et bilans*, Paris, Champion-Slatkine; investigates a variety of current issues, including reform of the orthography and the uses of computers in literary research.

Müller, B. 1985 *Le français d'aujourd'hui*, Paris, Klincksieck; Chapters 3 and 5 include discussion of the quantitative approach to lexicology.

Picoche, J. 1977 *Précis de lexicologie française*, Paris, Nathan, for a clear exposition of basic concepts relating to the structuring of the lexis.

Robins, R.H. 1967 *A Short History of Linguistics*, Harlow, UK, Longman

Saussure, F. de 1949 *Cours de linguistique générale*, Paris, Payot

Zipf, G.K. 1945 'The meaning–frequency relationship of words', *Journal of General Psychology* 33: 251–66.

Dictionaries and other works of reference

Académie française 1994 *Dictionnaire de l'Académie française* (vol. 1 A–E), Paris, Julliard
Bailly, R. 1968 *Dictionnaire des synonymes de la langue française*, Paris, Larousse
Bloch, O. and von Wartburg, W. 1950 *Dictionnaire étymologique de la langue française*, Paris, PUF
Centre de recherche pour un Trésor de la langue française 1971 *Dictionnaire des fréquences, vocabulaire littéraire des XIXe et XXe siècles* (4 vols), Paris, Didier
Hachette 1996 *Axis* (multimedia encyclopedia on CD-ROM), Paris, Hachette
Institut national de la langue française 1971–94 *Trésor de la langue française* (16 vols), Paris, Gallimard
Juilland, A., Brodin, D., Davidovitch, C. 1970 *A Frequency Dictionary of French Words*, The Hague/Paris, Mouton; based on a smaller, though more heterogeneous, corpus than the *Dictionnaire des fréquences*, and revealing similar membership of the 'core' lexis.
Larousse 1996a *Petit Larousse illustré*, Paris, Larousse
—— 1996b *Multimédia Encyclopédique* (on CD-ROM), Paris, Liris Interactive
Maquet, C. 1979 *Dictionnaire analogique: répertoire moderne des mots par les idées*, Paris, Larousse
Mel'cuk, I.A. 1984 *Dictionnaire explicatif et combinatoire du français contemporain*, Montreal, Presses de l'Université de Montréal; a detailed semantic analysis of about fifty lexical items, pinpointing fine distinctions of referential and connotative meaning and providing a lot of information on the collocations associated with these items. Such an explicit and thorough-going analysis shows just how approximate and elliptical is most of the semantic information given in dictionaries, which are necessarily limited by practical constraints of time, size and cost.
Péchoin, D. (ed.) 1992 *Thésaurus Larousse* Paris, Larousse
Picoche, J. 1994 *Dictionnaire étymologique du français*, Paris, Robert
Rey, A. (ed.) 1988 *Le Micro-Robert*, Paris, Robert
—— 1989 *Le Grand Robert de la langue française* (9 vols), Paris, Robert
—— 1993 *Dictionnaire historique de la langue française* (2 vols), Paris, Robert
Rey, A. and Rey-Debove, J. (eds) 1992 *Le Petit Robert de la langue française*, Paris, Robert
Rey-Debove, J. (ed.) 1990 *Le Robert méthodique*, Paris, Robert, a dictionary in which the entries are classified in terms of roots and affixes as well as words.

Chapter 2

The lexical foundations of French

THE LANGUAGE OF EMPIRE

Latin was originally the language of a small city-state in central Italy. By the middle of the third century BC the Romans controlled the Italian peninsula; two centuries later Spain, Sicily, Greece, Gaul and parts of Asia Minor and North Africa had become Roman provinces, and expansion continued into the second century AD. From the third century the Empire began a gradual decline, until Rome itself was overrun by the Visigoths in AD 410. But the 'pax romana' had brought two hundred years of stability and prosperity to the provinces of western Europe, enabling Latin to take root and displace the indigenous languages of much of the region.

Today we tend to think of Latin as the language of Cicero and Virgil: a highly inflecting language with strict grammatical rules, and a copious lexis adapted to the needs of a sophisticated urban society and the administration of a vast empire. As in any living language, however, there were differences between the forms appropriate to educated public discourse and writing, and those used informally, and lower down the social scale.

SPOKEN LATIN

It is the spoken form of Latin, often known rather unfortunately as 'Vulgar Latin', that was brought to Gaul by the legions, and then by merchants, administrators and settlers.[1] This is the form of Latin that can be considered the common ancestor of all the 'Romance' languages that subsequently emerged (see Map 1) and developed as national languages in their own right.

Vulgar Latin has come down to us through various sources, from graffiti preserved on the walls of Pompei and prayers and curses scratched on fragments of lead in sacred shrines, to literary texts: some of the comedies of Plautus and Petronius' famous *Satyricon* contain dialogue which reflects colloquial and uneducated speech. Even Golden Age writers like Cicero on occasion used colloquial expressions in their informal correspondence.

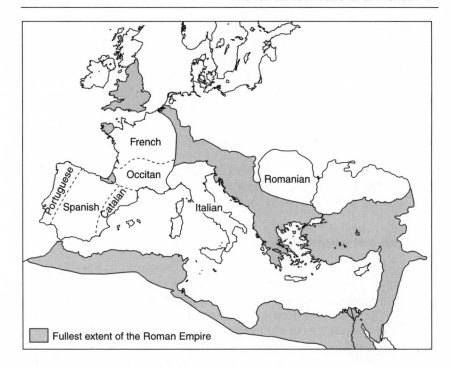

Fullest extent of the Roman Empire

Map 1 The Romance languages
Source: Adapted from Lodge 1993: 55

Other texts, such as cookery books or works on animal husbandry or practical medicine, written by and for people with an imperfect knowledge of the written norm, contain revealing 'mistakes' in grammar and spelling which shed light on the spoken language of the time. Such departures from the norm are increasingly common after the collapse of the Empire, when educational standards declined dramatically. Even more compelling evidence comes from didactic works like the *Appendix Probi* (third century AD), which explicitly upholds the written norm, warning against the use of forms which must have been in common use. Later, in the eighth century, the Reichnau Glossary, which was produced in northern France, gives us valuable information about the vernacular of the region, since it provides equivalents to Latin expressions in the Vulgate which the average reader would have had difficulty in understanding; hence *pueros* is glossed as *infantes* (> *enfants*), and *forum* as *mercatum* (> *marché*).

However, even without any contemporary written evidence, the methods of historical reconstruction, applied to the later forms of Romance, make it possible to reconstitute much of the phonological, grammatical and lexical system of the parent language (see Bynon 1977: 45–75).

There must have been a certain amount of regional variation across the

Empire, and even within the spoken Latin of Gaul, but this does not seem to have become marked until after the Germanic invasions of the fifth century. The invasions not only precipitated the final disintegration of the Empire but also accelerated the process of linguistic fragmentation and divergence. The sixth to ninth centuries are generally considered to be an intermediary period, in the course of which the Romance languages began to develop in embryonic form (see Lodge 1993: Chapter 3).

The majority of lexical items in the earliest French texts, and indeed the core lexis of the modern language, can be traced back to the spoken language of the imperial age. We should therefore look briefly at the lexis of Vulgar Latin: the ways in which it differed from that of the Classical language, and its main lines of development.

Reduction and regularisation

Classical Latin had a wealth of literary and philosophical vocabulary, with quantities of near synonyms in many fields; for example, *celer*, *velox* and *rapidus* all have the meaning 'swift', in slightly different, if overlapping contexts. The lexis of Vulgar Latin, restricted as it was to everyday discourse, and excluded from the language of law, administration, literature and formal rhetoric, was much more limited. Thousands of the words of Classical Latin were therefore absent or rarely used in the spoken variety. Although *pulcher* was the usual word for 'beautiful' in Classical Latin, it was *formosus* 'good-looking' that developed in Spanish to *hermoso* and in Romanian to *frumos*, while *bellus* 'pretty' gave rise to the modern French and Italian words.

In the course of such replacement, some quite major semantic shifts occurred; Classical *ignis* 'fire', for example, gave way to *focus* (> *feu* – originally 'hearth').

Words which belonged essentially to different registers in Latin often went their separate ways in different Romance languages; *comedere* (derived from Classical *edere*, to eat), seems to have been rather more refined than *manducare* 'to chomp or chew', which was probably slang in origin; the latter gave rise to French *manger* and Italian *mangiare*, and the former to Spanish and Portuguese *comer*.

Highly irregular verbs were often dropped in favour of regular verbs of the *-are* conjugation (which developed into the regular *-er* conjugation in French). Hence one of the most irregular of all Latin verbs, *ferre*, 'to carry', was replaced by *portare* (in Classical Latin, 'to transport').[2]

With such massive reduction taking place in the lexis, the word surviving in Vulgar Latin naturally tended to take on a broader meaning; for example the lexical distinction between *homo* ('man' in the generic sense of human being) and *vir* (a male of the species) in Classical Latin was lost when only *homo* was retained in early Romance.

The disappearance of a word may sometimes have been due to the avoidance of homophones, especially if they belonged to the same word class and were likely to occur in similar contexts; the fact that *homines*, the plural of *homo*, became homophonous with *omnes* 'all' following the loss of the unstressed vowel and the initial 'h', probably explained why the latter was abandoned in favour of *toti* (originally, 'whole, entire'). Similarly, the replacement of *os, oris* 'mouth' by *bucca*, originally meaning '(inflated) cheeks', and perhaps carrying something of the force of modern *gueule*, may have been due to the danger of a clash with *auris* 'ear'. (See Elcock 1960: 156–9, on the avoidance of homonymic clashes in Romance.)

Examples like the adoption of *manducare* and *bucca*, or the metaphoric substitution of *gamba* 'fetlock' for Classical *crus* 'leg', or *testa* 'earthenware pot' for *caput* 'head', demonstrate the more popular and expressive colouring of much of the lexis of spoken Latin.

The creation of new words

The long-established processes of suffixation and prefixation that had generated so many of the words of Classical Latin continued to operate on the roots which survived into Vulgar Latin and early Romance. Although many of the abstract nouns of Classical Latin had been lost, the suffixation of adjectives and verbs made the creation of new ones possible. For example, despite the loss of the Classical *pulchritudo* 'beauty', a new abstract noun could be formed by suffixing the adjective *bellus* to give *bellitas* (> *beauté*). Besides *-itas*, the nominal suffixes *-ia*, *-itia*, *-ura*, *-(i)tio*, and *-mentum* were productive, giving rise to forms like *fortia* (> *force*), *nutritio* (> *nourrisson*). On occasion, a suffixed noun was replaced by one with a different suffix; Classical *amicitia* gave way to *amicitas* (> *amitié*).

The popularity of diminutive nouns formed by a range of suffixes – *-ulus*, *-ellus*, *-icellus* or *-iculus* (as in *somniculus* 'snooze' (> *sommeil*)) – was probably due in part to their greater expressivity; in addition, the suffix gave more substance to monosyllables, and in some cases ensured the differentiation of potentially homophonous nouns; *sol* 'sun' was replaced by *soliculus* (> *soleil*), hence becoming distinct from *solum* 'earth'. In this case it is certainly difficult to imagine any genuine semantic function for the diminutive suffix.

Verbs too were given diminutive suffixes; again the advantage was that the resulting form belonged to the regular *-are* conjugation; e.g. *tremulare* (> *trembler*) supplanted the Classical *tremere*. The frequentative or intensive form of verbs was often preferred, no doubt for the same reason; for example the very irregular *canere* 'to sing' was replaced by *cantare* (> *chanter*). Suffixation also proved highly productive in Vulgar Latin in transforming nouns, adjectives and participles into verbs: *caballicare*

(> *chevaucher*), for example, was derived from *caballus* 'horse', and *sponsare* (> *épouser*) from *sponsus* 'betrothed'.

Common adjectival suffixes were *-alis* (> *-el*), *-ianus* (> *-ien*), *-osus* (> *-eux*), as in *zelosus* (> *jaloux*). Sometimes these were added, redundantly, to existing adjectives; *aeternus*, for example, being replaced by *aeternalis* (> *éternel*). It was not uncommon for nouns to be formed simply by adding an appropriate inflectional ending to a verbal root; e.g. *probare* 'to test', giving rise to *proba* (> *preuve*), and *dolere* 'to suffer', to *dolus* (> *deuil* – 'mourning'). This simple process of 'back formation', little used in Classical Latin, was to become highly productive, down to the present day (see Chapter Six). A change in word class is also involved when an adjective or participle is used elliptically to replace the noun it modifies; *hibernum* (> *hiver*) replaced *hibernum tempus* (literally, 'winter time'), itself a periphrastic substitute for the Classical Latin *hiems*; just as *pêche* developed from *persica* (*poma*), 'Persian (fruit)'.

Prefixes, often locative prepositions in origin, are frequently used to create new verb forms, such as *de+liberare* (> *délivrer*), *ad+colligere* (> *accueillir*), *ex+caldare* (> *échauder*, 'to scald'); often these phonologically more substantial forms survive, while the unprefixed verbs are lost. Prepositions were sometimes themselves prefixed by a preposition, like *ab+ante* (> *avant*), and *de+intus* (> *dans*), which originally had the more complex meanings 'from in front of' and 'from inside'.

Short adverbs of time and place in Classical Latin are often replaced by phrases, although subsequently reduced to a single morpheme by phonological change; *lors* can be traced back to *illa hora* 'at that time' and *ici* to *ecce hic* (literally, 'see here'). While in Classical Latin adverbs were formed by the addition of a short inflectional suffix to an adjective, in the later period we find compounds being formed from the ablative of the noun *mens* – *mente* 'in mind or spirit' – preceded by a modifying adjective; so that *bona mente* would mean 'in a good state of mind'. Such expressions were increasingly used to include non-human states or activities (e.g. *sola mente > seulement*), and the second element came to function as a suffix – the most productive of all in the modern language. Analytic comparatives, consisting of *plus* followed by the adjective, were increasingly preferred to the inflected comparative of Classical Latin; only a few high-frequency comparatives and superlatives escaped this trend, such as *meliorem* (> *meilleur*), and *pejor* (> *pire*).

The greater degree of transparency, that is, a clear relationship between form and meaning, displayed in most of the more analytic forms just mentioned, must have been one of the underlying reasons for the success of many early neologisms. *Matrastra* 'stepmother' (> *marâtre*), for example, consisting of *mater*, the root morpheme for 'mother' plus a pejorative suffix, replaced the opaque *noverca*, just as *patraster* 'stepfather' (> *parâtre* – now obsolete) replaced *vitricus*. Similarly the compound *calvas sorices* (> *chauves-souris*, 'bats', literally 'bald mice') replaced *vesperti-liones* and *sanguisuga* (> *sangsue* 'leech', literally 'blood-sucker'), *hirudo*. The latter compounds have retained their transparency over the centuries. However, the transformations wrought by phonological change have introduced a degree of opacity into many once transparent forms, such as *aubépine* (< *alba spina* 'hawthorn', literally 'white thorn'), or *lundi* (< *lunis dies*, 'the day of the moon' – it being the Roman practice to name the days of the week after the planets).

On the whole, compounding remains a much more limited means of producing new words than affixation, down to the present day; it is a derivational process which has always been more productive in Germanic languages than in Romance.

It will be seen from Chapter Six that the basic processes of word formation operative at this very early, formative stage of the language have remained the major and perennial source of lexical renewal for the language. External influences had also begun to shape the lexis of spoken Latin: some of these are discernible in all the Romance languages, while others were specific to the Latin of Gaul.

THE GREEK ELEMENT IN LATIN

For the Romans, the Greek language was both the repository of a great body of literature and scientific and philosophical thought, and the lingua franca of many of their provinces in the eastern Mediterranean.

As any dictionary of Classical Latin containing etymological information will reveal, Latin borrowed heavily from Greek. As Greek and Latin are cousins on the Indo-European family tree, assimilation of Greek loans was not a major problem; the two languages have similar inflectional systems, and the roots of cognate words are often recognisably related, such as Greek *pous* and Latin *pes* 'foot' or *neos* and *novus* 'new' – although the relationship is less obvious in other pairs of words, such as *hyper* and *super* 'above' or *pente* and *quinque* 'five'.

Many borrowings like *poema*, *philosophus*, *physica*, were made to supplement literary, philosophical and scientific terminology and were confined, initially, to written Latin, whence they were borrowed into French (see next chapter). Direct borrowings from Greek into French are rare before the Renaissance, when the revival of interest in the arts, science and literature of classical antiquity led to the rediscovery of many Greek authors.

The Old Testament was translated into Greek as early as the third century BC, while much of the New Testament and other Christian texts were written in Greek. It was also the first widely used liturgical language of the Christian Church. It was therefore natural that many borrowings should be made in this field via Low Latin (the written Latin of the early

Church), such as *ecclesia* (> *église*), *episcopus* (> *évêque*), *baptisma* (> *baptême*), *monachus* (> *moine*), *presbyter* (> *prêtre*) and *angelus* (> *ange*). These passed at an early date into Gallo-Romance and French, where they are found in the earliest texts.

In addition to these learned and semi-learned elements, words as common as *chaise, chambre, beurre, bras* and *pierre* derive from Latinised Hellenisms which passed directly into the spoken language. The names of plants, often used in cooking or in medicine, such as *persil* 'parsley', *baume* 'balsam', *trèfle* 'clover', *cerfeuil* 'chervil', *girofle* 'cloves', also derive ultimately from very early Greek borrowings.

THE CELTIC SUBSTRATE

The first stage of the colonisation of Gaul took place in about 120 BC, with the invasion of the southern Provincia Narbonensis (later 'Provence'), and the process was completed with the campaigns of Julius Caesar about seventy years later. The inhabitants of Gaul were mainly Celtic-speaking peoples whose ancestors had spread from south-central Europe between the eighth and fifth centuries BC, to inhabit large areas of northern and western Europe. When the Romans began to expand their Empire, they found Celtic neighbours in northern Italy, Gaul, the Iberian peninsula and the British Isles. What we know about the early Celtic languages has had to be gleaned from a small number of inscriptions, and through reconstruction based on knowledge of later forms of the languages. Figure 6 indicates which of these languages are still spoken, on the north-west fringes of Europe, and how they are related.

Even before the occupation of Gaul, the Romans had borrowed words relating to wheeled vehicles from their northern neighbours; a Celtic root Latinised to *carrus* is to be found in *char, chariot,* and *charrue* (originally,

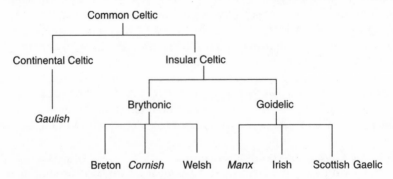

(The languages in italics are now extinct)

Figure 6 The Celtic languages

a wheeled plough); *caballus* is thought by some to be Celtic in origin, borrowed first with the meaning of 'packhorse' or 'nag', but supplanting *equus* in Vulgar Latin. A handful of other words, giving rise to modern French *bec*, *chemin*, *changer*, *alouette* 'lark', *tonne* 'barrel', *braies* 'breeches', *claie* 'hurdle', *combe* 'narrow valley' and *lande* 'moor' were also early borrowings, to be found in other Romance languages.

The towns of Gaul were romanised first, and schools and universities established, where the sons of Gaulish noblemen were soon eager to learn Latin. The way to Roman citizenship and to public office was open to free men of the Empire (from the time of Julius Caesar Gauls were appointed as senators to Rome); for the ambitious fluent Latin was an obvious necessity. We know very little about the rate of decline of Gaulish, except that it had probably died out by the sixth century; but there must have been a long period of bilingualism, with Latin being adopted first by the Gaulish aristocracy, at least in public life, while Gaulish survived longest in remote rural areas. It is perhaps predictable, therefore, that most of the words surviving from Gaulish concern rural and domestic pursuits.

Features of the landscape and types of soil bearing Gaulish names include *boue*, *talus* 'slope', *quai* (originally 'embankment'), *bourbier* 'quagmire', *glaise* 'clay soil'. Words connected with work on the land are especially prominent: *mouton*, *bouc* 'billy goat', *ruche* 'beehive', (originally 'bark', of which the Gauls made their hives), *raie* (originally 'furrow'), *soc* 'ploughshare', *javelle* 'sheaf', *glaner* 'to glean'. The fir tree (*sapin*) and the birch (*bouleau*) are indigenous to cooler northern climates rather than to the Mediterranean, while the yew (*if*) and the oak (*chêne*) had religious connotations for the Celts (*druide*, too, is from Gaulish). *Brasser* 'to brew' and *cervoise* 'barley beer', a doublet of Spanish *cerveza*, reflect Celtic drinking habits, while others (*borne*, *arpent*, *lieue*) are associated with the traditional demarcation and measurement of land. (The *lieue* or 'league' resisted the imposition of the Roman measurement of the *mille* or mile (a thousand paces), and only finally succumbed to the Revolutionary metric system.) Although the majority of the loans are nouns, a number of common verbs – *craindre*, *bercer*, *briser* – are Gaulish in origin.

In addition to direct borrowings, it is very likely that the form *quatre-vingts* is modelled on the Celtic system of counting in twenties, which survives in Irish and Welsh today.

Given that Gaul was not heavily settled by speakers of Latin, except in the south, it is surprising that the Celtic element in the lexis is so slight. Even if we add words scattered throughout other dialects of French and Occitan, and allow for the fact that many words must have persisted, unrecorded, into later stages of the language, it is still extremely modest: no more than 0.1 per cent of the lexis of modern French, according to Messner (1975). Brunot (1905–53, vol. 1: 22ff.) suggests that the adoption of Latin, especially in the countryside, was accelerated following the third-century incursions by Germanic tribes, who sacked towns and cities in Gaul. Many of the romanised Gaulish aristocracy left the towns to live on their estates, in close contact with those who actually worked on the land. Moreover, the workers increasingly consisted of slaves who had originated in other parts of the Empire, and did not have Gaulish as their mother tongue.[3]

For a long time it was thought that Breton speakers constituted a Celtic enclave surviving from Roman times. However, it is now clear that, while Gaulish may have survived in some parts of the peninsula, Breton was in fact brought by refugees from south-west Britain, emigrating across the Channel in the fifth and sixth centuries under pressure from the Anglo-Saxon invaders. A few words from Breton have filtered into French over the centuries, mostly referring to features characteristic of the sea shore: *goéland* 'seagull', *goémon* (a kind of seaweed), *bernicle* 'barnacle', *belon* (a type of oyster). They have also given the names for the prehistoric megaliths – *menhir*, *cromlech* and *dolmen* – to be found in Britanny. *Baragouin* 'gibberish' is thought to derive from the Breton for 'bread and wine', possibly as the kind of basic phrase a traveller in the region might pick up.

EARLY GERMANIC INFLUENCE

Like the Celts, Germanic-speaking peoples had had contact of various kinds with the Romans from the earliest days of the Empire (see Guinet 1982: Introduction). Above all, they were valued as fighting men, and came to form the backbone of the Imperial army. Many early borrowings are in fact associated with warfare and army life; terms like *werra* (> *guerre*), *helm* (> *heaume*), *raustjan* (> *rôtir*), *suppa* (> *soupe*) have their cognates in other Romance languages.[4] French, however, possesses more words of early Germanic origin than any other Romance language, owing largely to the invasions of the fifth century.

The Roman grip on Gaul had already been greatly weakened in the third century by the series of incursions from the East, which left the great arterial roads in disrepair, regional capitals sacked and destroyed and agricultural production significantly reduced. Although the Germanic invaders were expelled, or placated with federate status in exchange for promised military support, the stage was set for the final dissolution of the Empire.

The Visigoths sacked Rome early in the fifth century, and then swept on to southern Gaul and Spain. By the middle of the century the Saxons had settled along the Channel coast, and the Burgundians in an area corresponding roughly to modern Burgundy and Franche-Comté in the south-east, while the Alamans had established themselves in the north-east (later Alsace). In the north the Franks, led by Clovis, occupied an area stretching

Map 2 The Gallo-Romance dialects
Source: Lodge 1993: 72

from the Rhine to the Loire by the end of the century. They proved to be the most successful of the invaders, establishing dominance over the Burgundians and the Visigoths by the end of the sixth century. They were also the most important group from a linguistic point of view. Their original area of settlement corresponds very approximately to the region of the Langue d'Oïl, the group of northern dialects which emerged in the early medieval period (see Map 2). Of these, *francien*, the dialect of Paris and the Ile de France, was to become the national language of France.

To the south, the Langue d'Oc[5] was much less marked by Germanic influence, and remained closer to the other southern Romance languages, owing in part to the heavier and earlier romanisation of the region. The Franco-Provençal area is linguistically heterogeneous, showing features of both northern and southern varieties.

As with Celtic and Latin, there must have been a long period of bilingualism, with the difference that Frankish was the language of the conquerors, and continued to be used by the ruling élite up to the tenth century. This must account in large part for the proportionally greater imprint left by the Germanic superstrate, compared to the Celtic substrate.

The majority of the newcomers were soldiers and farmers, skilled in husbandry, agriculture and hunting, and these activities are reflected in the distribution of loan words from this period. Features of the landscape and their boundaries carry names of Germanic origin: *bois, forêt, bosquet, jardin, haie, marche* (in the sense of 'border'), as do tree names like *aulne* 'alder', *houx* 'holly', *hêtre* 'beech', *saule* 'willow', and products of the soil: *blé, framboise, cresson* 'watercress'. Most domestic animals keep their Celtic or Latin names, but the collective nouns *harde* and *troupeau* were borrowed, together with some names for wild animals and birds: *renard, héron, blaireau* 'badger', *caille* 'quail', *crapaud* 'toad'. *Epervier* 'sparrowhawk', *faucon, gerfaut* 'gyrfalcon' and *leurre* 'lure' reflect the Frankish passion for falconry. The borrowing of *mésange* 'titmouse' is probably due to the fact that the bird was protected by an ancient taboo, while the flight of the *freux* 'rook' was used in divination. *Hallier*, now meaning brushwood, but derived from the word for 'hazel', also carried religious significance, since fencing made of hazel branches was thought to have beneficial magical properties.

In the field of warfare we find *trêve* 'truce', *guet* 'watch', and the verbs *frapper, blesser, meurtrir, épargner* and *garder* (originally with the sense of 'guard'). Many terms for weaponry and armour, such as *haubert* 'coat of mail', *épieu* 'pike', *estoc* 'short sword' are naturally obsolete, although *flèche* and *hache* remain, having found new functions. Terms associated with horsemanship, such as *étrier* 'stirrup', *éperon* 'spur' and *bride* 'bridle', have also survived.

More domestic items include *banc, mijoter, cruche, loge, halle, fauteuil, danser, gratter, poche* and *bière* (in the sense of funeral bier; *bière* the drink is a later borrowing from Dutch). Although hardly engineers and architects on the Roman scale, the newcomers provided the basic building terms *maçon* and *bâtir*, originally 'to weave', relating to the use of interlaced twigs or willow shoots (*osier* – another Germanic borrowing) in domestic buildings.

It is thought that a whole range of borrowed colour terms – *blanc, brun, gris, fauve, bleu* (originally ranging from grey-blue to beige) – were first used to describe the nuances of colouring in horses; while *blond* was borrowed because of the typical hair-colour of the newcomers. *Savon* is thought to come from a Germanic word **saipon*, a substance used for washing and dying or bleaching the hair, adopted by the Romans.

A variety of words describing moral or psychological states and qualities

– *honte, hardi, haïr, orgueil* – were no doubt retained as forming part of a rather different system of ethics from that current in romanised Gaul.

The social structures which developed after the break-up of the Empire were also very different. The emerging hierarchical feudal system naturally drew much of its terminology from the language of the new ruling élite. Many existing terms, from *roi, duc, seigneur* and *comte*, down to the *vassal* and *serf*, were retained, albeit with different values; but new terms were added from Frankish, like *baron, marquis, maréchal* and *sénéchal*. Some began as relatively humble, even domestic roles, a *sénéchal* (< **siniskalk*, literally 'elder servant') being the chief steward in a household, and a *maréchal* (< **marhskalk*) the chief stableman, but they later came to signify elevated rank in the military hierarchy (see Matoré 1985). One might also associate the term *riche* (originally 'powerful') with this field.

The key term *fief* (< **fehu*, 'cattle') was a gift, usually of land, from the feudal lord to his vassal in return for loyalty and military support. It is possible that *gant* was taken from Frankish because of the symbolic role of the glove in ceremonies associated with the conferring of a *fief*, and with ritual challenges. *Ban* was first a feudal expression, meaning the body of vassals subject to a particular *seigneur*; then it came to mean the act of summoning one's vassals, and finally, any official summons or proclamation (hence *bans de mariage*). The related *bannière* was originally the banner under which the vassals assembled for war at their lord's behest.

We find a handful of Frankish terms connected with fishing and seafaring: *esturgeon* 'sturgeon', *hareng* 'herring', *bord* 'side', *mât* 'mast', *falaise* 'cliff', *écume* 'foam'; while the dialect of the Saxons on the Channel coast gave the compass points, *nord, sud, est* and *ouest*, and *bāt* from which *bateau* derived. Further contributions to this particular field, such as *tillac* 'upper deck', *étrave* 'prow', *hune* 'topmast', *vague, crique, flotte*, and *marsouin* 'porpoise', are traceable to Old Norse. This Scandinavian language, a member of the northern branch of Germanic, was spoken by the Vikings, who invaded and settled in the Normandy peninsula and lower Seine valley in the ninth century. (Although they rapidly abandoned Old Norse in favour of the local variety of Romance, a distinctive dialect emerged, which was to become the Norman French imported to England in the eleventh century.)

A few seafaring terms were later taken into Old French from the variety of Low German spoken in what is now Holland: *dune, hâvre* 'harbour' and *amarrer* 'to moor'. Later still, in the Middle French period, Dutch gave *bâbord* 'port' and *tribord* 'starboard'.

In addition to full lexical items, a handful of suffixes can be traced back to the early period of Germanic influence; *-aud* (< *-ald*) and *-ard/-art* were first productive in forming personal names – Bertaud, Guiraud, Renart –

and later derived nouns or adjectives with pejorative connotations, such as
salaud 'bastard', *pataud* 'clumsy', *vantard* 'braggart'. The suffix *-ard* was
very popular in the medieval period, giving rise to words which have
unfortunately disappeared, like *dormard* 'sluggard' and *mangeard* 'glut-
ton', but it has taken on a new lease of life in twentieth-century slang, as in
chauffard, *connard* and *motard*. The Germanic suffix *-enc* (> *-an*) denoting
origin, as in *paysan*, was less productive than *-esc* (> *-ais/-ois*), which fused
with the Greco-Latin *-isc* and Latin *-ensem*.

Germanic influence was even felt at the level of the phonological system.
It is rather rare for a phoneme to be borrowed; usually borrowings are
pronounced according to the existing phonological system. But the presence of a so-called 'aspirate h' in Modern French − that odd phantom
phoneme that occurs in words like *la haine*, *le heurt*, blocking the normal
processes of elision and liaison − usually means that the word can be traced
back to Germanic, where the 'h' was pronounced; in some dialects, a
genuinely aspirate 'h' is still to be heard.[6]

The form of individual lexical items was sometimes influenced by that of
the Germanic synonym, particularly if it resembled the Latin. Hence the
initial aspirate of Germanic **hoh* 'high' was transferred to the Latin *altus*
(> *haut*), and Latin *vespa* blended with Germanic *wefsa* 'wasp', to give
Gallo-Romance *wespa* (> *guêpe*).

More far-reaching changes were wrought in the phonology of the northern dialects, particularly the loss of unstressed vowels and the lengthening
and diphthongisation of stressed vowels, due in all probability to the strong
stress accent typical of Germanic dialects. Such major transformations,
which were also to have implications for the morphological structure of
the language, are responsible for the fact that French has moved much
further from the parent language than any other Romance language. (See
pp. 45–6 for a brief outline of some of the principal changes involved.)

The lexis of Old French contained about a thousand words from Germanic,
of which many, especially relating to feudal society, have disappeared.
Between three and four hundred remain, with perhaps one hundred and fifty
in general use. This figure may appear insignificant; but many of these words
lie at the heart of the modern lexis. They include not only everyday nouns,
like *besoin*, *bout*, *rang*, *housse*, *bord*, but adjectives: *sale*, *frais*, *laid*; verbs:
gagner, *gâcher*, *choisir*, *lécher*, *guérir*; and even the adverbs *guère* and *trop*,
which are on the borderline between lexis and grammar. Of the thousand most
frequent words in the language today (see Gougenheim *et al.* 1964), thirty-
five can be traced to this particular superstratum.

HISTORY IN PLACE NAMES

Place names are not strictly speaking part of the lexis, except in so far as
many common nouns contribute to their formation; some words in fact only

survive in this fossilised form. With the help of place names, and a few words borrowed into Celtic, we are able to shed just a little light on the dimly known era before the Celtic settlement of western Europe, when non-Indo-European languages were spoken by peoples like the Ligurians in the south-east, and the Iberians in the south-west, who spoke a language which was possibly the ancestor of modern Basque.

The names of major topographic features, especially mountains and rivers, are particularly resistant to change; it is thought that the Garonne and the mountain peaks Le Gar, and Le Ger of the Pyrenees, in addition to towns and villages like Le Cayrou, Le Cheyron and Beaucaire, all share the same root *gar-* or *kar-*, meaning 'stone', which is very similar to the ancient Basque *karri*. The pre-Celtic root *roc-*, which came to be used of easily fortified rocky crags, gave rise to the common nouns *roc* and *roche*, and is also to be found in place names like Le Roc, La Roche, La Rochelle, Rochefort, Roquefort and many more. The names of major rivers, such as the Rhône, the Loire and the Seine, also appear to be pre-Celtic.

Gaulish may be sparsely represented in the French lexis, but it has left its mark in the form of thousands of place names. As towns and villages were often established on fortified sites, the morphemes *-rato*, *-dunum* and *-durum*, all meaning approximately 'fortress', are combined with other elements; Issoire comes from *Iciodurum*, or 'fortress of Iccius', and Lyon from *Lugdunum*, Lug being the Celtic god of craftsmanship. It is common for the same elements to have evolved rather differently in different places; alongside Lyon we find Loudun, Laon, and even Leyden, in Holland. Another recurring place name is the Gaulish *Noviomagus*, literally 'new market', taking the modern forms of Noyon, Noyen, Nyons and Nouvion. The Celtic *lann-*, 'plain', often a sacred site or shrine, has a very wide distribution; Mediolanum, 'central plain or shrine' underlies modern Meillant, Meylan, Molain and Milan in Italy. (This root is cognate with the Welsh *llan-*, now meaning 'church'.)

The mixing of Latin and Celtic elements was common, as in the pleonastic hybrid Châteaudun. *-acum* is a Celtic suffix frequently added to Latin personal names (often adopted by the Gauls themselves); as words in the south underwent fewer phonological changes than in the north, we find many 'doublets' like southern Aurillac and northern Orly (< *Aureliacum*, roughly speaking 'Aurelius' place'), and *Quintiacum* gave rise to a whole range of names – Quinsac, Quincy, Quincié, Quincieux.

Latin-based place names indicate the ongoing importance of a town's defences, with dozens of names containing *château* and *châtel* (from *castellum*, the diminutive of *castrum*, 'fort'), scattered across the map of France. The adjectives variably precede or follow the noun, as in Châteauneuf and Neufchâtel. Many towns and villages were naturally founded on hills; hence the numerous names with *mont-*: Hautmont, Montaigu, Chaumont, Clermont, Montréal, Montpellier, etc.

The element *-ville* is traceable to the *villa*, or estate which formed the kernel of a village, often developing into a town: Grandville, Villefort, Villeneuve. Similarly, the suffix *-court* (< Latin *cohors*), as in Azincourt, referred originally to the farmyard, thence to the farm itself, and later to the village which grew up around it.

The distribution of place names gives us an idea of the density and extent of settlement by particular groups. The Germanic settlers, for instance, favoured the suffixes *-ville*, *-villiers* and *-court*, which were added to the landowner's name. These tend to cluster in the north and east of the country, where Frankish settlement was heaviest. Here too we find names formed from the Germanic *-bourg*, such as Cherbourg and Strasbourg. The Norse word for 'stream', *bec*, is to be found in Norman place names, like Houlbec and Briquebec, recalling names in the areas of Danish settlement in the north of England, like Troutbeck and Landon Beck (Norman Caudebec and Cumbrian Caldbeck are therefore variants of the same name, literally 'coldstream').

The Midi is rather different from the rest of the country, in having relatively few names of Celtic or Germanic origin. It was the most thoroughly romanised region, and one where the Gauls had not succeeded in ousting the earlier inhabitants, the Ligurians. The Latin suffix *-anus*, as in *Frontinianus* (> Frontignan) is therefore more common in the south than the Gaulish *-acus*. Many Gaulish cities were named after the dominant tribe of the area; Paris is derived from *Parisiis*, Reims from *Remis* and Poitiers from *Pictavis* (the Romans having supplied the locative ending *-is*, which explains the final *-s* of the modern spelling). But again, these are confined to northern and central France.

The Midi is also distinguished by the fact that centuries before the Roman colonisation, Greek cities had been established along the coast, as part of a network of trading posts and colonies that spread Hellenic civilisation round the Mediterranean. Marseilles (< *Massilia*, a hellenised name of unknown origin) became a very considerable centre of Greek culture, as well as a flourishing port. Agde comes from *Agathê* (*Tuchê*), short for 'Good (Fortune)'; Nice (< *Nikaia*) was named in honour of the Greek goddess of victory, while Antibes, across the bay, comes from *Antipolis* 'the town opposite'.

FROM LATIN TO FRENCH

The problem of assigning a date – however approximate – to the beginnings of French, as opposed to the later forms of spoken Latin, or 'Gallo-Romance', is one that continues to exercise scholars today (see Lodge

1993: 87–95, Wright 1982 and 1991). Linguistic change is so gradual that any date must be arbitrary. Moreover, people's perceptions of what language they speak are determined more by cultural and political factors than by linguistic facts. Nevertheless, for a variety of reasons, it is generally recognised that the earliest form of Old French dates from the ninth century. By that time, the spoken and written varieties were characterised by very different phonological, grammatical and lexical features – differences which had been accentuated by linguistic reforms introduced by Charlemagne in the late eighth century. These were designed to eliminate from written Latin much of the influence of the spoken language and to establish a more standardised pronunciation of Latin throughout his western empire. His reforms had the effect of highlighting differences between the two varieties which had hitherto been masked; no longer could the spoken language be considered a rough and ready form of Latin. By the ninth century a clear state of diglossia existed, which was to continue for the next six or seven hundred years.[7]

The fact that Latin with the revised pronunciation was no longer intelligible to speakers of the Romance vernacular is clear from the recommendation of the Council of Tours in 813, when priests were advised to deliver

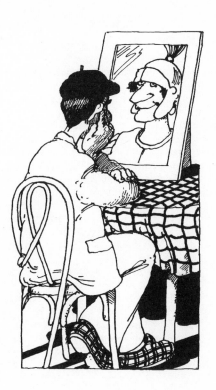

sermons in the *rustica Romana lingua*, that is the spoken Romance language, rather than Latin, 'so that all may understand what is said'.

Another factor in the retrospective recognition of French as a separate language is the appearance of what is considered to be the first French text: the Strasbourg Oaths (842). These were composed both in German and Romance, to be read aloud by two of Charlemagne's grandsons, Romance-speaking Charles and German-speaking Louis, who were in league against a third brother. The oaths were sworn in front of their respective troops who themselves took an oath of allegiance. From this and the more elaborate texts which were soon to follow we can appreciate the differences that distinguish early Old French from Latin, at every level. The fact that the written and spoken languages were to a high degree mutually unintelligible, that a different name was now given to the spoken variety, for which different spelling conventions were being developed, and that we can see the beginnings of a separate literary tradition, all combine to support the view that a language distinct from Latin had emerged.

But the illustrious ancestor was not to be forgotten; as the next chapter will show, French has always turned to the treasure-house of the Latin lexis, as an inexhaustible supply of new words.

NOTES

1 It could be glossed as 'of the people', since it is not pejorative in this context, but is rather related to the Latin *vulgus*, meaning 'people' or 'populace'. Nevertheless, it is a disputed term, and nowadays many scholars prefer to refer to 'spoken Latin'. More importantly, the notion of a clear-cut distinction between Classical and Vulgar Latin has been called into question. Classical and Vulgar Latin, rather than being two autonomous varieties, were the opposite ends of a continuous spectrum, with speakers' usage varying subtly, according to their level of education and the social context of the exchange.

2 This strong preference for regular verbs continued to make itself felt throughout the development of the language; in Old French, the irregular *gésir* (< *jacere* 'to lie') was still used, but was gradually replaced by *coucher*, and survives nowadays only in a few forms and contexts, such as inscriptions on tombstones: *ci-gît...* 'here lies...'. Today neologisms, approved or condemned, such as *solutionner* or *réaliser*, are often rivals to existing irregular forms (see Chapter Six).

3 For discussion of the Latinisation of Gaul, see Brunot 1905, vol. 1, Introduction, and Lodge 1993, Chapter 2.

4 There is a good deal of controversy surrounding the dating and precise provenance of Germanic borrowings, owing to similarities among the dialects involved, the paucity of attested written forms, and the remodelling of early borrowings under the later influence of Frankish cognates. One of the most detailed studies is provided by Guinet (1982), who bases his arguments largely on the phonological development of the forms in question.

5 The Langue d'Oïl and Langue d'Oc (the latter more recently termed 'Occitan') are so called because these were the words for 'yes' in the north and south, respectively.

6 The purely orthographic, non-aspirate 'h' of *l'homme* or *l'hôtel* was simply inserted as a reminder of the original Latin form, although it had been dropped from pronunciation during the Vulgar Latin period.

7 The notion of diglossia was first elaborated by Ferguson (1959), who defined it as a situation in which two related varieties coexist with complementary functions: a 'high' variety used in writing and in prepared speech, and a 'low' variety which is the language of everyday discourse. The high variety is no-one's mother tongue, and must therefore be consciously learnt; it is usually codified in terms of prescriptive rules, is stable over time and lacks internal variation. Being associated with the 'higher domains' of government, law, education and literature, it carries great prestige. The low variety tends to be more variable in time and space, is uncodified, and is generally felt to be inherently inferior to the high variety.

The term has been used rather more loosely, being extended to situations in which two quite distinct languages are involved, both of which may function as mother tongues for some sections of the population, so that there is not a clear complementarity of roles. Some would claim that a state of diglossia (in Ferguson's sense) already existed in Gaul, in the later days of the Empire.

PROJECTS

1 Trace the origins of the following words, whose etymons were neologisms in Vulgar Latin. Which expressions did they replace? Where possible, suggest an explanation for the replacement:

demain, pavillon, oublier, fromage, parler, abeille

2 Investigate the semantic development of the following early borrowings, and comment on their subsequent morphological productivity:

rang, bouc, guinder, gouverner, grève, fauteuil

Can you find words in other modern European languages which are ultimately relatable to these?

3 Trace the origins of the following place names. What does their etymology tell us about the topography or history of the places themselves?

Strasbourg, Chambord, Queiroux, Grenoble, Bagnères-de-Luchon, Tours

FURTHER READING

Brunot, F. 1905–53 *Histoire de la langue française des origines à nos jours* (13 vols), Paris, Armand Colin

Bynon, T. 1977 *Historical Linguistics*, Cambridge, Cambridge University Press

Dauzat, A. and Rostaing, C. 1963 *Dictionnaire étymologique des noms de lieux en France*, Paris, Librairie Guénegaud

Dauzat, A., Delandes, G. and Rostaing, C. 1978 *Dictionnaire étymologique des noms de rivières et de montagnes en France*, Paris, Klincksieck

Elcock, W.D. 1960 *The Romance Languages*, London, Faber and Faber; an overview of the development of the Romance languages from the Latin period to the beginnings of standardisation.

Ferguson, C.A. 1959 'Diglossia', *Word*, 15: 325–40. Re-printed in Giglioli, P.P. (ed.) 1972 *Language and Social Context*, Harmondsworth, UK, Penguin

Fierro-Domenech, A. 1986 *Le Pré carré*, Paris, Robert Laffont; a general demographic history of France, including an account of Celtic expansion, and the patterns of Germanic invasion and settlement.

Giglioli, P.P. (ed.) 1972 *Language and Social Context*, Harmondsworth, UK, Penguin

Gougenheim, G., Michéa, R., Rivenc, P. and Sauvageot, A. 1964 *L'Élaboration du français fondamental*, Paris, Didier; a list of about 8,000 words in order of decreasing frequency, established on the basis of a large corpus of recorded conversational French.

Green, J. 1993 'Representations of Romance: contact, bilingualism and diglossia' in Posner, R. and Green, J.N. (eds) 1993 *Trends in Romance Linguistics and Philology* (5 vols), Berlin/New York, Mouton de Gruyter; for a discussion of the status of different forms of Latin and early Romance, and the relationship between them.

Guinet, L. 1982 *Les Emprunts gallo-romans au germanique*, Paris, Klincksieck

Harris, M. and Vincent, N. (eds) 1988 *The Romance Languages*, London, Croom Helm; succinct outlines of the structure of the modern languages, linked to their historical origins.

Herman, J. 1975 *Le Latin vulgaire*, Paris, PUF Que Sais-Je?

Johnson, J. 1946 *Etude sur les noms de lieu dans lesquels entrent les éléments -court, -ville et -villiers*, Paris, Droz

Lodge, A. 1993 *French: From Dialect to Standard*, London, Routledge

Matoré, G. 1985 *Le Vocabulaire et la société médiévale*, Paris, PUF

Messner, D. 1975 *Essai de lexicochronologie française*, Salzburg, University of Salzburg

Nègre, E. 1963 *Les Noms de lieux en France*, Paris, Armand Colin

Posner, R. and Green, J.N. (eds) 1993 *Trends in Romance Linguistics and Philology* (5 vols), Berlin/New York, Mouton de Gruyter

Thévenot, E. 1972 *Les Gallo-Romains*, Paris, PUF Que Sais-Je? An introduction to the history of the Gallo-Romans: their social structure, religion, culture and economy, up to the time of the collapse of the Empire.

Väänänen, V. 1963 *Introduction au latin vulgaire*, Paris, Klincksieck

Wright, R. (ed.) 1982 *Late Latin and Early Romance in Spain and Carolingian France*, Liverpool, UK, Francis Cairns; investigates the complex relations between written and spoken varieties during this period.

—— 1991 *Latin and the Romance Languages in the Early Middle Ages*, London, Routledge

Chapter 3

Les racines nobles
Borrowing from Latin and Greek

A TWO-TIER LEXIS?

The single most striking feature of the French lexis is the lack of formal similarity between many words which are closely connected, morphologically, semantically and even etymologically. The relationship between *arbre* and *arboriculture* is reasonably transparent, but the same cannot be said of *oiseau* and *aviculture*, although ultimately they both share the same Latin root. Such discrepancies are largely due to the coexistence of words which have developed from the spoken language of Roman Gaul with words borrowed from written Latin and, to a lesser extent, Greek. These borrowed elements are termed *savant* or 'learned', since Latin and Greek were the languages associated with the 'higher domains' of theology, law, medicine, astronomy, philosophy and rhetoric, to which only the educated élite had access. Many have remained within such fields, or are restricted to formal and literary registers of the language; but others, such as *utile, nature, animal, facile,* are now in everyday use, and are quite unmarked, stylistically, although it is true that the very core of the lexis contains few such words. (Guiraud (1968b) calculates that only about 6 per cent of the words of *français élémentaire* are *savants*.) In this particular context, therefore, *savant* refers to a word's origins, rather than its current function.

THE EFFECTS OF PHONOLOGICAL CHANGE

As was suggested in the last chapter, French has been subject to even more phonological change than its Romance siblings; in many cases hardly a phoneme of the original word remains unchanged. Who could recognise *chaud* in the Latin *calidum*, *échelle* in *scala*, or *oiseau* in *avicellum*?

A few examples will give some idea of the scope and complexity of the changes that have taken place in the language over the last fifteen hundred years.

In a word like *calidum*, the final 'm' was the first element to be lost, in

Vulgar Latin, then the unstressed 'i' and 'u'; the now final 'd' was devoiced to 't', the initial 'c' became palatalised to the affricate /t∫/, like the English 'ch' in 'church', then simplified to the fricative /∫/, and 'l' before a consonant became vocalised to 'u'. In Old French the adjective would therefore have been pronounced /∫aut/.

Simplification of the diphthong /au/ to /o/ and loss of the final 't' in Middle French completed the transformation to the modern pronunciation /∫o/.

Other far-reaching changes include:

- the diphthongisation of many stressed vowels, so that Latin *pedem* gave modern *pied*, *mel* > *miel*, *pira* > *poire*, and so on;
- the voicing of p, t and k to b, d and g, between vowels, with the subsequent disappearance of d and g in this position, while b > v; hence *vita* > *vie*, *securum* > *sûr*, *ripa* > *rive*;
- the disappearance of 's' after a vowel and before a consonant, often lengthening the preceding vowel, which is now marked by a circumflex accent, as in *festa* > *fête*, *castellum* > *château*;
- the reduction or assimilation of the first element in many consonant clusters, so that *insula* > *isola,* and *deb(i)ta* > *dette;*
- the reduction of word-final 'a' to the central vowel /ə/, subsequently lost altogether in most northern dialects, but represented by 'e' in the orthography.

In principle, such phonological changes operate with absolute regularity; at a given time, in a given context, a particular sound will change in a particular way, throughout the lexis.[1] This regularity helps the linguist to date the arrival of a borrowing in the language, even in the absence of textual evidence; it is clear, for example, that *cause* (borrowed from Latin in the twelfth century, and forming a doublet with the indigenous *chose*) post-dates the palatalisation process, since the initial plosive has remained intact. As most Latin and Greek borrowings post-date the major phonological changes, they have stayed much closer to their original forms, despite a certain amount of Gallicisation to bring them into line with the phonology and morphology of French.[2]

When words that have undergone over a thousand years of phonological reduction and transformation are set in a paradigmatic relationship with the original Latin form – *œil* with *oculaire* or *oculiste*, or *mois* with *mensuel* – very considerable complexity is introduced into the morphological system of the language. The consequences for the lexical structure of modern French of the introduction of large numbers of learned borrowings are more fully examined in Chapter Six; in this chapter we are concerned rather with the reasons for the cultural dominance of Latin and Greek, and with the variety of ways in which they influenced French.

COMPLEMENTARITY AND RIVALRY BETWEEN LATIN AND FRENCH

The state of diglossia existing between Latin and the emerging Romance languages, mentioned in the last chapter, continued well into the sixteenth century. Throughout Europe, to be educated was to be able to read and write in Latin, since all valued sources of knowledge were enshrined in Latin texts. Nor was it confined to the written mode. Latin would have been heard in the streets of the Quartier Latin around the Sorbonne, which was founded in 1252 as a centre for theological studies; and European scholars with different mother tongues could converse freely with one another on any learned topic. Moreover, the grammatical rules of Latin had long been clearly established, as an immutable norm, even if they were not always observed. Compared to this permanence, invariability and universality, French in the early Middle Ages, as yet uncodified, with its dialectal variation and irregular morphology, must have seemed both anarchic and parochial.

Gradually, however, the hegemony of Latin gave way to French.[3] The northern dialects of the Langue d'Oïl, like those of the south, began to be used as a literary medium in the early medieval period. The very first compositions were works of popular piety, recounting the lives of the saints, such as the ninth-century 'Sequence of Saint Eulalia', about the fourth-century Christian martyr. Since such 'sequences' were designed to be sung in church by a choir, it was important that all the singers should use the same pronunciation, both for the sake of unison, and for the lines to scan properly. In other words, the initial use of an orthography which attempted to represent the vernacular with reasonable accuracy was motivated by very practical considerations. There followed epic poems like the Song of Roland, composed round about 1100, which tells of the exploits of Charlemagne's knights against the Moors in Spain. In the twelfth and thirteenth centuries, when greater stability and prosperity fostered a great flowering of artistic, literary and intellectual activity, progessively diverse types of text were produced: prose as well as poetry, historical and didactic works, and, increasingly, legal and administrative documents. By the end of the thirteenth century, *francien,* the dialect of Paris and the Ile de France, had emerged as the dominant variety of northern French.

The fourteenth to sixteenth centuries witnessed both a steady extension of the functions of French, and a parallel expansion in its vocabulary.[4] By a series of royal edicts from the mid-fifteenth century, the use of French in law and administration was greatly extended, at the expense of Latin. Finally, not only Latin, but other vernacular languages were excluded from this domain, by the Ordinance of Villers-Cotterêts of 1539, which decreed that throughout the realm legal records and court proceedings should be 'en langage maternel français et non autrement'.

Paradoxically, the wider adoption of French as a serious scholarly and literary language was also stimulated by the renewal of interest in the classical languages from the fifteenth century. The central pillar of the 'new learning' of the Renaissance was the study of the philosophy, literature and history of Christian and pagan antiquity, through a detailed and critical study of the original texts. Impetus was given to Greek studies by the arrival in western Europe of Byzantine scholars, following the fall of Constantinople to the Turks in 1453. Hitherto, Greek authors had been known largely through Latin translations, but in the sixteenth century a great body of literature, including works on mathematics, astronomy and medicine, became directly accessible to Western scholars. At the same time, in Italy, long forgotten manuscripts of the work of many Latin authors were brought to light and eagerly devoured, in the original and in translation. There was a movement to restore Latin to a form closer to that of the Augustan Age, divesting the language of the neologisms which it had accumulated as a result of centuries of use in diverse spheres. However, a purified, Ciceronian Latin was no longer adapted to an active role in government or law – even less to the description of new discoveries in science and geography. Hence this was a period of much debate about the role of French. Du Bellay's famous *Défense et illustration de la langue française* (1549) affirmed that the language was suited to all literary and scholarly purposes, although lexical and stylistic elaboration, using Latin and Greek as models, was needed to perfect it.

Even so, writers (including du Bellay himself) frequently moved between Latin and French, depending on their subject, and on the readership they had in mind. Montaigne expressed doubts about the durability of his *Essais*, written as they were in French, as the language seemed to him to be changing so rapidly that they would surely be incomprehensible to future generations.

In the seventeenth century, the great works of authors like Corneille and Racine, Molière and La Fontaine, Descartes and Pascal, demonstrated beyond all doubt the fitness of the language as a vehicle for the highest forms of literary and philosophical expression, while codification in the seventeenth and eighteenth centuries gave it the unity and permanence essential to any prestigious standard language.

Latin was nevertheless slow to die. The church and the legal and medical professions were, perhaps predictably, highly conservative in their attitude to language. When the great sixteenth-century surgeon, Paré, had the temerity to write books on his subject in French rather than Latin he was hounded and condemned by many of his colleagues. The Bible was translated into French in the sixteenth century, as a central tenet of the Reformation, although the Catholic Church remained for a long time opposed to allowing direct access to the scriptures. Education, largely under the tutelage of the church, remained dominated by Latin well into the eighteenth century. Even up to the early years of this century at the University of the Sorbonne doctoral theses in certain subjects were presented in Latin. The last bastion of Latin fell in 1964, when the Second Vatican Council decreed that mass be conducted in the vernacular.

PATTERNS OF BORROWING, FROM OLD FRENCH TO THE PRESENT DAY

Against this background, Latin and Greek were the most natural sources of lexical expansion, for a language which was gradually extending its functions to encompass every aspect of spiritual, intellectual and public life. Old French had remained lexically homogenous, enriched mainly by the internal processes of affixation and composition.[5] But in texts of a religious nature we already find substantial numbers of borrowings, among them *perdition, miracle, trinité, miséricorde, confession, divinité, rédemption,* while Greek (through the medium of Latin) gave terms like *sépulcre, chrétien, archange, apôtre.* Most such borrowings appear to have been taken from the Vulgate, the official Latin version of the Bible. In fields such as medicine, philosophy, law and administration, a more modest number of borrowings were made, including *élément, orient, équinoxe, solstice, dérogatoire, légataire, clarifier, administrer, oblique, mendicité, ultime* and *rhétorique.*

It was not until the fourteenth century, in the Middle French period, that Latinisms began to pour into the language. There was a growing demand for knowledge from a public largely ignorant of Latin, which led to a vast amount of translation into French. Inevitably, the response to a problem of translation was often to borrow the original expression, in more or less Gallicised form. Even where an indigenous word was available, or a neologism conceivable, the general preference was for a borrowing, in keeping with the seriousness of the subject matter.[6]

Greek borrowings in the Middle French period cluster in those fields in which the Ancient Greeks had been the early masters, such as medicine, which the Romans had adopted and elaborated. Hence terms, mediated through Latin, like *épiglotte, diaphragme, diarrhée, thorax, diabétique.* The Greek art of rhetoric, also adopted and transmitted by the Romans, was embodied in an elaborate terminology which has all but died out with the art itself, leaving only a few of the less arcane expressions – *métaphore, périphrase, antithèse* – in general use.

By the sixteenth century, the passion for Latinisms had been carried to such lengths by some authors that their texts were riddled with redundant and obscure expressions. It is this style that Rabelais parodied in the language of his scholar from Limoges, in *Pantagruel* (1532). And yet over half the terms that Rabelais, either inventing or imitating, intended as satire, such as *crépuscule, célèbre, capter, génie, indigène,* have become perfectly assimilated into the lexis.

Familiarity with Greek texts in the original, and their translation into French, led to a growing number of direct borrowings from Greek, such as *hygiène, larynx, symptôme, trapèze, hypothénuse.* As this handful of examples suggests, it was in the fields of science and medicine that Greek was to play a major role. In the sixteenth century, magic and science, astrology and astronomy, alchemy and chemistry, were not yet distinguishable. Nevertheless, the approach to the acquisition of knowledge was essentially empirical; there was intense curiosity about the workings of the natural world allied with great confidence in the powers of the human mind, which paved the way for the development of modern science.

From the seventeenth century, which marks the true beginnings of scientific method, based on observation and the systematic testing of rational hypotheses, the need for new scientific terminology increased exponentially. The productivity of the Greek morphemes *-scope* and *-mètre,* alone, as in *stéthoscope, périscope, magnétoscope, baromètre, photomètre,* and *thermomètre,* are indicative of the importance of precise observation and measurement in the new sciences.

In the Middle and early Modern French period many medieval anatomical terms were replaced by Latin borrowings, such as *abdomen* for *susventre,* but Greek tends to dominate in more recently created medical terminology. The basic anatomical term may be Latin-based or French – *veine, reins, foie, cornée* – but many of the adjectives relating to these body parts, or their associated diseases, are of Greek origin; hence we find *phlébite* (inflammation of the veins) paired with *veine, kératite* with *cornée, néphrite* with *reins.*

Besides medicine, chemistry is the science which has drawn most heavily on Greek roots. Lavoisier, considered by many to be the father of modern chemistry, is also largely responsible for establishing the bases of its terminology in the *Méthode de nomenclature chimique* (1787); the underlying principles of the nomenclature, and indeed many of the basic terms, such as *oxygène* and *hydrogène,* are in universal use today.

The vast majority of words of Greek origin in French (and other European languages) were not borrowed as fully fledged words, but as individual morphemes which were freely combined as the need arose. This morphological flexibility makes Greek ideal for the succinct naming of complex processes and substances. For example, *hyperchlorhydrie* (an excess of hydrochloric acid in gastric secretions) combines a compound stem – *chlor +hydr* – with both a prefix and suffix.

Despite the growing use of Anglicisms in science and technology, Latin and Greek are still the principal sources of scientific terminology, worldwide. Cottez' *Dictionnaire des structures du vocabulaire savant* (1988) is so organised that, as well as providing information on existing words, it sets out for the scientist in search of a new term the lexical material available; there may be a choice between Latin and Greek synonyms: *multi-* and *poly-*; *super-* and *hyper-*; *aqua-* and *hydro-*, and so on, are classed together. It is often the Greek morpheme that has proved the more productive.

Although numbers of learned words, with or without technical meanings, have been adopted into general usage, most words of this kind that have come into the language over the last two to three hundred years remain opaque to the average speaker. The strict diglossic divide may have come to an end with the Renaissance, giving much wider access to knowledge to those who could read their mother tongue, but one could argue that a new kind of division, between scientific and mainstream lexis, has taken its place, reinforcing the distinction between professional élite groups and the mass of the population.

TYPES AND FORMS OF BORROWINGS

Most of the borrowings that have survived filled a genuine need in the language, as it expanded into new domains. The elaboration of ecclesiastical terminology, or that of the developing sciences, mentioned above, are cases in point. Many borrowings however were shortlived; for example, *opposite, expecter* and *genius* can be found in texts of Middle or early Modern French, but are no longer in use. The verb *computer* did not succeed in replacing *compter*, nor the Greek-based *thésor* the existing term *trésor* (not, that is, until the twentieth century, when it was adopted in a Latinised form, *thésaurus*). Some borrowings actually replaced existing terms, a fact that can only be explained in terms of the potent attraction exercised by Latin. For example, Old French possessed the generic nouns *chauvesse* 'baldness' and *humblesse* 'humility', derived transparently from the adjectives *chauve* and *humble*. They were nevertheless supplanted by *calvitie* (< *calvities*) and *humilité* (< *humilitas*), just as indigenous *certaineté* and *seürtance* gave way to *certitude* (< *certitudo*).

In other cases, the borrowing came to coexist alongside the existing term, though always with a different semantic or stylistic function. The distinction between *frêle* and *fragile* remains quite subtle, while other 'doublets', such as *évier* and *aquarium*, or *métier* and *ministère*, retain few semantic links.

As is the case with most borrowings (see Chapters Four and Five), Latin and Greek words often have a much more specific meaning in French than in the original, since they are borrowed in a specific context. This is particularly true of scientific terminology of Greek or Latin origin; *diaphragme* simply meant 'partition' or 'barrier' in Greek, just as the medical term *ausculter* 'to auscultate' (< *auscultare*) meant 'to listen' in Latin. In the latter case the inherited form of the verb – *écouter* – has retained the much broader meaning of the original. Conversely, the learned *natif* (< *nativus*) is closer in meaning to the original than *naïf*, the indigenous development of the same etymon.

The meaning of the original Latin was ever-present in the minds of French writers, at least until the seventeenth century, and this meaning is sometimes grafted on to that of the French word; hence *gloire,* originally used in religious contexts with the sense of the glory of God, or the homage paid to God, took on the meaning of 'fame', or 'earthly glory', under the influence of the meaning of *gloria* (see Gougenheim 1970: 413ff.).

Most semantic borrowings of this kind, such as the seventeenth-century use of *admirer* to mean 'to wonder at', or eighteenth-century *candeur*, to mean 'whiteness', tend to be literary conceits which did not take root in the language. Perhaps one reason for this is that the new meaning is often far removed from the original; natural semantic developments tend to be gradual and to follow specific pathways (see Chapter Seven). Artificial, unmotivated extensions of meaning risk producing ambiguity, without necessarily introducing any new semantic distinction into the language.

The forms of borrowings were variably influenced by the pronunciation of the vernacular; the earliest borrowings were the most heavily Gallicised, so that they did not stand out as being distinct from indigenous words. Later borrowings tend to be closer to the original in form, and with these there is sometimes hesitation between a Gallicised and a Latinate pronunciation; for example, speakers vary between /kadrã/ and /kwadrã/ for *quadrant*, and between /kazi/ and /kwazi/ for *quasi*.

Most words borrowed from Latin and Greek lost their grammatical endings, and were assimilated to the inflectional morphology current in French at the time. Latin verbs of the *-are* and *-ire* conjugations, for example, were assigned to the *-er* and *-ir* conjugations. Latin masculine and neuter nouns lost their endings *-us* and *-um*, marking case and gender, and were generally assigned to the masculine gender in French, while the feminine nominal ending *-a* was replaced by the French equivalent *-e*. However, a relatively small number of nouns were borrowed with their inflectional ending – especially medical and legal terms, such as *sternum*, *rictus, duodénum, quidam*. Occasionally whole phrases may be borrowed: *quiproquo* (< *quid quo pro*), *et cetera, ad hoc, de cujus, in extremis, extra-muros, de facto*; even more rarely, an inflected verb is borrowed *tel quel*, such as *déficit* (literally 'it is lacking') – now a noun. Such inflected borrowings are still occasionally made, like the early twentieth-century medical terms *in vitro* and *in vivo*.

As part of the process of Gallicisation, the derivational affix of a Latin borrowing was often replaced by the indigenous affix which had developed from it; the suffix *-(i)tas* for example, was regularly replaced by *-(i)té*, and *-osus* by *-eux*. *Facilitas* was therefore borrowed as *facilité*, and *generosus* as *généreux*. Borrowing was not restricted to the adoption of whole words; roots and affixes drawn from Latin could be used in new combinations, such as *exact+itude*, *abdomin+al*.

Increasingly in Modern French, there is a mixing of elements of popular and learned origin, and of Greek and Latin morphemes, as in *polyvalent* or *télévision* (see Chapter Six). When a learned affix is in competition with its French counterpart, such as *-al* (< *-alis*) with *-el*, or *-ation* (< *-ationem*) with *-aison*, the borrowed affix usually proves to be the more productive. Such affixes were also used to Latinise existing words; *dérivation*, for example, replaced Old French *dérivaison*, and *interrompre*, *entrerompre*.

Roots also underwent phonological remodelling; it required only the addition of a vowel to Latinise Old French *verté* (< *veritas*) to *vérité*, and the reintroduction of the intervocalic consonant in *aorer* (< *adorare*) to restore the Latin form of the root. Not all such reworkings remained in the language; *rarité*, for example, was shortlived, as a rival to the indigenous *rareté*.

INTERNAL MOTIVATION FOR BORROWING

Quite apart from the general historical and cultural reasons for the heavy influx of learned words into French, there are functional reasons, internal to the language and usually connected with semantic overload, which have probably promoted the adoption of many loan words. The longer words have been in the language, the more nuances of meaning they tend to accumulate; they may also lose the meaning with which they were originally borrowed. The development of *blâmer* (< *blasphemare*) is examined in some detail by Chaurand (1977: 39); it was first used in religious contexts, with the meaning of 'blaspheme' – as in *blâmer le nom du Seigneur* – but was extended to secular contexts, with a meaning closer to that which it carries today. This polysemy is probably the reason for the reintroduction of *blasphémer*, with a specifically religious meaning.

Phonological change, progressively eroding the forms of words, was also undoubtedly indirectly responsible for some learned borrowings. As we saw in the last chapter, it had already resulted in the formation of large numbers of homophones in the early, Gallo-Roman period. Gougenheim (1970: 420) suggests that the confusion arising from the coexistence, in similar contexts, of homophones like Old French *seing* (< *signum*) and *saint* (< *sanctum*) prompted the replacement of the former by its learned counterpart, *signe*. Similarly, *envier* (< *invitare*), to invite or challenge, had converged with *envier* (< *invidiare*), to be jealous – which helps to explain the introduction of *inviter* in the fourteenth century.

Gougenheim cites a more complex case from the Middle French period, involving both semantic change and learned borrowing, as a response to a potential clash of this kind. By the fifteenth century sound changes had led the verbs 'to swim' (< Latin *natare*) and 'to knot' (< *nodare*), both present in the same broad semantic field of maritime activities, to have the same pronunciation *nouer*; he suggests that this is probably why the verb *nager* (< Latin *navigare*), originally meaning 'to navigate', came to mean 'to swim', with the borrowing *naviguer* coming in to fill the semantic gap, so to speak, left by this change.

He also suggests, more speculatively, that certain borrowings were blocked because they would have clashed with existing terms, while noting the occurrence of borrowings which provoked just such clashes; the existence of Old French *errer* (< *iterare*), meaning 'to travel', did not prevent the borrowing of *errer* (< *errare*) 'to err', although this meaning is now archaic. Possibly they were able to coexist because the latter was perceived as being a metaphorical extension of the former.

LATIN AND GREEK INFLUENCE ON ORTHOGRAPHY

Twelfth-century orthography, although showing a good deal of local and even personal, idiosyncratic variation, had reflected the spoken word reasonably accurately. Words like *pied*, *loup*, and *noeud*, in which the final consonant was no longer pronounced, were spelt *pie*, *lou* and *neu*. Some Latin influence is nevertheless discernible, in the form of additional letters which, in indigenous words, had long since ceased to be pronounced; *tens*, for example, was also spelt *temps* (< *tempus*).

From the late thirteenth century, when armies of lawyers' clerks were drawing up legal documents of all kinds in French, they introduced large numbers of 'silent' letters, at a time when the language itself was, in effect, evolving in the opposite direction. Hence the 'g' in *doigt* and *vingt* was added to recall the Latin *digitus* and *viginti*, the 'b' in *debte* and *doibt* was taken from Latin *debita* and *debet*, the 'mp' in *compter* from *computare*, the 'l' of *aultre* from *alterum*, and so on. False assumptions were sometimes made about the etymologies of words; Old French *lais*, for example, meaning 'bequest', was a back formation from the verb *laisser*, but was given the current spelling *legs* in the fifteenth century, in the belief that it was related to the verb *léguer* (< *legare* 'to bequeath'). Occasionally, the reintroduction of a letter led to its being actually pronounced; hence the modern pronunciation of *obscur* and *legs*, with the 'b' and the 'g' reinstated.

As we can see from some of the examples given above, not all such spellings were retained. Of those that were, it must be said in their favour that they often serve to distinguish homophones (a factor which no doubt appealed strongly to the lawyers' clerks). *Compter* and *conter*, for example, are homophones which, rather unusually, followed different paths of semantic development from the same Latin etymon.

Another effect of etymological spellings was to provide a formal link with related words, learned or otherwise; the connection between, for example, *temps* and *temporel*, or *grand* (pronounced and spelt *grant* in Old French) and *grandir* or *grandeur*, was made visible.

Before the advent of printing, in the late fifteenth century, the addition of apparently redundant letters also had the function of aiding the interpretation of handwritten texts, in which sequences including the letters m, n, u, i and v were often very difficult to differentiate. This problem no doubt also explains the practice of adding letters for which there was no etymological motivation, such as the silent 'g' to the indefinite article *ung*, and the substitution of 'y' for 'i' as in *amy* or *celuy*.

The influence of Greek orthography is immediately obvious in the use of the digraphs 'th' or 'ph' and 'ch' in words of Greek origin, such as *thème*, *physique* or *chaos*; these are in effect transliterations of Greek letters, devised by the Romans and carried over into French. 'Ch' in Greek borrowings is a transliteration of a sound absent from the French phonological system, in which it is sometimes borrowed as a fricative /ʃ/, as in *architecte* – that is, with the original value of the digraph in the French orthographic system – and sometimes as a velar plosive /k/, as in *archéologue*. Unlike 'th' or 'ph', then, this digraph has a double phonetic value.

Greek words originally pronounced with a velar plosive that were borrowed into Latin naturally tended to follow Latin conventions, and were represented by a 'c', as in *cataracte*. In more recent, direct borrowings, 'k' is often used, as a closer transliteration of the Greek, as in *kinésithérapeute* ('physiotherapist'); in some cases there is variation between the two: e.g. *kleptomane ~ cleptomane*.

From the sixteenth century, with the rapid increase in the printing of books in French, there was a pressing need to formulate a more standardised and accessible orthography. There was intense debate about the kind of system best suited to the language, some advocating a transparent, almost phonemic system, others extolling the advantages of the traditional, etymological approach. Ultimately, the traditionalists triumphed. Some improvements were made in the late sixteenth century, such as the introduction of accents on vowels, and the cedilla; 'i' and 'u' were given different values from 'j' and 'v', and many etymological spellings were gradually eliminated. But it was not until the nineteenth century, when major educational reforms were in train, that the system was more or less standardised.

The orthography of modern French, though fortunately divested of much of the hyper-Latinisation of Middle French, still bears the imprint of the cultural preoccupations of a previous age. Moreover the debate continues

to be revived with renewed fervour every thirty or forty years; impassioned polemics surrounded the modest spelling reforms of 1990, which proposed nothing more drastic than the removal of an occasional circumflex accent, or the substitution of 'f' for 'ph' in some obscure words of Greek origin.[7] Some would claim that French orthography is another of the cornerstones of the modern diglossic divide, accentuating the remoteness of the written norm from the spoken language. Full mastery of the orthography certainly remains a major educational and social hurdle.

With the exception of the question of orthography, the influence of both Latin and Greek has ceased to be a contentious issue. On the contrary, their contribution to the formation of a semi-universal scientific lexis has generally been welcomed. However, the influence of other, living languages, both symbolising and reflecting the political and economic relations between rival European powers, has often proved to be controversial, as we shall see in the next two chapters.

NOTES

1 See Price (1971) for a succinct description of the sound changes that took place from Vulgar Latin, and Pope (1961) for a more detailed account. See Bynon (1977: 24ff.) for a discussion of the notion of exceptionless 'laws' of phonological change.
2 The problem of dating Latin loans in French remains a particularly tricky one (see Pope 1961: 638ff.); the pronunciation of early borrowings from Latin tended to be strongly influenced by the pronunciation of early Old French; some words are semi-learned, in that they belonged to formal oral registers – restricted perhaps to prayers or hymns – and were therefore preserved from the effect of some of the sound changes to which thoroughly vernacular words were

subject. Moreover, the pronunciation of existing words was often remodelled, bringing it closer to that of the original Latin.

3 See Lodge (1993, Chapters 4 and 5) for a detailed discussion of the selection of spoken and written norms within France, and the progressive elaboration of the functions of French.

4 Guiraud (1966) estimates that over 40 per cent of the modern French lexis came into the language during this period, and that half of these words were taken from Latin or Greek.

5 See Godefroy (1961) or Walker (1982) for some idea of the productivity of these processes, which often resulted in a plethora of synonyms. For example we find series like *folesse, folage, foleté* and *foliance* and *grandure, grandise* and *grandité*, in Old French, all coexisting with much the same meaning.

6 See Brunot (1905–53, vol. 1: pp. 516ff.) for the opinions of fourteenth-century translators, such as Nicole Oresme, who favoured learned borrowing, and vol. 2, pp. 216ff., for contrary arguments advanced in the sixteenth century by writers and translators who felt that words should be drawn from French, so that the language might be made 'populaire, et facile à lire'. It was the views of the Latinisers that prevailed.

7 The official text of the reform is published in *Le Français dans le monde*, no. 239, February–March 1991, together with a summary of attempts at and opposition to spelling reform over the last century.

PROJECTS

1 Identify the origins of the following pairs of words, noting the semantic fields in which they originate, and trace their semantic development:

amande / amygdale	*cailler / coaguler*	*épice / espèce*
rançon / rédemption	*poison / potion*	*nourrisson / nutrition*

Can any tentative conclusions be drawn from these findings?

2 Find as many words as possible containing these (more or less synonymous) Latin- and Greek-based elements. Do any patterns emerge in relation to

(a) the structure of these words
(b) the semantic fields in which they occur?

Latin:	*puéri-*	*lumin-*	*quadro-*	*petr*	*magni-*
Greek:	*pédi-*	*phos-/photo-*	*tétra-*	*lith-*	*macro-/méga-*

Latin:	*utér-*	*aqu-*	*foli-*	*calor-*
Greek:	*hystér*	*hydr-*	*phyll-*	*therm-*

3 Identify the orthographic elements in the following words which:
(a) reflect their etymological origins rather than their pronunciation
(b) serve to disambiguate the word from a homophone
(c) connect it with morphologically related forms:

corps, porc, pied, poids, honte, huit, pouls

FURTHER READING

Ayres-Bennett, W. 1996 *A History of the French Language through Texts*, London, Routledge; the major developments in the orthographic system, as well as in the grammar and phonology of the language, are exemplified in a collection of texts dating from early Old French to the modern period.

du Bellay, J. 1549 *Défense et illustration de la langue française*, Paris, Arnoul l'Angelier

Brunot, F. 1905–53 *Histoire de la langue française des origines à nos jours* (vols 1 and 2), Paris, Armand Colin; for the historical background to learned borrowings in the fourteenth to sixteenth centuries.

Bynon, T. 1977 *Historical Linguistics,* Cambridge, Cambridge University Press

Catach, N. 1995 (6th edition) *L'Orthographe* Paris, PUF Que Sais-Je?

Chaurand, J. 1977 *Introduction à l'histoire du vocabulaire français*, Paris, Bordas

Cottez, H. 1988 (4th edition) *Dictionnaire des structures du vocabulaire savant*, Paris,Usuels du Robert

Godefroy, F. 1961 (reprinted from 1880) *Dictionnaire de l'ancienne langue française*, New York, Kraus Reprint Corporation

Gougenheim, G. 1970 *Etudes de grammaire et de vocabulaire français*, Paris, A. J. Picard

Guiraud, P. 1966 *Le Moyen français*, Paris, PUF Que Sais-Je?

—— 1968b *Les Mots savants*, Paris, PUF Que Sais-Je?

Kesselring, W. 1981 *Dictionnaire chronologique du vocabulaire français au seizième siècle*, Heidelberg, Winter; a year-by-year inventory of the first appearance of neologisms and borrowings during this period.

Lodge, R. A. 1993 *French: From Dialect to Standard*, London, Routledge

Matoré, G. 1985 *Le Vocabulaire de la société médiévale*, Paris, PUF

Pope, M. K. 1961 *From Latin to Modern French*, London, Butler and Tanner

Price, G. 1971 *The French Language: Present and Past*, London, Edward Arnold

Rickard, P. 1989 *A History of the French Language*, London, Hutchinson; for a summary of the development of the French orthographic system.

Walker, D.C. 1982 *Dictionnaire inverse de l'ancien français*, Ottawa, Editions de l'Université d'Ottawa

Zink, G. 1990 *Le Moyen français*, Paris, PUF Que Sais-Je?; for an account of the major lexical developments in the fourteenth and fifteenth centuries.

Chapter 4

The Romance contribution

Geographical proximity and complex economic and political relations have always promoted lexical exchange among the Romance languages of western Europe (see Map 1), more particularly when international trade and intellectual exchange began to develop, after the narrow feudalism of the early Middle Ages. The direction and extent of lexical influence have changed, according to shifts in the centres of economic and cultural dominance; more often than not, French has been the donor language. Influence from Romance languages outside French territory was slight, until the sixteenth century, but input from varieties spoken in northern France and the territory of the Langue d'Oc can be detected from the early medieval period.

THE NORTHERN DIALECTS

Francien, the dialect of Paris and the Ile de France, and ancestor of the standard language, was just one variety of the Langue d'Oïl until the late twelfth century. Other regions, notably Normandy, Picardy, and Champagne, were prosperous centres where court life fostered the use of the local vernacular for literary purposes. The Normans in particular could boast a kingdom which spanned southern Britain as well as much of northwest France, and which went on to establish bases in southern Italy and the eastern Mediterranean. But the growing importance of Paris, commercially, politically and intellectually made Francien a linguistic melting-pot which absorbed influences from other northern varieties, while gradually extending its influence over them (see Map 2).

Establishing the exact provenance of a word is often difficult, owing to the similarities that exist among the dialects of the Langue d'Oïl; nor is it always possible to distinguish between a borrowing and the phonological remodelling of a French word due to the influence of a regional cognate. Norman or Picard *biche* 'doe', for example, supplanted Francien *bisse*, and Norman *câble* Francien *chable*. The borrowing of a cognate does not necessarily entail the loss of the French word, if the two have become semantically differentiated. Hence we find the doublets *chevrette* 'young goat' from Francien and *crevette* 'shrimp', borrowed from Norman French in the sixteenth century, both from Latin *capritta*.

Closely parallel developments also mean that a dialectal word can often slide easily into place within an established series of words in French: for example, *crachin* 'drizzle', from Britanny, is formally and semantically in line with the existing *cracher* 'spit', *crachat* 'spittle', *crachoir* 'spittoon', etc.

Although words as common as *boulanger* or *cauchemar* 'nightmare' from Picard, or *flâner* 'to stroll' from Norman, which have no regional 'flavour', may be borrowed, most loans refer to phenomena typical of the region they come from.

In Chapter Two we saw the number of seafaring terms of Scandinavian origin which came into French via the Norman dialect: *vague, crique, flotte, tillac*, etc. In addition, Norman French gave words from the same field, of Latin origin, such as *pieuvre* 'octopus', *câble, s'enliser* 'to get stuck' and *vergue* 'yard' (of a sail).

The Walloon and Picard dialects of the north-east, the most important coal-mining area of France, have provided a whole range of terms relating to the industry, from *houille* 'coal', to *escarbilles* 'cinders', *grisou* 'fire-damp', and many technical terms unfamiliar to the general public, mostly dating from the late eighteenth and nineteenth centuries. A terrible mining accident in 1906 led to the Walloon word *rescapé* 'survivor' being taken up by the press, supplanting its cognate noun *réchappé* in the standard language. *Estaminet*, a working man's bar, is also from this source.

Early borrowings from the mountainous parts of the Franco-Provençal area reflect the physical environment: *avalanche, moraine, mélèze* 'larch' and local artifacts – *chalet* and *luge* 'sledge'. Most of these, like the word *alpes* itself, seem to have pre-Latin origins.

Predictably, regional dishes figure prominently among the borrowings into standard French, such as *choucroute* 'sauerkraut', *quenelles* (fish or meat balls) and *quiche* from the German dialect of Alsace, *hochepot* 'hot-pot' from the north-east and *mouclade* (mussels with cream) from the Charentes area.

Even allowing for the problems of determining the provenance of some words, and for the fact that many borrowed dialectal words relate to occupations which are now extinct, the quantity of loans from the northern dialects is modest; Guiraud (1968c) estimates that they amount to fewer than 500, entering the language at an average rate of about sixty per century. Rather more substantial has been the contribution of the southern dialects of the Langue d'Oc, or Occitan.

OCCITAN

The term 'Occitan' is to be preferred to 'Provençal', as the latter is often used ambiguously to refer to all the southern varieties, as well as to those specifically of Provence in the south-east. In addition, it is used of the literary koine, or semi-standardised variety, which enjoyed great prestige in the twelfth to thirteenth centuries; its themes and forms were copied, not only in northern France, but in Italy and Catalonia. Some borrowings from this field came into French in the medieval period: *ballade, aubade* 'dawn song' and *amour* itself. Later *troubadour* replaced the northern equivalent *trouvère*.

In close contact with the Mediterranean, the southern dialects are a source of loans relating to the sea: in the Middle Ages *cap* 'cape', 'head-land', *brume* 'fog', *cabestan* 'capstan', in the Renaissance period *aiguade* 'provision of water', *cargaison* 'cargo', and from the seventeenth century onwards terms such as *radeau* 'raft', *remous* 'eddies', *chavirer* 'to capsize' and *mistral*. Some technical expressions originating in this field, such as *(mettre) en panne* 'to bring a ship to', *déraper* 'to slip anchor' and *caler* 'to sit low in the water' have subsequently extended their meaning in other fields (compare the semantic development of other nautical terms, p. 160). To these may be added many more technical terms which would be familiar only to sailors. Guiraud (1968c) estimates that there are about ninety in the field as a whole.

Almost as productive – and more widely known – are borrowings from the semantic field of food; many of the fish and shellfish of the Mediterranean, the fruit and vegetables of the Midi and dishes derived from them carry Occitan names. The most familiar of the seafood are the *sole, sardine, daurade* 'gilt-head', *anchois* 'anchovy', *rascasse* 'scorpionfish', *thon* 'tuna', *clovisse* 'clam', *langouste* 'crayfish' and *poulpe* 'octopus'. (*Poulpe* is the Occitan equivalent of northern *pieuvre*, both derived from the Latin *polypus*.) *Concombre, datte, figue* and *ciboule* 'chives' are among the fruit and vegetables that have contributed to the variety of French cuisine. The south is known for its *escargots*, its delicately flavoured *ortolans* (small birds of the bunting family), and the hugely expensive *truffes* of the Périgord, in the north Occitan area. Among the dishes native to the Midi are the *cassoulet* from the south-west, the *panade* or bread soup, the more elaborate *bouillabaisse* with its accompanying *aïoli* sauce, and the *pissaladière*, or Provençal pizza from the south-east. The sweet *muscat* and the *muscadet* wines bear Occitan names, although the latter is now produced mainly around Nantes.

Examples of Occitan borrowings are also to be found in the names of animal species: *cigale* 'cicada', *rossignol* 'nightingale', *cigogne* 'stork'; in features of the landscape: *pic* 'crag', *brousse* 'bush', 'scrub', *garrigue* 'scrubland', *causses* 'limestone plateaux'; and some everyday terms whose connections with the south have been obscured by the passage of time: *casserole*, *terrasse*, *cadenas* ('padlock', a doublet of French *chaîne*).

REGIONAL BORROWINGS AND *NIVEAUX DE LANGUE*

The dominance of Parisian French has meant that writers, whatever their origins, have been loath to use regional expressions, except to lend local colour to their narrative or their characters. Even in the sixteenth century, when there was a certain vogue for dialect words, few found a permanent place in the lexis.

Everyday discourse, however, was less affected by such constraints. We have already seen how words relating to regionally based products, trades and occupations entered the standard language through dialects and regional languages. From the mid-nineteenth century, increasing centralisation of the administration and the very nature of modern industry led to dialects becoming less productive of technical terms. However, they have always been a rich source of slang and expressive vocabulary of all kinds (see pp. 206–7). *Bagnole* 'old banger', *moche* 'ugly' and *pleurnicher* 'to snivel' come from northern dialects, *baratin* 'sweet talk' and *truc* 'thingummy' from Occitan, *grolles* 'shoes' from Franco-Provençal, and so on. Some, such as *dupe* and *cambrioleur*, have come up in the world, and form part of the standard lexis; others have remained linked to informal or working-class speech (see pp. 203–5).

It is therefore a characteristic of dialectal and regional words that they originate at the bottom of the social ladder and – occasionally – work their way up to acceptability in the literary language; hence they follow the opposite route to that of learned borrowings from Latin and Greek, some of which 'trickle down' into general use.

ITALIAN INFLUENCE

Of all the Romance languages it is Italian that has had the most marked effect on French. At its peak, Italian influence was perceived to be of greater significance than the linguistic facts alone perhaps warranted, owing in part to the heavy concentration of borrowings in a single century. This influx coincided with a burgeoning nationalism in France, which engendered a strong reaction against Italian political influence.

The early period

To understand why the trickle of Italianisms which had been entering French in the Middle Ages reached tidal proportions in the sixteenth century, it is necessary to appreciate the growing economic importance of the city states of northern Italy.

The wealth of Venice and Genoa was founded on the twelfth-century revival of trade in Europe and the reassertion of European power in the Mediterranean. Silk and porcelain from China, Persian carpets, Syrian cotton, jewels and spices from India and the East Indies, all converged by sea or overland routes to ports on the eastern Mediterranean or the Black Sea. Venice dominated the sea-borne trade from Constantinople and the Levant, while Genoa controlled routes to the west, and south to the ports of North Africa. They were well-placed to link up with the cities of the Hanseatic League, which were clustered around the Baltic and the North Sea, specialising in the trade of timber, fur, woollens, minerals and fish. Hence the ports of northern Italy were for several centuries at the hub of trade in the Western world.

Italian merchants not only played a role in directly financing fleets of merchant ships and providing credit and insurance for trading ventures of all kinds; from an early date they became involved in financing the military campaigns of European monarchs, including crusades to the Holy Land. Trade, high finance, politics, diplomacy and war are all recurring themes when we come to look at the kinds of borrowings taken into French in the Medieval period.

The very earliest borrowings reflect Italy's role as the importer of luxury goods from the East: *sucre* (< *zucchero*) and *coton* (< *cottone*) are both from Arabic, like *avarie*, damage suffered by a ship or its cargo. Later Arabisms filtered through Italian include *matelas* 'mattress', *magasin* (meaning 'warehouse'), *gabelle* 'tax', *douane* 'Customs', *carat* 'carat', *nacre* 'mother-of-pearl', *massepain* (first meaning a casket for sweetmeats, later 'marzipan'), and the names of exotic animals like the *girafe* and the *civette* or civet cat, which produced musky secretions used in the fixing of perfumes. From Persian and Turkish Italian transmitted *sérail* 'seraglio' and *taffetas* 'taffeta', and from Greek *riz*.

Native Italian words for merchandise include *perle, lavande, grenade* 'pomegranate' and *porcelaine* (named after a shell with the same translucent properties). The key term *banquier* seems to have been borrowed before *banque* (originally a money-changer's counter) and *banqueroute* 'bankrupt', which was later displaced by *faillite*. Other basic commercial terms are *trafic, trafiquer* and *crédit*, and, naturally enough, the names for the Venetian and Florentine currencies, the *ducat* and the *florin*.

Shipping terms are important, in the overlapping fields of trade and naval warfare; many types and parts of boats are now obsolete, though *barque*, *poupe* 'stern' and *proue* 'prow' remain key terms,[1] and *esquif* 'skiff' and *corsaire* (originally 'pirate', later the small fast vessel used by them) are still in use. Terms relating to the repair and construction of ships include *calfater* 'to caulk', and *arsenal*, originally from Arabic *dār sinā'* 'dock-yard' (by the fifteenth century Venice had by far the largest docks and ship-building yards of Europe). The less technical of terms for weather conditions include *tramontane* (north wind), and *sirocco* (south-east wind). Other non-technical loans connected with navigation are *pilote* and *escale* 'port of call'.

Military borrowings begin in the fourteenth century, with *canon* and *bricole* 'siege catapult', new developments in armaments at the time; this category is one of the most productive in the fifteenth century, a period when the French kings Charles VIII and Louis XII made attempts to seize Naples and Milan, often with the support or collusion of other Italian states. Some loans, such as *investir* 'to besiege', *citadelle* and *escalade* 'scaling' remind us that long sieges were a common feature of warfare at the time, with the loan verb *saccager* 'to pillage' recalling the customary reward for the victorious troops. Other military terms include *brigade*, *alarme* (< *all'arme* 'to arms'), *embusquade* 'ambush', *escarmouche* 'skirmish', *escadre* (originally 'brigade') and *escadron* 'troop of cavalry'. The earlier medieval loan *brigand* had originally meant simply foot-soldier, but rapidly acquired the pejorative connotations it has today.

It may seem surprising that the basic term *soldat* was borrowed, since a range of expressions – *soudoyer*, *homme d'armes* and *sergent* – already existed in French; but as Hope (1971: 673) points out, a new type of professional private soldier was emerging in the standing armies of Europe, very different from the temporary conscripts and mercenaries of the feudal era, and a new designation was required.

The first loan to appear in the field of what might be termed international relations is *espion* in the thirteenth century. *Ambassade* and *ambassadeur* follow in the fifteenth, together with *chiffre*, originally meaning 'code' or 'cipher' (hence the derived form *déchiffrer* 'to decipher'). Fourteenth-century *courrier* and fifteenth-century *poste* bear witness to the importance of swift communications in both diplomacy and commerce. (*Courrier* first meant the bearer of the message rather than the correspondence itself, while *poste* referred to the relays of post-horses for carrying mail, that Italy was the first to organise.)

The handful of loans connected with the court foreshadow an influence which would figure prominently in the sixteenth century. The key term *courtisan* 'courtier' was borrowed, in a slightly different form, as early as the mid-fourteenth century; *marquis* was adopted as a remodelling of French *marchis*, while the terms *banquet*, *caresse*, *cadence*, *discourtois*, *guirlande* 'garland', *panache* 'plume', *lustre* 'light', 'splendour', *escrime* 'fencing', give a flavour of the lifestyle and pastimes of the court. There are very few literary or artistic terms at this stage; we find only *dôme* (with reference to Italian architecture), *dessin*, *mosaïque*, *médaille* and *nouvelles* (short stories, such as those written by Boccaccio).

Borrowing was therefore well under way before the sixteenth century; Hope (1971) lists 28 loans in the thirteenth century, 59 in the fourteenth

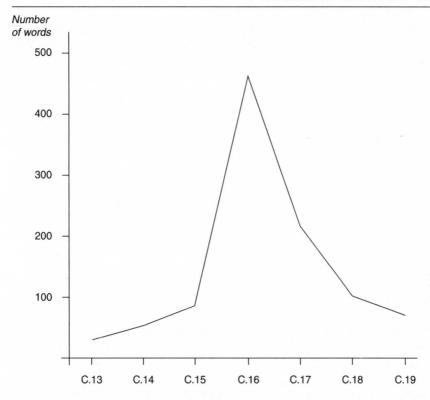

Number of words

Figure 7 Italian borrowings in French from the thirteenth to the nineteenth century
Source: Hope 1971

and 91 in the fifteenth. But these seem meagre beside the surge of Italian-isms we find in the sixteenth century, which reach a total of 462.

The High Renaissance

The great concentration of wealth of the cities of northern Italy, coupled with their prolonged contact with the highly sophisticated civilisations of the Near and Far East, had set the scene for the great flowering of intel-lectual and artistic activity of the Renaissance. Italian universities drew students and scholars from all over Europe to participate in the New Learning, and they took home with them a taste for Italian literature, music, art and fashion. François I, an enthusiastic collector of Italian art and builder of the château at Blois, invited the greatest artists of the day, like Leonardo da Vinci and Cellini, to his court.

The first decades of the sixteenth century were a continuation of the trend established in the previous century, but the rate of borrowing increased rapidly, reaching a peak from 1540–60 (about eighty per decade at this point). There was then an abrupt diminution to something like the previous level of influence. As Hope demonstrates, both the quantitative patterning of borrowing and the types of field affected can be related to the nature and intensity of relations between the two countries.

Direct political influence must be in part responsible for the mid-century rise in the rate of borrowing. Henri II, who married Catherine dei Medici in 1533, came to the throne in 1547; on his death in 1559 she became Regent, and continued to dominate French politics during the reigns of her sons Charles IX and Henri III.

Court manners, amusements and dress are reflected in the kinds of loan which proliferate as the century progresses: *politesse*, *délicatesse*, *courtisane*, *courtiser*, *machiavélique*, *intrigue*, *supercherie* 'trickery', *favori*, *créature* (both in the sense of protégé or favourite), *festin* 'banquet', *masque*, *ballet*, *mascarade* 'masked ball', *travestir* 'to disguise', *s'amouracher* 'to become infatuated', *caprice*, *pommade*, *escarpin* 'dancing slipper', *cabriole* 'leap', 'caper', *brocart* 'brocade', *capuchon* 'hood', *ombrelle*, *parasol*, *turban*.

It is perhaps not too far-fetched to detect the atmosphere of court gossip in some of the expressive terms relating to human personality – *jovial*, *leste* 'sprightly', *poltron* 'craven' and *humoriste* (originally 'moody'). It has also been suggested that even the abstract verbs *manquer* and *réussir* began in court circles as power-laden words, adopted partly because of the way the existing semantic fields were structured (see Chaurand 1977: 75–6).

We cannot really separate the life of the court from influence in the literary and artistic fields, since the court was the main source of patronage. It is in the sixteenth century that the first of many terms relating to musical genres and instruments are borrowed: *e(s)pinette*, *trombone*, *contrebasse* 'double bass', *fugue*, *madrigal*, *cantilène*, *sérénade*, *sourdine* 'mute', *duo* and *trio*. In a field where French had hitherto been the donor language, we find the loans *sonnet*, *stance* 'stanza' and *tercet* 'triplet'. The growing influence of Italian art and architecture can be seen in terms like *belvédère*, *pilastre*, *piédestal*, *arcade*, *façade*, *frise*, *corniche* 'cornice', *arabesque*, *esquisse* 'sketch', *estampe* 'engraving', *figurine* and *relief*, as well as the key terms *architecte* and *architecture*.

All of the above found a permanent role in the French lexis, but there were many modish and ephemeral Italianisms of the kind parodied by Henri Estienne in his *Dialogues du nouveau langage français italianisé et autrement déguisé* (1578), in which two courtiers debate the pros and cons of Italian influence. Estienne considered that *courtisanismes* and *singularités courtisanesques* constituted a threat to the language. In a largely bilingual court, what we now call code-switching must indeed have been common, and the fashion for Italianisms was picked up by some writers. The phenomenon was, however, restricted in scope to a small social group over a limited period of time, and could hardly threaten the wholesale transformation of the French lexis.

Beyond immediate court circles we also find increased influence in the fields of military and naval terminology, due no doubt to continued French involvement on Italian soil. François I laid claim to Milan and Piedmont, where he met with some success. However, at the time the private armies of the Italian states were in many ways more rationally structured and better trained than their French counterparts and the influence of their organisation, tactics and armaments can be seen in loans like *bataillon*, *colonel*, *caporal*, *généralissime*, *escorte*, *fantassin* 'foot soldier', *balle* 'bullet', *cartouche* 'cartridge', *sentinelle* 'sentry', *espadon* 'broadsword', *taillade* 'slash', *estocade* 'death-blow', *cavalerie*, *infanterie*, and even the basic verb *attaquer*. Interestingly, just as *soldat* had found a niche in a changing semantic field, *cavalier* came to be seen as more appropriate to modern warfare than its doublet *chevalier* which was heavy with the accumulated social and moral connotations of medieval chivalry.[2]

Surviving nautical terms include *fanal* 'ship's lantern', *frégate* 'frigate', *môle* 'jetty', *mousse* 'cabin-boy', *remorquer* 'to tow', *bourrasque* 'squall', *strapontin* (originally 'hammock'). At this time we find the first appearance of *boussole*, the magnetic compass manufactured in Italy in the fourteenth century, which helped to revolutionise navigation.

Commercial terminology is not quite as prolific as in the preceding period, but some key words still make their appearance: *escompte* 'discount', *faillite* 'bankruptcy', *bilan* 'balance sheet', *liquide* (of assets, etc.) *numéro* (first a serial number on merchandise). There are also a few exotic imports; *caviar* and *turban* can be traced back to Turkish, and *sorbet* to Arabic. More common are local exports, especially food products – *parmesan*, *vermicelle*, *brocoli*, *saucisson*, *semoule* 'semolina', *marrons* 'chestnuts', *citrouille* 'pumpkin'.

By the end of the sixteenth century the areas of the lexis affected by Italian influence therefore reflect not so much relations based on commercial exchange as the response of an urbane society eagerly embracing the refinements and innovations of a superior cosmopolitan culture; social and intellectual involvement was intensified by the close military and political ties between the two countries.

The decline in borrowing later in the century no doubt reflects the changing political climate of the time. A strongly Italianised court over a period of several decades inevitably engendered bitter resentment of foreign influence, as can be seen in Estienne's writings. Catherine's personal unpopularity was increased by the widespread belief that she was responsible for much of the religious strife in the country, including the infamous Saint Bartholomew Massacre in which 3,000 Protestants were put to death.

Nevertheless, Italian linguistic influence continued at a significant level over the next three centuries. During this period, it is above all the artistic and musical genius of Italy that leaves a mark on the French lexis.

Waning lexical influence from the seventeenth century

With Marie dei Medici as the wife of Henri IV, and later Regent, and the Florentine Mazarin as one of the most powerful figures of seventeenth-century France, it is not surprising that Italian remains the primary source for borrowings. (Hope (1971) lists about two hundred items for this century.)

It is art and architecture that constitute the largest single category of loans at this time. Ancient Rome was a model and an inspiration for architects of the day, and Italian expertise was called upon in the design and execution of many of the most ambitious architectural projects of France, including the palace of Versailles. Some major architectural features are *coupole, rotonde, mezzanine, salon* 'reception hall'; while decorative details include *cariatide* and *fronton* 'pediment'. In sculpture and painting we find loans like *torse, fresque, pastel, miniature*. The importance of this field, culturally and psychologically, can be seen in the way in which terms initially connected with painting are a focal source of metaphor and metonymy; technical expressions like *attitude, costume, svelte, calque, reflet* and *élève* (originally artist's pupil or apprentice) were subsequently extended in meaning and passed into general usage. The popularity of the *commedia dell'arte* reached a peak in the seventeenth century, and some of its stock characters like Scaramouche were adopted in the French theatre; among these, Tartuffe, immortalised by Molière, and Polichinelle achieved the status of common nouns referring to human stereotypes, while the costume of Pantalone is responsible for the common noun *pantalon*. In all probability *improviser* and *tremplin* (then, 'trapdoor') can be traced to the same source.

Some of the hitherto most productive fields, such as warfare, show a marked decline, as France abandoned its ambitions in the Italian peninsula. The military innovations of the *bombe* and the *cantine* 'field canteen' did however prove to have staying-power.

Borrowings connected with trade continued, but at a modest level. Disruption of the overland trade routes to Asia and increasing competition from the sea routes which had been opened up by the great navigators of Portugal and Spain, both to the east, and west to the New World, led to a decline in Italy's economic power. By the end of the century Holland and England were dominant in international trade, and German bankers had assumed greater importance in the world of finance.

However, a few terms for luxury goods, like *(soie) grège* 'raw silk', and *filigrane* 'gold thread' were borrowed, while Italian *travertin* and *granit* were prized building materials. One or two luxuries arrived from the East, notably *mousseline* 'muslin' and *café*. Food is a semantic category which has provided a steady lexical input, from seventeenth-century *macaroni*, *céleri* and *estouffade* (a kind of stew) to eighteenth-century *chipolata* and *cantaloup*, nineteenth-century *biscotte*, *polenta*, *ravioli*, *risotto* and *sabayon* 'zabaglione', and twentieth-century *lasagne*, *minestrone*, *pizza* and *osso buco*. Some of these should perhaps be considered **pérégrénismes**, to use Deroy's term (1956: 223) – that is, words with a distinctly 'foreign flavour', that have remained marginal to the lexis, rather than fully integrated loans.

The last concentrated influx of borrowings came in the field of musical terminology, largely owing to the brilliance and popularity of Italian opera. It begins in the seventeenth century, with the introduction of *opéra* itself, *récitatif* and *sonate*. In the eighteenth century, we find a flood of loans designating musical instruments, types of singer, genres, tempi and notations: *mandoline*, *violoncelle*, *pianoforte*, *cantatrice*, *castrat*, *contralto*, *alto*, *solo*, *oratorio*, *aria*, *cantate*, *tempo*, *adagio*, *allegro*, *andante*, *piano*, *presto*, *forte*, *fortissimo*, *crescendo*, *arpège*, *finale* and many more. (Here again, many of these might be considered *pérégrénismes*, particularly in the light of the un-Gallicised suffixes -*o* and -*a*.) In all, they total about fifty, or half the entire intake for the century.

The flood subsides in the following century, although music is still the single most important category, with about twenty terms, including *brio*, *imprésario*, *diva*, *maestro*, *libretto*, *trémolo*, *coda*, *piccolo*. (*Fiasco* was first associated with operatic flops, before becoming generalised.) The other arts are somewhat eclipsed, with only a handful of loans relating to art and architecture, such as *putto* 'cherub' and *aquatinte*.

In this later period influence is not only much reduced, but diffused across an apparently random collection of fields. Consciousness of the *mafia* and its activities may explain the latter borrowing, together with that of *vendetta*. Criminal slang of Italian origin also makes its appearance at this point, and continues into the twentieth century: *camoufler* (originally 'to trick'), *gonze* 'bloke' and *gonzesse*, and more recently *saccagne* 'knife' and *rengracier* 'to back off'.

SUFFIXATION AND ASSIMILATION

In the examples given above a number of derivational suffixes recur, most notably -*esque*, -*ade* and -*issime*. Highly productive in Italian, the latter was used in French both for superlatives like *grandissime*, and honorific titles like *Généralissime* and *Illustrissime*; many, like *ignorantissime*, were short-lived, while a few, like *richissime* and *rarissime*, remain. The role of intensifier seems to have been filled more successfully by the classical prefixes *hyper-*, *super-*, *ultra-* and *archi-* (see p. 198).

The suffix *-esque* (originally Germanic) was first introduced in loans like *grotesque*, *burlesque* and *pittoresque*, and later occasionally suffixed to non-Italian elements, as in *moliéresque*, *livresque* and twentieth-century *ubuesque*. *-ade* proved to be more productive, occurring not only in loans but with French roots – usually verbs, to signify a repeated or vigorous action: *bousculade* 'scramble', *glissade* 'skid', *engueulade* 'slanging match', *embrassade* 'hugging', *œillade* 'come-hither glance'. Its origins in French loans have occasioned much debate (see Hope 1971: 601–9); as we have seen, it occurs in borrowings from Occitan – *ballade*, *aubade*, etc. – and from Spanish (see below), while in northern Italy it is a common variant of the Tuscan *-ata*. It seems that it was established at an early date in French, primarily through contact with Occitan, and that later Italian forms ending in *-ata* were remodelled accordingly. Etymologically, *-ata* corresponds to French *-ée* (so that *chevauchée*, for example, is the cognate of Italian *cavalcata*), but this suffix was no doubt too different for any synchronic connection to be made with *-ade*, so it is not introduced into Italianisms.

Such is not the case for most cognate suffixes in French and Italian; for example, *-ier* and *-iere*, *-in* and *-ino*, *et* and *-etto*, *-ure* and *-ura* are transparently related, and only minimal adjustments are needed to Gallicise the Italian form. Hence *balletto* was borrowed as *ballet*, *politezza* as *politesse*, and so on.

Naturally many of the words borrowed from Italian have existing cognates in French. Where the two terms have developed clearly differentiated meanings, as is the case with *échelle* and *escale*, they coexist just like forms which have no etymological connections. If, however, the words are virtually synonymous, the loan often displaces the native word. *Espion*, for example, replaced Old French *espie*, *embusquer*, *embuschier*, and *canaille*, *chiennaille*.[3] Where the meanings of cognates overlap there may be some jostling for position before the semantic territory of the two terms becomes settled. A particularly interesting case here is that of *attaquer* and *attacher*. The latter already fulfilled some of the functions of modern *attaquer*, but the meaning 'attack' later became exclusively associated with the loan (see Hope 1971: 158).

As we shall see in more detail in the next chapter, with reference to cognate Anglicisms, it is not unusual for the meaning of the foreign word to be transferred; examples already cited above are the use of *liquide* as a financial term, and the pejorative overtones added to *créature*.

THE INFLUENCE OF SPANISH, PORTUGUESE AND CATALAN

Compared to Italian, the languages of the Iberian peninsula have not had a profound effect on French, despite their proximity to French territory. The cultures have remained more distinct, and many words of Spanish origin are still somewhat marginal to the French lexis. The major contribution of Spanish and Portuguese has rather been as intermediaries for the transmission of words which have come from much further afield.

Only a handful of early loans from Spanish survive, such as *baie*, *tournesol* 'sunflower' and *infant* 'infante'. From the sixteenth century, wars with France, and Spain's importance as a maritime power, led to borrowings like *parade, camarade, casque* 'helmet', *pinasse* 'pinnace' (a small, light boat), *caboter* 'to hug the coast'. More nautical terms followed in the seventeenth and eighteenth centuries: *flotille, embarcation, embarcadère* 'landing stage', *récif* 'reef'.

Courtly influence on French society in the sixteenth and seventeenth centuries is reflected in loans like *romance, quadrille* and *sarabande*. The Spanish orthographic innovation of the *cédille* (< *zedilla*, or 'little z') was to prove useful in attempts to rationalise the orthography of French in the sixteenth century.

Spanish colonisation of parts of Central and South America, and involvement in the slave trade, account for sixteenth- to seventeenth-century loans like *nègre, mulâtre* 'mulatto' and *quarteron* 'quadroon'. Many of the products of the region are taken from indigenous languages (see 'Words from the New World', below). The Spanish presence in Central and South America has left its mark on American English as well as on the languages of Europe, in the form of words which are familiar to most people through American westerns; the French versions of Hispano-American loans are *lasso, rodéo, ranch, cañon*.

For the most part, Spanish borrowings from the eighteenth century onwards conjure up stereotypical images of Spanish life and culture: *mantille, duègne, gitan, sombrero, sieste, macho*, and all the terminology relating to bullfighting: *torero, toréador, picador, matador, corrida*, and so on. The words associated with traditional Spanish music – *guitare, flamenco, boléro, castagnettes, paso-doble*, – form a significant category, together with more recent Latin American developments like *rumba* and *tango*. The popularity of dishes like *paella* and *gazpacho* have brought them, at least marginally, into the French lexis.

Only the seafaring terms *galère* 'galley' and *misaine* 'foresail' can be traced with any certainty to Catalan (though the latter seems to have passed through Italian); Portuguese also gave a number of words associated with the sea: *sargasse, cachalot* 'sperm whale', *vigie* 'crow's-nest' or 'lookout', *caravelle* (a sailing ship of the type used by Columbus). Other indigenous Portuguese loans recall Portugal's heyday as a trading and colonial nation; their African voyages no doubt inspired *pintade* (< *pintada* 'guinea-fowl'), *paillotte* (< *palhota* 'straw hut'), *coco* and *fétiche* (< *feitiço*, literally 'charm' or 'spell'). In the Indian subcontinent they coined *cobra de capel*, literally 'hooded snake' (> *cobra*), *casta* 'breed' (> *caste*), *cerval* 'tiger-cat' (> *serval*), while the French version of *balhadeira* 'dancer' – *bayadère* – came to be used specifically of professional Indian dancers. The words *favela* 'shantytown' and *bossa nova*, now known throughout Europe, were born in Portugal's former colony of Brazil, while *crioulo* (> *créole*) was used first of the European cattle, then of the European settlers born in the Caribbean.

Like the Spanish, the Portuguese naturally borrowed from the languages of their colonies and trading-posts, and some of these were also to find a place in the French lexis (see below).

'EXOTIC' BORROWINGS IN THE ROMANCE LANGUAGES

After a period of several centuries when the Mediterranean was at the crossroads of trade in the Western world, the sixteenth century saw massive global expansion of trade and colonisation, following the discovery of the New World and the opening up of direct sea routes to India and the Far East. The consequences of these contacts, as far as the lexis of French is concerned, tended to be indirect, with the other Romance languages acting as intermediaries.

We have already seen how Italian passed on loans, such as *sucre* or *turban*, from the major languages of the Near and Middle East – Arabic, Turkish and Persian, which themselves interacted in complex ways. Some Arabic loans like *minaret* and *muezzin* reached French through Turkish, itself an important intermediary owing to the extent and duration of the Ottoman Empire. The form of the French word *café* also suggests that it was not taken direct from Arabic *qahwa*, but came through Turkish *kahvé*.

The same etymon may develop along different pathways; Persian *diwān* came into French through Turkish as *divan*, while in a separate development it found its way into the language as *douane*, through Arabic and then Italian. The relatively few loans from Turkish itself tend to be either trading terms through Italian, like sixteenth-century *caviar* and *bergamote* (a pear-like fruit) or later borrowings from a variety of fields, such as *kiosque, odalisque, bey, caïque, gilet* and *baklava*.

Direct loans from Arabic

By the middle of the eighth century, the Arabs had conquered vast tracts of territory: eastwards as far as the frontiers of China, and westwards across

North Africa and into Spain. Their advance was only halted at Poitiers in 739 by the Franks, so that they were obliged to withdraw behind the Pyrenees. Southern Spain was to remain under Arab control until the Reconquest in the thirteenth century and it was not until 1492 that the kingdom of Grenada was finally conquered.[4]

Contacts with China, Persia, India and Byzantium combined to produce an Islamic civilisation of great refinement, where architecture and the decorative arts, music and poetry were developed to the highest degree. The sciences of mathematics, astronomy, chemistry and medecine all flourished at a time when Europe was still suffering from the effects of the barbarian invasions. In the ninth century, for example, when Paris was a modest town of a few thousand inhabitants, Cordoba was the largest city in western Europe with a population of over half a million, boasting some of the finest buildings of the Western world, and a university of international renown.

The crusades of the eleventh and twelfth centuries, both in Spain and in Palestine, brought the French into direct contact with this civilisation. A few direct borrowings date from this period: *gazelle*, *tasse*, *jupe* (then a loose outer garment), *tambour* 'drum', *barbacane* (fortification around a gateway or bridge).

It was not until French colonisation of parts of North Africa in the nineteenth century that renewed contact with Arabic speakers brought in direct borrowings from the dialects of Algeria, Tunisia and Morocco. Some of these refer to local phenomena: *oued* (rocky watercourse), *souk* (oriental market), *chéchia* 'fez', *méchoui* 'barbecue', *marabout* 'hermit' or 'shrine', *merguez* (spicy sausage), *burnous*, *haschisch* and *couscous*; others are colloquialisms, often referential equivalents of existing terms: *kif-kif* 'the same', *ramdam* 'noise', 'uproar' (< 'Ramadan'), *toubib* 'doctor', *salamalecs* 'greetings', *clebs* 'dog', *maboul* 'crazy', etc. (see p. 207).

Arabic loans via the Iberian peninsula

In the medieval period it is through Spanish that most Arabic loans came into both French and other European languages. In a largely bilingual population, they passed easily into the local Romance tongue: several thousand words of modern Spanish, including everyday terms like *aceite* 'oil', *marras* 'long ago', and *hasta* 'until' are from Arabic.

Among those which filtered through to French are *hasard* (from the Arabic for dice), *amiral* (< *al-'amir*, 'prince' or 'commander'), while *auferrant* (< Arabic *al-faras* 'horse') was one Old French term for warhorse. Another generic term for horse in Arabic, *al-hisan*, survives as *alezan* 'chestnut', while *genet* 'jennet' (a small fast horse) comes from the name of a Berber tribe. Within the same broad semantic field we find *algarade* (originally a surprise attack; later an outburst or tirade).

Various fruits and vegetables originated as far afield as China, and a number of terms underwent Arabic influence on their passage to Europe. *Aubergine*, for example, from Arabic *al-badinjān*, originated in Persian, and reached French through Catalan. *Orange* is another word which can be traced back to Persian, via the Arabic *naranj*. We have already seen (p. 30) how the peach was known to the Romans as the *persica (poma)* or 'Persian (fruit)' (> *pêche*); the same word was Arabised as *al-berchiga*, (> *alberge*), referring to the now neglected clingstone, which is related to the peach and the nectarine. Although the apricot itself comes from China, *abricot* stems from a Latin word *praecoquum* or 'early-ripe (fruit)', which was Arabised to *al-barqūq*, and then reached Europe through the Iberian peninsula.[5]

Medieval science and Arabic loans

Besides these borrowings, relating to everyday life and commerce, and passed on by word of mouth, there is an important group of Arabic words relating to science, which were disseminated throughout Europe via medieval Latin. (From the twelfth century, following the reconquest of northern Spain, Toledo was an important centre for the translation of Arabic texts.)

Alchemy, the forerunner of modern chemistry, was one of the most important fields, linguistically speaking. From Arabic came not only *alchimie* and *chimie* (< *al-kimiya* 'transmutation'), but also *élixir* (< *al-iksir*), *alcool* (< *al-kuhl*, powdered antimony, later 'essence' or 'distillation'), *alcali* (< *al-qali* 'soda') and *alambic* (< *al-anbiq* 'still'). *Carafe* (< *gharaf*) may also be associated with this field, and perhaps *sirop* (< *sharab*), in medieval times a medicinal potion. Another Latinised Arabism (originally from Persian) was *azurrum*, ground lapis lazuli used in the manufacture of glass; now it is a purely poetic word (as in *la Côte d'Azur*).

Arabic gave to the science of astronomy a large number of technical terms, of which a few are in common use today, such as *almanach*, and *nadir* (the point in the cosmos directly below the observer), as opposed to the *zénith* (< *samt* meaning 'direction'). The plural of *samt* gave *azimut*, surviving in the idiom *tous azimuts* 'in all directions'.

The related science of mathematics, which was greatly advanced by the adoption of the Arabic numerals, has taken the key word *algèbre* (< *al-jabr*, literally 'reduction') from Arabic. This was the title of a famous work by the ninth-century mathematician Al-Khawarizmi, whose name was Latinised to Algoritmus (hence *algorithme*) which was used to mean mathematics in general in the medieval period, but became a more specific technical term in the sixteenth century. The notion of 'zero', crucial to modern mathematics, was brought by the Arabs from India; the medieval Latin version of the Arabic word *sifr* was *zephirum*, which gave both *zéro* (through Italian) and *chiffre* (from Italian, which had taken it from Spanish).

Arab scholars were thus a vital cultural link with Greek science and philosophy, which had been largely lost to Europe during the early Middle Ages. It was through Arabic translations of Greek scientific works that the works of Aristotle and Ptolemy were rediscovered in the West, and that advances in world geography and map-making became possible. This cultural connection can be seen in many borrowings from Greek to Arabic; of the examples given above, the terms *alchimie*, *élixir*, *alambic* are ultimately from Greek. The name for the guitar, which was to become Spain's national instrument, so to speak, can also be traced back via Arabic (*gitar*) to Greek *kithara*, a kind of lyre; the latter etymon is also the origin of the oriental *sitar*, and the European 'zither'.

Loans from India and the Far East

When Portugal opened up the sea-route round Africa to India and the Far East in the early sixteenth century, the overland caravan routes were gradually eclipsed, and we find later borrowings coming through the languages of the European colonial powers, rather than through Arabic or Turkish. For example, Portuguese mediated *mandarin* and *bambou* from Malay and *typhon* from Chinese. Via Portuguese French also acquired *calicot*, *mangue*, *cachou* (used as a breath-freshener) and *cari* 'curry', all taken from Tamil. (*Cari* was replaced this century by *curry*, from the English version of the same Tamil word.) English was again the vehicle for *catamaran* and *patchouli* from Tamil, and *tussor*, *bungalow*, *mohair* and *pyjama* from Hindi.

Linguistic influence was of course mutual. *Véranda* (< *baranda*) is a nice example of a much-travelled word, first exported to India by the Portuguese in the sixteenth century, only to be brought back to Europe three centuries later by another colonial power (see Map 3).

Words from the New World

In the sixteenth century it was the Spanish and the Portuguese who first established colonies and trading posts in Central and South America. From the languages of Mexico and Peru – areas with immensely productive silver mines – the Spanish took the names for other valuable products, and local flora and fauna. These then found their way into other European languages; *quinine*, *chinchilla*, *alpaga*, *coca*, *puma*, *lama*, *condor*, *pampa*, *caoutchouc* 'rubber', *vigogne* 'vicuña', can all be traced by this route to Peruvian languages. From Mexico came *avocat*, *cacao*, *chocolat*, *tomate*, *coyote*, *ocelot* and *cacahuètes* 'peanuts', while the languages of the Caribbean gave *tabac*, *hamac*, *iguane*, *pirogue*, *patate* 'sweet potato', *goyave* 'guava', *maïs* 'maize' and *cannibale* (originally *caribal*, or inhabitant of the Caribbean).

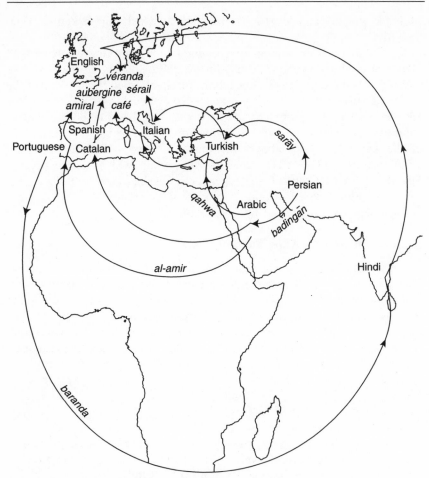

Map 3 Some much-travelled loan words

One of the most heavily colonised areas of South America was Brazil, where over three million slaves were transported by the Portuguese from their West African trading posts and colonies. At the same time African plants and animals were exported; hence *banane* and *macaque*, brought from Brazil but of Bantu origin. Words from the Tupi languages of Brazil were disseminated through Portuguese – again, a mixture of valuable products and exotic flora and fauna: *ananas* 'pineapple', *acajou* 'mahogany', *cobaye* 'guinea-pig', *manioc, tapioca, cougar, jaguar, piranha.*

These words from distant corners of the globe are few, and marginal to the lexis as a whole. But as markers of the European colonial enterprise they have a significance beyond lexical statistics. They might even be considered what Matoré (1953) terms *mots témoins*, or words that are symbolic of some key social or economic phenomenon of their time. By their very nature, such loans demonstrate that relations with these countries were based above all on trade. When we come, in the next chapter, to look at the influence of France's near neighbour and chief rival at the height of the colonial era, we will find that a much more complex array of semantic fields is involved, as well as much heavier borrowing, reflecting the complexity and intensity of relations between the two countries.

NOTES

1 These are good examples of loans where southern Romance forms are almost identical, and where the historical linguist must glean additional clues from the type of text in which the first attestations occur, in order to determine the provenance of the loan.

2 In effect, the military functions of the medieval *chevalier* were now fulfilled by the *cavalier*, while his social functions passed to the *courtisan*. See Gougenheim (1970: 356–67) for discussion of the social and linguistic contexts which led to the borrowing of such apparently redundant cognates.

3 In so far as some Italian borrowings enter into a lexical paradigm with existing French words (*canaille*, for example, with *chien* and *festin* with *fête*), the allomorphic complexity of the language is increased (see Chapter Six), since the Italian root has usually undergone fewer phonological changes than the French. The introduction of Italian loans has therefore much the same effect in this respect as the influx of Latin borrowings discussed in the last chapter. (*Canin*, for example, is a fourteenth-century Latinism sharing the same root as *canaille*.)

4 French *Matamore* (< *Matamoros*, literally 'Moor-killer', a stock comic character of the Spanish theatre, later meaning 'braggart') is a sixteenth-century reminder of the long struggles in the peninsula against the Arab occupiers.

5 The forms of words provide clues as to the route they have followed. It is typical of Arabisms of the Iberian peninsula that they are prefixed by the definite article *al-* – often with assimilation of the 'l' to the following consonant. Arabisms in Italian, however, tend to be borrowed without the article; hence we find pairs like Italian *cotone* (> French *coton*) and Spanish *algodon*, from Arabic *(al-)qutn*. Similarly the word for 'rice' took on an Arabised form in Spanish (*arroz*), but remains un-prefixed in Italian *riso* (> French *riz*). Another indication of Arabisation is the change from 'p' to 'b', since Arabic does not have a 'p' sound. This is clear from the examples of *abricot* and *alberge* just given, and from other borrowings like *babouche* 'slipper', which comes from Persian *papouche*.

PROJECTS

1 What do the following loan words have in common?

faïence, bougie, mousseline, cantaloup, calicot, bungalow

2 Choose a dozen Romance borrowings from those given in this chapter; check on their pronunciation and note words to which they appear to be formally and semantically related in French. Suggest to what extent they have been morphologically, orthographically and phonologically assimilated into the language.

(You may find it useful to begin by reading the section on assimilation in the next chapter.)

3 Trace the route taken by the following loans into French, relating this where possible to external historical factors:

artichaut, mosquée, azerole, satin, moire, magazine, kaki, gilet

FURTHER READING

Chaurand, J. 1977 *Introduction à l'histoire du vocabulaire français*, Paris, Bordas

Deroy, L. 1956 *L'Emprunt linguistique*, Paris, Belles Lettres

Estienne, H. 1885 [1578] *Deux dialogues du nouveau langage français, italianisé et autrement déguisé*, Paris, Ristelhüber

Gougenheim, G. 1970, 'De "chevalier" à "cavalier" ', in *Etudes de grammaire et de vocabulaire français*, Paris, A. J. Picard

Guiraud, P. 1968c *Patois et dialectes français*, Paris, PUF Que Sais-Je?

Hope, T.E. 1962/3 'Loan words as cultural and lexical symbols', *Archivum Linguisticum* 14 (2) and 15 (1)

—— 1971 *Lexical Borrowing in the Romance Languages*, Oxford, Blackwell; the most detailed and up-to-date analysis of lexical exchange between French and Italian, from the Middle Ages to the mid-twentieth century, against the background of the cultural and political history of the time. (He revises some of Wind's datings.)

Ifrah, G. 1985 *Les Chiffres: histoire d'une grande invention*, Paris, R. Laffont, shows how this field, culturally and lexically, owes much to the civilisations of the Near East and South Asia.

Walter, H. 1988 *Le Français dans tous les sens*, Paris, R. Laffont; see pp. 324–6 for references to recent studies in French dialectology.

Wind, B.H. 1928 'Les mots italiens introduits en français au XVIe siècle', doctoral thesis of the University of Amsterdam, Deventer; dates and categorises the bulk of Italianisms in French for this period.

Chapter 5

English influence
Good neighbours or false friends?

The influence of English on the French language has proved to be the most contentious linguistic issue of the twentieth century, provoking more popular polemics and government intervention than either spelling reform or the widening gap between the written norm and spoken usage. The debate is often couched in highly emotive terms, with metaphors of pestilence, disease and war enlivening the pages of learned journals and the conclusions of official commissions:

> On pourrait... comparer l'effet de l'emprunt abusif au mécanisme par lequel telle cellule, mal préparée à se défendre, devient monstrueuse et prolifère aux dépens de tout le corps, jusqu'à le tuer... [1]

In 1964, with his book *Parlez-vous franglais?*, an exercise in eloquent rhetoric and amusing pastiche rather than a work of scholarship, René Etiemble helped to mobilise influential sections of public opinion against the threat of American English, perceived as both a symptom and a tool of military and economic domination in the postwar period: 'pour gagner tout à fait sa partie, il faut que ce dollar tue notre langue'. The idea that language is inseparable from culture and thought, and that linguistic influence necessarily entails the adoption of alien ways of behaving and thinking is a recurring theme in Etiemble's work: 'dispensons-nous d'emprunter, avec le vocabulaire des Yanquis, les défauts et les vices qu'il annonce'.

Chapter Eleven shows such reactions to be rooted in French cultural and political history. In this chapter we shall examine the linguistic facts of the case. In so doing, English influence will be seen to be inevitable, but perhaps less invasive than many have feared.

Some statistics may help to put the debate in perspective. Robert's *Dictionnaire d'anglicismes* (1980) contains 2,620 borrowings from English, but some of these are archaic, and many belong to technical semantic fields. In a recent edition of the *Petit Larousse*, a non-technical dictionary which aims to reflect current linguistic usage, only 350 of the 45,000 entries are of English origin (Trescases 1979). Among the 650 words that Rolland and Laffitte (1995) calculate to be the 'hard core' of the French lexis today, there are no English borrowings. The effects of English must therefore be sought less in the shared lexis of most French speakers than in peripheral, specialised terminologies.

English is much more of a lexical hybrid, with more than 20,000 words of French origin (see Baugh 1951: 214–5), not to mention the many Latin borrowings which further enhanced the Romance element. Fluctuations in the intensity and direction of linguistic influence, and in the fields affected, can only be explained in terms of the social history of the two nations.

CONTACT AND EXCHANGE

The histories of France and Britain have been more closely intertwined than those of any other two countries in Europe; centuries of conquest and settlement, of political alliances and protracted wars, of cultural, scientific and commercial exchange, have all left indelible traces on the two languages. Following the Norman invasion, French was the language of the ruling class in England for more than two centuries. As Figure 8 indicates, 40 per cent of French borrowings into English entered the language in the thirteenth and fourteenth centuries.[2] Even after the medieval period, French continued to be an important source of borrowings for English until well into this century.

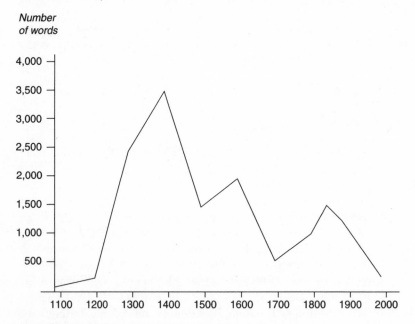

Figure 8 Gallicisms in English from 1100 to the present
Source: Adapted from Gebhardt 1975

French influence can be seen in all areas of the English lexis, providing such commonplace terms as 'country', 'village', 'city', 'chair', 'table', 'river', 'branch', 'people', 'pleasure', 'beauty'... Only the absolute core of the lexis, for example basic terms for the physical environment, such as 'wind', 'rain', 'sun', 'earth', 'sky', major body parts like 'head', 'hands', 'belly', 'feet', or the closest family relationships, escape the influence of French; 'mother' and 'father', 'brother' and 'sister', 'son' and 'daughter' are Anglo-Saxon in origin, while 'aunt' and 'uncle', 'cousin' and 'grand-parent', one step removed from the nuclear family, are French. And if we find 'belly' a touch on the crude side, the more refined French 'stomach' is a ready near-synonym, just as we can opt for 'perish' rather than 'die', or 'desire' rather than 'lust'.

The stylistic resources of the language have thus been greatly enhanced by contact with French, with the patterns of synonymy still broadly reflecting the hierarchical relationship between the two peoples at a formative stage in its history. The vast bulk of French borrowings have been fully assimilated into the language, phonologically, grammatically and orthographically.

By comparison, as shown in Figure 9, the influence of English on French was minimal before the mid-seventeenth century, and even now is of modest proportions. In other words, significant borrowing was only initiated following the period of standardisation and codification of French, and reached a peak at a time when the language had assumed the symbolic value of the nation. Assimilation – both psychological and linguistic – has therefore been much more problematic.

The few early borrowings include the points of compass – *nord, sud, est, ouest*, taken from Anglo-Saxon, the ancestor of English, and the root *bāt* 'boat' which acquired the suffix *-el*, to give modern *bateau. Milord* and *parlement* survive from the fourteenth century, and from the sixteenth century a few words relating to English institutions and religious and philosophical ideas start to make their appearance, such as *jury, puritain, Utopie...*

The arrival of thousands of Protestant Huguenot refugees in England in the late seventeenth century increased contact between the two countries; *rosbif, boxe, punch* (the drink), *boulingrin* (< 'bowling-green') date from this period. That the parliamentary system became a particular focus of interest is clear from borrowings such as *communes, vote, parti, coalition, session*. Voltaire himself spent three years in England, resulting in his *Lettres philosophiques* (1733), which, with other works like his *Eléments de la philosophie de Newton*, helped to stimulate interest in many of the political and philosophical ideas and scientific theories current in Britain at the time. In his work we find some of the first uses of scientific terms like

*Number
of words*

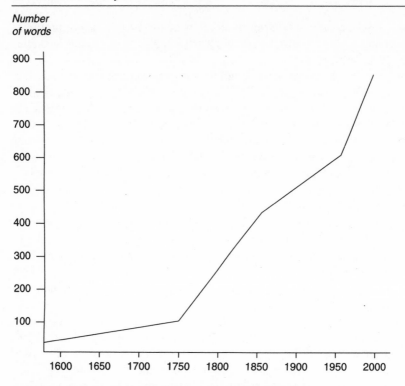

Figure 9 Anglicisms in French from 1600 to the present
Source: Adapted from Gebhardt 1975 and Trescases 1982

spectre 'spectrum' and *réfracter*, and, in the political field, literal translations like *libre-penseur* and *balance des pouvoirs*.

The pastimes and fashions of the leisured classes inspired a veritable
wave of *anglomanie* in the French, reflected in the latter half of the eighteenth century in borrowings like *dandy, sport, redingote* (< 'ridingcoat'),
plaid, plum-pudding, whisky, gin, jockey, club, whist, some of which
generated derived forms like *whisteur* and *clubiste*.

Although the Revolution interrupted such activities, political terminology continued to flow across the Channel in both directions, producing
Anglicisms like *ultimatum, pétition, opposition, constitutionnel, majorité,
motion*. Social *anglomanie* resumed early in the nineteenth century, as
symbolised by the founding in 1834 of the prestigious Anglo-French
Jockey-Club (still in existence). From this period date borrowings like
*match, handicap, fairplay, snob, flirt, tweed, blackbouler, poker, book-
maker*, and later in the century *garden-party, ferryboat, shampooing,
walkover, record, hockey, tennis, football, rugby*. We should however
remember that influence was reciprocal during the eighteenth and nineteenth centuries. French was not only the diplomatic language of Europe, it

acted as a kind of lingua franca for the ruling élite. It was the language of the Russian court when Russian itself was considered the language of the peasants. Aristocratic English households had a French governess, and polite conversation was sprinkled with French expressions: 'la crème de la crème', 'connoisseur', 'recherché', 'bon ton', 'parvenu', 'élite', 'liaison'... From the field of diplomacy in the nineteenth century English imported 'détente', 'rapprochement', 'fait accompli', 'entente cordiale', 'communiqué', 'attaché', 'protocol', and many more.

The traditional pattern of French as a donor language and English as the recipient only really changed in the mid-nineteenth century, when the British Empire reached its apogee, controlling vast natural resources across the world, which served to fuel the Industrial Revolution at home. The linguistic effects of an economically powerful and technologically advanced neighbour are nicely exemplified in the terminology associated with the development of railways in France (see Wexler 1955).

Originally developed to pump water from mines, the steam engine was soon exploited to power other types of machine. Locomotives were first used to move coal from the mines, and ultimately to provide a nationwide transport system for goods and passengers, and Britain was the first country to have an extensive rail system. The new technology began to be imported into France in the late eighteenth century, initially to link mines to the canals and rivers which were the main means of transport for heavy goods. Many of the key terms involved were either direct borrowings from English, or loan translations, like the early *machine à vapeur*, from 'steam engine'.

To begin with, as in any new and rapidly expanding field, there were competing terms for key concepts. *Locomotive* (a newly derived noun in English) alternated with *moteur mobile, chariot locomoteur* or *locomoteur*. It took some time before the borrowing *rail* came to be used to the exclusion of *barreau* or *ornière*, for *tunnel* to take over from *gallerie*, *percement* or *(passage) souterrain*, and *tender* from *allège* or *fourgon d'approvisionnement*. Another English neologism, 'viaduct', was borrowed as *viaduc*, on the pattern of the existing *aqueduc*.

While *wagon* became established early on to mean goods wagon, it still remains in competition with *voiture*, in the meaning of 'carriage for passengers'. *Train* already existed in French as a verbal noun, but its specific semantic development in this field was probably determined by the meaning of the English cognate word – as is often the case.

A number of the terms were by no means complete newcomers. *Rail* had been borrowed into English in the fourteenth century, but subsequently lost in French. *Tunnel* can also be traced back to an Old French word, related to Modern French *tonnelle* 'bower', 'arbour' and *tonneau* 'cask'.

A brief examination of this single field therefore demonstrates the diverse nature of English influence. It ranges from borrowings of words which are quite foreign to French, through Latin neologisms, to reborrowings of words of French origin, and more indirect loan translations and the semantic remodelling of existing words. Borrowings, whatever their form, do not however monopolise the field; Wexler shows how many words are drawn from the existing terminologies of road and canal transport, or of mining and iron foundries. He shows too how some English terms were taken in for only a brief period of time, before being supplanted by indigenous words. A detailed examination of the growth of other technical terminologies might well show the same pattern of early variability and heavy borrowing, followed by later stabilisation and a reassertion of indigenous terms.

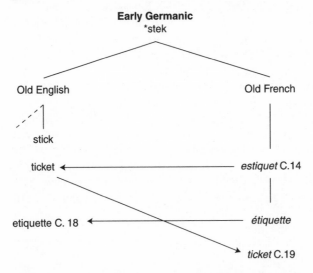

Figure 10 Ticket and related items in English and French

The history of another 'reborrowing' used in this field, *ticket*, and of words related to it, exemplifies the closeness and complexity of relations between the two countries over the centuries. As Figure 10 shows, it can be traced back to an early Germanic root, which gave rise to the English verb 'stick' and also to an Old French verb meaning 'to fix', from which were derived the nouns *estiquet* and *estiquette*. The former was taken into English in the sixteenth century, with a specialised, legal function, and evolved new meanings, including that with which it was reimported into France in the nineteenth century. One of its new roles was in the technological revolution mentioned above. In the meantime, *estiquette* had continued to develop, resulting in the polysemous *étiquette*, borrowed into English in the eighteenth century with the meaning of 'system of court precedence and ceremonial'. Thus a single ancient root adopted by both languages has moved between the two, changing as the two nations evolved socially and technically, supplying terms in fields of special interest or expertise in the two nations.

The twentieth century saw English influence in an increasing range of activities, not only sport and industry, but fashion, commerce, science, technology, entertainment and the growing mass media. The following examples give a flavour of the variety of semantic fields affected during the first half of the century:

> *cardigan, jersey, pullover, pyjama, blazer, smoking, camping, building, shopping, weekend, lobby, gangster, talkie-walkie, telex, gadget, dumping, reporter, chèque, yacht, jazz, barman, show business, boycotter, film, star.*

According to Trescases (1982), a more detailed, decade-by-decade breakdown of the statistics given in Figure 9 would actually show a dip in English borrowings in the first thirty years of this century. He sees in this a reflection of the decline of Britain as a world industrial and military power during this period.

Renewed impetus was given to the flow of English borrowings from the 1930s, when the United States began to dominate the world scene, militarily and economically. Its commercial growth and expansion coincided with the development of mass means of communication, with all their potential for the marketing of both products and ideas. It is precisely at this point that the number of borrowings from English into French exceeds French borrowings into English, for the first time in their history.

In the dreary postwar years the American lifestyle, with products to match, was especially appealing to the young. Fashion, food, pop music, entertainment, sports and high technology all took on an American flavour. (It is from this period that Hagège (1987) suggests it is more appropriate to talk of *franricain* than *franglais*, the term made famous by Etiemble.) Again, a random selection of borrowings demonstrates the range of fields affected:

> *drugstore, snackbar, hotdog, hamburger, ketchup, bestseller, cornflakes, chips, bluejean, eyeliner, sweater, tee-shirt, bikini, bowling, surfing, jogging, bulldozer, jet, jeep, rock, marketing, western, hitparade, fan, gag, flashback, zoom, clip, design.*

The saturation of certain fields, like drugs, with words from American English – *dealer, shit, brown sugar, joint, trip, sniffer, se fixer, speeder –* has reinforced the feeling in some quarters that *cocacolonisation* is responsible for any number of social ills.

Borrowings have become much more visible – and audible – over the last fifty years, owing to the growth of advertising and of the mass media generally. On a stroll around a popular shopping area the eye is bombarded with fragments of English in shop names, slogans or products: *sweat-shirts, compacts discs (sic), prix discount, Restaurant-Grill, Beauté-club, air conditionné, Bookiniste, Chequepoint, posters, cookies, Shampoo-Brush*, etc., while neon signs in Pigalle shout *Peepshow, Sexshop, Striptease*. Despite their high visibility, and the anguish they cause to defenders of the language, most such forms represent less a serious undermining of French by a tide of alien borrowings than the use of international 'tourist-speak', largely ephemeral and marginal to the concerns of the average citizen.

Although the press is often blamed for the propagation of Anglicisms, they are only found in any numbers in certain types of text; an article on rap music in a teen magazine will be crammed with them, while a piece of political analysis in a serious daily may have none at all. Typically, the pages devoted to sport, showbusiness and fashion yield the highest concentration.

In addition, there are the less conspicuous but more numerous borrowings to be found in specialised technical and scientific terminologies. They may be used by relatively few speakers, but there is a growing tendency for such vocabulary to find its way into everyday speech (see Gilbert 1973). Most French speakers can use technical terms like *laser* or *antibiotique* more or less appropriately, even if they could not provide a scientific definition. And in an area like home computing, words that began as obscure technical terms, like *interface, back-up* or *login* are becoming household words for the younger generation.

Even marginal areas of the lexis, like acronyms and other abbreviations, may show Anglo-American influence. One could argue that *UNESCO* and *UNICEF* have the advantage of being pronounceable as words. The increasing adoption of *USA* is less easily explicable, except perhaps as a kind of visual icon, seen on labels, products, films and TV screens in a wide variety of contexts. *PC* and *CD* may be used by speakers who also use the French 'long' forms *micro-ordinateur* and *disque compact* – perhaps as more informal variants. The abbreviation *Mr.* is not infrequently used as a substitute for *M.*; in its favour, it can be argued that the English form avoids the ambiguity often inherent in the French, which may stand either for *Monsieur* or for a first name beginning with 'M'.

ENRICHMENT OR REDUNDANCY?

Where imported goods or ideas are concerned, it is natural that the name should come with the referent. There are certainly many historical precedents like *cachemire* or *mousseline* from the Middle East, *tomates, patates* or *chocolat* from the New World, or notions developed as part of a philosophical, artistic or cultural movements, like *Weltanschauung* or

Leitmotiv from German. How, then, can one object to *hamburger*, *western*, or *jogging*? For good or ill, these foreign referents have been embraced by large sections of the French population; the words are therefore 'emprunts de nécessité', to use Deroy's term (1956).

What is more disturbing to many observers of the language is the apparently redundant nature of some recent newcomers. At first sight many borrowings appear to trespass on the semantic space of indigenous words. Why is there a need for *caméra* when *appareil-photo* already exists? Apart from its brevity, it has the advantage of referring, in French, to a particular kind of camera, one used for taking moving pictures; in other words it has been adopted with a more restricted meaning than the original, polysemous word. This greater specificity is characteristic of most borrowings. As noted with *ticket* and *étiquette*, words are generally borrowed in a particular context, with a meaning relevant to that context, even if over time the meaning is extended.

As Figure 11 suggests, English and French have exchanged what appear to be synonymous items; in their native habitat 'cake' and *gâteau* are generic terms, but are borrowed as hyponyms, or semantically subordinate terms, according to the recipients' stereotyped notion of the other nation's confectionery; *du cake* is rather dull fruit cake, while a 'gateau' is a multi-layered dessert only manageable with a fork.

Borrowings may also serve to introduce finer lexical distinctions into an existing field, without new referents necessarily being involved. There has, for example, been much debate about the redundancy of *shopping*, which has become emblematic of English influence. But *faire du shopping* implies a pleasurable browse for items like clothes or a new table-lamp, not a quick dash round the supermarket, which is *faire des courses*. The

cake   *gâteau*

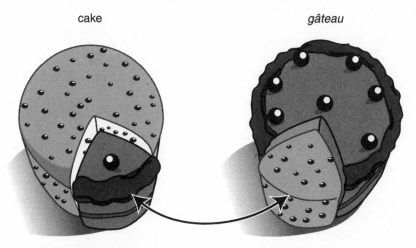

Figure 11 Borrowings and hyponymy

borrowing surely fills a semantic need, when shopping has become a major leisure activity.

Regardless of its origin, once established in the language a word will start to undergo the normal processes of semantic change, expanding and diversifying (see Chapter Seven). *Tennis* now refers to tennis shoes or plimsolls, as well as the sport, just as *un jogging* means a tracksuit, and *un bowling* means a bowling alley.[3]

The latter extension from activity to place where the activity occurs is a common one in French; hence the polysemy of *camping*, *golf* or *parking*. It is not always clear whether such forms result from the ellipsis of longer expressions (*terrain de golf* giving *golf*, and so on) or from direct semantic shifts. Either way the result in synchronic terms is the same: a lexical item differing in meaning from that of the original. When single words are clipped, as in *snack* from *snackbar*, or *self* from *self-service*, the contrast with the meaning of the shorter form in English is even more marked.

Words like *pressing* 'dry cleaner's', *brushing* 'blow-dry' and *smoking* 'dinner jacket' seem to have been adopted from the outset with meanings different from those in English, and for that reason are sometimes referred to as 'false Anglicisms' (see Spence 1987). So too are words which are new combinations of English morphemes, like *rugbyman*, or *tennisman*; but since the morphemes involved here occur in other genuine borrowings like *barman*, such words can be seen as the result of normal derivational processes, which recombine existing morphemes.

Although most borrowings fulfil a new semantic function in the lexis, there are cases where newcomers have driven out existing terms. Many examples are to be found of Old English words being supplanted by French imports: *eam*, for example, gave way to 'uncle', *twiewifing* to 'bigamy', and *unwisdom* to 'ignorance'. But the conditions under which borrowing took place, and the relationship between the two languages, were so different from those of today that we should not necessarily predict a similar fate for many modern French words. A more apt parallel might be between the present situation and that in the sixteenth century when Italianisms were in fashion (see Chapter Four). Many borrowings vanished after enjoying a brief vogue; a few hundred came to play a useful role alongside existing words.

As far as English influence is concerned, only well into the twenty-first century will we be able to see if some French words have been eliminated by current English rivals – whether, for example, *chandail* is definitively replaced by *pull* or *sweater*. What is clear is that one can already point to Anglicisms that have not survived, or that have a distinctly outmoded flavour. Some of the borrowings that disturbed Etiemble thirty years ago – *déterrent*, *barracks*, *steamer* – are now nowhere to be found.

The most vulnerable borrowings are naturally those referring to ephemeral phenomena; *tea-cosy* and *bloomer* are confined to a few early twentieth-century dictionaries; *dropout* is a moribund reminder of the 1960s. Clearly, redundant words are unlikely to survive unless they can find a new role for themselves. Hence nineteenth-century *mackintosh* never succeeded in establishing itself in the face of the indigenous *imperméable*, and *tea-room* flourished for only a decade or two, as a synonym of *salon de thé*. In the Gulf War, *char* was more in evidence in the media than *tank*; and estate agents now use *immeuble* and *(salle de) séjour* much more widely than *building* or *living*.

An Anglicism seems to have the best chance of surviving not only if it represents some new concept or invention, but if it also has the advantage of brevity. One can see why large stores prefer *escalator* to *escalier mécanique*, why the officially proposed *disque audionumérique* stood little chance against *compact disque*, and why *lobby* may well survive, in competition with *groupe de pression*. Not only are the English terms less of a mouthful, they are often convenient for newspaper headlines, like *crash* and its derived verb *se crasher*, used quite widely in the press of air disasters. (It remains to be seen whether these newcomers will forge a permanent role for themselves, with this very specific meaning, or whether *s'écraser* will reassert itself.)

Some apparently redundant Anglicisms are in fact thriving. How did *pull* and *sweater* manage to establish themselves, when *tricot*, *chandail*, *gilet* and *maillot* surely covered the ground quite adequately? *Challenge* came in originally as a sporting term, but has since broadened its field of reference so that it now encroaches on the territory of *défi* and *gageure*.

BORROWINGS IN SHEEP'S CLOTHING: COGNATES AND CALQUES

Borrowings of a different kind arise from the very intimacy of the relations between the two languages, and their shared propensity for borrowing from Latin and Greek. Every English-speaking student of French (and vice versa) rapidly becomes aware of the pitfalls of *faux amis*, or words which look alike if not identical in the two languages, but which almost invariably differ semantically. Their meanings may differ radically, like 'trivial' and *trivial* 'vulgar'; more frequently – and more insidiously – they may overlap, so that on some occasions it is in fact appropriate to use the cognate term. For example, *développer* may in some cases be the appropriate translation of 'develop', but in many contexts *élaborer*, *créer* or *fonder* would be more accurate. *Opportunité* is now widely used in the English sense of 'chance' or 'favourable situation', while traditionally in French it means 'opportuneness' or 'suitability to the occasion'; that is, it refers to an abstract quality, rather than a specific event or occasion. But if a situation is endowed with *opportunité* in the abstract sense, then it is likely to be an 'opportunity' in the English sense. In other words the meanings are closely connected, and we see just this kind of natural semantic shift occurring in words, independently of any external influence (see Chapter Seven). However, words like *occasion* and *possibilité* already cover the semantic ground of English 'opportunity', and the increased polysemy of the French word simply obliges the hearer to rely more heavily on the context to interpret the utterance correctly.

One could argue that in some cases, such as the use of *réaliser* in the English sense of 'become aware of', the borrowed meaning is sufficiently different from the original – 'to bring about, carry out' – that confusion as to which meaning is intended is unlikely to arise. The popularity of the new interpretation is probably strengthened by the fact that *réaliser* is a one-word, regular verb, unlike the indigenous alternative, *se rendre compte de*.

In many cases, then, the context serves to eliminate any potential ambiguity, but in others, *emprunts clandestins*, like the use of *versatile* 'inconstant', 'unreliable' with the English meaning in mind may lead to serious misunderstanding.

Less pernicious than semantic borrowing is the direct, morpheme-for-morpheme translation of English expressions. Some, like *gratte-ciel* for 'skyscraper', may result in successful figures of speech – lively without being obscure, and conforming to a morphological pattern which is productive in French. Such 'calques', or 'loan translations', have a long history, like *haute trahison*, from the seventeenth century, or *franc-maçon* from the eighteenth. Like semantic borrowings, calques are extremely common in bilingual situations, when speakers are constantly moving between the two languages. Hence Canadian French is particularly prone to them, producing expressions such as *éléphant blanc* or *melon d'eau* (see Pergnier 1988).

Some calques are clearly redundant, in that an appropriate term already exists; the process may nevertheless be a useful source of new terminology, as many entries in the official *Dictionnaire des néologismes* testify (see 'Solutions' below). Calquing is not always successful, however. Pergnier (1989) quotes the expression *le sexe sûr*, which mystified him on first hearing. The context eventually revealed that what was being referred to was 'safe sex', but someone unfamiliar with English might well find it difficult to decode. (It is the polysemy of both *sexe* and *sûr* that makes the phrase opaque.) How much clearer would be his proposed *l'amour sans risques*!

THE ASSIMILATION OF ANGLICISMS

As we have indicated above, the semantic assimilation of borrowings, as opposed to calques, appears to be subject to a process of self-regulation, whereby the language takes in words with a restricted meaning, compared to the original; new meanings subsequently develop as the need arises.

Stylistic differentiation may also occur, with an indigenous term being used in formal written style, and an English borrowing in more everyday conversation (see Marcellesi 1973). For example, a computer expert may use *software* (or more probably *le soft*), when chatting to a colleague, but revert to *logiciel* in written mode, or when talking more formally.

Whether or not Anglicisms are semantically assimilated, it is often argued that many do not match the phonological, orthographic or morphological patterns of French, and remain audibly and visibly 'foreign' to the system.

Orthographic and phonological assimilation

The ease with which orthographic and phonological integration can take place varies a good deal, depending on the form of the original. English words of Romance origin can often be made to look and sound French with only minimal adjustments to the pronunciaton and spelling: such is the case with *comité, promotion, inflation, déodorant, suprématie, contraception*, and many more. Some of these are not even acknowledged as borrowings in dictionaries. In addition, such words are usually relatable to existing lexical items. The Romance origins of English *festival* mean that it is perfectly camouflaged within the lexical paradigm *fête, fêter, festin, festivité*. A French speaker may also be able to connect the borrowing *missile* with existing words like *mission* and *missive*, not only because of the formal identity of the root, but also because they all share the more tenuous semantic link of 'something which is dispatched' – for whatever purpose.

Other English borrowings, usually of Germanic origin, remain lexically isolated even after centuries of cohabitation. This is true of *redingote, bouledogue, mildiou* and *boulingrin* (with only the *boul-* of *boulingrin* lending a little transparency to this particular borrowing). These do, however, conform to the phonological patterns and orthographic conventions of the language; they contain no unusual combinations of sounds or letters, and their pronunciation is absolutely predictable from the spelling. One can surmise that *boulingrin* was originally an interpretation of the English orthographic form 'bowling-green' (what one might call a 'visual borrowing'), with the sequences 'in' and 'een' of the English being interpreted as nasal vowels. The vowels were then committed to writing following the conventions of the French system. *Bouledogue* and *mildiou*, on the other hand, seem to be 'aural borrowings' – that is, they approximate to the original English pronunciation, which the spelling has been modified to reflect.

More recent borrowings, however, tend to retain the English orthography, while the pronunciation may vary between the visual and the aural. For *charter*, for example, the *Dictionnaire des mots contemporains* gives the pronunciations /ʃartɛr/, /ʃartœr/ and /tʃartœr/; the first form is a visual interpretation of the English word, the last an aural version, and the second has elements of both. Most dictionaries are not helpful in this respect; they either assign one (often arbitrarily selected) pronunciation to the borrowing, or give none at all. (An exception is Martinet and Walter's *Dictionnaire de la prononciation de la langue française, dans son usage réel*, based on a survey of speakers' usage.)

The English agentive suffix '-er' is variably realised as either /ɛr/ or /œr/, the latter being an approximation of the English pronunciation, or possibly due to the influence of the parallel suffix *-eur*. Occasionally the spelling too may be variable: we find for example both *supporter* and *supporteur*.

The general trend is for the pronunciation of more recent borrowings to reflect the English form more closely. This can be seen in the different treatment given to the two (English) homonyms 'punch' (the drink), dating from the seventeenth century, and 'punch' the boxing term, borrowed early this century. They are differentiated in French, with the former being pronounced /pɔ̃ʃ/ with a nasal vowel (not the /œ̃/ that the spelling implies, but one that is more widely used), whereas the latter, /pœnʃ/, has an oral vowel plus nasal consonant, as in English.

A similar pattern is detectable in the pronunciation of English borrowings beginning with 'j', the earlier ones tending to be pronounced with the French fricative /ʒ/, as in *jersey*, *jockey*, while in twentieth-century borrowings like *jet* or *job* the English affricate /dʒ/ predominates. As such borrowings have become widely used in French, the two English affricates /tʃ/ and /dʒ/ can now be considered marginal phonemes of the language, together with the velar nasal /ŋ/, disseminated through the many borrowings or new formations suffixed by '-ing'. (The curious variant of /smatʃ/ for *smash* (in tennis), with its substitution of the typically English affricate /tʃ/, is perhaps a mixture of hypercorrection and the influence of *match* /matʃ/.)

English words containing an 'h' are very variably treated, often depending on the speaker's knowledge of English, and on how well established the word has become. But generally the sound is simply omitted, and cannot therefore be given phonemic status.

Forms initially established as visual borrowings may be subsequently remodelled, to match the English pronunciation more closely. *Meeting* was occasionally spelt *métingue*, indicating an earlier, visual pronunciation, although /mitiŋ/ is now the norm. A detailed analysis of the kind of data provided by Martinet and Walter could reveal whether speakers are moving increasingly to forms that are closer to the original pronunciation. It has been suggested (Warnant 1968) that *club* has actually developed two contrasting forms, correlating with two distinct meanings: the 'visual' form /klyb/, meaning a political or literary association, and /klœb/, used for sporting clubs – a more recent semantic extension.

A degree of variability of pronunciation is perhaps inevitable in borrowings (one has only to think of the different pronunciations of 'buffet', 'niche' or 'garage' in English). Martinet and Walter found seven different pronunciations for both *steward* and *walkover*. However, it is generally accepted as desirable that every word should have a single written and phonological form, in the standard language. As far as the written form goes, this requirement is generally met by borrowings in French, which, apart from the earliest forms, usually retain the English orthography. This undoubtedly gives rise to problems for the French speaker, since the conventions of the orthographic systems of English and French are so different. Some sequences of letters occur with different values: French 'ch' usually represents /ʃ/ (more infrequently /k/, as in *archaïque*), while English 'ch' has the value /tʃ/. Other sequences of letters simply do not occur in French, as in 'cr*aw*l', 'cl*ow*n', '*knock*out'.

Compared to English orthography, the French system is relatively free of ambiguity; it is usually possible to predict the pronunciation of a word from its spelling. It does however carry a good deal of redundancy, in that there are usually several different ways of spelling a single phoneme, particularly where vowels are concerned. (The phoneme /o/, for example, may be spelt 'au', 'eau', 'o' or 'ô'.) The addition of substantial numbers of words in which French phonemes are expressed through yet more sequences of letters is bound to increase both redundancy and ambiguity in the system. (The example of English orthography does however suggest that a language can tolerate a good deal of both.)

Morphological assimilation

As regards inflectional morphology, the assimilation of Anglicisms presents few problems. The majority of borrowings are nouns, which have minimal inflection in both languages, and it is simple to form the plural by the addition of the orthographic 's' of French – happily coinciding with the English plural form. The few adjective which have been borrowed, such as *cool* or *clean*, are treated in the same way. In the cases where the English plural is '-es', there is hesitation between extending the regular French form, and retaining the English ending. So we find variation between *sandwichs* and *sandwiches*, and *matchs* and *matches* – though the latter in each case seems to be increasingly preferred. The same is true of irregular English plurals; both *barmans* and *barmen* are found, but more usually the latter. Where the English has a plural for garments like 'jeans', 'shorts', 'pyjamas', and so on, French uses a singular, *un jean, un short*, on the pattern of *un pantalon, une culotte*.

The gender of nouns rarely poses a problem, especially if parallel suffixes are involved: *promotion* and *interférence* will obviously become feminine, while *pandémonium* and *isolationnisme* will be masculine. Otherwise the majority of nouns are given the 'unmarked' masculine gender. Only occasional hesitations arise, for example with *interview*, which does not have a specifically feminine ending, but is usually treated as such, perhaps on analogy with *entrevue*. A similar explanation may be given for the feminine gender of *star*, influenced perhaps by *vedette*. *Détective*, despite its feminine suffix, is assigned masculine gender as it refers to a male-dominated profession.

Feminine gender agreement is rarely made, unless the word has been borrowed with a Romance suffix, so that *snob* or *sexy*, for example, will remain unchanged. Since there are so few, and since absence of gender marking is not uncommon in French, this cannot really be considered a departure from the morphological rules of the language.

Borrowed verbs, also relatively rare, are assigned to the *-er* conjugation, as with *shooter*, *stopper*, *interviewer*, although occasionally the suffix *-iser* is used, as in *sponsoriser*, *squatteriser*.

Once borrowed, words are subject to the derivational processes of the language. Sometimes whole lexical paradigms are established: *filmer*, *filmage*, *filmique*, *filmothèque*, *filmologue*...

Like Greek or Latin roots that have been borrowed into the language (see Chapter Three), English elements can combine with others to form hybrid compounds, like *surbooking*, *top niveau* or *autostop*. Calqued compounds may be remodelled to fit the French order of 'modified + modifier' as in *planning familial*, *table ronde*; *disque compact* is now the recommended equivalent of 'compact disc', although *compact disque* and even *CD* seem to be preferred. Calqued noun + noun combinations often retain the original order of 'modifier + modified' of elements, as in *science-fiction*, this structure being particularly favoured in the naming of hotels and restaurants: *Le Terrasse Bar*, *l'Europe Hôtel* – perhaps dating back to the Edwardian era, when the British colonised the Côte d'Azur in winter months.

Compound adjectives of origin, like *sud-américain*, *nord-vietnamien*, are sometimes frowned upon as being calques of the English equivalents. It is, however, difficult to imagine another way of deriving a reasonably concise and unambiguous adjective or adjectival phrase from *l'Amérique du Sud*, or *le Vietnam du Nord* (now often itself calqued as *le Nord-Vietnam*).

Other syntactic phenomena, like the placing of adjectives before nouns, and the use of adjectives as adverbs in certain registers (*Souriez jeune!*), have been laid at the door of English influence. But since a number of words with this double function have existed in the language for a long time (*chanter faux*, *voir clair*, etc.; see Ewert 1954: 144–5), this explanation is unconvincing.

Degrees of assimilation

In addition to the semantic and formal assimilation of borrowings, there is a sense in which a word becomes psychologically assimilated, so that the average speaker is unaware of its origins. This is certainly the case with early borrowings, such as *parlement* or *nord*. They are both everyday terms with no unusual orthographic or phonological characteristics, and they can be related formally and and semantically to other words in the language.

At the other end of the scale, a foreign word may be introduced into a text or an utterance as a consciously alien element, isolated by italic print, or inverted commas, often to add 'local colour' to a text. Such *pérégrénismes* usually retain the original spelling, and in spoken form attempts may be made to approximate to the foreign pronunciation. A *pérégrénisme* is often short lived, but its appearance may be the first step to a more permanent place in the lexis. Newspapers often introduce a word, like 'leadership' or 'coach', in the context of a British or American story, perhaps on the assumption that no precise cultural equivalent exists in French. Eventually the italics or inverted commas may be dropped, implying that the writer assumes that the reader is familiar with the word.

Some *pérégrénismes* may retain a permanent but marginal place in the lexis, as words which are felt to be foreign, and which are often orthographically and phonologically unassimilated, designed primarily to demonstrate the speaker's erudition or social class. This is the case with quite a few eighteenth- and nineteenth-century French borrowings into English, like 'recherché', 'cri de coeur' or 'haute cuisine'. Other *pérégrénismes* may form part of a specialised terminology, like Japanese terms relating to judo. Usually only the largest dictionaries include such expressions, which are then marked as being foreign words, rather than assimilated words of foreign origin.

SOLUTIONS

Anglo-American influence on the language has triggered a range of responses, from bitter chauvinism to the measured analysis and monitoring of the phenomenon by professional linguists. It has also inspired attempts to impose legal constraints on the use of Anglicisms (an issue discussed in Chapter Eleven). Most importantly, the debate has demonstrated beyond all argument the need for a wealth of new terminology, finally conquering the traditional mistrust of neologisms.

Rational government measures have included the setting up of *Commissions ministérielles de terminologie*, from 1973, to propose new expressions in thirty-six specialist fields, including tourism, medicine, computing, electronics, insurance, agriculture, aeronautics, finance and many others (see Chapter Eleven).Their proposals, published at regular intervals, show clearly that a major aim is to implant French alternatives to English terms, before the latter can become established.[4] (English equivalents are given, as expressions to be avoided, alongside most of the entries.)

Occasionally, an entrenched foreign borrowing is given the seal of approval, though here the French speaker often faces the problem, mentioned above, of interpreting a written form which does not conform to the conventions of French orthography. To minimise this difficulty, Gallicisation of the spelling of borrowings has been proposed, for example *jerricane* rather than *jerrycan*, and *bouldozeur* instead of *bulldozer*. Alternatively, a more 'French' pronunciation of the orthography is suggested: pipeline is admissible, but only provided it is pronounced *à la française* (i.e. /piplin/). Management is similarly allowed, if it is pronounced /manaʒmã/. On the whole, both writers and dictionaries have been reluctant to adopt Gallicised spellings, although some, like *tacle* for 'tackle' and *drible* for 'dribble', are quite widely used. Occasionally minor modifications to a borrowing are proposed, to bring it into line with existing French morphemes (for example, *conteneur* is the proposed Gallicisation of 'container').

The problem is that French speakers are now directly and frequently exposed to both written and spoken forms of English, through the education system and the media. It is difficult for them to abandon what they know to be the original form of the word, without appearing uneducated or old-fashioned. Many borrowings thus seem likely to remain orthographically anomalous forms, and to vary in their pronunciation.

Attempts at Gallicisation of the derivational morphology of borrowings can be seen in the official substitution of the native *-age* for the ubiquitous *-ing* (with as yet modest success), so that *kidnappage* is a possible alternative to *kidnapping*, and *caravanage* to *caravaning*. Trescases (1979) notes a decline in the use of *-man* as a sporting suffix, possibly due to the irregularity of the plural forms, and to the need to find a simple feminine form (*tenniswoman* or *yachtwoman* being undeniably clumsy). New sports tend to take the suffix *-eur* or *-iste*, and existing forms may be remodelled; for example, *joueur de rugby* nowadays rivals *rugbyman*.

Many official terms are simply calques of the English expression: *écran tactile* for 'touch screen', *souris* for '(electronic) mouse', *industrie du spectacle* for 'show business'. Others involve the extension in meaning of an existing word, as when *lifting* 'face-lift' is replaced by *lissage*, and *rush* (the cinematographic term) by *épreuve*. Given the already polysemous nature of many terms, this process is likely to increase the possibilities of ambiguity and reliance on context for the appropriate interpretation. Some periphrastic recommended forms, like *avion à réaction* for 'jet', or *exposition interprofessionnelle* for 'trade show', although unambiguous, will surely be disadvantaged by their sheer length.

The traditional source of technical terms has for centuries been the *racines nobles* of Latin and Greek (see Chapter Three). Some have the disadvantage of being opaque to many French speakers – which is the primary objection levelled at English borrowings. *Oléoduc* and *gazoduc* (oil and gas pipelines), modelled on *viaduc* and *aqueduc*, are no doubt reasonably accessible; but *ondes décamétriques* and *ondes kilométriques*, suggested as replacements for the established *ondes courtes* and *ondes longues*, presumably on the grounds that the latter are calqued on English, are both lengthy and obscure. The originally proposed *astronef* 'spacecraft', a blend of scientific and archaic morphemes, has given way to the more easily interpretable calques: *vaisseau spatial* or *véhicule spatial*.

The 'official' *mercatique* does not seem to have made headway against *marketing*, perhaps because the latter has already become too well entrenched, and is at the heart of one of the semantic fields most heavily affected by English.

Given the tradition of using Latin and Greek for technical terminology, it is not surprising that foreign borrowings that have drawn on these languages are accepted without comment. Thus *téléphone* and *kérosène* (English neologisms) and *protoplasme* and *aspirine* (from Germany) have slipped into French virtually unnoticed.

French is of course rich in non-classical, native lexical resources. One might predict that the neologisms most likely to succeed are in fact derived forms based on roots and affixes of long standing, which are both concise and accessible to the average speaker, like *jardinerie* for 'garden centre', *vraquier* (from *vrac*) for 'bulk carrier', or *télécopieur* for 'fax machine'. Fresh metaphors too can be lively and memorable, like *chandelle* for 'lob' in tennis, *remue-méninges* for 'brainstorming'. *Mémoire vive*, telescoped to *MEV*, is surely more transparent in French than is 'Random Access Memory' (RAM) to an English speaker. The acronym *CB* for 'Citizen Band (radio)' has been borrowed, but naturalised by means of a cunning reformulation as *canaux banalisés*.

The campaign to oust the foreign invader has clearly inspired defenders of the language to an impressive display of lexical creativity. One only has to look at the range of alternatives suggested for *fast food* – *restovite*, *restauration rapide*, *prêt-à-manger*, *plat-minute*, *BGV* (*bouffe à grande vitesse*) – to know that, whatever problems the French language may be facing, it is certainly not lacking in richly inventive lexical resources.

THE OUTLOOK

There have been many doom-laden prophesies about the 'death' of French, or at least the complete hybridisation of the lexis. A brief look at two fields often quoted as being among those most heavily permeated with Anglicisms might help us to see if these fears are justified.

Terminology relating to personal computers and their associated software is naturally particularly vulnerable to the influence of American English, since so much of the market is controlled by American companies. A glance at computer manuals or computer games on sale in France would tend to confirm this. There have however been remarkable successes for French alternative terms. In the very early years, *computer* was used, but it has been replaced by the official *ordinateur* (even if *PC* rivals *micro-ordinateur*). *Informatique* acts as a more generic term than either 'comput-ing' or 'computer science' in English, with the advantage that it reflects more accurately the activities involved: not so much number-crunching as the processing of information of all kinds. Moreover it lends itself to useful derived forms like *informaticien* and *informatiser*. It seems to be the source of a proliferation of new terms ending in *-tique*, such as *télématique*, *documentique*, *bureautique*, *éditique*, all involving the computerisation of existing systems (see Reboul 1994). *Matériel* and *logiciel* have made good headway against *hardware* and *software*, and have opened the way to further neologisms on the same pattern: *ludiciel* (games software), *didac-ticiel* (educational software) and *progiciel* (software package), which are much more concise in French than in English. *Passerelle* (literally 'gang-way' or 'footbridge') is a graphic, parallel metaphor for 'gateway', like *ardoise* (literally 'slate') for 'note pad'. Detailed studies are required, to monitor the evolution of this field which, although technical, is rapidly becoming a part of daily life. A superficial glimpse suggests that French is at least holding its own on this particular territory, although whether it can meet the challenge of the Internet, on which English is likely to become the lingua franca, remains to be seen.

Sport is a field which has absorbed large quantities of borrowings from British and American English, from the nineteenth century. Any sports page of a newspaper will yield a substantial number. The proportion never-theless remains relatively small. An impression of dominance is given because these words occupy key positions – the names of sports, terms which are common to many sports like *match*, *score*, *handicap*, *open*, etc. This has been demonstrated in a detailed analysis carried out by R. Galis-son (1978) on the vocabulary of football, the most popular of all imported sports, with highly developed technical, journalistic and slang terminolo-gies. Among these, English plays a relatively minor role; only about 3 per cent of the technical terms Galisson gives are English – though they are among the most frequent. He claims that many sporting Anglicisms are on the wane, with indigenous words like *arbitre* and *match nul* replacing *referee* and *draw*. Some, he suggests, are used primarily by journalists as handy synonyms, to avoid repetition: in one article or commentary, *shooter* may vary with *tirer*, and *goal* with *gardien de but*.

The most striking revelation of his study, confirmed in Doillon's dic-tionary *Argots et néologismes du sport* (1993), containing about three thousand entries, is the great wealth of metaphorical terms which have been created to describe all aspects of sporting activities. An easy shot at goal is *un caviar*; *faire la dentelle* is over-elaborate play that doesn't make much headway; a slippery rugby ball is *une savonette*, and so on.

Slang aside, French has evolved complex indigenous terminologies for those sports widely practised in France, like football or rugby, as can be seen from an examination of Pétiot's or Failliot's recent sporting diction-aries. It is only in less popular sports like golf that substantial borrowings are to be found. The terminology of the recently imported sport of judo is, predictably, full of Japanese expressions.

Sport is an area to which the official *Commissions de terminologie* have paid little attention; the evidence suggests that, left to their own devices, French speakers have the confidence and imagination to devise as many new terms as are needed.

The media are often accused of disseminating quite redundant Anglicisms, and it is not difficult to find absurdly modish examples of the kind parodied by Etiemble. This is perhaps inevitable when journalists live in a world dominated by English-language news media; they are constantly obliged to draw on material in English, from the press or news agencies, translating and editing under pressure to meet deadlines. The brevity of many English words also makes them temptingly suitable headline material.

Above all, glamour, power and modernity are still associated with the United States, and while this is the case, American English is bound to retain its allure. The position of English as a world language is unchal-lenged, and the growth of multinational companies and worldwide com-munication systems of all kinds is likely to favour it still further. So, while the lessons of history show that languages tend to shrug off redundant items and retain only those which can play a useful role, the French are right to keep a wary eye open for their language. However, the violence of the reactions in some quarters, the kind of arguments used in the debate, and the various attempts at intervention by the government can hardly be explained in terms of the linguistic facts alone. They may be seen rather as a response to specific political and economic circumstances, set against a long tradition of linguistic conservatism and control. It is this tradition that is examined in Chapter Eleven.

NOTES

1 From the introduction to the official *Guide des mots nouveaux* (1985), by Philippe de Saint Robert, *Commissaire général de la langue française.*
2 The figures are based on Mossé's study (1943) and Gebhardt (1975). Together with the earlier analyses carried out by Jespersen (1905) and later Baugh (1951), they show the heaviest borrowing taking place in the period when English was re-establishing itself as the language of the state. The terminology required in the higher domains of law, administration, education, and so on, was naturally enough drawn largely from the language of the former rulers.

3 There seems to have been quite a lot of lexical movement in the field of sportswear. *Training(s)* briefly took on the meaning of 'trainers' and 'tracksuit'; but *jogging* has taken over the latter function, while *baskets* are used for the former. Even more recently, *bowling* has been used to refer to the loose, short-sleeved shirt worn by players.

4 The work of each Commission is published as it is completed in the *Journal Officiel de la République Française*, and these lists are periodically collated in a *Dictionnaire des néologismes officiels*. The proposals are also popularised in books like Voirol's *Anglicismes et anglomanie* (1993), which includes additional suggestions, especially for more everyday terms, which are considered beyond the scope of the Commissions.

PROJECTS

1 With the help of English and French dictionaries, trace the history of *pudding*, *nurse*, *palace*, *label*, *standard*, *turf*, and of etymologically related words. Present this information in diagrammatic form and comment on any changes of meaning involved.

2 Check on the pronunciation of the following borrowings, both with native speakers and in a number of French dictionaries:

meeting, job, jazz, gadget, budget, shampooing, chewing-gum, sweater, outsider, iceberg, club

Note how many forms each takes, and whether these are visual or aural, and suggest whether it is possible to relate any of your findings to the date of entry of the item into French.

3 Examine the range of meanings of the following pairs of words in English and French, and determine whether there is semantic overlap:

control / *contrôler*   attractive / *attractif*   confidence / *confiance*
agenda / *agenda*   informal / *informel*   conference / *conférence*

Suggest words in French which might be more accurate translations of the English, in specific contexts.

4 Examine the following proposed equivalents for English terms:

English:	zapping	tour-operator	hovercraft	design	pace-maker
French:	*pianotage*	*voyagiste*	*aéroglisseur*	*stylique*	*stimulateur cardiaque*
English:	shopping	hot dog	overdose	chat-show	casting
French:	*magasinage*	*sauci-pain*	*surdosage*	*infovariétés*	*distribution des rôles*

Which of the following devices have been used to provide the French term?
(a) semantic extension of existing term
(b) neologism using French morphemes
(c) neologism using Latin or Greek morphemes
(d) calque
(e) periphrasis
(f) Gallicisation of the English term
Suggest how successful you think they are, and why.

5 Take a range of French newspapers and magazines. Which publications gener-

ally contain most Anglicisms, and within each publication which type of column or topic elicits the largest number? Do some of the English expressions appear to you to be *pérégrénismes*, rather than assimilated borrowings?

6 With the help of dictionaries of Anglicisms and the intuitions of native speakers, suggest whether the following terms are redundant in French, or whether they have forged a specific semantic role for themselves:

business, box-office, boss, speech, puzzle

FURTHER READING

Baudot, J., 1992. *Fréquence d'utilisation des mots en français écrit contemporain*, Montréal, Presses de l'Université de Montréal; based on a corpus of twentieth-century fiction and journalistic texts.

Baugh, A.C. 1951 *A History of the English Language*, London, Routledge and Kegan Paul

Baugh, A.C. and Cable, T. 1978 (3rd edition) *A History of the English Language*, London, Routledge and Kegan Paul

Bécherel, D. 1981 'A propos des solutions de remplacement des anglicismes', *La Linguistique* 17: (2) 119–24

Brunet, E. 1981 *Le Vocabulaire français de 1789 à nos jours* (3 vols), Paris, Slatkine-Champion; vol. 3 is an alphabetical list and analysis over time of the 900 most frequent words in the corpus.

Catach, N., Golfond, J., Denux, R., 1971 *Orthographe et lexicographie*, Paris, Didier; both for general discussion of French orthography, and for suggestions about the orthographic treatment of borrowings.

Darbelnet, J. 1976 *Le Français en contact avec l'anglais en Amérique du nord*, Québec, Presses de l'Université Laval

Deroy, L. 1956 *L'Emprunt linguistique*, Paris, Belles Lettres

Doillon, A. 1992 *Argots et néologismes du sport*, Paris, Amis du lexique français

Dubois, J., Guilbert, L., Mitterand, H., Pignon, H. 1960 'Le mouvement général du vocabulaire français de 1949 à 1960, d'après un dictionnaire d'usage', *Le Français moderne*, April/July

Etiemble, R. 1964 *Parlez-vous franglais?* Paris, Flammarion

Ewert, A. 1954 *The French Language*, London, Faber and Faber

Failliot, P. 1995 *Dicosport 95*, Suresnes, DPS; first published in 1988, and regularly updated since

Fantapie, A. 1984 *Dictionnaire des néologismes officiels*, Paris, Franterm

Gebhardt, K. 1975 'Gallizismen im Englischen, Anglizismen im Französischen: ein statistischer Vergleich', *Zeitschrift für Romanische Philologie* 91

Gilbert, P. 1973 'Remarques sur la diffusion des mots scientifiques et techniques dans le lexique commun', *Langue française* 17

Hagège, C. 1989 *Le français et les siècles* Paris, Odile Jacob

Jespersen, O. 1905 (10th edition 1982) *Growth and Structure of the English Language*, Oxford, Blackwell

Koessler, M. 1975 *Faux-amis des vocabulaires anglais et américain*, Paris, Vuibert

Lalanne, P. 1957 *Mort ou renouveau de la langue française*, Paris, Editions André Bonne; a work which is typical of the highly politicised rhetoric which appeared in the postwar period: 'les anglicismes montent à l'assaut de notre langue en raz-de-marée'.

Lenoble-Pinson, M. 1991 *Anglicismes et substituts français*, Paris, Duculot

Mackenzie, F. 1939 *Les Relations de l'Angleterre et de la France d'après le vocabulaire*, Paris, Droz; contains a detailed historical analysis of the first attested occurrences of Anglicisms and Gallicisms, up to 1939.

Marcellesi, C. 1973 'Le langage des techniciens de l'informatique: quelques aspects de leur vocabulaire écrit et oral', *Langue française* 17.

Martin, R. (ed.) 1971 *Dictionnaire des fréquences, vocabulaire littéraire des XIXe et XXe siècles*, Paris, Didier

Martinet, A. and Walter, H. 1973 *Dictionnaire de la prononciation de la langue française, dans son usage réel*, Paris, France-Expansion; a survey of the pronunciation of difficult words or words of foreign origin.

Mossé, F. 1943 'On the chronology of French loan words', *English Studies* 25 (1).

Pergnier, M. (ed.) 1988 *Le Français en contact avec l'anglais (en hommage à Jean Darbelnet)* Paris, Didier-Erudition; a collection of papers on developments in Canadian French.

——— 1989 *Les anglicismes*, Paris, PUF; objective, unpolemical discussion of recent Anglicisms and their assimilation.

Pétiot, G. 1982 *Le Robert des sports*, Paris, Robert

Reboul, S. 1994 'Le vocabulaire de la télématique du discours au lexique', doctoral thesis, Université de Paris X

Retman, R. 1978 'L'adaptation phonétique des emprunts à l'anglais en français', *La Linguistique* 14 (1): 111–24; an analysis of 583 terms from the *Journal Officiel*; he finds that the extension of the meaning of existing words is the device most heavily used in the proposed alternatives to Anglicisms.

Rey-Debove, J. and Gagnon, G. 1980 *Dictionnaire des anglicismes*, Paris, Robert

Rolland, J.-C. and Laffitte, J.-D., 1995 *Dicofle* (on diskette), Sèvres, Centre International d'Etudes Pédagogiques; a core lexis obtained by comparing the analyses of Baudot, Brunet and the word list of *Le français fondamental*.

Saint Robert, P. de 1985 *Guide des mots nouveaux*, Paris, Nathan

Spence, N.C.W. 1987 'Faux amis et faux anglicismes: problems of classification and definition', *Forum for Modern Language Studies* 23 (2), April

Trescases, P. 1979 'Les Anglo-américanismes du Petit Larousse Illustré de 1979', *French Review* 53 (1); a study of the *PLI* 1960–79, carrying on from Dubois's comparison (1949–60). (His analysis suggests there may have been a deceleration in the rate of borrowing.)

——— 1982 *Le Franglais vingt ans après*, Montreal/Toronto, Guérin, *Langue et Société* series

——— 1983 'Aspects du mouvement d'emprunt à l'anglais reflétés par trois dictionnaires de néologismes', *Cahiers de lexicologie* 42 (1)

Voirol, M. 1993 *Anglicismes et anglomanie*, Paris, Centre de formation et de perfectionnement des journalistes; a mini-dictionary of 250 Anglicisms and proposed alternatives, designed for journalists.

Warnant, L. 1968 *Dictionnaire de la prononciation française*, Gembloux, Belgium, Duculot

Wexler, P. 1955 *La Formation du vocabulaire des chemins de fer en France (1778–1862)*, Geneva, Droz

Chapter 6

New words for old
The derivational processes of French

External borrowing is the kind of lexical renewal of which speakers are most aware, and which attracts most public comment. Nevertheless, the most important source of new words in French has always been the exploitation of the internal lexical resources of the language: the combining and recombining of existing lexical elements. Over the centuries, families of words, or lexical paradigms based on a common root, have been elaborated: *symbole, symbolique, symboliser, symboliquement, symboliste... discret, indiscret, discrètement, discrétion... histoire, préhistoire, historien, historique, historiquement... penser, repenser, impensable, pensée, penseur...* Half an hour spent with a dictionary – especially one like the *Dictionnaire du français contemporain*, organised by lexical paradigm – will demonstrate the wide variety of **affixes** (either prefixes, added before the root, or suffixes, added after it), which are available to the language.

It is important to distinguish such **derivational** affixes, which have the function of creating new lexical items, from **inflectional** affixes (like verb endings), which carry grammatical information (see Chapter One p. 3).

Compounds, or words consisting of elements which can themselves function as independent words – such as *gentilhomme, tire-bouchon, pomme de terre* – also constitute an increasingly important part of the lexis. These are discussed in the second major section of this chapter. The first section, however, is devoted to an examination of prefixation and suffixation, since these are the processes which have proved to be the most productive in French, as in other Romance languages.

AFFIXATION

The following questions are fundamental to an investigation of how these derivational processes work:

- On what grounds can we divide words into morphemes, and classify these as roots or affixes?

- What is the function and meaning of affixes?
- How predictable are the forms of both roots and affixes?
- What are the limitations on the ways in which these elements can combine?

The following sections will outline answers to these questions, and then discuss briefly some of the theoretical issues that they raise. The section on further reading indicates where a much fuller examination of these topics may be found.

Determining the morphological structure of words

The morphological analysis of some words, and indeed of whole lexical paradigms, may be quite straightforward. In the series *symbole*, *symbolique*, *symboliser*... etc., the root /sɛ̃bɔl/, corresponding to the form of the noun, remains unchanged in form and meaning throughout the paradigm. The suffixes *-ique*, *-iser*, etc., are to be found elsewhere in the language, producing adjectives and verbs respectively: *état* → *étatique*, *étatiser*; *alcool* → *alcoolique*, *alcooliser*... In other words, the division of words into separate morphemes is based on formal distributional and semantic criteria: identical or similar sequences of phonemes can be identified as belonging to the same morpheme, if they share the same meaning or function.

It is important to specify 'identical *or similar*' sequences of phonemes,

since the root morpheme of a lexical paradigm may be variable in form; for instance, in the series *histoire, historique*, etc., the root is sometimes /istwar/, sometimes /istɔr/. /istɔr/ is a **bound** form – i.e. it cannot stand by itself as a word, but it is clearly relatable to the **free** form /istwar/, of which it may be considered an **allomorph**, or variant. And the semantic relationship between *histoire* and *historique* is exactly the same as that between *symbole* and *symbolique*. Similarly, two major allomorphs of the root exist in the paradigm *musique, musical, musicien, musicalité*: /myzik/ and /myzis/ – the first free, the second bound. This alternation of free and bound allomorphs in the root is an extremely common pattern within lexical paradigms in French.

In many cases, however, the analysis is less simple. For example, it is not immediately obvious how a word like *concevoir* should be analysed. *Concev-* can clearly be separated from *-oir*, as it occurs elsewhere, before other inflectional suffixes, as in *concevons, concevais*, etc. But is *concev-* itself a single morpheme, or a sequence of prefix+root: *con+cev*? Relying again on distributional criteria, one can find the sequence *-cev-* occurring in other verbs, like *décevoir, recevoir, percevoir*, just as *con-* occurs in other verbs, such as *contenir, convaincre, conformer*, where it is more obviously a prefix, since *tenir, vaincre* and *former* occur independently. Moreover all the *-cevoir* verbs form part of lexical paradigms which pattern in the same way: the corresponding nouns are *conception, déception, réception, perception*. The verbs also inflect in the same way: *conçu, déçu, reçu; conçoivent, déçoivent, perçoivent...* These are all indications that they share the same root morpheme, *-cev-* ; it just so happens that in these verbs we are dealing with a bound root, which has no free counterpart.

The importance of finding recurring forms, with a shared meaning or function, as a means of identifying the constituent morphemes of words, can be further illustrated by analysing a word like *image*. Is this one morpheme or two? *-age* clearly exists as a suffix in words like *garage, emballage, élevage*, in which it serves to derive a noun from a verb. However, one would not wish to segment *image* as *im-age*, since no verb **imer* exists. The fact that *image* is feminine, whereas *garage*, etc., are all masculine, gives us an additional clue that *image* is in fact morphologically simple, a single morpheme, like *page* or *cage*. (Although there is a marked tendency for morphemes to consist of one syllable in French, they may be of two or more – witness the monomorphemic *magasin, éléphant, marjolaine, ganglion, quolibet...*)

While roots in French may be bound or free, affixes are nearly always bound. Exceptions to this are a few prefixes like *contre-, sous-* and *pour-*, as in *contredire, sous-entendre*, and *poursuivre*, which have the same form as free-standing prepositions. Since these words consist entirely of free forms, there are grounds for considering them compounds, like *bonhomme* or *bienfait*. But as the distribution of *contre-, sous-* and *pour-* corresponds more to that of bound verbal prefixes like *re-* or *pré-* in, for example, *redire* and *prédire*, this is how they are generally analysed.

So far, it has been implied that words are just linear sequences of morphemes. In fact we should recognise that they have an internal structure, just as sentences do. There are two possible ways of analysing a word like, say, *inutilement*, consisting of prefix, root and suffix. We postulate either that the negative prefix *in-* is added to the adverb *utilement*, as in A, or that the adverbial *-ment* has been added to the adjective *inutile*, as in B.

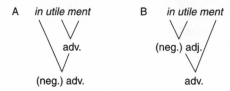

If we examine the function of negative *in-*, we find that it habitually prefixes adjectives: *injuste*, *indirect*, *inhumain*. But we never find it as a prefix to a single-morpheme adverb, like *vite* or *bien*. On distributional grounds, then, we must prefer B as representing the internal structure of the word, since this configuration clearly links *in-* to the adjective, rather than the adverb.

The function of suffixes

In the discussion that follows, it is useful to distinguish the notion of **stem** from that of **root**. A stem is a morpheme or sequence of morphemes which is available for affixation; i.e. it may be morphologically simple or complex. So *musical* is a (complex) stem since a further suffix can be added: *musicalité*, *musicalement*. A root on the other hand is the morpheme which remains when all affixes have been removed; in this case, *musique* /myzik/. Another way of looking at this is to say that single-morpheme stems can be referred to as roots.

The primary function of derivational suffixes in French is to change the syntactic category or **word class** of the original stem. So *-al*, as in *musical*, *national*, *original*, derives adjectives from nouns. From a semantic point of view, the suffix adds little to the meaning of the root noun; definitions of such adjectives in a dictionary will simply refer the reader to the lexical entry of the noun; *national* will be defined as 'relatif à la nation', *musical* as 'propre à la musique', and so on. Similarly, words containing the productive verbal suffix, *-ifier*, added to adjectival stems, as in *purifier*, *simplifier*, *clarifier*, will be given a semantic definition of the type 'rendre (plus) pur, simple, clair', etc. Verbs changed to nouns by the suffix *-ation* (e.g. *réalisation*, *confrontation*) will be defined as 'action de réaliser, de confronter'. One can argue that such semantically 'transparent' suffixes have a basically syntactic function, and in some theoretical models they are indeed treated as part of the syntactic component of the linguistic description (see Spencer 1991).

Table 1 shows most of the class-changing suffixes of French, together with the type of stem to which they are usually added. (A full inventory of derivational affixes can be found in the introduction to the *Grand Larousse de la langue française*, and the *Robert Méthodique* provides detailed entries for affixes, specifying their range of functions and meaning.)

Table 1 Class-changing derivational suffixes

Nominal suffixes		
On adjectival stems:	*(i)té, -esse*	*beauté, absurdité, tendresse*
	-eur, -itude, -ie, -tion	*hauteur, amplitude, jalousie, discrétion*
	isme, -iste, zéro	*nationalisme, royaliste, calme*
On verbal stems:	*-(a)tion, -age, -ment*	*animation, mariage, consentement*
	-ure, -ance, -aison	*blessure, croyance, comparaison*
	-ade, -erie, -ée	*rigolade, bouderie, assemblée*
	-ant, -eur, -oir(e), zéro	*assistant, menteur, baignoire, dîner*
Adjectival suffixes		
On nominal stems	*-al, -el, -able, -eux*	*original, formel, rentable, boueux*
	-aire, -é, -if, -ique	*bancaire, affairé, fautif, catastrophique*
	-esque, -ais, -iste	*romanesque, français, impressionniste*
	-ien, -ard, zéro	*parisien, soiffard, orange*
On verbal stems:	*-able/-ible, -ant, -eur*	*buvable, divisible, militant, flatteur*
Verbal suffixes		
On adjectival stems:	*-iser, -ifier, zéro*	*nationaliser, solidifier, aveugler*
On nominal stems:	*-iser, -ifier, zéro*	*alcooliser, codifier, masquer*
Adverbial suffixes		
On adjectival stems:	*-ment, zéro*	*facilement, faux*

A number of generalisations emerge from Table 1:
- The widest array of suffixes is available for the production of nouns and adjectives.
- At the other end of the scale, there are only two ways of producing adverbs, both based on adjectival stems; moreover, adverbs themselves do not act as the stem for new words.
- Most suffixes occur only once – i.e. they have a single class-changing function, though nouns and adjectives can be seen to be overlapping categories, as they share a number of suffixes, such as *-iste* and *-eur*.

This overlap of nouns and adjectives is due in part to the operation of **conversion** or **zero affixation**, by which a word changes its syntactic category without the addition of an affix. Adjectives transfer to the category of nouns (*du calme, les responsables, les riches, les pauvres...*) much more frequently than the reverse. This type of conversion is sometimes due to **ellipsis**, or omission of a head noun. (It is quite obvious that ellipsis has occurred in cases where the gender of the noun remains marked on the former adjective: *une (danse) polonaise* 'a polka', *une (chanson) berceuse* 'a lullaby'). But some words, such as the twentieth-century *raciste*, seem to have had the double function of noun and adjective from the beginning.

There is currently a vogue for the creation of abstract feminine nouns ending in the essentially adjectival suffix *-ique* (*l'historique, la symbolique, la poétique*), which could be analysed either as cases of conversion, or as derivable from an underlying noun phrase of the type *la technique/étude/ discipline...*. Nouns like *le pour, le contre, le pourquoi, le comment, le devoir, le pouvoir*, derived from prepositions, adverbs or verbs, are best analysed as cases of conversion rather than ellipsis, as it would be difficult to reconstruct longer, underlying noun phrases from which they might have been derived.

In Table 1, the verbs *masquer* and *aveugler* are listed as being derived from a noun and an adjective respectively, by conversion, or zero affixation, rather than by suffixation. This is because *-er* is an inflectional suffix, and therefore part of the grammatical system of the language, rather than a genuine derivational suffix like *-ifier*. It permutes with other inflectional suffixes like *-é, -ais, -ons*, and is lost altogether in the third person of the present tense of the verb. The noun is therefore identical in form with the root morpheme of the verb.

Conversely, nouns can be derived from verbal stems by conversion. For example, *offre* is derived historically from *offrir, vol* from *voler, demande* from *demander*. Such forms are considered by some linguists (who take *-er* and *-ir* to be derivational affixes) to be cases of **back formation** (*dérivation régressive*). This is a process connected with suffixation, in that it involves reanalysis of the morphological structure of a word by speakers who assumed that there must be a corresponding suffixless noun, since so many such pairs exist. (In much the same way English *burgle* was formed from *burglar*, on analogy with forms like *teach ~ teacher*.) Similarly in French *aristocrate* was formed from *aristocratie*, and *géographe* from *géographie*, presumably on analogy with existing forms like *bourgeois ~ bourgeoisie*, while the recent adjective *performant* post-dates the Anglicism *performance*, the analogy here being with pairs like *élégant ~ élégance, belligérant ~ belligérance*.

Back formation is impossible to distinguish from suffixation, in terms of its synchronic effect; the result in both cases is two words, one a suffixed version of the other.

Class-maintaining suffixes

Some suffixes do not change the word class or syntactic category of the stem. Such morphemes tend to be rather unproductive, compared to the class-changing type, but they do have a relatively clear semantic function. For example, 'X+*erie*' is used to mean the place where 'X' is made or sold, as in *laiterie, bijouterie, serrurerie*. The (approximately) parallel series of 'agentive' or 'occupation' nouns ending in *-ier* are often affixed to the same root, meaning 'producer/seller of X': *laitier, bijoutier, serrurier*. The suffix *-iste*, when denoting occupation or profession, can also be added to nouns: *journaliste, artiste, standardiste*...

'X+*ée*' usually means 'quantity contained by X', when 'X' is a noun (equivalent to 'X+ful' in English): *une bouchée, une cuillerée, une assiettée, une brassée, une poignée*...

Class-maintaining suffixes added to adjectives or verbs often have an attenuating or pejorative function; *-âtre*, equivalent to '-ish' in English, though less productive, is limited to some colour adjectives, such as *rougeâtre, jaunâtre, verdâtre*, and a handful of others: *douceâtre, folâtre*... One may contrast the meanings of *sauter* 'to jump' and *sautiller* 'to hop', *pleuvoir* 'to rain' and *pleuvasser* 'to drizzle'. Sometimes different suffixes can be applied to the same verbal root, with subtle nuances of meaning; *pleuvoter* and *pleuviner* exist alongside *pleuvasser*; *écrivailler* and *écrivasser* may both be translated as 'to scribble'; while *toussailler*, and *toussoter*, from *tousser* 'to cough', are difficult to translate both briefly and accurately. The suffixes used to create the diminutives of nouns too, are numerous, but individually, quite unproductive (see Hasselrot 1972). One finds, for example, *frère ~ frérot, oiseau ~ oisillon, chanson ~ chansonnette, goutte ~ goutelette, diable ~ diablotin*.

The function of prefixes

Most prefixes are class maintaining; a handful are highly productive, and have a clear semantic function. Like suffixes, they tend to be associated with specific syntactic categories, as indicated in Table 2.

The only really productive verbal prefixes are: *dé(s)-* implying 'undoing the action of X', *re-/ré-* implying either backward motion or repeated action, and the reciprocal *(s')entre-*. A whole range of less productive prefixes have basically locative or, more rarely, temporal functions: *incorporer, amener, survoler, transporter, préétablir, antidater*. Some of these recur – even less frequently – with adjectives or nouns: *préscolaire, présélection*.

Forms like *adoucir* and *engraisser* are traditionally viewed as being simultaneously prefixed and suffixed, a process given the rather unwieldy name of **parasynthesis**. If however we consider the *-er* and *-ir* suffixes to

Table 2 Derivational prefixes

Verbal prefixes	
dé(s)-, re/ré-, (s')entre-	déshabiller, déplaire, refaire, réorganiser, s'entraider
co-, in-, sur-, trans-	coexister, incorporer, surmonter, transparaître
pré-, a-, en-	préexister, adoucir, engraisser

Adjectival prefixes	
in-, anti-, pro-	injuste, anticommuniste, pro-Chinois
super-, hyper-, ultra-, extra-	superfin, hypernerveux, ultra-rapide, extra-fort,
archi-, inter-, trans-, sur-	archiplein, international, transafricain, surhumain

Nominal prefixes	
non-, contre-, dis-	non-intervention, contre-mesure, disproportion
avant-, co-, para-	avant-bras, co-auteur, parapluie

be inflectional rather than derivational, as suggested above in relation to the verbs *masquer* and *aveugler*, we should then class *en-* and *a-* as class-changing prefixes: *en-* changes nouns to verbs (cf. *emboîter, enrober, embourgeoiser...*), and *a-* in *adoucir, amollir, alourdir*, derives verbs from adjectives.

The only highly productive adjectival prefix is *in-* and its variant forms (not to be confused with the locative, verbal *in-*). *Anti-* became extremely popular in the eighteenth century, when it was essentially a political affix, and is now found increasingly in scientific, technical and commercial vocabulary: *antirouille, antichar, antivol, antitache, antigel...* Although these more recent forms have a nominal base, they are used both nominally and adjectivally: *le meilleur antigel, des missiles antichars, un système antivol.*

The range of hyperbolic prefixes – *super-, extra-* and *ultra-*, borrowed from Latin, and *hyper-* and *archi-*, from Greek – can encode subtle meaning differences; *ultra-* implies excess, *archi-* the top position in a hierarchy; *extra-* implies the quality has been reinforced or added to; *hyper-* is often used in medical terminology. These prefixes have naturally proved irresistible to advertisers, who tend to use them indiscriminately (see Chapter Nine).

Nominal prefixes are both rare and non-productive, with the recent exception of *non-*. The semantic function of *para-* 'protecting against', as in *parapluie*, is now more frequently fulfilled by verb + noun compounds with *pare-: pare-brise, pare-chocs, pare-balles, pare-boue, pare-feu.*

Again the adverb appears to be something of a derivational dead-end, in having no prefixes at all associated with it.

The meaning of affixed words

Among the examples given so far are a number of affixes which, while being identical in form, have quite different meanings and functions. The verbal prefix *in-* of *incorporer, infiltrer, inhaler,* which has a loosely locative interpretation, cannot be identified with the negative, adjectival *in-* of *indiscret, injuste* and *inutile.* The adverbial *-ment* of *rapidement, purement, lentement* is also clearly distinguishable from the nominal *-ment* of *tremblement, mécontentement, ralentissement.* These examples simply demonstrate that affixes, like whole words, can be homonymous, and as such have quite separate lexical status.

A rather different case is that of the nominal suffix *-(i)té,* as in *beauté, banalité, solidité,* for which the first semantic definition given in most dictionaries is something like 'caractère de ce qui est X' – 'X' being the adjective which is the stem of the word. But as well as referring to the abstract quality, the noun often refers to someone or something endowed with that quality, so that *une beauté* is also 'une femme très belle', *une banalité* is 'une idée, un propos, un écrit banal', and so on. Nouns derived from verbs, like *construction, écriture, enregistrement,* often mean both the action and the result of the action: 'la construction de la maison a pris deux ans'; 'la construction s'est effondrée'.

The nominal suffix *-eur,* as in *chanteur, menteur,* etc. usually stands for a human agent; but sometimes it refers also to an instrument or machine performing the same task; hence the ambiguity of *calculateur:* 'une personne qui sait calculer' or 'une machine à calculer '. The feminine form is frequently used with the latter function, as in (the again ambiguous) *balayeuse* 'street sweeper' or *moissonneuse* 'harvester'. Since the *-eur ~ -euse* suffix can have an adjectival function (as indicated in Table 1), such nouns possibly result from the ellipsis of a feminine head noun: *une (machine) moissonneuse.*

The difference between these examples and the cases of homonymy mentioned earlier is that the grammatical function remains the same for all the *-ité, -tion* and *-eur ~ -euse* words, and one can see that there are close semantic connections between the different interpretations. In Chapter Seven, where we look more closely at semantic change, we find precisely such 'metonymic' shifts; the result of an action is identified with the action itself, a quality with something possessing that quality, and so on. Here we are dealing not with separate, homonymous words, but with single lexical items, which have a variety of related meanings – in other words, with cases of polysemy (see Chapter One). The dividing line between homonymy and polysemy is not always clear. For example, although *re-* or *ré-* is always prefixed to a verb, it has two semantic functions, as suggested above: repetition as in *redemander* or, more rarely, movement away from, as in *repousser, rejeter.* Are these sufficiently distinct to warrant setting up two quite separate, homonymous prefixes?

Polysemy in one word may be carried over into words derived from it. For example, *appui* and *appuyer* both carry the literal and metaphorical meanings of 'support'. But frequently the polysemy of the stem is resolved in the derived forms. *Prolonger* (to extend in time or space) has two corresponding nouns: *prolongement* (spatial extension), and *prolongation*, which refers to time. The two meanings of *aveugler* – 'to blind' both literally and metaphorically – are differentiated even more clearly in the corresponding nouns: *cécité* (by substitution of a completely different stem) means literally 'privé de vue', while the normally derived *aveuglement* now means only 'blindness' in the sense of irrationality, as in 'dans l'aveuglement de la passion'.

There are a few examples of affixation with little semantic or syntactic effect. *Attacher* and *rattacher* can be used more or less interchangeably, while *remplir* has replaced the now archaic *emplir*, and has no reiterative value. Occasionally synonymous suffixed forms exist, like *bredouillage* and *bredouillement* 'stammering'. Both *arrosage* and *arrosement* 'watering' have the same meaning, but the latter is old-fashioned and little used. *Arrivée* and *arrivage* could both be translated by 'arrival', but the latter is used of goods rather than people. In other words, there are often subtle semantic or register differences corresponding to derived forms with a common root. But perfect synonymy is rare in morphologically complex forms, just as it is in the lexis as a whole.

Even when we are dealing with a highly productive affix, the meaning of the derived form is not always predictable. One of the commonest suffixes deriving adjectives from verbs – X+*able* – can usually be interpreted as 'can be X-ed', as in *buvable, mangeable*. However, *aimable* no longer means 'lovable' but rather 'pleasant' or 'amiable'. The productive negative prefix *in-* which appears to occur in *impertinent* does not mean the opposite of *pertinent* 'relevant', but 'cheeky'. One may be able to set up a general rule about the function and meaning of a given affix, but there are always exceptions. The problems such cases pose for a formal description will be addressed briefly later in the chapter. But it is not surprising that discrepancies of this kind occur; once a word has been formed, it develops semantically as a unit, largely independent of the words to which it is historically related.

Predicting the form of derived words

Earlier we saw how there is often variation in the form of the root morpheme: *histoire ~ histor-ique, musique ~ music-ien, mou ~ moll-esse, cercle ~ circul-aire, chaud ~ chal-eur*. Sometimes the variation is predictable from the phonological context – in which case we can talk of the forms being **phonologically conditioned**. Compare the following pairs of words:

nation	/nasjɔ̃/	*national*	/nasjɔnal/
nom	/nɔ̃/	*nommer*	/nɔme/
petit	/pəti/	*petitesse*	/pətitɛs/
grand	/grɑ̃/	*grandeur*	/grɑ̃dœr/

In each pair, a vowel-final form of the root alternates with a form ending in a consonant, which appears before the vowel of the suffix; for example, /pəti/ alternates with /pətit/. (This variation is masked in the orthographic representation, which reflects the pronunciation of an earlier period, when word-final consonants were pronounced.)

In addition, the final nasal vowel of the free form /nasjɔ̃/ or /nɔ̃/ alternates with an oral vowel followed by a nasal consonant when the root is affixed: /nasjɔn-al/ and /nɔm-e/.

Many linguists would account for these alternations by deriving both variants from an underlying form which in these cases is close to the affixed variant. Hence in a formal description /nɔm/ would be the lexical entry for *nom*, with

1 a rule which nasalises the vowel, if there is a final nasal consonant, followed by
2 a rule which deletes the final consonant.

Together these give the surface pronunciation of the free form /nɔ̃/. Neither rule applies to the derived form /nɔm+e/, as the /m/ now precedes a vowel. For the adjectives *grand* and *petit* (underlying forms /grɑ̃d/ and /pətit/) only the rule deleting the final consonant applies. Again, the final consonant of the root remains in the suffixed forms, *grandeur* and *petitesse*.

Various theoretical models have been developed to describe the phonological form of words, and a proper discussion of even one of these would take us far beyond the scope of this book.[1] Suffice to say that any adequate description has to find some way of accounting for such widespread alternations. They occur, after all, in inflectional paradigms (the masculine and feminine forms of the adjectives, *petit ~ petite*, *grand ~ grande*) and the rules operate even across word boundaries, producing 'liaison' forms: *un bon ami* /œ̃bɔnami/, *un petit arbre* /œ̃pətitarbr/, etc. Most linguists therefore agree on the desirability of rules like (1) and (2), which are both simple and productive.

However, many allomorphs occur which are not predictable in this way from the environment. It would be a good deal more complex, for example, to devise rules which formally relate /istwar/ and /istɔr/, or /mu/ and /mɔl/ – although this has been done. There are allomorphs where the variation is even more marked, as in *cercle ~ circul-aire*, *païen ~ pagan-isme*, *loi ~ lég-al*. It would be extremely 'costly', in terms of number and complexity of phonological rules, to derive these pairs from a single base form of the root; moreover, some of the rules required would apply to only a small handful of lexical items.

The historical reasons for such unpredictable alternations are twofold.

First, the language has been subject to very considerable phonological change, from Vulgar Latin onwards (see Chapter Three, pp. 45–6). What is more, sounds developed differently according to context; for example, consonants in syllable-initial position tended to survive better than those at the end of syllables. Hence the vocalisation of syllable-final 'l' to 'u' in Old French giving, for example *cou*, from Latin *coll-(um)*, but its survival at the beginning of the second syllable in *collier*, from Latin *collarium* 'necklace'. Vowels taking primary stress, which in Vulgar Latin was on the final syllable of the stem, were lengthened or changed in other ways, while vowels with secondary stress often remained unchanged. Latin *mar-* (under primary stress) gave French *mer*, but in the suffixed form *marin* (< Latin *marinus*), the vowel is unchanged. The same vowel alternation /ɛ ~ a/ occurs in *mère* (< Latin *mater*) and *marraine* 'godmother' (from *matrina*) and many others. It follows that many words which were transparently related in Latin have developed much more complex and irregular formal relationships. Nearly two thousand years of phonological change have resulted in radical allomorphic variation.

Second, as has been indicated in Chapter Three, French has borrowed from Latin throughout its history, especially in order to create derived, suffixed forms. Thus indigenous *larme* (< *lacrima*) has undergone considerable change, but to create the corresponding adjective, the Latin form has been borrowed with an appropriate suffix: *lacrymal*.

Borrowing is responsible for the alternations in *objet ~ object-if*, *corps ~ corpor-el*, *cercle ~ circul-aire*, *île ~ insul-aire*, *doigt ~ digit-al*, and many more.

Dauzat (1937) suggests that Latin borrowing in derived forms is common partly because so many indigenous words end in a vowel. Since many suffixes begin with a vowel, suffixation would give rise to the awkward juxtaposition of two vowels, when French favours sequences of consonant+vowel. For example, rather than deriving an adjective directly from the existing noun *ami*, Latin *amical(is)* was borrowed. To the same phonological effect, an additional 'parasitic' consonant is sometimes introduced in derived forms, as in *numéro ~ numérot-er*, *Congo ~ Congol-ais*, *abri ~ abriter*, *banlieue ~ banlieus-ard*, on analogy with the very large numbers of forms, like *petit ~ petitesse*, which show such alternations. The argument is not entirely convincing, as Dauzat himself points out, since borrowing of derived forms occurs even when the French root ends in a consonant. One can conceive of adjectives like **dimanchal* or **évêqueux*, corresponding to the nouns *dimanche* and *évêque*; but what we find are the borrowings *dominical* and *épiscopal*.

So far, only variation in the root morpheme has been discussed. But the forms of suffixes vary in just the same way, when a further suffix is added. The suffix *-ique* /ik/ as in *électr-ique* has the variant /is/ when it is itself suffixed: *électr-ic-ien*, *électr-ic-ité*. In other words, the form of a morpheme is frequently influenced by the morpheme that follows it.

The same phenomenon can be observed in prefixes. It is they, rather than the roots to which they are attached, that vary. The highly productive 'negative' prefix in *inutile, indiscret, imprudent, inactif*, is a good example. Two major allomorphs occur: /ɛ̃/ before most consonants, and /in/ before a vowel. It is relatively simple to derive both from an underlying form /in/; in fact the required rules of vowel nasalisation and consonant deletion have already proved necessary, to account for the suffixed forms discussed earlier.[2] In much the same way, *dé-* occurs before consonant-initial roots, and *dés-* before vowels, as in *dévoiler* and *dépolitiser*, versus *désarmer* and *déshabiller*.

In most of the examples taken so far there has been at least some degree of phonological similarity in the roots of words which form lexical paradigms. However, there are a substantial number of cases where words are in a paradigmatic relationship, although their forms have nothing in common. Although *semaine/hebdomadaire*, and *jeu/ludique* are in the same lexical relationship to one another as *complément* is to *complémentaire*, or *sphère* is to *sphérique*, it is counter-intuitive, to say the least, to think of *hebdomad-* and *semaine*, or *lud-* and *jeu*, as being variants of the same root morpheme. The reason for these alternations is again borrowing, but this time of a historically unrelated form (in the case of *hebdomadaire*, from Greek). Such lexical replacement is known as **suppletion**, and obviously has the effect of increasing the overall opacity of the lexicon.[3]

The combinability of roots and affixes

Table 1 showed that most suffixes can be added only to stems of a specific category, usually with the function of effecting a change of word class. There are, however, a number of suffixes for any given function, such as the formation of nouns from verbs, or adjectives from nouns, and at first the choice of affix appears to be arbitrary. If *curiosité* can be derived from *curieux*, why not **gloriosité* from *glorieux*? Since *glorieux* corresponds to *gloire*, why do we find *historique*, and not **historieux*, corresponding to *histoire*? Since the negative prefix *in-* is so productive, one might expect to find **invrai*, as well as *invraisemblable*. And since we have *journée* and *soirée*, corresponding to *jour* and *soir*, why not **nuitée*, corresponding to *nuit*? (The latter has in fact been coined, but failed to take root like *journée* and *soirée*; see Duchesne and Leguay's *Dictionnaire des mots perdus* for many examples of this kind.)

Some linguists claim that certain lexical gaps occur owing to a principle of natural economy at work in the language; **invrai* is not derived from *vrai*, nor **gloriosité* from *glorieux*, because *faux* and *gloire* already exist. In a formal description there would be a blocking mechanism, preventing the derivation of, for example, the negative of *vrai*, if an adjective with precisely that semantic interpretation was already in the lexicon. This implies an important assumption about language, namely that synonyms are automatically excluded, and many linguists would dispute this.[4] It would certainly not apply to English in the latter case, where 'untrue' and 'false' happily coexist.

For a number of linguists, including Corbin (1987) and Zwanenburg (1983), lexical gaps are apparent rather than real; they claim that there are many virtual or potential words, which have just not been 'actualised', but which should be considered part of the lexical system of the language. In Corbin's model, productive derivational processes are allowed to operate freely, without any 'weeding out' of non-occurring forms.[5]

Some 'potential' words do not occur for semantic or pragmatic reasons; to put it more simply, one would have no cause to use them. For example, although *dé-* is a highly productive verbal prefix, it does not occur with the verb *cuire* (and many others), since *cuire* refers to processes which cannot be 'undone'. Nouns like *poignée, cuillerée, bouchée, bolée, brassée*, meaning 'quantity contained by...', were referred to earlier. It is not surprising that we do not find, for example, **une piédée* (*a footful). But advances in organic chemistry might one day lead to the creation of **décuire*; and **une piédée* would no doubt be a perfectly viable concept for a French-speaking chimpanzee....[6] These 'gaps' have everything to do with the world we live in, but little to do with the internal organisation of the lexicon.

Still other 'gaps' may be due to social or cultural constraints. There is no accepted feminine version of *mineur* or or *éboueur*, because these are jobs which are not traditionally done by women in France. Given the changing nature of social structures and conventions, this is the type of gap most likely to be filled (see Chapter Eight).

Lexical gaps aside, we are still faced with the problem of explaining why a particular verbal root is nominalised by, say, *-ment* rather than *-age* or *-tion*. Some processes are simply statistically more frequent than others, and the popularity of any given affix varies in time. Computer-based technology now makes it possible to scan huge databases from different periods, to have a reasonably accurate view of the changing patterns of affixation in a language. In data drawn from two editions of the *PLI* around the middle of this century, for example, Dubois (1962) reports *-age* as becoming rather more productive than *-ment*, but *-(a)tion* nouns being more popular than either of these. One reason for the increase in *-(a)tion* words is the growth of verbs in *-iser* and *-ifier*, which necessarily form their verbal nouns with this suffix, e.g. *pétrifier ~ pétrification, nationaliser ~ nationalisation*, etc. (see also Goosse 1975, on this trend). Adjectives ending in *-able* or *-ible* invariably form nouns in *-ité: possible ~ possibilité; comptable ~ comptabilité; fiable ~ fiabilité*; whereas monomorphemic adjectives, verbalised with *-ir*, then form nouns ending in *-ment* or *-age*, almost invariably affixed to the 'long' form of the verb: *rouge ~ rougir ~ rougissement*; *doux ~ adoucir ~ adoucissement*; *blanc ~ blanchir ~ blanchissement* or *blanchissage*. In other words, there is a high degree of predictability in the sequencing of suffixes.

Some of the constraints on the way suffixes combine, and indeed the form of the root to which they are added, can be explained in terms of the distinction between 'popular' and 'learned' morphemes.

'Popular' versus 'learned' elements

These terms, which are essentially translations of the French *populaire* and *savant*, have already been used in Chapter Three, in a diachronic context. But they can also be useful in helping us to make generalisations about the language as it is today.

Traditionally, words or morphemes are said to be **popular** if they have developed from Vulgar Latin or came into the language at a very early stage, while **learned** forms have been borrowed at a later date from Classical Latin, or Greek – usually from the late fourteenth century onwards. Since the same etymon is often involved in learned and popular forms, we find historically related pairs occurring, of both roots and affixes. Just as *frêle* and *fragile* can both be traced to Latin *fragilis*, so *-aison* and *-ation*, as in *terminaison* and *explication*, stem from Latin *-ation(em)*.

One could argue that this distinction is of purely historical interest, and need not be made in a synchronic description of the language. However, there are distributional grounds for classifying both roots and affixes as learned or popular[7]. There is a tendency for learned roots to take learned affixes, and popular roots to be matched with popular affixes. For example, the learned *stranguler* (< Latin *strangulare*) is nominalised with a learned suffix, *strangulation*, while its popular counterpart *étrangler* has a popular suffix, *étranglement*. Similarly, the lexical paradigm associated with the verb *louer* (< *locare* 'to hire') contains two root allomorphs, the popular form *lou-* and the learned form *loc-*. *Lou-* is associated with popular affixes in *lou-age*, *lou-eur*, while *loc-* is to be found with learned suffixes in *loc-ation* and *loc-ataire*.

However, there are not always two root allomorphs which can be neatly classified in this way. For example, there is only one allomorph of the nominal root *forme*, which has a corresponding adjective *formel*, with a popular suffix. But if further, learned suffixes are added, we find learned *-al* occurring in the stem: *formalité*, *formalisme*. On the other hand, *-el* remains if a popular suffix is added: *formellement*. It looks as if such roots may be classified as either 'popular' or 'learned'.

So far, so good. But more problematic cases occur. The ubiquitous *-iste* (borrowed ultimately from Classical Greek) is increasingly added to home-grown roots, as in the neologisms *jardiniste* 'landscape gardener' and

voyagiste 'tour operator'. *Chosifier* and *chosification* are even more striking examples, as *chose* is the most prosaic of words, but here takes
essentially 'learned' suffixes. Despite this, it is a perfectly respectable,
technical term in philosophy. (The synonyms *réifier* and *réification* conform to the 'learned root + learned suffix' constraint, with the root being
borrowed from Latin *res* 'thing').

Such hybrid words often sound a little incongruous, as if one were
mixing registers; as Pichon (1942) says: 'il y a toujours gaucherie à
attacher un suffixe savant à un radical de la souche authentique'. As
learned affixes are generally more productive nowadays than those of 'la
souche authentique', we will no doubt witness a progressive erosion of this
binary 'popular v. learned' distinction.

A number of other anomalies occur. For example, nouns suffixed with the
supposedly learned suffix *-tion* are given the (popular) adjectival suffix *-el*
(as in *conventionnel*, *dérivationnel*, *sensationnel*), although the learned
equivalent *-al* is available and productive. The picture with prefixes is
even less clear. The correlation between prefixes and roots, or prefixes
and suffixes, in relation to the popular–learned distinction is patchy to say
the least.[8]

There is no general agreement on how to incorporate these facts in a
formal description of the language. As is frequently the case, the linguist
must choose between capturing a partial generalisation (at the expense of
listing substantial numbers of exceptions), and missing the generalisation
altogether.

Derivational processes and linguistic theory

Word formation was the poor relation in the early models of linguistic
theory, developed in the 1960s. Interest was then focused almost exclusively on syntax, where spectacular advances were being achieved. Syn-
tactic-style transformations were therefore used to derive many
morphologically complex words; for example, a nominalisation rule would
derive 'the destruction of the town by the soldiers' from the full sentence
'the soldiers destroyed the town'. These efforts foundered, for reasons
Chomsky discusses in his 'Remarks on nominalization'[9].

More recent approaches have tended to take individual morphemes as the
basic input to the lexicon; each morpheme is given separately, with its
phonological form, word class (in the case of roots), and semantic interpretation. A set of word formation rules then specify which affixes may be
added to which roots (e.g. that the prefix *dé-* can only be added to a root
marked as a verb). Then follows a set of phonological rules, of the type
indicated on p. 113; the final output represents the actual spoken form of
the derived word, together with its meaning. Linguists differ in how they

handle each of these stages in the generation of words. The phonological form of the morphemes entered in the lexicon may be more or less 'abstract' – i.e. removed from the surface pronunciation of the morpheme; the more 'abstract' the base form, the more complex will be the later phonological rules. Two alternative forms of a morpheme may be entered together (e.g. the 'learned' and 'popular' allomorphs), with no attempt to derive one from the other; the word formation rules simply specify which allomorph is to be selected for which affix. Corbin inclines to the latter approach, giving for example the two forms of the root *bœuf ~ bov-in* separately, while Schane (1968 and 1973) sets up one underlying abstract form from which both can be derived. Some linguists choose to limit the scope of the word formation rules, to generate only words actually used by native speakers, while others (like Zwanenburg and Corbin) are not bound by this constraint, and allow the generation of all 'potential' words in the language. Zwanenburg does however build in a 'blocking' mechanism to rule out potential synonyms like **gloriosité*.

Particular theoretical problems are posed by the semantic opacity of many derived forms in French. At the beginning of this chapter it was suggested that on distributional grounds we can recognise words like *con-cev-oir, re-cev-oir*, etc. as being morphologically complex; all the elements recur elsewhere in the language, and the verbs enter into similar inflectional and lexical paradigms. The difficulty is that of assigning a meaning to the root – and indeed to the prefixes in these cases. Semantically, the words are indivisible units. This is often the case with words that have bound roots – especially those carrying prefixes inherited from Latin which are no longer productive. What common meaning can one assign to the root *-stit-* in *constituer, restituer* and *prostituer*, or to *-sist-* in *consister, persister* and *désister*?

An even tougher problem arises with words like *quatorze* or *royaume* (cited by Corbin). One may wish to recognise a morpheme *quat-* or *roy-* on the basis of comparison with words like *quatre, quarante*, or *roi* and *royal*. But the remaining elements *-orze* and *-aume*, apparently functioning like suffixes, are found nowhere else. It is therefore impossible to assign to them either meaning or a clear grammatical function. Non-recurring roots are also found. One might wish to recognise two morphemes in a word like *formidable* – but that raises the problem of how to categorise *formid-*. (Just the same problem arises with the non-recurring roots of English 'uncouth' or 'reckless'.)

Corbin's solution is to recognise such words as complex but non-derived forms; that is, they are entered as complete words in the lexicon, together with their meaning, rather than being derived through word formation rules. But they are assigned a morphological structure, and are subject to the same phonological rules that act on other derived forms.

The same treatment can be given to words which appear to have been derived via productive processes of affixation, but whose meaning is not derivable from that of their constituent elements, like *impertinent* and *aimable*, mentioned earlier. *Impertinent* will be entered as a unit, together with its semantic interpretation, but will be assigned the structure *in+pertinent*, with the nasalisation and consonant-deletion rules specified on p. 113 applying to the prefix. In the freely derived *imprudent*, however, the meaning of the word is derived from that of the root adjective plus that of the negative prefix, through the mediation of the word formation rules.

It has been impossible in the space available here to do more than touch on one or two of the issues which arise when one attempts to formalise the properties of derived words. The scope of the lexicon, and the type of rules it contains, will depend very much on the nature and scope of rules formulated for the other components, semantic, syntactic and phonological, which interact with it.

COMPOUND WORDS

A substantial part of this chapter has been devoted to the processes of affixation, partly because these constitute such a productive source of new words in French, and partly because they raise the most important theoretical issues. No new theoretical problems arise from the analysis of compound words; again it is a question of specifying which combinations of morphemes are possible, and of dealing with morphologically complex words which are semantically opaque. (For instance, just as non-recurring morphemes like the *formid-* of *formidable*, or the *-aume* of *royaume*, occur in affixed words, so do elements of compounds like the *rez* of *rez-de-chaussée* 'ground floor', which is restricted to this item.

The formation of words by combining free morphemes (rare in the parent language) has become an increasingly important process in French. The diversity of possible internal structures should be clear from the following range of examples:

noun + adjective	*chaise longue, pied-noir*
adjective + noun	*sage-femme, gentilhomme*
adjective + adjective	*sourd-muet, aigre-doux*
noun + noun	*porte-fenêtre, mot-clé*
noun + preposition + noun	*hôtel de ville, arc-en-ciel*
verb + noun	*tire-bouchon, couvre-feu, casse-pieds*
verb + verb	*laissez-passer, savoir-faire*
preposition + noun	*en-cas, presqu'île*
adverb + verbal participle	*clairvoyant, bienveillant, déjà vu*

Occasionally, whole sentences may be used as words: *un certain je ne sais quoi, le qu'en dira-t-on* 'gossip'. (It is clear that these are being used as nouns, as they are preceded by an article.)

This handful of examples is enough to demonstrate that compounds are overwhelmingly nouns, whatever their internal structure. Only the sequence adjective + adjective, and the adverb + present participle (and, more rarely, verb + noun compounds, like *casse-pieds* or *casse-cou*) function as adjectives. In verb + noun compounds the noun generally acts as the object of the verb. In noun + noun compounds the second noun usually modifies the first in some way – although the precise semantic relationship between the two varies a good deal.[10] *Une pause-café, un passage piétons, un thé citron* may in fact be considered abbreviated versions of longer phrases, *une pause pour le café*, etc., where the relationship is spelt out. More rarely, the nouns are in a semantic relationship which corresponds to a coordinate structure; *une porte-fenêtre* is both a door *and* a window.

Problems of definition

The orthography of the above compounds is somewhat arbitrary, in that some are written as one word, some as separate words, and some with hyphens. It is obviously of no help in either establishing or reflecting the status of these expressions as words. The formal criteria generally used to distinguish between a compound word and a phrase are those of **internal cohesion** and **semantic opacity**. The elements within a compound remain immutable. One cannot talk about **une chaise très longue*, or **un en-tout-cas*; nor can verbs within compounds inflect in the normal way. The meaning of a compound often cannot be derived from the current meaning of its parts. *Un hôtel de ville* is not a type of *hôtel, une sage-femme* is not the same as *une femme qui est sage, un gentilhomme* is not necessarily *gentil*, and so on.[11]

Once a sequence of morphemes starts to be used as a single unit, its meaning can change, without regard to the meaning of its component parts. Since the process of fusion is gradual, compounds of long standing, like *sage-femme* and *gentilhomme*, are usually furthest, semantically, from the present meaning of their component elements. It is often harder to distinguish compounds from phrases in sequences which have been combined more recently. Should *voiture de sport* or *livre de poche* be considered compound words or phrases? They are relatively transparent, semantically, but phrases of this structure also tend to have internal cohesion. Mitterand (1968: 63) and Spence (1976: 21–40) discuss this problem, and that of differentiating compounds from derived forms. Set phrases (*locutions*), such as *prendre feu* or *avoir beau* are often recognised as an intermediary category; these are discussed in detail in Guiraud (1962).

While formal criteria can be used to distinguish the two end points of this continuum – with an immutable and highly opaque word (such as *sage-femme*) at one end, and a freely generated syntactic phrase (such as *dans mon garage*) at the other – categorical distinctions are difficult to make in the middle ground. We have to fall back on the admittedly very vague criterion of frequency of use.

Neo-classical compounds

The definition of compound words could be extended to cover words consisting of roots borrowed from Classical Latin or Greek, like *téléphone* (called *recomposés* by Martinet (1967)); one could simply define a compound as a word consisting of two or more root morphemes – either bound or free. There are huge numbers of such words in French, as in other European languages, but mostly occurring in rather specialised, technical fields. Large dictionaries like the *Grand Larousse de la langue française* (*GLLF*) give these roots separate lexical entries, and often devote articles to the phenomenon in their introductions.

The main formal difference between these and indigenous compounds is that the latter consist of free roots, whereas those of the former are bound. (It is in the nature of Latin and Greek roots to be bound, since these are highly inflecting languages.)

Although most neo-classical compounds are new combinations of classical roots, rather than being borrowed as words, it is unusual for Greek and Latin to be mixed. The morphemes in *microscope*, *téléphone* and *monopole* are Greek; those in *aqueduc*, *ambidextre*, *somnambule* and *suicide* are from Latin. Purists may look down on hybrid forms, such as *polyvalent* or *thermostat* (Greek + Latin), but the absence of Latin or Greek from most school curricula means that they are increasingly unlikely to shock the average French speaker.

More and more frequently Greek or Latin roots are combined with French ones, as in *télévision* and *autoroute* and (more recently) *multirisque* or *télécarte* 'phone card'.[12] This pattern has been adopted to create what might be called 'pseudo-classical' compound adjectives, of the type *socio-culturel* or *franco-allemand*, where the first adjective has been clipped and given the typically Greek linking vowel -o-. More ephemeral hybrids like *câlinothérapie* 'stroking therapy', *crapauduc* 'underpass for toads', or *pifomètre* (literally 'nose-meter', i.e. intuition) rely for their comic effect on the incongruous juxtaposition of homely, everday term and learned morpheme.

Greek compounds predominate, particularly in the more specialised terminologies of medicine, chemistry, and other branches of science and technology. (In the introduction to the *GLLF* nearly five times as much space is taken up by the list of Greek roots, compared to Latin ones.) This is partly because the process is indigenous to Greek, while compounds

were rare in Latin. The order of the elements occurs as in Greek, too, with the modifying element preceding the head, as in *hippodrome* (literally a horse-track) – contrary to the more usual order of 'modified + modifier' in French. As with native French compounds, a variety of different semantic relationships may hold between the root morphemes; *hydrophobie* means 'fear *of* water', whereas *hydrothérapie* means 'treatment *using* water'.

Unlike compounds consisting of free morphemes, neo-classical forms can usually be suffixed: *microscopique, suicidaire, monopoliser,* etc. On the rare occasions when indigenous compounds are suffixed, as in *mots-croisiste* (from *mots-croisés*), meaning 'crossword enthusiast', the resulting word is awkward and unconvincing; the neo-classical equivalent – *cruciverbiste* – may be comically pretentious, but it is more faithful to established patterns of word formation.[13] This type of word thus combines morphological flexibility with the encapsulation of a large quantity of information. Add to this the traditional prestige of the donor languages, enhanced by their role in the international lingua franca of science and technology, and one can see why such terms are likely to continue to proliferate.[14]

CURRENT TRENDS IN WORD FORMATION

Besides this continuing expansion of neo-classical forms in technical and scientific fields, a number of tendencies characterise the derivational processes of twentieth-century French, with some becoming particularly marked in the postwar period. Compounds combining verb + noun and noun + noun have proved enormously popular. The former may refer to people, in informal registers, in which case they can act as adjectives or nouns: *lèche-cul*, *pique-fesses* 'nurse', or to gadgets and machines: *lave-vaisselle*, *tourne-disque*, *chauffe-eau*. Noun + noun combinations either result from ellipsis of longer forms (*un café à la crème > un café crème*), or are created *tels quels*: *le cinéma vérité*, *un roman fleuve* – in which case the semantic interpretation is often somewhat opaque. (Ellipsis may be carried further still, with *un café crème* becoming simply *un crème*, and *des chaussures de basket(ball)* becoming *des baskets*.) They are particularly favoured in the language of commerce and advertising – *une boisson télévision*, *un prix choc*, *un coin cuisine* – where brevity and novelty are both modish and practical. Maybe it is part of their attraction that the reader/hearer has to puzzle out the missing semantic link.

This trend to brevity is even more striking in the **clipped forms** which are so characteristic of informal varieties of contemporary French. Most commonly, the final syllable or syllables of a word are dropped, as in *sympa(thique)*, *mon beauf(rère)*, *le petit-déj(euner)*... As we can see, the process is no respecter of morpheme boundaries. Much less frequently, the initial syllable(s) are lost, as in *(omni)bus* or *(ca)pitaine*.

A few date back to the early years of this century or earlier: *piano*, *stylo*, *métro*, *cinéma*. Here, the longer forms *pianoforte*, *stylographe*, *métro-politain*, *cinématographe* have virtually ceased to exist, so that the clipped versions are no longer informal variants, and can be considered thoroughly lexicalised. (*Métro* is the result of both ellipsis and clipping since the original full form was *chemin de fer métropolitain*.)

When the long form is a neo-classical compound the abbreviation often takes place after the linking -*o*-, as in *aristo(crate)*, or *porno(graphique)*, which has become something of a marker of informal register in the lexis. It is sometimes extended to forms which contain no -*o*- in the original – hence *intello* for *intellectuel* and *dico* for *dictionnaire* – and has the additional effect of maintaining the favoured syllable structure of the language, which is a consonant followed by a vowel.

Since the semantic interpretation of an item relies to a large extent on the linguistic and social context, we should not be surprised to find most clipping occurring in small, closely knit social groups with shared knowledge and interests. It is therefore highly characteristic of slang and informal professional jargon, which are discussed in Chapter Ten. The clipping of *Saint Tropez* to *Saint Trop'*, and the double clipping of *le boulevard Saint Michel* to *le boul' Mich'*, implies a kind of affectionate identification with these places. The clipping of the names of products, companies, newspapers or magazines (*Libé* from *Libération*, or *Nouvel Obs* from *Nouvel*

Observateur, MacDo for *MacDonald's*) must therefore be very gratifiying to the directors – if indeed it is not actively promoted by them.

With the loss of so much phonological material in the course of clipping, homophones naturally arise; for over fifty years *micro* has been the clipped form of *microphone*. More recently, it has come to be used for a microwave oven – *un (four) micro-(ondes)* – and even more recently, one finds references to *la presse micro*, i.e. relating to microcomputers. As with all homophones, the reader/hearer relies on the context to select the appropriate interpretation.

Speakers tend to be very aware of clipping as a sociolinguistic phenomenon, partly because it is so at odds with the normal processes of word formation, but even more because it is especially characteristic of the language of the young, and often results in forms which are obscure to the outsider (see Chapter Ten). This in turn feeds the widespread anxiety about the direction French is taking, and especially about the widening gap between the written norm and spoken forms of the language. However, since most clipped words remain informal variants of the full forms, and are subject to quite rapid turnover, they remain marginal to the lexical system; the long-term effects on the language are therefore unlikely to be significant.

The combination of clipping and compounding gives rise to **blends** (in French, *mots-valises* or *mots-centaures*) which, in their novelty and brevity, again find popularity with journalists and the promoters of new products or services. The process of synthesising music is sometimes referred to as *acousmatique* (< *acoustique* + *automatique*?); the gourmet in constant search of new culinary experiences is a *gastronomade*; baby-worship or *bébolâtrie* is successfully exploited by advertising copywriters. The professional wordsmith Finkielkraut (1979) has even produced a dictionary of humorous blends like *délicaresse* (= 'étreinte très douce'), *fliction* (= 'histoire policière') and *bidingue* (= 'qui délire entre deux langues'). But here we are venturing into the uncharted margins of the French lexis, where a word lasts, at most, as long as an advertising campaign. One of the few blends to find a more permanent place in the language is the term *franglais*, popularised through Etiemble's various diatribes against English influence.

Another phenomenon, which is immediately obvious on opening any French newspaper, is the proliferation of **acronyms** (in French, *sigles*), or sequences of initial letters, usually standing for the name of an organisation. (Increasingly, they are written without full stops.) Some are so rarely used in their full form that many French speakers would be hard pressed to provide it. (How many Parisians know that *RATP* stands for *Régie autonome des transports parisiens* or *RER* for *Réseau express régional*?)

Acronyms were little used in French before the middle of this century; since then they have mushroomed, with virtually every newly formed organisation or large company being referred to by its initials. This can no doubt be explained both by the growth of bureaucratic or commercial organisations, at a national and international level, and by the constraints of the modern media, where time and space are at a premium. Acronyms which have really become common currency (some even finding a place in dictionaries) are those concerned with aspects of bureaucracy which impinge heavily on everyday life: *les HLM* (*habitations à loyer modéré*), *le SMIC* (*salaire minimum interprofessionnel de croissance*), *les ZUP* (*zones à urbaniser en priorité*), *la TVA* (*taxe à la valeur ajoutée*).

Names may be conceived with the resulting acronym in mind; hence the artfully named *AMAT* (*Association de la Musique et des Arts Tchèques*); and it seems a shame that the term *ECU* (European Currency Unit), ingeniously recalling the ancient coinage of France, has now been replaced by the plebeian clipped form, the *Euro*.

The most successful acronyms are often those that form a pronounceable word. *L'OTAN*, *l'ONU* or *le CAPES* are rarely pronounced letter by letter. Even un-French consonant clusters are not a bar to pronounceability; witness the adoption of the popular *FNAC* /fnak/ chain of book and record stores or the huge *CNIT* /knit/ commercial centre at la Défense, as one-syllable words. The most heavily used may be 'naturalised' further as ordinary words, and entered as such in some dictionaries, acquiring accents where necessary: *le Capès*, *le smic*. Such transformations are inevitable when the acronym operates as the root of a newly derived word. Hence a member of the *CGT* (*Confédération générale du travail*) is a *cégétiste*, and a graduate of the *ENA* (*Ecole normale d'administration*) is an *énarque* (modelled on *monarque*?). *ONU* has given rise to *onusien*, *onufier*, *OTAN* to *otaniser*, *SMIC* to *smicard*.

It may be the pronounceability of the English acronyms *UNESCO* and *UNICEF* which has caused them to be borrowed, rather than translated. It is harder to find an explanation for the fashionable use of *USA* (pronounced letter by letter) to replace *Etats-Unis*. Organisations which are clearly foreign often retain their original acronym, with gender being assigned according to that of the cognate head noun in French; hence *la RAF*, *la CIA*, *le FBI*. The foreign pronunciation of the letters may even be used: for example, *la BBC* is either /bibisi/ or /bebese/.

Given the French predilection for word play, it is not surprising to find joke acronyms being devised by the young, smart 'Saint-Germain-des-Prés' set, rather as 'OTT' or 'sweet FA' are used in English. So *PPH* (*passera pas l'hiver*), or even worse, *PPLW* (*passera pas le weekend*) refer to the crumbling older generation; other stereotypes include the Parisian equivalent of the Sloane Ranger – *BCBG* (*bon chic bon genre*) – and the well-heeled *CPFH* woman (*collier de perles, foulard Hermès*).

Despite the prominence of acronyms in the contemporary media, it is again difficult to see in them a real threat to the traditional processes of word formation. Full lexicalisation, as with the borrowed *radar*, is extremely rare. The majority of acronyms are the names of organisations and therefore proper nouns, and, as such, remain marginal to the main body of the lexis. Moreover, they are heavily used only in certain types of written text, and most of the phenomena they represent are essentially ephemeral.

NOTES

1 Schane (1968) was one of the first to investigate French morphology and phonology using an early generative model. In 1973 he advocated an even more 'abstract' phonological representation, explicitly in order to relate 'learned' and 'popular' roots, like *mère* and *matern-el*. The works of Dell (1973 and 1979), Zwanenburg (1983) and Corbin (1987) represent further developments of generative theory in this area, applied to French.
2 Other phonologically conditioned allomorphs of this prefix occur: for example before /r/, /l/, /m/ or /n/ (i.e. liquids or nasals), assimilation of the nasal consonant occurs, giving *irréel, illégal, immortel, innombrable*, etc. These may be pronounced with either a single or a double consonant; in formal terms, an optional consonant-reduction rule would have to be added to that of assimilation.
3 It is not an easy matter to decide where allomorphic variation ends and suppletion begins. If we set aside etymological considerations, and look only at the degree of formal similarity of morphemes, we might decide (like Corbin (1987) and many other linguists) that *épiscopal* should be treated like *hebdomadaire*, since it is impossible in both cases to set up phonological rules which will relate these adjectives to their corresponding noun. Others, like Spencer (1991) recognise 'partial suppletion' in cases like *épiscopal*.
4 Corbin, for one, is unimpressed by this argument, and points to cases of synonymy which undermine it.
5 One is tempted to think that this line is adopted because it tidies up an otherwise messy system, and hence simplifies the linguist's task. It also mirrors the widely accepted notion of 'linguistic competence', developed initially to account for the creativity of the syntactic component. There is some support for this approach from the sort of derived forms that children use (see Corbin's appendix: 'Corpus de néologismes enfantins'); they produce forms like *poubellier* instead of *éboueur*, *visitation* instead of *visite*, *abandonnement* instead of *abandon*, *se dégarer* as the opposite of *se garer*. See also Corbin and Corbin (1982) for a fuller analysis.
   The forms demonstrate that the children have internalised certain rules of lexical production (apparently favouring affixation rather than conversion), which are part of the adult system, but they have not as yet learnt the exceptions to these rules. For Corbin and others, what is important is describing the rules – the speaker's 'lexical competence', not the 'accidental' departures from them. For a contrasting, traditional view, see Dauzat (1937) and Ullmann (1952), who stress the relatively unproductive nature of the derivational processes of French, up to the twentieth century.
6 There is again a parallel with syntax here; these words conform to the rules of word formation, but are semantically aberrant, just as Chomsky's well-known sentence 'colorless green ideas sleep furiously' is perfectly well formed, grammatically, but would be ruled out by the semantic component.
7 In Zwanenburg's study of deverbal derivation (1983), the distinction is fundamental to his theoretical framework.

8 Some partial correlations are discussed in Zwanenburg (1983: 58). For example, popular *dé(s)-* tends to correlate with popular roots, and learned counterpart *dis-* with learned ones. The latter also co-occurs only with nominal *-tion*, while *dés-* appears with all the major nominal suffixes *-age*, *-ment* and *-tion*.

9 This early approach to derivational morphology has however been immortalised in the introductions to dictionaries like the *DFC* and the *GLLF*, which suggest that many derived words should be analysed as reduced forms of sentence-like structures.The main problem, as we have seen, is the unpredictability of the form and meaning of derived words. See Spencer (1991) for a clear summary of the arguments involved.

10 Noun + noun compounds exist which can be traced back to the medieval period, for example *bain-marie*, *hôtel-Dieu*, and place names like *Mont St-Michel*, *Ville l'Evêque*. These are relics of Old French nominative + genitive constructions, where such relationships were originally marked by inflection, rather than with a preposition; so that *hôtel-Dieu*, for example, was equivalent to *hôtel de Dieu*; but the construction had fallen out of use by the Middle French period.

11 Compounds consisting of adjective + noun usually date back to the Old French period, when word order was much freer.

12 Although *télé-* and *auto-* function as roots in the original languages, there are strong arguments for analysing them as prefixes in French. For example, *therm-* is clearly a root in *thermal*, but *télé-* and *auto-* are never suffixed in this way. They only fill the first slot in words, that is, they have a distribution more typical of prefixes. Similarly the Greek-based morpheme *-logue*, a root in Greek, patterns more like a suffix in French.

13 Only a few suffixed compounds of the non-classical type exist, such as *tire-bouchonner* and *gentilhommière*. Words like *banqueroutier* or *bouleverser* are former compounds whose stems have coalesced to the point of becoming single morphemes. Dauzat (1937) shows how on occasion French is obliged to borrow a derived form, owing to the difficulty of suffixing compounds; for example *ferroviaire*, the adjective corresponding to *chemin de fer*, comes from Italian.

14 See Cottez' dictionary (1988), which gives large numbers of Greek and Latin roots recurring in scientific and technical terminology; these are also classified separately according to the notions they express, so that *beaucoup* is shown to correspond to both Greek *poly-* and Latin *multi-*, and so on. As a number of the entries indicate, even these classical roots are subject to homonymy and polysemy, with *auto-*, for example, meaning 'self' (as in *autofinancement*, *autobiographie*), or 'relating to motor vehicles' (e.g. *autocar*, *autoroute*).

PROJECTS

1 Identify the constituent morphemes of the following words as root, suffix or prefix, bound or free, and indicate the meaning or function of each, justifying your analysis where possible with reference to words similar in form and meaning:

décalage, courage, carnaval, carnivore, exaucer, excaver, document, régiment, maison, livraison, champignon, champêtre, famine, gamine

2 Establish lexical paradigms based on the following roots:

rouge, noir, blanc, vert, pourpre, bleu
pomme, olive, orange, abricot, cerise

Note parallels and discrepancies in these paradigms. Do there appear to be any lexical gaps? If so, suggest how they might be explained.

3 Demonstrate the internal structure of the following words with the help of branching tree-diagrams (justifying these by referring to the distribution and function of the affixes in other words):

dépersonnalisation, réutilisabilité, ininflammable, transméditerranéen

4 (a) Check the various meanings of the following verbs. Which might be considered cases of homonymy, and which are polysemous?
(b) Check on the form and meaning of nouns derived from these verbs. Identify those cases where the meaning of the derived noun corresponds to only one meaning of the corresponding verb:

arrêter, voler, assembler, déchirer, tenter, décoller, se dégonfler

5 Establish lexical paradigms for the following root nouns, and suggest which allomorphs of the root and which associated affixes might be considered 'popular' or 'learned':

fruit, lait, raison, école, racine, sec, nœud, mûr

6 Suggest half a dozen 'potential' words, which do not (yet) occur in French for (a) pragmatic and (b) social reasons. Suggest a few more which would be ruled out as ill formed by word formation rules in a formal description.

7 On the basis of the following words (and any others you can think of ending in *-ier*), how many different semantic functions can be identified? Would you consider these to be cases of homonymy or polysemy?

encrier, poivrier, meunier, routier, teinturier, pommier, cerisier, policier, laitier, cendrier, charcutier, prunier

8 Which suffixes are used to indicate 'inhabitant of'? Can any semantic nuances be distinguished among them? Which appear(s) to be the most productive? (Include in your analysis the derived forms corresponding to *Pays Bas, Belgique, Danemark, Turquie, Yemen, Terre de Feu, Chartres, Chantilly.*)

FURTHER READING

Battye, A. and Hintze, M.-A. 1992 *The French Language Today*, London, Routledge; see Chapter 3 for a discussion of some of the problems relating to the formalisation of both the inflectional and derivational morphology of French.
Calvet, L.-J. 1980 *Les Sigles*, Paris, PUF Que Sais-Je?; looks at the history of *siglaison*, and analyses it as both a social and a linguistic phenomenon.
Chomsky, N. 1970 'Remarks on nominalization', in R. Jacobs and P. Rosenbaum (eds) *Reading in English Transformational Grammar*, Waltham, Mass., Blaisdell
Cottez, H. 1988 (4th edition) *Dictionnaire des structures du vocabulaire savant: éléments et modèles de formation*, Paris, Usuels du Robert
Corbin, D. 1987 *Morphologie dérivationnelle et structurale du lexique* (2 vols), Tübingen, Germany, Max Niemeyer Verlag; elaborates a theoretical model of that part of the lexical component generating affixed words, with morphemes as the basic lexical elements, taking into account problems posed by the formal and semantic irregularity of such forms. See her bibliography for the theoretical background of these issues.

Corbin, D. and Corbin, P. 1982 *La Part de l'autonomie dans la construction de la compétence lexicale*, Lille, Actes du 54e congrès de l'AGIEM

Dauzat, A. 1937. 'L'appauvrissement de la dérivation en français', *Le Français moderne* 5.

Dell, F. 1973 *Les Règles et les sons: introduction à la phonologie générative*, Paris, Hermann; exemplifies an early model of generative phonology, with about half the book being devoted to specific problems raised by French data.

—— 1979 'La morphologie dérivationnelle du français, et l'organisation de la composante lexicale en grammaire générative', *Revue Romane* 14

Di Sciullo, A.M. and Williams, E. 1987 *On the Definition of Word*, Cambridge, Mass., MIT Press; they argue that compounding in French is essentially the lexicalisation of syntactic processes, not a derivational process carried out by word formation rules.

Dubois, J. 1962 *Etude sur la dérivation suffixale en français moderne et contemporain*, Paris, Larousse

Dubois, J. and Dubois, C. (eds) 1971 *Introduction à la lexicographie: le dictionnaire*, Paris, Larousse

Dubois, J. and Guilbert, L. 1961 'Formation du système préfixal intensif en français moderne et contemporain', *Le Français moderne*, April

Dubois, J., Guilbert. L., Mitterand, H. and Pignon, H. 1960 'Le mouvement général du vocabulaire français de 1949 à 1960, d'après un dictionnaire d'usage', *Le Français moderne*, April/July, and in Dubois, J. and Dubois, C. 1971 *Introduction à la lexicographie: le dictionnaire*, Paris, Larousse

Duchesne, A. and Leguay, T. 1988 *L'Obsolète, dictionnaire des mots perdus*, Paris, Larousse

Finkielkraut, A. 1979 *Fictionnaire*, Paris, Seuil

Gertner, M.H. 1973 *The Morphology of the Modern French Verb*, The Hague, Mouton; discusses the form and meaning of derived verbs, in a generative framework.

Goosse, A. 1975 *La Néologie française aujourd'hui: observations et réflexions*, Paris, Conseil international de la langue française

Guilbert, L. 1975 *La Créativité lexicale*, Paris, Larousse; see Parts 2 and 3 for a comprehensive discussion of the derivational processes of French, including neo-classical composition.

Guiraud, P. 1962 *Les Locutions françaises*, Paris, PUF Que Sais-Je?

Hasselrot, B. 1972 *Etude sur la vitalité de la formation diminutive française au XXe siècle*, Uppsala, Sweden, Almquist och Wiksells

Marchand, H. 1951 *Esquisse d'une description des principales alternances dérivatives dans le français d'aujourd'hui*, Lund, Studia Linguistica vol. 5: 95–112; one of the first linguists to suggest a formal distinction between *savant* and *populaire* forms – with an intermediary category of *mi-savant*.

Mitterand, H. 1968 *Les Mots français*, Paris, PUF Que Sais-Je?; for a brief summary of the derivational processes of French.

Pichon, E. 1942 *Les principes de la suffixation en français*, Paris, D'Artrey

Retman, R. 1980 'Un inventaire des suffixes adjectivaux du français contemporain', *Le Français moderne* 48 (1): 6–14; list of adjectival suffixes in decreasing order of frequency, with comments on their functions and on current trends.

Rey, A. 1968 'Un champ préfixal: les mots en "anti-" ', *Cahiers de lexicologie* 12

Rey-Debove, J. (ed.) 1990 *Le Robert méthodique*, Paris, Robert; a dictionary classifying its entries broadly in terms of their constituent morphemes, rather than by word.

Schane, S.A. 1968 *French Phonology and Morphology*, Cambridge, Mass., MIT
    Press
——— 1973 'Sur le degré d'abstraction de la phonologie du français', *Langages* 32,
    December
Spence, N.C.W. 1976 *Le Français contemporain*, Munich, Wilhelm Fink Verlag
Spencer, A. 1991 *Morphological Theory: an Introduction to Word Structure in
    Generative Grammar*, Oxford, Blackwell; traces the development of the gen-
    erative approach to both inflectional and derivational morphology, from its
    beginnings in the 1960s to the present day.
Ullmann, S. 1952 *Précis de sémantique française*, Berne, Francke; stresses the
    opacity of the French lexis (pp. 125–131), contrasting the derivational processes
    of French with those of German and Italian.
Zwanenburg, W. 1983 'Productivité morphologique et emprunt', in *Studies in
    French and General Linguistics*, supplement to *Linguisticae Investigationes*
    10; looks at the theoretical implications of deriving 'learned' adjectival and
    nominal forms from verbal stems.

A number of journals have devoted issues to the kind of topic discussed in this
chapter, among them *Langages* 36, December 1974 and 1978, June 1985; *Langue
française* 2, May 1969 (*Le lexique*), 30, May 1976 (*Lexique et grammaire*), and 96,
December 1992 (*La productivité lexicale*); among the most relevant issues of
Cahiers de lexicologie are 45, 1982, 51, 1987, and 53, 1988.

Chapter 7

Cognitive processes and semantic change

THE BASIC ISSUES

Browse through a handful of entries in any substantial monolingual dictionary, and it will be obvious that the meaning of most lexical items has undergone considerable change; sometimes earlier meanings are lost, more often they are retained, with the result that polysemy is the norm rather than the exception.

Why is meaning so volatile? What causes semantic change? Is it quite random, or is there any discernible pattern to the way in which changes occur?

These questions raise further, fundamental questions about the relationship between language, thought and reality – questions which have been debated for centuries by philosophers and linguists. Those which are most relevant to an investigation of semantic change may be summed up as follows:

- Does a structured, physical reality exist objectively, independent of any conceptual or linguistic system associated with it? Or is reality structured only through human thought and language?
- Since languages are organised in different ways, does this imply different underlying conceptual systems?
- If the latter is indeed the case, is the way we think strictly determined by the language we happen to speak, or are our thought processes sufficiently flexible to enable us to grasp conceptual systems different from our own?
- Do the conceptual systems embodied in a given language combine to form some kind of coherent 'world view'?

A whole range of views is possible, depending on whether one answers 'Yes', 'No', or 'To some extent' to these different questions. The position taken here could be termed one of mild relativism.[1]

Some aspects of reality clearly lend themselves more readily to being conceptualised in certain ways rather than in others, but we cannot claim that one conceptual system is a more accurate representation of reality than any other.

The most fundamental parts of our whole conceptual system – such as the way we think of time, space, and motion – are largely determined by a combination of basic bodily experiences and innate cognitive processes. As these are largely, if not wholly, shared by all human beings, one would expect similarities in the structuring of basic concepts, in all languages. However, differences between languages clearly exist, even in the most fundamental conceptual fields, and these need to be accounted for.

The conceptualising processes that are part of our general cognitive development are so rich and flexible that we are able to categorise our experience in a wide variety of different ways; indeed, it is common to have alternative representations for the same notion, even within one language (see below for alternative conceptualisations of time in French).

We should not therefore be surprised if no truly coherent 'world view' can be inferred from the study of any given language – despite the still widely held belief that every language is imbued with a unique spirit: *le génie de la langue*.[2]

Moreover, many of our concepts are shaped by our social environment; the notions of politeness, greed, cleanliness, adulthood, leisure, hospitality, and so on, are part of the fabric of any society, though experience of other social systems is usually required for us to realise that they are highly variable concepts. We therefore expect, and find, a good deal of variation when we investigate the linguistic organisation of such areas of experience. The ways in which the French lexis reflects social attitudes, past and present, are examined in the next chapter.

This chapter will show how two basic conceptual processes predominate in both thought and language: metaphor and metonymy are at the root of how we think and how we verbalise our thoughts; they are also responsible for much semantic change.

METAPHOR

In the first verse of Verlaine's poem 'Chanson d'automne', we find an elaborate accumulation of metaphors:

Les sanglots longs
Des violons
De l'automne
Blessent mon cœur
D'une langueur
Monotone.

In the first three lines the sound of the autumn wind is likened to that of violins, which is in turn compared to a weeping human voice. It is clear from the next three lines that autumn, season of decay and prelude to winter, stands for the poet's own melancholy frame of mind.

Although it is as a literary device that we are most familiar with the term, metaphor plays a far greater role in human experience. When children are exploring their environment, in the early stages of language acquisition, we find that they over-extend the words in their personal lexicon. All metal implements may become 'scissors'; 'door' may refer also to gates, corks and box-lids; the moon, a grapefruit, a car headlight, may all share the same name.[3]

Later in life a child describes his first earache: 'Mummy, an elephant stamped on my ear.' Here, his (presumably indirectly acquired) knowledge of elephants – their weight and strength and tendency to blunder about not looking what they are stepping on – is used to convey an unpleasant bodily experience.

In all these cases, the child is drawing analogies between familiar objects or situations and new objects and experiences. Some shared feature or features, real or imagined, enable him to categorise the world around him, using the limited linguistic means at his disposal. Extension of this kind, based on perceived similarity, is also a form of metaphor.

The impulse which gave rise to the conscious and complex metaphors of the poet may be different from the connections made by the child, but the basic conceptual process is the same.

METONYMY

However, when a child uses 'hat' to refer not only to all kinds of headgear, but also to a hairbrush, she is making a quite different kind of connection. Hat and brush co-occur in the same environment; both come into contact with the child's head. This relationship is one of spatial contiguity, and extensions or substitutions made on the basis of this type of relationship are metonymic. A similar kind of over-extension takes place when a child uses the same word to refer both to her plastic duck and the bathwater it is floating in, or to her mug and the milk she habitually drinks out of it.

It is a short step from spatial to temporal metonymies. Having her bath one evening, a four-year-old complains 'Are you washing me blind?' – not an expression she has acquired direct from an adult, but one in which the processes of cause and effect are clearly verbalised. Lexical innovations connecting activity and goal, instrument and process, and changes of state can be seen in examples like 'Water the dirt off my stick'; 'On va poissonner [= aller à la pêche]'; 'Il m'a désendormi [= réveillé]'.

The range of such connections made by the child foreshadows the variety of metonymic relations we discover on analysing adult vocabulary.

A biologist observing the reproductive behaviour of sandworms notes that on certain nights he can observe them in shallow water without the help of a torch, since the moon is full. On just such nights their activity is at its peak. The biologist then pursues the line of thought that the phase of the moon and sexual activity of the worms are – unlikely as it may first seem – related. The connections being made are less obvious than in the child, but the process of linking contiguous phenomena in a given field of experience is essentially the same for the child and the scientist.

Metaphor, then, whether conceptual or linguistic, consists of linking two phenomena which have no apparent logical connection, drawn from realms of experience which are generally quite distinct, but in which a similarity of form, function or effect is perceived.

In metonymy, the two phenomena involved coexist within the *same* domain of experience, and may be linked by any of an immense range of spatial or temporal connections. A may be a part or a property of B, A may be used to produce or cause B, A may be the place where B occurs, and so on. On the basis of such connections, expression A may replace expression B, or vice versa.

Stereotypically, the scientist is thought to make use of metonymic reasoning, proceeding analytically by logical steps, from the phenomenon under study to others which impinge upon it; while the poet relies on intuitive, imaginative associations, bringing together elements which occur in quite different spheres. And yet some of the greatest scientific insights have depended on the association of two apparently quite unconnected notions. Newton under the apple tree, Archimedes in his bath, in a flash of inspiration, connected an everyday experience with a scientific problem with which they had been wrestling. Einstein associated mass and energy, two concepts which had hitherto been considered as belonging to separate branches of physics. Similarly, it took a sustained effort of the imagination to conceive of electricity, magnetism and gravity as being related forces. Such insights were not achieved by the controlled, meticulous observation of cause and effect which is often thought of as typical of a scientist's way of working.[4]

Conversely, the analysis of any literary text will show how writers make constant use of contiguous relationships, for example to condense the essence of character or a situation by focusing on a significant detail, as we shall see in the concluding section to this chapter.

Metaphor and metonymy are therefore fundamental to the way experience is conceptualised and conveyed to others. For the developing child, they are crucial to coping with the mass of sensory information with which he is bombarded daily. For the scientist and poet they may be more consciously manipulated, but they are just as vital to the exploration and verbalisation of everyday experience.

INNOVATION, CLICHÉ AND DEAD METAPHOR

From Aristotle's *Poetics* onwards, studies of metaphor have tended to focus on its use in literature, often as a superficial rhetorical embellishment of 'ordinary' or 'literal' language. And yet we can hardly open our mouths without using metaphorical expressions. *La tête d'une épingle, au pied de la falaise* or *le dos d'un livre* are no longer thought of as being figures of speech, bringing together animate and inanimate semantic fields. There is no other obvious way of referring to that particular part of a pin, cliff or book; they are simply the prime signifiers for these referents.

In such cases the metaphors are usually referred to as 'dead' or 'lexicalised'. One could argue that as long as the original meaning is still operative, the metaphor, although 'naturalised' in its new setting, is still recognisable on reflection as a metaphor, however hackneyed.

This is not true of expressions which, while metaphorical in origin, are now no longer used in their original sense. *Muscle*, for example, comes from *musculus* the diminutive of 'mouse', and the new sense had already become lexicalised in Latin. (*Moule* meaning 'mussel' is a parallel metaphorical development of the same etymon.)

Arriver and *aborder*, originally nautical metaphors, have retained a measure of transparency, since speakers can relate them synchronically to *bord* and *rive*; while *accoster*, from the same semantic field, is perhaps more tenuously connectable to *côte*. There are large numbers of words which used to refer to physical actions, but are now used exclusively for psychological states or intellectual or verbal activity, such as *divertir* (originally 'to turn aside'), *penser* (< 'to weigh'), *offenser* (< 'to hurt' – physically), *supposer* (< 'to place beneath') or *comprendre* (< 'to grasp'). (*Saisir*, on the other hand, can be used in both the abstract and the original, physical sense.) 'Fossilised' metaphors conjure up no images for French speakers unless, perhaps, they have a very good knowledge of Latin.

An original, 'live' metaphor, on the other hand, like a good joke, derives its effect from a combination of shock and recognition. As the poet Reverdy puts it: 'Plus les rapports des deux réalités rapprochées seront lointains et justes, plus l'image sera forte…'.

In his description of the island where Robinson Crusoe is shipwrecked Michel Tournier (1967) elaborates a sequence of metaphors which express the castaway's changing relationship with the island ('Speranza') and his spiritual and psychological development. At one point Crusoe crawls into a tiny cave in the heart of the central mountain, where he undergoes a profound transformation:

Speranza était un fruit mûrissant au soleil dont l'amande nue et blanche, recouverte par mille épaisseurs d'écorce, d'écale et de pelures s'appelait Robinson.

Closer to the fully lexicalised expression than to the original metaphor comes the cliché – the common currency of everday conversation and a boon to the hard-pressed journalist or hack novelist.

Elle a une voix d'or.
Un manteau de neige couvrait le paysage.
On n'a plus besoin du parapluie nucléaire de l'Otan.
Le bras de fer entre les deux présidents continue.

Some may find their way into dictionaries, others will fall out of favour, to be replaced by marginally fresher images.

None of these categories, except for metaphors of the fossilised type, can be clearly separated one from the other. The most well worn image is after all fresh and striking the first time we hear it.

Idioms, or lexicalised phrases, rather than individual lexical items, are often metaphors summing up common situations and attitudes of mind:

Il s'est brûlé les doigts dans cette affaire.
Pourquoi te mettre à plat ventre devant lui?
Il faut jouer cartes sur table.
Tu as vraiment mis les pieds dans le plat.
Je me trouve assis entre deux chaises.

Such expressions differ from image-based proverbs such as:

Chat échaudé craint l'eau froide.
Pierre qui roule n'amasse pas mousse.
Le vin est tiré, il faut le boire.

In these examples the function of the proverb is essentially didactic, and its form symmetrical and lapidary. As condensed, memorable images proverbs represent one form of transmission of the shared beliefs and values – and perhaps prejudices – of a community. Parables, fables, fairy tales and myths are all elaborated forms of metaphor, whether one interprets them as folk wisdom or as expressions of the collective unconscious.

METONYMY IN EVERYDAY LANGUAGE

Metonymic expressions, like metaphors, are assimilated into the general lexis to differing degrees. Few speakers would be aware that *bureau*, *viande* or *fiacre* are metonymic in origin, though one might guess at the origins of *secrétaire*, *compagnon* or *potage*. Although *argent* has been extended metonymically, to refer not just to the precious metal, but to the coins made out of it, and then, further still, to refer to currency in any form, including the intangible kind that can be stored and transferred electronically, the original meaning has been retained; we can therefore consider these to be cases of lexicalised but not yet fossilised metonymy.

Journalistic clichés of the metonymic type like

Cette année c'est un Belge qui endosse le maillot jaune

to designate the winner of the Tour de France, or

> Le drapeau palestinien va-t-il enfin flotter sur les territoires de la Cis-Jordanie?

to refer to the possibility of political autonomy for the Palestinians, may lack originality, but they have the advantage of providing a visual image which symbolises the event in question. When the French Prime Minister says he is reluctant to use 'la politique de la chaise vide' in negotiations with his European partners, he is both avoiding the harshness of the term *véto* and giving us a snapshot of the negotiating table where the future of Europe is being debated.

It is sometimes possible to place both a metaphorical and a metonymic interpretation on an expression. The lexicalised **bras d'un fauteuil** is both a limb-like extension and the place where the human arm actually rests; i.e. it can be seen as anthropomorphic and metaphoric, or spatially contiguous and metonymic. This is rather different from an expression in which metaphor and metonymy are involved in two consecutive stages of semantic change, as in 'Cela a été un vrai Trafalgar' – meaning an enterprise ending in catastrophe. The expression is metaphoric in comparing two disastrous events, but metonymic in that the name of a place has come to stand for what happened there.

METAPHOR, COMPARISON AND SIMILE

Comparisons and similes are figures of speech which are clearly closely related to metaphors, since some perceived similarity or analogy is involved in all three cases. If we refer to a person as (1) *Ce vieux renard*, or if we say (2) *Il est comme un renard*, or (3) *Il est rusé comme un renard*, in all three cases the subject is being compared to a fox, but in (2) and (3) the comparison is overt, and in (3) we are told in precisely what way he resembles a fox. Three elements are involved: the subject or 'tenor', i.e. that which is being described, the 'vehicle', or that which the tenor is being compared to, and the 'ground' or feature(s) shared by the tenor and vehicle.[5]

When the grounds for comparison are spelt out as in (3), the figure of speech is known as a simile. These are frequently quite conventional, and are given in any good dictionary: 'il est bête comme un âne... gras comme un pape... sobre comme un chameau... malin comme un singe', etc.

In a comparison, as in similar grammatical structures – *pareil à...*, *semblable à..., ressemble à...*, etc. – only the tenor and vehicle are given; the shared property has to be guessed at by the hearer.

In metaphors, the vehicle replaces the tenor and it is up to the hearer to realise that the sentence is not to be taken literally, and to imagine the shared features which gave rise to this transfer.

In most similes, the ground is a prototypical characteristic of the vehicle and they tend to recur in may different languages; in western European culture at least, donkeys are thought of as stupid if patient, pigs dirty and greedy, popes rich and well nourished, and so on. Others are more idiosyncratic. While in English one says 'as thin as a rake' or 'poor as a church mouse', in French one is *maigre comme un clou* or *pauvre comme Job*. Oysters are stereotypically uncommunicative in English, but plain stupid in French.

Some similes, especially in informal registers, deliberately flout the hearer's expectations by using grounds which are hardly defining characteristics of the vehicle in question.

If we say someone is *con comme un cornichon* or *bête comme un pied*, or that something is *simple comme bonjour*, it is the very quirky improbability of the juxtaposition, allied with a certain perverse logic, that appeals.

In certain structures, like 'Martineau, ce renard qui...', the tenor and vehicle are both given, but no overt comparison is made; these may be considered intermediate structures between comparison and full metaphor.[6] Similarly, in compounds like *un bateau-mouche, le roi soleil*, the two elements being compared are juxtaposed. Or they may be linked by the copula verb *être*:

> Un vieux qui meurt, c'est une bibliothèque qui brûle.
> (Ammadu Hampaté Bâ)

We should perhaps question the notion of a metaphor involving the replacement of one term by another, as being rather simplistic. Metaphors carry with them a whole range of associations on which we can draw, in order to interpret the apparently anomalous expression. The individual's interpretation will depend in part on the context in which the metaphor is used, in part on the complex pattern of beliefs and associations that he shares with other members of his speech community. If we speak of a surgeon being *un vrai boucher*, we are not simply stating that he is professionally incompetent. *Boucher* brings with it an array of assumptions, overtones and prejudices which it would be impossible to paraphrase succinctly – still less reduce to a single expression.

THE SOURCES OF METAPHOR

The body and personification

We have mentioned lexicalised metaphors like *le pied de la falaise* and *la tête d'une épingle*; but there is nothing strikingly similar between the base of a cliff and human feet, or a human head and the round end of a pin. The human body has been chosen as a vehicle because it is so central to our experience, not because parts of it happen to resemble many things in the world around us. The multiple dictionary entries for *tête*, *œil*, *main*, *pied*, *doigt*, *cou*, *dos* and words for many other external parts of the body demonstrate the importance of this conceptual field as a source of both metaphorical *and* metonymic extensions, as the following examples illustrate:

> Juste un doigt de whisky, s'il te plaît.
> Pour démarrer, appuyez sur le doigt de contact.
> Ses yeux tombèrent sur le tapis.
> La soupe était couverte d'yeux de graisse.
> Il a l'oreille du ministre.
> Tenez la marmite par les oreilles.

As with metaphor, metonymy relies on context to enable the reader/hearer to choose the most likely interpretation, presumably dismissing as improbable the ghoulish implications of the literal interpretation of some of the above.

Since we are primarily physical beings interacting constantly with our physical environment and experiencing the world through our bodies, it should not surprise us that the flow of metaphor is generally from the physical to the abstract. Rarely do we find transfers from abstract to physical – though poets may well exploit the shock value of such unusual images (see the concluding section of this chapter).

Not only body parts, but human and animate attributes of all kinds are projected onto the inanimate and the non-human. Animals and plants may be given names which are essentially humanising metaphors: *le saule pleureur*, *la mante religieuse*...; verbs which normally are limited to human subjects may follow inanimate or abstract nouns: *un ciel menaçant*, *la fortune lui a souri*....

Fields which remained for a long time relatively unelaborated, like taste and smell, but in which a rich technical and aesthetic terminology has developed, for example to describe all the subtle attributes of wine and perfume, draw heavily on personification:

> Constitué sans défaut, ce vin est discret mais élégant... Un vin généreux... aimable... tendre et expressif... fessu et bien habillé... aucune agressivité... il a du caractère...

The device can of course be carried to extremes of preciosity:

> Ces vins ont traversé le temps avec une belle santé. Les rides ont embelli les visages, et les cheveux blancs les ont singulièrement anoblis...

Personification is a favourite trick of the copywriter; a product can be endowed with endearing or enviable human qualities, and a relationship contrived between product and potential consumer:

Nouvelle Kadett – conçue pour vous séduire...
Velouté, tu me mets la pulpe à la bouche...
Carte Bleue Visa – elle parle toutes les langues...

This kind of device is explored more fully in Chapter Nine.

Explaining the emotions

Just as we use our bodies and human characteristics of all kinds to conceptualise the world around us, we also use metaphors from the external world to articulate bodily and emotional sensations.

Let us take one example – viewing the body as a container. In a sense, this is already a literal truth, in that substances are taken into the body, and other substances expelled from it. Our skin envelops a complex mass of tissue, muscles, bones and internal organs to which orifices give limited access, and which, in cases of illness or violent trauma, may be exposed.

But the body may also be seen as a container of the emotions.Take the following – fully lexicalised – expressions:

Il était plein/rempli de joie.
Il n'a pas pu contenir son émotion.
Il se sentait complètement vide.
Après la mort de son enfant, elle s'est renfermée en elle-même.
Sa colère ne s'extériorise pas.
Sa passion, trop longtemps contenue, a explosé.
La joie éclatait sur son visage.
La tendresse m'a inondé le cœur.
J'ai le cœur qui déborde.

Emotion here is seen as varying in physical pressure, and/or as being a fluid substance. Indeed, the basic verbs associated with emotion, *exprimer* and *réprimer*, come from the Latin verbs meaning to push out and to push back.

Other 'liquid' metaphors would be:

Ils essayaient d'endiguer leur chagrin.
Il faut canaliser tes forces.
Il m'a fait bouillir d'impatience.
Dans mes lettres je déversais tout mon enthousiasme.

One can see why these fields, of containment, heat, pressure, liquid have proved such fruitful sources of images, at once expressing and in a sense explaining the sensations associated with anger, fear, joy, etc.[7] On the one hand, real physiological effects correlate with emotions. The bodily posture of someone who is depressed is bowed, with limbs drawn in towards the body, eyes downcast or closed; the cheerful individual literally reaches outwards to others and the world in general. Fear, shock, embarrassment, rage, cause one to turn pale, or red, to sweat, to shake. One's temperature and blood pressure may rise from extreme emotion; tears, vomiting, even haemorrhages may result.

The behaviour of liquids mirrors some of these effects. They are more volatile than solid substances, they can be compressed, they expand when subjected to heat; if the container is inadequate they may then become dangerous, like emotions which are out of control.

A closer examination of the field would show that anger and lust are associated with heat, with or without a liquid element, whereas more positive emotions are associated with cool liquids in a state of motion.

Many other metaphors are available for the expression and exploration of emotions. An analysis of spatial images of the vertical and horizontal axes would show a very widespread analogy of up = good; down = bad: *être porté aux nues*; *avoir le moral très bas*; *tomber dans une dépression*; *toucher le fond de l'abîme*; *être au septième ciel*. *Déprimé* is yet another fossilised spatial metaphor from Latin.

The analogy stems partly from bodily experiences, and partly no doubt from practices and beliefs concerning death and the afterlife, such as the association of the earth with burial, the sky with heaven, hell with an underworld, and so on. Of course it is also very likely that beliefs about the afterlife are themselves rooted in bodily experience.

Conceptualising time

In French, as in many languages, prepositions do double duty in expressing relationships of time and space: *dans l'avenir, dans le jardin; en Bretagne, en été; être à Paris, arriver à temps...* – the examples are legion.

Time may be spatialised in linear fashion, for example with verbs of movement like *suivre, précéder* or *s'étendre* being used in temporal expressions. But if we say: 'Pour moi, jeudi est un jour creux', or 'Il ne sait pas comment remplir ses jours, après la mort de sa femme', a more specific form of spatialisation has occurred; time is being viewed as an empty container waiting to be filled by events and activities.

Alternatively, time is seen as a valuable commodity. Verbs like *gaspiller, gagner, perdre, économiser, épargner, dépenser* can all be used in relation to time. This chimes with the usual practice of paying people according to the amount of time they put in, rather than on the quality or quantity of the end product.

Fundamental notions such as time, which are not apprehended primarily through vision, are frequently given alternative conceptualisations in this way. Like the blind men describing the elephant, we attempt through a series of incomplete analogies to build up a complete picture of a complex phenomenon.

Making sense of the senses

The way in which the five senses are interrelated is a subject of fascination and controversy for linguists, poets and neuro-physiologists. **Synaesthesia** was the term used, initially, to describe the transfer of perceived sensation, from one sensory mode to another. (There are people, for example, who strongly associate specific words with specific colours.) The term has been extended to cover the metaphorical description of one sense in terms of another.

In some cases this might be expected; there are obvious physiological connections between smell and taste, and tactile sensations in the mouth are an important part of the enjoyment of eating and drinking. *Rêche* has come to mean not only rough to the touch but harsh on the palate; in medieval French the verb *tâter* was used for a time to mean 'taste' – surviving only in *taste-vin* 'tasting cup'.

Links between taste, touch and smell and the functions of seeing and hearing are much more remote. And yet metaphorical extensions from, say, touch to sound, or between sight and sound, are common. A colour can be *criard*, a sound can be *sombre*; *aigu* started as a touch adjective, but can also be used of sound; *âpre* has been extended even further, from touch to taste, smell and sound.

Is there simply a random exchange of terms among the senses, with rather more among those that are physiologically related? Or is there some clear pattern in the way such extensions take place?

J.M. Williams (1976) suggested, on the basis of a detailed study of the history of sense words in English, and a more superficial investigation of Japanese, and of a number of Indo-European roots, that in all languages transfers can take place only in certain directions, between certain senses.[8]

For example, terms for touch can be transferred to any of the senses (*un accent **pointu**, un goût **râpeux**, une voix **dure/perçante**, une lumière **douce***). Words for sound on the other hand can only be shifted to colour: *une **gamme** de couleurs, du gris avec des **notes** rouges*; and colour words to sound: *un timbre **clair*** or *une voix **incolore***.

To the five senses Williams adds the notion of dimension, which may be perceived through sight or touch, and subsequently transferred to other senses (*à voix **basse**, un vin **plat**, un visage **haut** en couleur*).

The constraints on the types of transfer which can be made, according to Williams, are set out in Figure 12. Touch is shown to be the starting point, so to speak, for many sense terms, while taste is a sensory dead end.

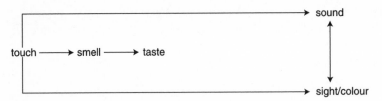

Figure 12 Synaesthetic transfer

Williams' thesis is convincingly argued for English, but no similar study has been carried out for French. At this point we can only say that, at first glance, similar constraints appear to hold. It may be that the thesis is valid universally for synaesthetic extensions which have been lexicalised. Creative writers, however, are certainly not constrained by such rules.

The comparisons used by Baudelaire in his 'Correspondances' do bring together touch and smell, but also describe scent in terms of sound and colour:

Il est des parfums frais comme des chairs d'enfants,
Doux comme les hautbois, verts comme les prairies...

It is perhaps natural that poets should draw on other senses to describe taste and smell especially, since these are fields which are relatively poorly provided with terminology, compared with those of sight and sound.

We have already noted the wine-writer's predilection for personification. Sensory metaphors, too, abound – again often breaking Williams' 'laws' of synaesthetic transfer:

Le nez et la bouche sont typiquement 'jaunes', avec des arômes de morilles et de noix...
En bouche il y a du relief et du volume, mais il souffre d'une certaine dureté...
Bouche souple mais bien construite...
Bouche ronde et ample, sans aucune lourdeur...
La bouche commence sèche et vive, puis se développe en puissance sans perdre son équilibre...

It will be seen that kinaesthetic images, drawing on bodily perceptions of weight and balance, help the writer to express the finest nuances of taste and smell. These two most important senses for the connoisseur are referred to metonymically as *la bouche* and *le nez*, whereas the relatively superficial role played by one's visual impression is expressed through metaphor as *la robe*.

METAPHOR AS CONCEPTUAL TOOL

It should be clear by now that metaphor is far from being a literary embellishment, or an alternative, if more vivid, way of naming a referent. A metaphor entails the fusion of two areas of experience, and once the vehicle field has been 'activated' terms from this field may be exploited to throw further light on the field to which the tenor belongs.

This is particularly true if the vehicle field is richly structured. Take for example the field of motion, in relation to human beings. We set off from fixed points, with goals in view, which we reach, or fail to reach, possibly changing direction, or turning back en route. These are primary concepts which a child learns to use at an early stage, and for which every language has an abundance of terminology.

But the semantic field to which, say, *idée* belongs is not so well endowed, at least with terms that can be taken in a primary, literal sense. To elaborate this lexical field, many languages, including French and English, have recourse to metaphors of motion: 'Je suis arrivé à cette conclusion...'; 'Je pars du principe que...'; 'Je n'ai pas très bien suivi son argument'; 'Il m'est venu à l'esprit que...'; 'Son nom m'est complètement sorti de la tête'...

Without such metaphors, it is difficult to see how abstract concepts of this kind could be manipulated at all; as Kittay (1987) puts it, metaphor 'provides epistemic access to the referent not otherwise available'.[9] It may even make possible the elaboration and articulation of quite new concepts, becoming a 'generator of hypotheses'.

Alternative metaphors may be needed to conceptualise different aspects of the same phenomenon, so that electricity, for example, may be viewed simultaneously as a fluid and as a mass of particles. The extended metaphor of body as machine led to impressive advances in medicine, but has resulted in neglect of a more holistic approach to health.

Metaphors are invaluable tools but can impose dangerous limitations, if taken literally.

METONYMIC CONNECTIONS

Metonymic shifts have been likened to the effect of a searchlight picking out different objects in a scene; a more appropriate analogy might be that of a camera focusing on different aspects of a scene. From a general view of a room or landscape it may move in on a seated figure or a rumpled bed, or show in close-up some small detail: hands, eyes, a bunch of keys, an empty glass.

Conventionalised metonymies – linguistic or visual – often involve the salient characteristic of an object or person standing for the whole. Dress, of which uniforms are a central example, plays a highly symbolic role in most cultures. Some have become verbal metonymies: *les casques bleus*, *les sans-culottes*, *les bérets rouges*, *les bas bleus*, *les blousons noirs...* Such cases, where a part stands for the whole, are possibly the commonest form of metonymy, and as such have been given the separate label of **synecdoche**.

Not surprisingly, parts of the body (usually the part relevant to the function under focus) are used in this way, to stand for the whole person:

Il a dix bouches à nourrir.
La construction a manqué de bras.
On a partagé le butin par tête.

The notion of synecdoche is usually broadened from the relationship 'part–whole' to include that of 'specific–generic'; in other words, a hyponym may replace a superordinate term (see Chapter One, p. 8). Thus *panier*, originally 'bread-basket', now means a container of variable size and function. On a more global scale, *l'Homme* may be used generically to refer to all human beings, of both sexes, while *la Femme* refers only to all women.

A particular brand name may come to stand generically for all products of that type: *Thermos* and *scotch* 'sellotape' are well-established examples, while *kleenex*, *bic* 'biro' and *boules quiès* 'ear plugs' are relative newcomers.

The converse process is to substitute superordinate for hyponym, that is a generic for a specific term. Fossilised examples of this type would be *chantre* (< Latin *cantor*, meaning 'singer', now 'cantor' in a church or synagogue), *traire* (< *trahere* 'to pull', now meaning 'to milk') or *Bible*, deriving ultimately from the Greek word for book. Here, the referential value of the term is reduced.

This is often used as a stylistic device to avoid repetition, or focus on a particular attribute or function of the referent. When writing about Cézanne, for example, one could use a superordinate term – *le peintre, ce génie* – instead of repeating his name. Such cases involve not a close-up but a long shot, so to speak, of the referent, placing it in a wider context. The result is hardly felt to be a figure of speech, as it entails no departure from the literal truth.

No doubt because of its 'distancing' effect, the use of a superordinate is favoured in euphemism, as in *la mécanique* for the guillotine. Similarly, *garce* (originally simply the feminine equivalent of *garçon*) came to mean a particular kind of girl; *fille* has followed much the same route. Extreme cases are the use of *chose* or simply *ça* to refer to anything unmentionable – usually sex (see next chapter).

Many other metonymic relations besides that of inclusion are possible. *Verre* and *argent* can refer both to the substance itself and to something made from it. **Material for artefact** metonymies can also be seen in *des marbres* for marble statues, or *des cuivres* meaning brass instruments, or copper cooking utensils.

A further extension of *verre* is **container for contained** as in 'Il a bu trois verres'. Similarly, if we are told 'Il possède une cave magnifique' or 'Il aime la bouteille' the more likely interpretation is the metonymic one.

Place for activity that takes place there, or the people who work there, is often used in relation to institutions or seats of power: 'L'Elysée/ la Maison Blanche/ le Kremlin a annoncé que...'.

When a chain of events is involved, one may stand for another; typically some **preliminary action** may substitute for a final result or goal. For instance, in slightly formal style, one might say 'Mon mari m'a offert un pull pour mon anniversaire', rather than 'Il m'a donné un pull...'. *Offrir* is literally a preliminary to the act of giving, but the sentence in no way implies the gift might have been rejected. *Baiser* is an interesting example of this type. The sixteenth-century poet Lemaire de Belges listed the five *poincts en amour*, with the kiss being the penultimate stage of the process: 'regard, parler, attouchement, baiser et don de mercy'. Already at that period a polite euphemism, it has become the everyday, albeit vulgar, term for love-making, and further polite substitutes have had to be found. Metonymic shifts of this kind, literally stopping short of the taboo referent, lend themselves especially well to the expression of euphemism.

Similar side-stepping takes place when politicians in power talk of *demandeurs d'emploi* or *chercheurs d'emploi* rather than *chômeurs* – another euphemistic shift, but this time substituting **effect for cause.**

Metonymy is sometimes seen as 'abstract', and lacking in visual impact, when compared with metaphor. This is true for some types of metonymy, such as that which substitutes **quality for possessor** of that quality, as when one refers to a person as *un génie, une beauté*, or in talking about *la jeunesse d'aujourd'hui*. But **instrumental metonymies** in particular are often more concrete and vivid than their literal alternatives; for example, 'Sa bouche l'a trahi', rather than 'Ses paroles...'. Instrumental metonymies which have now become fully lexicalised include *la langue* meaning language and *le style* (< Latin *stilus*, 'pen'). Verb-noun compounds such as *tord-pif* 'handkerchief', *écrase-merde* 'beetle-crushers', or *tire-gosses* 'mid-wife' lend themselves particularly well to slang metonymies of this kind.

The shift from action or **process** to the physical **result** or **means** of that process are very common in French; *bâtiment, voiture, élite, nourriture, confiture* were all originally de-verbal nouns signifying the process of building, transporting, choosing, and so on.

Plants and animals are often named according to their **habitual behaviour**, or **habitat**, or **food**: *le tournesol* 'sunflower'; *une (tortue) bourbeuse* 'mud turtle'; *un pique-bœufs* 'ox-pecker'. Fully lexicalised but more or less transparent animal names of this kind are *huîtrier* 'oystercatcher', *fourmilier* 'anteater', *sangsue* 'leech', *sauterelle* 'grasshopper', whereas the origins of *orfraie* 'sea eagle' (< Latin *ossifraga*, literally 'bone-breaker') or *furet* 'ferret' (< *furittus*, 'little thief') are much more opaque.

Categorising humans in this way is common in slang and informal registers generally. Foreigners are jokily identified with their national dish – *des couscous, des rosbifs, des macaronis...*; the terms *bavard* and *pique-argent* tell us something of the popular mistrust of lawyers; while fear of the needle has perhaps inspired *pique-fesses* for 'nurse'. When someone is characterised as *très 'm'as-tu vu'* we know what irritating attention-seeking behaviour to expect. But in expressions like *lèche-bottes* 'boot-licker' or *bouche-trou* 'stopgap', the behaviour or function involved is to be interpreted metaphorically.

Both popular and technical names for plants draw on metaphor as well as metonymy. The family of *ombellifères* have their flowers arranged like umbrellas, while *dent-de-lion* recalls the serrated shape of the leaf. The more widespread name for the latter is *pissenlit*, a metonymy indicating the plant's diuretic properties. (According to the medieval 'doctrine of signs' the form of plants often contained divine clues as to their potential uses; for example, the branching roots of the *pulmonaire* resemble the lungs and were therefore considered efficacious in treating them.)

This brief survey has simply focused on the commonest types of metonymy. It is clear that, just as metaphor may link almost any pair of semantic fields, metonymic connections are as varied as the spatial and temporal relations which can hold between any two objects or events.

METONYMY AND ELLIPSIS

In discussing the twentieth-century trend towards brevity in matters of word formation (Chapter Six) we saw how abbreviation can operate above the level of the individual word, reducing whole phrases to a single lexical item. Hence *une horloge à pendule*, becomes *une pendule*, *du vin de Champagne*, *du champagne*.

The semantic effect of ellipsis is usually a metonymic shift – in the latter examples the part stands for the whole, and place of origin for the product. In these two cases, as in *une (automobile) Renault*, *un (café) crème*, the gender of the noun provides a clue that ellipsis has taken place. In addition, changes in word class, usually from adjective to noun, may similarly point to elliptical origins: *des (boucles) anglaises*, *des (huîtres) portugaises*.

Some nouns traceable to this kind of ellipsis have lost all adjectival function, like *route* (< *(via) rupta*, literally 'broken road'), whereas *meubles* (< *(biens) meubles* 'movable goods') survives as an adjective only in legal terminology.

However, without the formal clues of gender and word class one cannot demonstrate conclusively that a short form has actually been derived from a longer expression. How would one set about proving that *un génie* is derived from *un homme de génie*, or even that *les jeunes* comes from *les jeunes gens*? It is difficult to believe that in 'Maastricht risque de provoquer la chute du gouvernement', *Maastricht* is literally a shortened version of a longer phrase like 'Le débat suscité par l'accord de Maastricht'.

We have simply to recognise that metonymy involves conceptual as well as linguistic short cuts. The compression and economy characteristic of much metonymy lies in this mental leapfrogging of redundant information, which can be supplied by the listener or reader from the context.

LITERARY IMAGERY

For Jakobson and Halle (1956), metaphor and metonymy are central to every symbolic form of human expression, from dreams to the visual arts to language in all its manifestations. But they see them less as processes which are complementary and intertwined, rather as disjunctive forces – 'metaphoric and metonymic poles' – separately characteristic of specific linguistic disorders, or literary styles or genres. For them, metaphor is the natural vehicle for poetry, metonymy for prose. At the same time, they claim that metonymy is the hallmark of the realist school, while metaphor is characteristic of romanticism and symbolism, which preceded and followed it.

Certainly, a writer like Zola is master of the salient detail which provides a precise, vivid sketch of a scene:

> Un murmure courut la poissonnerie, toutes les têtes, sur le trottoir, se rapprochèrent, causant vivement.
>
> (*Le Ventre de Paris*)

In Flaubert on the other hand synecdoche often serves a rather different purpose, pinpointing a detail which symbolises some aspect of a character's personality. The first thing that Charles notices about Emma Bovary is her hand:

> . . . pas belle, point assez pâle, peut-être, et un peu sèche aux phalanges, elle était trop longue aussi et sans molles inflexions de lignes sur les contours.

We know that we are not to expect a conventional romantic heroine.

Again, it is Léon's hands which Emma notices when she walks alone with him for the first time:

> Elle remarqua ses ongles, qui étaient plus longs qu'on ne les portait à Yonville. C'était une des grandes occupations du clerc que de les entretenir; et il gardait, à cet usage, un canif tout particulier dans son écritoire.

The detail sums up the combination of shallow sophistication and vanity which will contribute to Emma's downfall.

Metonymic connections are sometimes widely spaced, and may only be identifiable as symbolic threads when the whole narrative has run its course. In *L'Assommoir*, for example, metals of various kinds recur, usually with metonymic values; *le zinc* is the working material used by the central character, Coupeau, who is a *zingueur* or roofer; but it is also the bar of the café which represents the snare of alcoholism that he fears, but to which he, like his father, eventually succumbs.

As Jakobson and Halle noted, symbolist poetry is rich in 'figures of similarity'. Some of Baudelaire's comparisons shock the reader by reversing the usual direction of transfer, drawing the vehicle from an abstract field, to describe something physical:

> La lune, froide et claire comme un doute...

Or, describing the very physical effects of death:

> Et le ver rongera ta peau comme un remords
> (Remords posthume)

We have already seen how the directional 'law' of synaesthetic transfer is no barrier to the poet, in Baudelaire's 'Correspondances', where

> Les parfums, les couleurs et les sons se répondent...

But such images are not the monopoly of symbolist poets. Zola celebrates the smell of cheeses in Les Halles, in a joyous accumulation of musical images:

Le parmesan jetait par moments un filet mince de flûte champêtre, tandis que les brie y mettaient des douceurs fades de tambourins humides... Cette symphonie se tint un moment sur une note aiguë du géromé anisé, prolongée en point d'orgue.

(Le Ventre de Paris)

The metaphor is resumed and developed in fugue-like fashion two pages later.

Possibly the commonest type of metaphor in poetry or prose, as in the general lexis, involves rendering the inanimate animate or human. This is exploited to the full in Zola's *La Bête Humaine*, as when Jacques' beloved engine, the *Lison*, is derailed:

La Lison, renversée sur les reins, le ventre ouvert, perdait sa vapeur par les robinets arrachés, les tuyaux crevés, en des souffles qui grondaient, pareils à des râles furieux de géante...

Towards the end of the novel, when Flore is advancing along the railway track to her death, a sequence of parallel images of increasing intensity describes the light and noise of the oncoming train. At first, she is aware only of 'une petite étoile scintillante et unique au fond d'un ciel d'encre'. Then

l'effroyable grondement approchait, ébranlant la terre d'un souffle de tempête, tandis que l'étoile était devenue un œil énorme, toujours grandissant, jaillissant comme de l'orbite des ténèbres... L'œil se changeait en un brasier, en une gueule de four vomissant l'incendie, le souffle du monstre arrivait, humide et chaud déjà, dans ce roulement de tonnerre, de plus en plus assourdissant.

Proust's images, on the other hand, rely less on dramatic sensory impact than on subtle psychological connections, which are frequently metonymic in nature. Genette (1972: 41–63) points out how the vehicle of the metaphor or comparison is often contiguous, in time or space, with that which is being described. In

La mer déjà froide et bleue comme le poisson appelé mulet

the form of the figure of speech is clearly a comparison, but the relationship between tenor (*la mer*) and vehicle (*le poisson*) is essentially synecdochic.

Similarly, in Saint-Pol-Roux's description of Penelope's unwelcome suitors:

Dans leur haleine d'ail coassent des grenouilles
(Le Palais d'Ithaque)

we have on the surface a (synaesthetic) metaphor, relating smell and sound; but at the same time *grenouilles* provides the vehicle for a further image,

referring to the owners of the *haleine d'ail* – hence taking the reader back
to the original tenor. Literary imagery, then, can be not only 'lointain et
juste' but densely packed and finely structured, interweaving metaphor and
metonymy.

A subtle form of metonymy, particularly favoured by poets, has been
given the separate label of *hypallage*. In transferring an adjective from
some contiguous element – which may or may not be named – the writer
achieves great economy of expression. In

> Je suis d'un pas rêveur le sentier solitaire
> (Lamartine)

the adjectives *rêveur* and *solitaire* in fact refer to the poet.

Similar transference occurs when Baudelaire describes the street scene at
the beginning of 'La Belle Inconnue':

> La rue assourdissante autour de moi hurlait...

To use *hurler* and *assourdissante* here may look at first sight like a form of
personification; but there is metonymic displacement, in that it is the
people and traffic thronging the street rather than the street itself that are
creating the hubbub. In a less poetic context, the expression *un malade
imaginaire* involves just the same elliptical semantic shift.

The great classical dramatists of the seventeenth century are renowned for
their restraint in the use of metaphor. The images that are used tend to be
conventional rather than innovative: love as illness, or as fire, are commonplace:

> Plus j'apprends son mérite, et plus mon feu s'augmente...
> (*Le Cid*)

> Un même coup a mis ma gloire en sûreté,
> Mon âme au désespoir, ma flamme en liberté.
> (Ibid.)

When an image is elaborated, the effect is expository and cerebral rather
than visceral:

> Ah! qu'avec peu d'effet on entend la raison,
> Quand le cœur est atteint d'un si charmant poison!
> Et lorsque le malade aime sa maladie,
> Qu'il a peine à souffrir que l'on y rémédie!
> (Ibid.)

Corneille and Racine draw much more on metonymy, again of a conventional kind. *Couronne* and *sceptre* stand for earthly power, *le Ciel* for
divine authority. Synecdoche here involves not a striking visual detail but
substitution, for example of *tête*, to refer to the whole person:

C'est générosité quand pour venger un père
Notre devoir attaque une tête si chère.

(Ibid.)

Similarly *bras* or *main* are recurring metonymies used when the role of the
character is essentially instrumental or agentive:

Que peut-on m'ordonner que mon bras n'accomplisse?

(Ibid.)

Et demande pour grâce à ce généreux prince
Qu'il daigne voir la main qui sauve la province.

(Ibid.)

Emotions are described metonymically in terms of their physical effects:

Que la loi du combat étouffe vos soupirs...

(Ibid.)

Similarly, *rougir, pleurer, trembler* are used, again conventionally, for the
emotions of which these actions are the physical expression.

Some metonymies tend towards abstract grandeur. In *Le Cid* the king
declaims

Ce que n'a pu jamais Aragon ni Grenade
Ni tous vos ennemis, ni tous mes envieux...

Here, the ruler is identified with the place where he exercises authority. Or
a quality may be used to stand for a person possessing that quality:

... Qui
Laisse le crime en paix, et poursuit l'innocence...

A generic term may replace the specific hyponym, with an accompanying
explanatory circumlocution appropriate to the context. The sun, for example, is

L'astre dont la présence écarte la nuit sombre.

These are all what we might term amplifying metonymies, where an
expression is replaced by one loftier and broader in scope.

In the hands of lesser writers there is a danger of such oblique figures of
speech becoming pretentious. When Molière wishes to parody the excesses
of the *précieuses*, he uses elaborate and pointless metonymies. Chairs are
'les commodités de la conversation,' and a mirror, 'le conseiller des
grâces'. These are both metonymies of function, but of a very marginal
and abstract kind. Irritation arises from the effort one must put into decoding them, for very little reward. In other words, the effect is the
opposite of the graphic precision of successful metonymy.

One approach to the study of figurative language in literature is to investigate the 'dominant images' in a writer's work, sometimes interpreting these as subliminal expressions of childhood experiences or other deep-seated preoccupations, often buried in the subconscious. Examples are the recurring insect images in Sartre, and images of the sea in Alain-Fournier (see Ullmann 1977).

Such accumulations of metaphor are by no means confined to the literary sphere; the way in which clusters of lexicalised metaphors reveal more generalised social and psychological preoccupations is one of the themes explored in the next chapter.

NOTES

1　Benjamin Lee Whorf and his teacher and mentor, Sapir, brought these questions to the fore earlier this century, subscribing to the view that:

> the 'real world' is to a large extent unconsciously built upon the language habits of the group. We see and hear and otherwise experience largely as we do because the language habits of our community predispose certain choices of interpretation...
>
> (Whorf 1956)

Whorf supported this hypothesis with data from Hopi, a language of Central America, whose structures he claimed were radically different from those of European languages. For him, it followed that Hopi ways of thinking were very different from those of Europeans.

Black (1969) showed how it is possible to put a wide range of interpretations on the 'Sapir–Whorf hypothesis', depending on how a number of key terms are defined. He warns of the circularity inherent in claiming that linguistic structures actually determine behaviour, if the only behavioural evidence we have for this comes from these same linguistic structures. Lucy (1992) reviews the lines of research that have since been pursued, in the investigation of the relationship between language and thought.

2　This is probably a translation of the German *Sprachgeist*. The belief that a nation's language and culture are a manifestation of the shared moral, aesthetic and intellectual values of that nation was very popular from the late eighteenth to the mid-nineteenth century, emerging from the romantic movement, with its emphasis on the indigenous ethnic roots of European cultures.

Despite the absence of any hard evidence, the theory remains remarkably tenacious; originally a reaction against the classical, universalist tradition, its attraction today may be partly explained as nostalgia for the cultural diversity of the past, in the face of increasing cultural conformity. The role it has played in the French normative tradition is examined briefly in the final chapter.

3　Clarke (1993) describes studies of the child's acquisition of lexis in a variety of languages. Studies of acquisition in French children are discussed in Aimard (1974 and 1975).

4　Numerous illustrations from art and science can be found in Arthur Koestler's *Act of Creation*, in which he explores the sources of human creativity. He shows how two major processes are involved: what he calls 'bisocation', in which 'independent, autonomous matrices are brought together in the creative act', and 'association', 'which operates among members of a single pre-existing matrix'.

These correspond closely to the notions of metaphoric and metonymic conceptualisation.

5 These ideas are elaborated in I.A. Richards' *Philosophy of Rhetoric* (1936), a seminal work which establishes the centrality of metaphor as the 'omnipresent principle' at the heart of language.

6 The multiplicity of structures employed to make such connections, and the stylistic effects involved, are investigated in depth by Christine Brooke-Rose (1970).

7 Lakoff's *Women, Fire and Dangerous Things* (1987) is a study of the mind through an analysis of the ways in which we categorise objects, events, sensations and ideas. He suggests that categories do not exist in an objective, disembodied way, but arise from creative conceptual processes, in which the body and sensory perceptions play a central role.

Some of the ideas in this book were adumbrated in Lakoff and Johnson (1980); here they show how metaphors are so closely woven into thought and language that we are scarcely aware of them; but analysis reveals how our concepts are structured and in part determined by such apparently 'dead' figures of speech.

8 Williams proposes a biological explanation for his theory, in terms of the historical evolution of the senses, from touch, found in the simplest organisms, to sight and hearing in the more advanced. This sequence parallels the maturation process of the newborn child, with sight and hearing being the last sensory areas to mature fully.

9 Kittay views metaphor in the context of a philosophical framework which stresses the context-dependent nature of language; more specifically, she argues that metaphor involves bringing together two semantic fields, so that the structured relations within one field radically affect those of the other.

PROJECTS

1 Find a dozen metaphorical idioms involving body parts, such as *se mordre les doigts*, *toucher du doigt*, and suggest non-metaphorical alternatives. Can they usually be translated by similar metaphors in English?

2 Taking any short text – a poem, an article, an extract from a novel – identify all cases of metaphor and metonymy, and suggest whether these figures of speech are clichés, or live, lexicalised or fossilised metaphors or metonymies.

3 Compare a short English text full of live metaphor with one or more professionally translated versions in French. Comment on the problems of translating figurative language and the efficacy of the solutions proposed by the translator(s) of the text.

4 Taking a range of lexicalised metaphors referring to states of mind (e.g. *vacillant*, *accablé*, *posé*) suggest whether any broader underlying metaphors are detectable.

5 Examine the conceptual field of either physical combat or eating and drinking, and see how many metaphorical expressions you can find utilising such terms. On the basis of these findings, what conclusions can one draw about the phenomena that are typically considered as, on the one hand, enemies or quarry, and on the other, as consumable?

FURTHER READING

Aimard, P. 1974 *L'Enfant et son langage*, Villeurbanne, Editions Samép
—— 1975 *Les Jeux de mots des enfants*, Villeurbanne, Editions Samép
Black, M. 1969 'Some troubles with Whorfianism', in *Language and Philosophy: A Symposium*, ed. S. Hook, New York, New York University Press
Brooke-Rose, C. 1970 *A Grammar of Metaphor*, London, Martin Secker and Warburg
Clarke, E. 1993 *The Acquisition of the Lexicon*, Cambridge, Cambridge University Press
Genette, G. 1972 *Figures III*, Paris, Seuil
Henry, A. 1971 *Métonymie et métaphore*, Paris, Klincksieck; reviews previous approaches to the study of figurative language in literature and provides a detailed analysis of figures of speech in works of a range of French authors.
Kittay, E.F. 1987 *Metaphor: Its Cognitive Force and Linguistic Structure*, Oxford, Clarendon Press
Jakobson, R. and Halle, M. 1956 *Fundamentals of Language*, The Hague, Mouton
Lakoff, G. 1987 *Women, Fire and Dangerous Things*, Chigaco, University of Chicago Press
Lakoff, G. and Johnson, M. 1980 *Metaphors We Live By*, Chicago, University of Chicago Press
Lucy, J.A. 1992 *Language Diversity and Thought*, Cambridge, Cambridge University Press
Richards, I.A. 1936 *The Philosophy of Rhetoric*, Oxford, Oxford University Press
Tournier, M. 1967 *Vendredi, ou les limbes du Pacifique*, Paris, Gallimard
Ullmann, S. 1977 *The Image in the Modern French Novel*, Cambridge, Greenwood Press
Whorf, B.L. 1956 *Language, Thought and Reality*, Cambridge, Mass., MIT Press
Williams, J.M. 1976 'Synaesthetic adjectives: a possible law of semantic change', *Language* 52 (2)

Chapter 8

Lexis in society

In Brunot's famous phrase, 'les mots sont les témoins de l'histoire'; the sources upon which a language draws, indigenous or external, the semantic fields which are subject to expansion or contraction, the twists and turns of an individual word's semantic history, can all be given a socio-historical explanation. They reflect changes in the broad social structure of the nation, its changing relations with other countries and the cultural and economic preoccupations of its speakers.

We have already seen, in Chapters Two to Five, why certain external sources of the lexis became important at different periods; a more internal, structuralist-inspired approach to the study of lexical change consists in investigating the development of specific semantic fields. Some fields may change rather gradually, while others can be dramatically restructured, with lexical material mushrooming or dwindling, as society itself undergoes radical change.

The lexis of medieval French, for example, was perfectly adapted to its institutions, its cosmological and theological systems, the idealised and actual forms of chivalry, and the intricacies of medieval warfare. The profusion of specific verbs in Old French for stabbing, slashing and hacking with a variety of weapons (see Matoré 1985: 100, 163) gives us some idea of the violence of the times, and the importance of the prowess of the individual in face-to-face combat. As lifestyles and social structures change, specialised terms of this kind are either lost or take on totally different functions. The once highly elaborated terminology of hunting, for instance, has all but vanished, surviving only for the handful of speakers who can still use eight different words for a wild boar of different ages, or twelve terms describing the shape of a stag's antlers (see Lenoble-Pinson 1977). For the most part, terms from such a field survive only in semi-opaque idioms such as *bête noire* (originally used for wild boar and other dangerous quarry), *être aux abois* 'to be at bay', or *donner le change à quelqu'un* 'to throw someone off the scent'. Many obsolete terminologies are to be gleaned from the examination of early texts; others, relating to less aristocratic pursuits, may have left little in the way of written records.

Today, more detailed monitoring of lexical change is possible, thanks to the assiduous work of teams of researchers, and the production of regularly updated dictionaries.[1] The comparison of different editions of *dictionnaires d'usage*, such as the study undertaken by Dubois *et al.* (1960) in relation to the *Petit Larousse*, has proved a particularly fruitful way of pinpointing areas of the lexis undergoing major change. It is clear that this century huge numbers of new words have been created or borrowed to match technical and scientific advances. Moreover many, as Gilbert (1973) noted, are finding their way into general parlance.

Dubois *et al.* observed that hundreds of new terms in fields such as biology, medicine, psychiatry, telecommunications and the petro-chemical industry appeared in the *PLI* between 1949 and 1960. In technological fields substantial numbers of words also disappeared, since inventions and techniques are themselves subject to rapid turnover (*pickup* meaning 'record-player' is now classified as *vieilli* in the *PLI*, as no doubt will *machine à écrire* within a generation). The terminology of pure science, on the other hand, tends to accumulate, since scientific theory itself is cumulative; only occasionally do revolutionary new ideas render earlier theories and their terminology obsolete.

Another broad field in which there has been a veritable explosion of lexical activity in recent years is that of sport. The sheer volume of new words, imported or invented, to be found in generalised dictionaries of sport, like the *Robert des sports*, and the *Dicosport*, or in the many specialised terminologies that have been published, tells us a lot about the social and economic importance of sports, both as group activities and as part of the leisure industry.[2]

THE STRUCTURE OF SEMANTIC FIELDS

Numbers of words alone can only indicate which areas are a focus of interest at a given period. According to Matoré (1953), working within the structuralist tradition, the meaning of individual items – particularly those embodying social and cultural values – can only be properly understood in relation to other words within the same field, to which they are closely connected. Such intimately structured subsets of the lexis reflect the structure of the social context from which they arise. For Matoré, therefore, the study of the lexis is above all 'un instrument efficace d'enquête sociologique', ultimately 'capable d'expliquer l'évolution d'une civilisation'.

Only the closest study of texts enables the researcher to decode the interlocking *signifiants* of an earlier period so that they yield up a full picture of the life of their time. Matoré has applied this socio-structuralist approach to great effect, in studies of the lexis at periods as diverse as the nineteenth century and the Middle Ages (see 'Further reading' below). He shows, for example, how the word *chevalier* can only be understood, in a medieval context, as one of the many terms forming the elaborate hierarchy of the *noblesse*; this in turn is only definable in relation to the other two major social divisions of the period, the *clercs* and the *vilains*.

Society has changed so radically that none of these can be considered key terms today. *Bourgeois*, however, emerged from relative obscurity to play a central, and finally dominant, role in the field of social hierarchies. In the eleventh century certain towns were given the special status of *francs bourgs*, and were exempt from the legal control of the local landowners or clergy. The inhabitants of the *bourgs*, the embryonic middle class, rising from the ranks of the *vilains*, made money through property and trade, rather than land and taxation, prerogatives of the aristocracy and the church. In Molière's *Le bourgeois gentilhomme*, the *bourgeois* is seen in relation to the aristocracy, from above. His social pretensions are portrayed as absurd, but in reality, as the paradoxical title implies, the bourgeoisie were already penetrating the ranks of the aristocracy. By contrast, in the nineteenth century, the opposition is not so much *bourgeoisie–aristocratie* (since the former had emerged from the Revolution as the principal controllers of power and wealth), as *bourgeoisie–prolétariat*. The term *capitaliste* became closely associated with *bourgeois* at this time, and both were used as synonyms for oppressors of the working class, in a variety of revolutionary movements, well into the twentieth century.

Another important contrast, dating also from the nineteenth century, is that of *bourgeois–artiste*, in which the *bourgeois* is viewed as materialistic and philistine. Over the centuries the term has thus accumulated an array of (largely negative) moral, political and intellectual connotations, so that its precise interpretation today will depend on who is using the term, of whom, and with what intentions.

As Matoré suggests, some key words may refer to ideal human types, against whom people could consciously measure themselves and others, as touchstones for the moral and intellectual values of their time. In the medieval period, for example, the *preux* or *prodome* (later *prud'homme*, with a very different meaning) was the noble warrior par excellence, inspired by loyalty to his feudal lord and by his religious faith. The seventeenth-century *honnête homme* exemplified the qualities appropriate to a more social, courtly role, and the eighteenth-century *philosophe*, while profoundly ethical in his motivation, was endowed with powers of the intellect which were not defining characteristics of either the *prodome* or the *honnête homme*.

From the nineteenth century we no longer find universally accepted social models; as Matoré (1953: 69) observes: 'A partir de la Révolution, ce ne sont plus des types humains qui expriment la société, mais des principes.' The earlier, monolithic social hierarchy gave way to more fragmented and fluid movements, organisations and ideologies – social, political, aesthetic and other. Hence the popularity of the suffix -*isme*, discussed below.

CENTRES OF EXPANSION

If we turn from the internal structure or development of a field to the relationships between fields, we can see how at different periods, certain fields act as focal areas, or 'centres of expansion' upon which others can draw (see Ullmann 1962: 214).

The probably universal predilection for spatial metaphors (discussed in the previous chapter), allied to the socio-economic importance of modes of transport, has made the latter a perennial source of lexicalised metaphors, and favoured the transfer from the terminology of one form of transport to another.

Although today the average French speaker probably rarely sets foot on a ship or a barge, the earlier importance of sea-borne and river-borne traffic[3] is detectable in the wealth of terms, now relating not just to locomotion but to all kinds of human interaction and endeavour, which were nautical in origin, as the etymologies of verbs such as *arriver*, *aborder*, *accoster*, *démarrer*, *embarquer*, *débarquer* reveal. Echoes of this once dominant field are also to be found in surviving idioms, such as *mettre les voiles* 'to clear off', or *prendre la barre* 'to take the helm', and proverbs like *Selon le vent, la voile* (i.e. one must adapt to circumstances).

With the development of aviation and then space travel, this remained the natural source of supply for many new terms, as Guilbert (1965) demonstrated in his study of this particular field; *pilote*, *balise*, *navigation*, *gouvernail*, *aéroport*, *vaisseau spatial*, the root -*naute* itself, as in *cosmonaute* or *astronaute*, all show their nautical origins, just as the 'docking' manoeuvre between spacecraft and space station is referred to in French as either *amarrage* or *arrimage* – alternative nautical metaphors. Rather unusually, *aiguillage* and *aiguilleur*, now most commonly associated with the control of air transport, were drawn from rail transport, referring to the shunting or switching of trains from one track to another.

The railways transformed the economic and social fabric of Europe and were a powerful symbol of modernity and change for much of the nineteenth century. It was a centre of attraction which left its mark on the common fund of everyday expressions, such as *dérailler* 'to go off the rails', *remettre sur les rails*, *vivre sur rails*, *ne pas courir sur les mêmes rails*, etc. – although the latter has been largely replaced by the more up-to-date technological metaphor *ne pas être sur la même longueur d'ondes*.

More recently still, space technology has provided a range of metaphors using *orbite*: *mettre sur orbite* 'to launch'; *vivre en orbite*, *entrer dans l'orbite de quelqu'un*, and so on. Similarly the dramatic 'countdowns' to take-off which characterised the launching of manned spacecraft in the

1960s and 1970s gave *compte à rebours*, now used for the approach of any imminent and irreversible event. If a person's actions are *téléguidés*, or *télécommandés*, they are being manipulated by unseen forces.

It will be particularly interesting to monitor the currently developing fields of telecommunications and computer technology. At the moment they are undergoing rapid evolution, and are therefore drawing on other sources, rather than, as yet, acting as donors. *Convivial* 'user-friendly' has already established itself as something of a key term (as a metaphor drawn from the area of human relationships it has a reassuringly non-technical sound). The purveyors of software for microcomputers realise how important it is to develop a terminology which will encourage the widest possible market. Hence the use of homely metaphors like *puce* for 'microchip', or *souris*, the direct translation of English 'mouse', while the inspired French equivalent of 'wysiwyg' ('what you see is what you get') is the proverb-like *tel écran, tel écrit*.

One can thus see how the lexis is constantly recycled; focal semantic fields are the channels through which much of the material is directed, supplying metaphors to feed other developing areas of the lexis. Equally, everyday terms may be put to specialist, technical use.

THE RISE AND FALL OF AFFIXES

Although discussion of changes in semantic fields tends to focus on lexical items as key units, there is no reason why humble affixes too should not come to play a pivotal role in the development of a semantic field. They are after all often consciously referred to as significant elements – as when the lay person complains about the proliferation of '-isms' or '-ologies', symbolic of mysterious and exclusive areas of knowledge to which most people do not have access.

The processes of affixation in closely linked fields such as science, technology, industry, commerce and economics would certainly repay detailed investigation. The suffixes *-iste* and *-isme*, for example, are interesting as elements which were almost dormant in the language for many centuries, only to become two of the most productive of the twentieth century (see, for example, Dubois 1962, Dubois and Dubois 1971, Quémada 1993). Originally Greek, they were borrowed into Latin in the Classical period, but were little used until the eighteenth century, when the French political scene teemed with theories and dogmas. They came to stand for allegiance to a particular political faction or ideology: *royalisme, anarchisme, girondisme, dantonisme, terrorisme*, etc. (see Frey 1925). They have continued in this role, as new ideologies and movements have been formulated (*communisme, fascisme, socialisme...*), but have also spread to movements, beliefs and theories in other fields, such as literature, art and science: *impressionnisme*, *symbolisme*, *surréalisme*, *darwinisme*, etc.

As a suffix designating someone trained in a particular branch of science, *-iste* is often suffixed to the Greco-Latin *-ologie*, as in *zoologiste*, *biologiste* (in this context *-ologiste* and *-ologue* are occasionally in competition, as in *gynécologiste* and *gynécologue*, or *paléontologiste* and *paléontologue*). Is it the desire to add a prestigious scientific cachet to less strictly scientific professions that has given rise to words like *jardiniste* for 'landscape gardener' (as opposed to the *jardinier* who does the spadework), *voyagiste* 'tour operator' or *visagiste* 'beauty consultant'? Or does it constitute a recognition of the growing use of technology in these fields?

The suffixes *-isme* and *-iste* have steadily gained ground too in the growing fields of leisure and sports activities, from the nineteenth century *athlétisme* and *alpinisme* to more recent sports like *cyclisme*, *parachutisme*, and *motonautisme*. All in all, these suffixes have acted as trace elements marking the most culturally important of developing semantic fields.

Anti- has had a not dissimilar history to *-isme* and *-iste*, in that it took off as a political prefix in the late eighteenth century in the field of politics, as in *antipopulaire*, *antireligieux*, *antimonarchique*, *antipatriotique*, and continues to be productive in this role.[4] But it too has broadened its scope and moved into both scientific and commercial fields, in items like *antibiotique*, *antigel*, *antihistaminique*, *antichar*, *antirides*.

As a linguistic symptom of the growing commercialism of the latter half of the twentieth century, we could take the example of the suffix *-erie*, which Dubois (1962) refers to as being on the wane in the 1950s. Traditionally meaning the place where things are made and sold, or the process of production, as in *boulangerie*, *serrurerie*, and with parallel agentive forms ending in *-er* or *-ier*, it was associated with small-scale production by skilled workers. According to Dubois the suffix 'est lié au stade artisanal de la production, et disparaît avec lui'. For example he noted the disappearance from the Petit Larousse of words like *boutonnerie* 'button factory' and *zinguerie* 'zinc manufacturer's'; over seventy disappeared in the decade under investigation, while less than half a dozen new forms made their appearance. However, over the past twenty years the rash of signs for shops or in department stores, announcing *bagagerie*, *jardinerie*, *gadgeterie*, *sandwicherie*, *omeletterie*, *croissanterie*, *crêperie* suggests that the suffix has found a new commercial role, especially in relation to fast-food outlets.

WORDS AND STEREOTYPES

When fields of experience involving power relations are involved, the words associated with them do not remain neutral. As we have seen, words like *bourgeois*, referring to key protagonists in such fields, acquire negative or positive ethical connotations – a process that C.S. Lewis (1960) called 'the moralisation of status words'.

The etymologies of *gentilhomme*, *noble*, *franc*, *courtois* and *généreux* demonstrate how positive qualities invariably come to be associated with the ruling élite. *Franc*, with its wide range of contemporary meanings, from the abstract adjective to the coin, was originally simply the name of the Germanic tribe which invaded and settled in the northern part of Gaul in the fifth century, and eventually gave France its name. Chaurand (1977: 53–66) traces the two major parallel semantic developments of this tribal name, one connected with the special legal status enjoyed by the Franks, and the other with the qualities of openness and sincerity with which they were supposedly endowed.

At the lower end of the social scale, *peuple* acquired a complex range of meanings, not all disparaging, though collocations such as *le bas peuple*, *le petit peuple*, *la lie du peuple*, and the very fact that it was often used in opposition to *noblesse* or *bourgeoisie*, reveal negative connotations. More recently *populace* and *plèbe* came to be used pejoratively of the lower classes. An added dimension to these correlations of social class with moral qualities is the 'country–town' opposition, where the town is associated with polish, education and refinement, and the country with all that is ignorant, coarse and unmannerly. The etymologies of the root morphemes of *urbanité* (< Latin *urbs* 'town'), and *civilisation* (< *civis* 'citizen') bear witness to this. By contrast, *rustre* 'loutish' comes from the originally neutral *rusticus*, 'of the country', just as *vilain* comes from *villanus* – originally a worker on the *villa*, or country estate. The development of *piètre* 'wretched' from *pedestris* 'on foot' shows how the horse was one of the most powerful of early status symbols, just as many idioms have entered the language which associate horse-riding with power and control: *avoir le pied à l'étrier*; *être ferme sur ses étriers*; *être bien en selle*; *tenir la bride haute à quelqu'un…*

Mistrust and fear of the foreigner are so widespread that it is no surprise to find xenophobia enshrined in language. The objectionable or contempt-ible characteristics and habits of foreigners crop up in all kinds of idioms and collocations; England is *la perfide Albion*; French has *filer à l'anglaise*, where the English talk of 'taking French leave'; 'French letters' are *capotes anglaises*; *une querelle d'Allemand* is an unprovoked dispute; Greeks are mendacious and untrustworthy, Turks pitiless, Belgians stupid, Corsicans vengeful and lawless. The speech of foreigners is the object of particular mistrust; *hâbleries* 'bragging' and *palabres* 'long-winded discussions' were borrowed from Spanish, and *baragouin* 'gibberish' from Breton, although these do not have pejorative connotations on their home territory. (Going much further back, of course, *barbare* originated as the Greeks' onomatopeia for the unintelligible speech of foreigners.) Regional stereo-types, perpetuated in proverbs, are also common: 'Garde [= garde-toi] d'un

Gascon ou Normand; l'un hâble [= se vante] trop, l'autre ment'; 'Qui fit Breton fit larron' – and so on.

The underdog, the provincial and the foreigner may be given a hard time, linguistically; but when it comes to negative stereotyping it is women who are the target of by far the widest array of abusive and disparaging terms.

WOMEN AND WORDS

Even if one had no knowledge of the deep-rooted and pervasive differences in power and status between the sexes, it could be deduced from an examination of words relating to men and women, in French and no doubt many other languages. Certainly the reader will be able to draw close parallels with English.

Guiraud's *Dictionnaire érotique* (1978a) alone contains hundreds of terms of abuse applicable to women, most being synonyms for prostitute. *Garce*, for example, once simply the feminine equivalent of *garçon*, can be used to mean 'prostitute', or something as vague as 'bitch'. Other originally neutral terms which have taken on sexual connotations are *maîtresse* and *courtisane*; in certain contexts, even the generic *femme* or *fille* can be used in this way. Occasionally, a word for prostitute, like *nana*, loses its abusive force and is simply an informal term for 'woman'. Frequently animal images are used: *une sale bête, une poule, une vache, une chienne chaude*.

Other terms, such as *boudin* 'fat lump', *vieille peau, pouffiasse, grognasse* (all approximately 'old bag'), refer rather to a woman's sexual unattractiveness. *Laideron*, though masculine in form, refers only to ugly young women or girls.

The importance attached to a woman's appearance is also revealed, conversely, by the wealth of adjectives relating to female beauty: *jolie, belle, charmante, ravissante, mignonne, plantureuse, bien roulée, voluptueuse*, etc. There are relatively few terms, either positive or negative, relating specifically to the physical appearance of men. Those that exist usually indicate physical strength: *bien bâti, bien baraqué, costaud*.

Another aspect of the asymmetry of the lexis with regard to the sexes is the use of the masculine form as a generic, to include the feminine – a form of polysemy which operates at both the lexical and grammatical level. *L'Homme* can refer to the human race in general, as in *les droits de l'Homme*. Similarly a masculine noun or pronoun can refer to both sexes; *les étudiants de la Sorbonne* would not normally be interpreted as referring only to the male students. (*Femme* is of course polysemous but in a different way, designating both the female of the species and a woman defined in terms of her socio-legal status – as *la compagne de l'homme*, as some dictionaries put it.)

As awareness of lexical asymmetries has grown, there has been an increasing tendency to include the feminine form: *lecteurs/trices*, *un(e) technicien(ne)*, although these are somewhat inelegant. (This particular problem arises from the fact that in French, unlike say, English or Turkish, grammatical gender is strongly marked.) The solution is sometimes to find a singular generic noun instead, if necessary with a suitable adjective: *l'humanité* or *l'être humain* can be substituted for *l'Homme*, *le corps estudiantin* for *les étudiants*, *le lectorat* for *les lecteurs*, and so on.

Not infrequently, there is no feminine equivalent of a masculine noun, especially, though not solely, where it is a question of occupations only recently open to women. *Ingénieur, chauffeur, médecin, écrivain, auteur, sculpteur, professeur*, and many more, can be 'feminised' by the formation of a rather clumsy compound, like *une femme-médecin*,[5] while women in high office are given titles like *Mme le Préfet*, or *Mme le Ministre*.

A variety of morphological resources do however exist in the language, to derive feminine forms on the pattern of *acteur/actrice*, or *chanteur/chanteuse*, by the addition of an orthographic *e*, or by simply changing the gender of the noun with no modification of its form, particularly if it already ends in an *e*, as with *juge* or *ministre*. Just such new forms were suggested by a government *Commission de féminisation des noms de métier*, set up in 1984, which resulted in an official *circulaire* two years later (see Figure 13).[6] Responses to these proposals were unfortunately hostile or sluggish, and usage in France still lags behind that in other francophone countries such as Canada and Switzerland (see Oliviéri 1988).

It seems there is generally less resistance to the 'feminisation' of lower status jobs; in the university hierarchy for example *une maître assistante*, derived from *un maître assistant*, is often used for a female (junior) member of the teaching staff, but *Mme le maître de conférence* is generally retained for a more senior post.

One argument against using certain feminine forms, such as *ambassadrice, préfète* or *mairesse*, is that these words are already used to denote '*wife of* the ambassador, prefect or mayor, etc'.[7] (It is not clear how one should address the husband of a woman who achieves high office of this kind...)

There are fewer problems when it comes to finding masculine equivalents in professions hitherto dominated by women; a male nurse is an *infirmier*, and a social worker an *assistant social* – both back-formations from the feminine form. When men began to take on the role of midwife (*sage-femme*), the solution was not so obvious; *accoucheur* was one possibility, but the officially accepted term appears to be the sonorous Greek-based *maïeuticien*, proposed by the French Academy.

Interestingly, there seems to have been greater symmetry in the naming of occupations and professions in the Middle Ages, when a woman could be a *barbieresse* or a *miresse* (the feminine of *mire* (= *médecin*)). According

**Règles de féminisation des noms de métier,
fonction, grade ou titre**

Les féminins des noms de métier, fonction, grade ou titre sont
formés par application des règles suivantes:

1.   L'emploi d'un déterminant féminin: une, la, cette.

2.   *a*) Les noms terminés à l'écrit par un «e» muet ont un masculin
et un féminin identiques: une architecte, une comptable...

Remarque. – On notera que le suffixe féminin «esse» n'est plus
employé en français moderne: une poétesse...

b) Les noms masculins terminés à l'écrit par une voyelle autre que
le «e» muet ont un féminin en «e»: une chargée de mission, une
déléguée...

c) Les noms masculins terminés à l'écrit par une consonne, à
l'exception des noms se terminant par «eur», ont:

– un féminin identique au masculin; une médecin...;

– ou un féminin en «e» avec éventuellement l'ajout d'un accent
sur la dernière voyelle ou le doublement de la dernière consonne: une
agente, une huissière, une mécanicienne...

d) Les noms masculins terminés en «teur» ont:

– si le «t» appartient au verbe de base, un féminin en «teuse»: une
    acheteuse...;

– si le «t» n'appartient pas au verbe de base, un féminin en
«trice»: une animatrice...

Remarques:

– l'usage actuel a tendance à donner un féminin en «trice», même
à des noms dans lesquels le «t» appartient au verbe de base: une
éditrice...;

– dans certains cas, la forme en «trice» n'est pas aujourd'hui
acceptée; dans ce cas, on emploiera un féminin identique au masculin: une auteur...

e) Les autres noms masculins terminés en «eur» ont, si le verbe de
base est reconnaissable, un féminin en «euse»: une vendeuse, une
danseuse...

Remarque. – Le suffixe féminin «esse» n'est plus employé en
français moderne: une demanderesse...

Si le verbe de base n'est pas reconnaissable, que ce soit pour la
forme ou le sens, il est recommandé, faute de règle acceptée, d'utiliser un masculin et un féminin identiques: une proviseur, une ingénieur, une professeur...

Figure 13 Circular on feminisation, *Journal Officiel* 16 March 1986

to Melka and Zwanenburg (1993) it was only in the sixteenth century that legal and social constraints began to place stricter limits on the roles women could play (though they rarely had access to roles involving real power, such as high government office).

Today, even where an apparently equivalent feminine form does exist, it may well not correspond in status to that of the masculine noun. The role of a *gouverneur* is very different from that of a *gouvernante*, and *un secrétaire* performs some high administrative or political function, as opposed to the humbler tasks assigned to *une secrétaire*. A *couturier* is a dress-designer, a *couturière* a dress-maker. Sometimes the feminine form signifies a specifically sexual role, as in *maîtresse*, *courtisane* or *entraîneuse*, unlike the masculine equivalents. Feminine suffixes may be used inventively in an ironic or flippant way, as in *cheffesse* and *chauffeuse*, while the farcical and cheerfully sexist nature of the film *Le Gendarme et les Gendarmettes* can be guessed at from the title. Established and apparently status-neutral expressions with such feminine suffixes may in fact carry negative connotations; neither *une poétesse* nor *une doctoresse* could expect to be taken

as seriously as their male counterparts. Small wonder, then, that women in high-status professions are often reluctant to use feminised forms.

As Yaguello (1987) points out, other significant asymmetries exist, which involve the habitual collocation of lexical items. The phrase *caprices féminins* is a cliché, much like *le beau sexe*, *le sexe faible* and *le deuxième sexe*, which all refer to women. *Homme* occurs in expressions indicating positions of power and prestige: *homme du monde*, *homme de bien*, *homme d'armes*, *homme de loi*, *homme d'état*, *homme d'affaires*; *femme* and *fille* are found in expressions designating much humbler, even disreputable roles: *femme de ménage*, *femme de chambre*, *femme de mauvaise vie*, *fille de joie*, *fille publique*. Not surprisingly, when the same adjective occurs with *homme* or *femme*, the feminine expression often has sexual connotations; the *honnête homme* of the seventeenth century was the epitome of the distinguished, witty and cultivated gentleman; *une honnête femme* was simply one who was chaste, or faithful to her husband. The differences in the semantic development of analogous terms, like *compère* and *commère*, is also significant, with *commère* acquiring the additional meaning of 'gossip', which gives rise to the derived form *commérages*.

Yaguello also notes the insidious sexism to be found in dictionary definitions, and in the kind of examples and quotations which are used to illustrate the use of a feminine noun, as opposed to its masculine counterpart. The definitions of *homme*, *femme* and *fille* again are especially revealing, with *femme* and *fille* being defined in relation to marriage and childbearing, and *homme* denoting on the one hand the generic term for the human race, and on the other a person fulfilling a wide range of social roles, such as those indicated above; in addition, defining characteristics of *l'homme* viewed as an ideal are given: 'les qualités de courage, de hardiesse, de droiture propres à son sexe' (*Petit Robert* 1990). Sometimes, an apparently sex-neutral adjective is given in a dictionary, but the examples suggest that it is more appropriately applied to women, as with *bavard*; examples like *une femme bavarde*, *une voisine bavarde*, *une petite fille bavarde* predominate in a number of dictionaries.

The 'folk wisdom' enshrined in sayings, proverbs and catchphrases which feature women, like 'Cherchez la femme', or 'Sois belle et taistoi' tell the same tale. One has only to check the entry for *femme* (subclassified under *la vie domestique*) in the Robert *Dictionnaire de proverbes et expressions*, to find a long list of pejorative maxims, such as 'Foi de femme est plume sur l'eau'; 'A qui Dieu veut aider, sa femme meurt'; 'Où femme il y a, silence il n'y a'; 'Il faut aux filles des hommes ou des murailles'; and so on. (The parallel entry for *homme* shows that the word occurs in expressions which make generalisations about the behaviour and fate of human beings, irrespective of sex.)

All in all, the images of women projected by the language are largely negative: desirable but fickle, faithless, empty-headed and loquacious. No doubt these are outdated prejudices for the majority of speakers, but it may take a long time for the accumulated mysogyny of centuries to work itself out of the language.

Dictionaries play a delicate role here; their task is to reflect current usage, and not to take any kind of ideological stand. However, compiling a dictionary is such a major undertaking that existing material tends to be reused from one edition to the next; lexicographers need to look rather carefully at fields where social attitudes have in fact undergone significant changes. (Beaujot's study (1978) suggests that some adjustments have been made in at least one *dictionnaire d'usage*.) It will be interesting to monitor lexical entries in these sensitive areas over the coming decades, and see what changes occur.

EUPHEMISM, DYSPHEMISM AND TABOO

In all societies there are certain areas of experience that are particularly emotionally charged, and that it is difficult or even dangerous to talk about directly. These range from religious taboos, with interdicts on naming God or the devil, at the risk of incurring their wrath, to social inhibitions about discussing bodily functions openly. Formal religion may have lost much of its power, but subjects such as serious illness, death, sex and madness remain potential linguistic minefields in Western society.

Indirect, even placatory ways are found to talk about such threatening topics. Gravestones and obituary notices supply numerous examples of largely metaphorical substitutes for *mourir*: 'notre père s'est éteint... s'est endormi... nous a quittés...'. Comforting metaphors of this kind suggest that death comes as easily as the snuffing out of a candle, that it is not the end of existence, merely an interval of sleep, that it is a journey to another place, and so on. The formal *décéder* similarly comes from the Latin verb 'to go away', just as the somewhat archaic *trépasser* meant originally 'to cross over', and *périr* comes from the Latin 'to pass away'.

Violent death has spawned many euphemisms, often in informal registers of the language, with humour covering the underlying unease. *Tuer* itself is slang in origin, from the Latin *tutari*, 'to take care of'. The Revolution saw a spate of new expressions, often couched in black humour, which refer to death by the guillotine: *le fauteuil révolutionnaire, se faire raccourcir, baiser la veuve, mettre la tête à la petite fenêtre* (see Walter 1989). Modern understated slang euphemisms for killing include *expédier* and *buter* (much like English 'bump off').

As beliefs or attitudes change, so do the fields which are felt to be taboo.[8] It would be excessively coy today to refer to a pregnant woman as being *dans*

un état intéressant. Such *euphémismes de bienséance* are still in operation, however, when it comes to the bodily processes of excretion. To use the basic verbs *pisser* and *chier* still involves breaking a social taboo. The commonest euphemistic substitutes, *aller aux toilettes*, *faire ses besoins*, are typical in that metonymy, a kind of linguistic sidestepping or over-generalisation is used (see Chapter Seven) to achieve a distance from the taboo subject. But foreign languages can be a useful cloak, too; English has supplied *aller aux waters* or *aller aux WC*. Learned terms drawn from Latin or Greek have a similar distancing effect. *Uriner* and *excrément* are both essentially high-register words borrowed from Latin. Often, as in this case, no really neutral term is available; one must choose between a euphemism and a **dysphemism**, that is, a term which is intentionally offensive.

It has been suggested (Lefkowitz 1989) that one of the major functions of the word game *verlan* (see pp. 212–14), for secondary school pupils at least, is to provide a semi-euphemistic disguise for otherwise taboo words; one can dare to say *teub* (= *bite* 'penis') or *deumer* (= *merde*), where the original would be beyond the pale.

It is also possible to flirt, so to speak, with a forbidden word by radically changing its pronunciation, retaining perhaps only a consonant or vowel of the original; hence *mince!* for *merde!* and *fichtre!* for *foutre!* This device seems especially common in blasphemous expressions, that is, using sacred names as exclamations of anger and surprise, as in *sacré nom d'une pipe!* (= *du Christ*), *sacré bleu!* (= *Dieu*) and *diantre!* for *diable!* As established religion has become less central to many people's lives, so have oaths lost much of their force, and been replaced by swear words drawn from other fields. In Quebec, however, it seems that such expressions still flourish. *Christ* and a wide range of substitutes such as *cric*, *clis*, and *Christophe* are used, as well as terms drawn specifically from the Catholic mass: *calice*, *tabernacle*, *hostie*, *ciboire* (see Charest 1974).

Once an expression has become firmly associated with a taboo subject, it becomes taboo itself; in other words, a euphemism may become dysphemistic, and a new replacement must be found, which explains in part the accumulation of synonyms in particularly highly charged fields, like that of 'prostitute' mentioned above. When *baiser* became a polite euphemism for *foutre* (now scarcely used except in a metaphorical sense – see below), it too became socially unacceptable and new euphemistic terms like *coucher avec*, *avoir des rapports avec* were then required.

The large numbers of synonyms in such fields cannot however be explained solely in terms of rapid euphemistic replacement. Paradoxically, taboo areas are centres of attraction as well as repulsion; hence the numerous dysphemisms which also cluster around these topics. This is especially true in the unfettered lexis of informal registers, which are least subject to polite social constraints. Hence the labelling of many dysphemistic terms as *populaire*, *argotique*, or *familier*, as well as *vulgaire*, in dictionaries.

The breaking of a taboo can provide a powerful emotional release; it is exhilarating to venture momentarily into forbidden territory – and survive. Moreover the use of a taboo word is a display of courage or aggression on the part of the speaker, and is thus the perfect vehicle for insult.

Gros mots in French, as in many western European languages, are drawn above all from the semantic fields of sex and excretion (see Figure 14 and Guiraud 1975). The key taboo words are *foutre*, *cul*, *con*, *couilles*, *chier* and *merde*, which act as stems for whole paradigms of pejorative words: *foutoir*, *foutaise*, *foutriquet*, *foutraque*; *emmerder*, *merdoyer*, *merdique*, *merdeux*; and so on. Such words serve to express contempt, often with aggressive overtones, as do *se foutre de* in the sense of 'taking the piss', and *baiser* in the sense of 'taking for a ride'.

The link between sex and violence is apparent in the range of brutal slang metaphors for the sexual act, with woman as object: *cogner*, *sabrer*, *marteler une femme*, *tirer un coup*. (It is worth remembering here the etymology of *vagin* – 'scabbard' in the original Latin.) When woman is the subject the verbs are generally intransitive or reflexive in form, and passive in meaning: *se donner*, *se laisser aller*, *tomber*...

Conversely, *foutre* can be used of violent actions: *se foutre par terre*, *foutre en l'air*, *foutre à la porte*, and even as a substitute of *faire*, the transitive verb par excellence – as in *Qu'est-ce que tu fous là?* In turn, *faire* can be used as a synonym for *foutre* in its literal sense, as in *il se l'est faite* 'he got laid'.

In his extensive analysis of sexual terminology, Guiraud (1978b) exam-

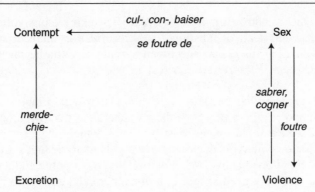

Figure 14 Lexical transfer among taboo fields

ines the complex semantic relationship between sex, violence and con-tempt. His principal thesis is that 'l'activité sexuelle est la forme exem-plaire de toute activité, et plus précisément, de toute activité transitive'. The male role is taken as a metaphor for action, energy and creativity, while the female role (object of the transitive action), is equated with passivity and inaction, owing in part to the human tendency to conceptua-lise in oppositional, polarised terms. According to Guiraud, such is the power of this metaphor, deeply rooted in the subconscious, that it has come to be taken literally, giving rise to many of the beliefs about what con-stitutes masculinity or femininity. It is consistent with his thesis that *con* and *cul*, both used for 'vagina', are the basis for many insulting, contemp-tuous expressions, while none of the dozens of synonyms for 'penis' are used in this way. (The disparaging use of *andouille*, and the derived forms of *couille – couillon, couillonner –* he explains as denoting ineffectual, incomplete attempts at the sex act, and therefore worthy of contempt.)

On entering such territory, we have clearly moved beyond Matoré's notion of linguistic investigation as 'un instrument efficace d'enquête sociologique'; Guiraud's study shows that it may also be used as a tool with which to probe the human psyche. Whether the conceptual connec-tions he reveals are universal – (a Jungian might claim they emanate from the collective unconscious) – could only be determined by extensive cross-cultural studies. The extent to which they influence the attitudes and behaviour of speakers is also open to investigation; other patterns of linguistic behaviour mentioned earlier in this chapter certainly tend to reveal similar stereotyping with regard to male and female roles, and corroborating evidence from non-linguistic behaviour would not be hard to find.

So far, the lexis has been looked at in rather broad terms, at the macro level, so to speak, perhaps giving the impression that it is a homogenous system to which all have equal access, and of which all make similar use. Closer investigation reveals a more complex, multi-dimensional picture: one of overlapping systems which the individual uses to express his or her identity, often in response to changes in role and situation. It is these functions of the lexis that are explored in the next two chapters.

NOTES

1 See for example Gilbert (1971 and 1987), and Quémada (1993).
2 See the bibliography given in the *Robert des sports* or the *Dicosport*.
3 One of the reasons for the early prosperity of Gaul, under the Romans, was the natural network of rivers linking many parts of the country – later to be developed by a complex canal system.
4 Frey (1925) discusses a range of affixes which became productive at this time, in the same field; some, like *-icide*, as in *liberticide, patricide*, on the pattern of *régicide*, were short-lived; others, like *anti-* and the hyperbolic prefixes, *ultra-* and *archi-*, found a more permanent and generalised role in the language.
5 Gilbert (1987) found a score of new compounds of which the first element was *femme-*, indicating the increasing range of occupations open to women, from *femme-pilote* and *femme-détective* to *femme-gangster*.
6 A *circulaire* is in effect a series of government recommendations, but it does not carry the weight of an *arrêté*, such as those published concerning the avoidance of Anglicisms (see Chapter Eleven).
7 This defining of a woman in terms of her husband is borne out by all kinds of linguistic and social conventions, to say nothing of legal distinctions: a woman takes first her father's and then her husband's family name. Significantly, there is something odd about referring to a man as *le veuf de Sophie* 'Sophie's widower', whereas *la veuve de Bertrand* 'Bertrand's widow' sounds quite natural; *veuf* is a much later formation – a lexical afterthought as it were, derived from the feminine form, as indeed is the English equivalent.
8 The current concern with avoiding giving offence to people from minority groups of all kinds, including people with physical or mental handicaps, may lead to the use of euphemism, such as *non-voyant* for *aveugle*. The problem here is that a euphemism implies that the referent itself is in some sense taboo – potentially threatening or embarrassing – which of course runs counter to the aims of politically correct language.

PROJECTS

1 Using a large monolingual dictionary, like the *TLF* or the *Grand Robert*, examine the origins of the following idioms:

avoir voix au chapitre; *entrer en lice*; *se remettre en selle*; *sans tambours ni trompettes*; *être au septième ciel*; *saigner quelqu'un à blanc*

From which semantic fields do they come? Find other expressions which originated in the same fields, and suggest why these were centres of attraction in the past.

2 Speculate on the reasons for the recent renaissance of the suffixes *-ité* and *-itude* in words like *berbérité, islamité, québécité, francitude, négritude*, and in any other expressions you may know of the same type.

3   With the help of recent monolingual dictionaries, or dictionaries of neologisms, examine the development of the elements *télé-*, *auto-* and *euro-* over the last fifty years. In what fields are they particularly productive?

4   Using a computerised literary database, such as the quotations provided in the *Robert électronique*, compare the way in which *vertu* collocates with, on the one hand, *femme* and *fille*, and, on the other, with *homme*. Do specific senses of *vertu* predominate in either case?
Using the same database, investigate the number of occurrences and range of meanings of *coquet* and *coquette*.

5   Examine the formulation of job offers in the classified advertisement sections of the French press. To what extent are feminine forms included?

FURTHER READING

Allan, K. and Burridge, K. 1991 *Euphemism and Dysphemism: Language Used as Shield and Weapon*, New York, Oxford University Press

Beaujot, J.-P. 1978 'Idéologie de la langue et idéologie du dictionnaire', *Bulletin du centre d'analyse du discours* 3, Université de Lille III; examines entries relating to male and female roles in the *PLI* from 1906 to 1978, and notes the disappearance of some asymmetries in dictionary definitions.

Charest, G. 1974 *Le livre des sacres et blasphèmes québecois*, Montreal, L'Aurore

Chaurand, J. 1977 *Introduction à l'histoire du vocabulaire français*, Paris, Bordas

Dubois, J. 1962 *Etude sur la dérivation suffixale en français moderne et contemporain*, Paris, Larousse; notes trends in the development of suffixes, especially in scientific and technical fields, based on a comparison of the 1906 and 1961 editions of the *PLI*.

—— 1963 *Le Vocabulaire politique et social en France de 1869 à 1872*, Paris, Larousse; an essentially structuralist study of key terms, such as *classe*, *travailleurs*, *clergé*, *bourgeoisie*, and so on, at a time when France was passing through a period of social and political upheaval.

Dubois, J. and Dubois, C. 1971 *Introduction à la lexicographie*, Paris, Larousse; includes 'Le mouvement général du vocabulaire français de 1949 à 1960, d'après un dictionnaire d'usage', which analyses changes taking place in entries in the *PLI* for this period.

Failliot, P. 1995: *Dicosport 95*, Suresnes, DPS; first published in 1988, and regularly updated since.

Frey, M. 1925 *Les transformations du vocabulaire français à l'époque de la révolution*, Paris, PUF

Gilbert, P. 1971 *Dictionnaire des mots nouveaux*, Paris, Hachette; detailed entries of about 6,000 neologisms appearing during the 1950s and 1960s.

—— 1973 'Remarques sur la diffusion des mots scientifiques et techniques dans le lexique commun', *Langue francaise* 17

—— 1987 *Dictionnaire des mots contemporains*, Paris, Usuels du Robert; an extended and updated version of the *Dictionnaire des mots nouveaux*.

Graddol, D. and Swann, J. 1989 *Gender Voices*, Oxford, Blackwell; provides a good overview of research carried out on English, in relation to language and gender.

Guilbert, L. 1965 *La Formation du vocabulaire de l'aviation*, Paris, Larousse

Guiraud, P. 1975 *Les gros mots*, Paris, PUF Que Sais-Je?

—— 1978a *Dictionnaire érotique*, Paris, Payot

—— 1978b *La Sémiologie de la sexualité*, Paris, Payot

Houdebine-Gravaud, A.-M. 1987 'Le français au féminin', in *La Linguistique* 23, (1); analyses reactions to legislation on the feminisation of titles and professions.
Journal Officiel de la République française1986 'Féminisation des noms de métier, fonction, grade ou titre', 16 March; reprinted in *Dictionnaire des néologismes officiels*, 1988, Paris, Direction des journaux officiels
Lefkowitz, N.J. 1989 'Verlan: talking backwards in French', *French Review* 63 (2): 312–22.
Lenoble-Pinson, M. 1977 *Le Langage de la chasse: gibiers et prédateurs*, Brussels, Facultés universitaires Saint-Louis
Lewis, C.S. 1960 (2nd edition, reprinted in 1991) *Studies in Words*, Cambridge, Cambridge University Press
Matoré, G. 1951 *Le Vocabulaire et la société sous Louis-Philippe*, Paris, Droz
—— 1953 *La Méthode en lexicologie*, Paris, Marcel Didier
—— 1985 *Le Vocabulaire et la société médiévale*, Paris, PUF
—— 1988 *Le Vocabulaire et la société du XVIᵉ siècle*, Paris, PUF
Melka, F.J. and Zwanenburg, W. 1993 'Femme et féminin en ancien français', *Cahiers de lexicologie* 62
Oliviéri, C. 1988 'Vers une langue non-sexiste', *Diagonales* 8, supplement 220 of *Le Français dans le monde*; reviews legislation and usage in the field, in France and Canada.
Petiot, G. 1982 *Le Robert des sports*, Paris, Robert
Peytard, J. 1977 'Néologisme préfixé et diffusion socio-linguistique en français contemporain', *Le Français moderne* 4.
Quémada, B. 1993 *Mots nouveaux contemporains*, Paris, Klincksieck; a continuation of the extensive collection of neologisms (listed alphabetically and by theme), previously published annually as *Matériaux pour l'histoire du vocabulaire français*, from 1970, also by Klincksieck.
Rey, A. 1990 *Dictionnaire de proverbes et expressions*, Paris, Robert
Ullmann, S. 1962 *Semantics: An Introduction to the Science of Meaning*, Oxford, Blackwell
Walter, H. 1989 *Des mots sans-culottes*, Paris, R. Laffont
Yaguello, M. 1987 *Les Mots et les femmes*, Paris, Payot; for the most comprehensive survey of the topic in relation to French.

Chapter 9

Lexis in context

Geographical diversity within languages has long been an object of study for linguists. However, it is only over the last thirty to forty years that the work of linguists like Labov and Trudgill has revealed variation which correlates not with region, but with membership of a specific social group, or with the situation in which an utterance occurs. The language used by a head of state addressing the nation on television will have little in common with that of a farm worker telling a joke in a bar, even if they were born and brought up in the same village. It is this kind of linguistic variability, as reflected at the level of lexis, that this chapter seeks to explore.

LINGUISTIC VARIETIES

A very broad range of both personal and situational factors combine to influence a speaker's (largely unconscious) choice of pronunciation, grammatical forms and vocabulary. When a signifiant number of linguistic features – specific sets of grammatical structures, phonological features and lexical items – habitually co-occur in the speech of a group or even an individual, we can recognise the existence of a 'variety' of the language. As Hudson (1996: 22) puts it: 'We may define a variety of a language as *a set of linguistic items with similar social distribution.*'

One variety may carry special prestige, as the standardised written form or the language of the ruling class, and be thought of as *the* language, but all varieties are describable linguistic systems. Although the traditional focus has been on 'correct' usage, it makes more sense to think in terms of appropriateness. As far as the lexis is concerned, if one is to be convincing as a speaker of a language, one's use of lexical items must not only be referentially accurate, it must also be appropriate to the social context in which the items are used. (A poetic or literary expression in a mundane exchange about the weather will be perceived as comic or stilted or simply bizarre, just as an utterance normally used to a small child will strike the hearer as condescending, over-affectionate or inappropriate in some other way.)

However, all individuals play so many social roles, adjusting their language accordingly, that one would hardly expect linguistic varieties to be autonomous, discrete systems, clearly demarcated one from another. Rather, they merge and overlap, to differing degrees. Typically, a given linguistic feature, especially at the levels of phonology and grammar, is simply used more frequently in one variety than in another. This makes varieties slippery both as concepts and as objects of linguistic description; which is not to say that we should be deterred from attempting to describe complex variation of this kind – we just have to be aware of the difficulty of drawing neat boundaries round varieties. It is however possible to make some very broad distinctions between varieties, according to the kind of extra-linguistic variables with which they correlate, and which may therefore be assumed to determine them, at least in part.

Register

Features of the situation in which the discourse or utterance takes place play a dominant role. These will include the personal relationship between the speakers (close friends of the same age, boss and employee, husband and wife, doctor and patient...), the social setting in which the exchange takes place (work, home, a large social gathering...) and whether the exchange is one-to-one or one-to-many.

For example, if there is social distance between the speakers, because of differences in their relative status, power, age, or simply because they do not know one another, and if the setting is a public one with a serious social function, such as a law court, a job interview or presentation of a business scheme to a client, the language used is likely to be formal and the participants will be on their 'best behaviour', linguistically speaking. They will be more likely to conform to the standard variety, in grammar and pronunciation, and will choose lexical items that might be judged stilted in less formal circumstances.

It is often the case that the formality of the setting will override the informality of the relationship between the participants; two close friends, when called upon to debate a serious topic in front of television cameras, are unlikely to use the same style of speech as they would discussing the same topic over a meal at home. Situationally determined varieties of this kind are often called 'registers' or, in French, *niveaux de langue*.

Social dialect

Characteristics of the speakers themselves, such as age, sex and social class also influence patterns of speech. Any clearly defined social group, with a sense of common identity, may develop a distinctive social dialect, or 'sociolect'; the group may be as restricted as a single street gang, or as broad as an entire socio-economic class.[1] In a sense, standard French may be considered a sociolect, in that it is spontaneously used more readily by upper-class speakers, while lower down the social scale, as Françoise Gadet (1989 and 1992) demonstrates, rather different grammatical structures and features of pronunciation can be observed. It is sometimes said that social class in France corresponds to less clearly marked linguistic differences than in Britain; certainly regional accent is rather less of a social marker in France.

Occupational style

The 'field of discourse' or subject matter of an utterance may be a powerful factor in determining linguistic usage, especially at the lexical level. This is particularly true of technical and professional fields, where a great deal of specialised terminology (often perceived as 'jargon' by the outsider) is necessarily used. Plumbers, lawyers, garage mechanics, diplomats, gardeners, musicians, all use terms which are either unique to their occupation, or to which they give a unique interpretation. *Aiguille* has different, technical meanings for a botanist, a zoologist and a geologist, as well as its everyday meaning. This kind of topic-associated variety is often known as 'occupational style'.[2]

Expressive function

The lexis may also indicate a speaker's personality, mood or attitude to the addressee or to the topic under discussion. If one talks of someone being *maigrelet*, *maigrichon* or *maigriot* rather than simply *maigre*, a more negative value judgement is often implied. Conversely, *mince* or *svelte* have positive connotations, just as *potelé* implies pleasantly plump, as opposed to the neutral or disparaging *gras* or *gros*.[3]

When a range of lexical items is available, expressing differing degrees of intensity of some phenomenon (such as *malpropre*, *sale*, *crasseux*, *dégueulasse*, or *surpris*, *étonné*, *stupéfait*, *abasourdi*, *ébahi*), selection of the most intense or hyperbolic item may signal the speaker's subjective emotional state – enthusiasm, anger, disgust or astonishment – rather than an objective expression of reality. Such emotive use of language is more likely to be found in relaxed exchanges within a peer-group setting than in carefully monitored formal registers of language.

Mode of communication

The mode through which language is transmitted – whether in spoken or written form, in a face-to-face exchange, or via a telephone or microphone – may well affect register. It is sometimes assumed that written language is bound to be formal and standardised. There is a certain correlation between formal register and written text, in that many texts, from novels to public notices, are forms of communication between people who have never met, and which are open to the public gaze. Moreover, the whole historical process of language standardisation has tended to focus on written French as the enduring form of the language, the vehicle of law, administration, literature and education, and for centuries the prerogative of the élite. Even the least formal text, such as a quick note to a flat-mate about feeding the cat, may be influenced by the habits long associated with writing in other more formal situations; moreover, it cannot rely on the non-verbal information available in a direct encounter.

However, a sharp distinction between the written and spoken modes is not really possible; some spoken forms of language, such as prepared formal speeches and lectures, are based on written texts, even if they are not actually read aloud; while some texts, like scripted dialogues, are designed to be spoken and to sound like spontaneous speech. Moreover, this century has seen a broadening in the range of lexis considered appropriate to a literary text, with writers like Céline in the postwar period using forms in narrative that are clearly drawn from informal spoken discourse.

Register, sociolect and occupational style are recognised as distinct types of linguistic variety, within which the mode of communication and expressive function may act as additional determining variables. Although such concepts can form the basis of a useful framework for discussing variation in French, it is not difficult to think of recognisable varieties which do not fit neatly into a single category. Correspondence relating to business or administration, for example, constitutes a type of text where occupational style and register are inextricably mixed. The specialised lexis of a particular occupational group is usually involved, but register plays an important role too, in that business letters are generally forms of communication between people who have never met, and they express the respectful formality considered appropriate to the written mode, to the social distance involved and to the impersonal nature of the transaction. Beyond the usual grammatical and lexical markers of formal register, and the specialised vocabulary required for the subject under discussion, this kind of text is also marked by a range of specific formulae, especially at the beginning and end of the letter. Manuals such as Ponthier's *Le grand livre de la correspondance commerciale et des affaires* (1978) help to instruct users in the implications of *Cher Monsieur*, as opposed to simply *Monsieur*, as an opener, and in the subtle nuances of *nos sentiments les meilleurs*, versus *nos sentiments devoués* or *respectueux*, in the closing formula.

Occupational style is to an extent independent of register; in a court of law, the relevant occupational style, at least on the part of the professional participants, is necessarily going to correlate with the grammatical forms and standard pronunciation appropriate to a formal, public and indeed ritualised occasion. But two close colleagues discussing the technicalities of a court case in their office, while retaining the use of much specialised terminology, will probably use grammatical and phonological forms of informal conversation. Here, lexis signals occupational style, while other linguistic features (possibly including low-register lexical items) reflect the informality of the setting and the personal relations involved.[4]

Register and sociolect, however, are intimately linked. It often happens that a variety which developed as the everyday mode of communication of the ruling élite (i.e. a sociolect), carries such prestige that it becomes the vehicle for formal written and spoken communication for the entire community – in other words, it acquires the function of a register. Conversely, positive qualities stereotypically associated with working-class speech have often led to features of this sociolect being adopted by speakers higher up the social scale, for purposes of relaxed, informal communication (see Trudgill 1972 and Giles and Powseland 1975). The social and stylistic mobility of lexical items is discussed in more detail in the next chapter.

LINGUISTIC VARIETIES AND LEXICAL LABELS

Most dictionaries use a range of *marques d'usage* (what are here called 'lexical labels'), to give some indication of the field, register or sociolect to which particular words or phrases are appropriate, and whether they are in current usage or somewhat archaic. Near-synonyms are also often provided in dictionary entries; for example *amuser*, *désennuyer*, *divertir*, *égayer*, *récréer* are added to the entry for *distraire* in the *PR*. As well as helping to pinpoint the denotational value of the headword, this practice gives readers a choice of items which may be appropriate to other registers, so that they are not obliged to reach for a thesaurus in their search for the *mot juste*. In addition, the expressive force or intensity of a word is marked in some dictionaries, such as the *DFC*, which uses arrows to indicate relative intensity. Hence ↑ is used to signal 'of greater intensity' and ↓, 'of lesser intensity'; for example the entry for *angoisse* is followed by 'synonymes: ↓peur, ↑épouvante'.

Words which belong to a specific field of discourse, or have a specialised meaning within such a field, carry a field label. The noun *domestique*, for example, as well as its usual meaning of 'servant', occurs in the field of *cyclisme*, with the meaning of member of a racing cyclist's support team. As the preceding chapter shows, it is very common for items to be transferred from one field to another in this way, with long-established words being recycled for use in the expanding areas of science and technology. (A whole line of development of modern science is discernible in the spread of the term *atome* from the field of philosophy to that of chemistry, and finally of nuclear physics.)

These field labels are potentially as numerous as the fields themselves, and vary a good deal from dictionary to dictionary. Some *dictionnaires d'usage*, by their very function, consciously exclude technical terms, and therefore use a narrower range of *marques d'usage*. In larger dictionaries, broad fields such as the law are often subdivided into *droit fiscal*, *droit commercial*, *droit civil*, *droit criminel*, and so on.

Most dictionaries include chronological labels: if a word is somewhat outdated it may be labelled *vieilli*; if it is considered actually obsolete it may be *vieux* or *archaïque*. On the other hand, what one dictionary may class as *vieux* or *vieilli*, another may see as *littéraire* – not surprisingly, since words are obviously still to be found in literary texts after they have disappeared from spoken usage, and may continue to be appropriate to certain types of modern text. *Soutenu* and *soigné*, labels sometimes used of formal registers, may also overlap with labels indicating literary or old-fashioned usage; *défunt* 'deceased' and *opulent* 'wealthy' are both 'soutenu' in the *TL*, but '*littéraire*' in the *PLI*.

The blending of occupational style and formal register that we noted in relation to commercial and administrative language, as well as the inherently conservative nature of such language, are reflected in the variety of labels assigned to expressions like *époux* 'spouse' – both '*admin.*' and '*noble*' in the *DFC* and '*littér.*' and '*dr.*' in the *PR*. For other expressions there is greater consensus in the labelling; most dictionaries agree that *trépas* 'death' is a literary word, whereas the synonym *décès* is more likely to be used in administrative and legal language.

The existence of an 'unmarked' register is tacitly recognised by the omission of any label for the majority of items in the dictionary. Such items belong to a register that many linguists would consider *courant*, or appropriate to the conversation of educated speakers who are acquainted, but not necessarily friendly, possibly in a slightly formal situation. The term is somewhat ambiguous, in that it can also be used to mean 'in current use', in opposition to labels like *vieux* or *vieilli*; in other words it can be used as a chronological marker as well as a marker of register.

If the relationship between the speakers is closer, and the situation more informal, then they may move into a register termed *familier*: not strictly adhering to the grammatical norm, and using lexical items that would be incongruous in a more formal setting, but which in no way mark the speakers as uneducated. The label *populaire*, however, is often used with pejorative overtones, and implies the word is characteristic of the social dialect of the relatively uneducated lower working class; the label may be considered a tacit warning to the reader to avoid such items as being *déclassants*!

Vulgaire is another pejorative *marque d'usage*, which is generally attached to non-euphemistic words involving taboo subjects, such as sex and other bodily functions, for example *péter*, *pisser* or *couilles*. Some words may simply be banned from a dictionary altogether. It was 1977 before the venerable *con*, established in the language for over a thousand years, found its way into the *PR*, for example, although the derived form *connerie* was admitted at a much earlier date.

To complicate matters still further, what some dictionaries consider *familier*, and others *populaire* or *vulgaire*, are elsewhere classed as **argotique**; the definition of *argot* is itself a complex matter, which is discussed in the next chapter. Traditionally, an *argot* is defined as the lexis of a tightly knit, exclusive social or professional group (the earliest known *argot* being that of criminal gangs) – in other words, as being the lexical component of a sociolect. Some linguists and lexicographers, however, see it as characterising the lower echelons of the scale of *niveaux de langue*. This is partly due to the fact that, as we shall see, many words become upwardly mobile; they may originate in a working class *argot*, but later be adopted by the wider community. (The conversation of Brétecher's well-known cartoon strip characters, middle-class left-wing intellectuals, is liberally sprinkled with expressions of this kind, perhaps as an indication of solidarity with the working class.) It is hardly surprising, then, to find variable labelling of 'non-standard' expressions: *flinguer* 'to shoot', is considered *argotique* by the *PLI*, *populaire* by the *DFC* and *familier* by the *PR*. Such discrepancies are legion.

In an attempt to reduce this stylistic complexity to some kind of order, linguists have devised frameworks within which near-synonyms may be classified. Batchelor and Offord (1993a and b), for example, propose a three-term system – broadly speaking *familier–courant–soutenu*, numbered 1–3 respectively, so that *sympa* is labelled 1, *aimable* 2 and *affable* 3. The system acts as a good rough-and-ready guide for the student of French who wishes to avoid serious stylistic lapses, even if it is an inevitable over-simplification of the linguistic reality. The more highly structured classi-ficatory frameworks which have been proposed are too rigidly symmetrical to encompass the messiness of the data.[5] Corbin (1980) demonstrates very lucidly why these efforts are doomed to failure; he does not however propose any more workable framework.

Discussions of *niveaux de langue* in relation to lexis also tend to neglect the fact that 'synonyms' are usually referentially as well as stylistically different.[6] *Succomber* is, in one of its senses, a near-synonym of *mourir*, and is sometimes given the label *soutenu*, but *succomber* is more specific in that it carries the added implication of dying of wounds or an illness, after a period of time. *Invectiver* is not only of a higher register than *insulter*; it implies sustained and elaborated insult.

In fact a difference in reference – often discernible in the case of verbs, in the range of subjects or objects they can take – may be causally related to a difference in register. The fact that *inhumer* can only be used of human bodies, while *enterrer* can be used of any physical object, is probably one reason for the more elevated tone of the former. Similarly, *destituer* may be seen as a high-register equivalent of *congédier*; this is not unconnected with the fact that the object of *destituer* must be a person of high office, while *congédier* can be used of employees at any level.

While most low-register or slang lexical items are marked in some way in French dictionaries, it is not unusual for words which would only be found in formal discourse to remain unmarked, rather than carry the label *soutenu* or *littéraire*. Such is the case of, for example, *éconduire* 'to dismiss', *immondices* 'refuse' and *désobligeant* 'disagreeable' in the current *PR* – all of which would be unlikely to occur in casual conversation. Underlying this absence of marking is a tacitly normative, bipolar classification of words as either 'standard' or 'non-standard'; the former are left relatively undifferentiated, while non-standard items are seen as being in need of labels as a kind of linguistic health warning.

It is said that near-synonyms tend to cluster in the lower registers. This is undoubtedly true of certain semantic fields, for reasons that are discussed in the next chapter. While in 'standard' varieties there is only one *courant* term for 'drunk', *ivre*, together with the literary *aviné*, and the legal–administrative *en état d'ébriété*, there is a wealth of synonyms among the ranks of words classified as *familier, populaire* or *argotique*: *soûl, plein, gris, schlass, bourré, blindé, rétamé*, etc. On the other hand, there are a number of *courant* to *soutenu* synonyms for *ivre*, used in its abstract, figurative sense: *exalté, transporté, excité...* Conversely, in the more abstract semantic field of time, we find a cluster of 'high-register' near-synonyms: *transitoire, éphémère, fugace*, and at least a couple of *courant* terms: *passager* and *momentané* – but no low-register term springs readily to mind.

No doubt such striking differences in the stylistic elaboration of certain semantic fields could be given a socio-psychological explanation of the kind suggested in the preceding chapter.

LE FRANÇAIS SOUTENU – AND BEYOND

The most formal register, appropriate to texts or discourse where the topic is a serious one, the setting public and the interlocutors usually unknown to the writer or speaker, will be marked by strict adherence to the grammatical norm, as laid down in 'bibles' of correct usage, such as Grevisse's *Le bon usage*. Moreover, there is likely to be considerable complexity of syntactic structure, with many embedded clauses, inversions of subject and verb, and use of the subjunctive, where these might well be avoided in *français courant*.

In the spoken mode, pronunciation will be standard, with few if any regional features, little elision of unstressed vowels or reduction of consonant clusters, and observance of all permissible liaison forms, such as *extrêmement‿heureux, amis‿intimes*.

Here, however, we are primarily concerned with the representation of register at the lexical level. It is significant that English has borrowed the expression *le mot juste* from French. The importance given to the selection of precisely the right word can be traced back to the concern for clear definitions of words in dictionaries, evident from the seventeenth century, with its acute awareness of lexis as a marker of style. This tradition is reaffirmed in modern manuals designed for people who wish to express themselves clearly, precisely and elegantly, usually in the written mode. Emphasis is placed on exploiting the full richness of the standard lexis.

Guides to good style, such as Legrand (1972) or Georgin (1953), advise that generic verbs like *faire* be avoided, if a more specific term is available: instead of *faire un trou*, *percer un trou* is recommended; *fournir un grand effort* is felt to be more elegant than *faire un grand effort*, *contracter des dettes* preferable to *faire des dettes*, and so on.

In other words, *le bon usage* requires knowledge of the way in which often low-frequency lexical items co-occur. A good dictionary will at least provide clues about such collocational restrictions in their entries, usually in the form of illustrative sentences. It will indicate, for example, that *détenir*, in the sense of 'possess', can be used with abstract object nouns like *secret*, *record* or *pouvoir*, but not with concrete nouns like *voiture*.

Most *dictionnaires de synonymes* are expressly designed to distinguish between words which are very close in meaning, but which collocate with different items. Verbs are limited according to the semantic range of their subject or object, and adjectives by the semantic features of the noun they modify. So it will be specified that *édifier*, in the literal sense of 'build', can be used of large buildings like *temple* or *palais*, but not of more humble structures like *garage* – except, of course, with ironic intent.[7]

Legrand also recommends the avoidance of catch-all nouns like *chose*, again proposing more semantically specific terms appropriate to the context; for example, *vertu* could substitute for *chose* in the sentence 'l'humilité est une chose bien rare'. Similarly, specific nouns are felt to be preferable to the neuter pronoun *cela*, so that

Vous aimez votre patrie; ce sentiment vous honore

is suggested, rather than

Vous aimez votre patrie; cela vous honore

Often a phrase or even a whole clause may be more succinctly replaced by a single word which contains the equivalent semantic information:

La ville a été complètement détruite

could be rephrased as

La ville a été dévastée

and the relative clause in

La guerre qui a lieu maintenant...

could be replaced by a single adjective:

La guerre actuelle...

In other words, conciseness, specificity and avoidance of ambiguity are the key features of 'good' French, at the lexical level.

At the other end of the register scale, it is of course very common to find semantically empty terms, like *chose*, *truc* or *machin*, the pronoun *ça*, the phrase *il y a*, being used over and over again in casual conversation. The over-use of hyperbolic terms – *extra*, *fantastique*, *fabuleux* – diminishes their expressive force and reduces them to simple terms of approbation. The innermost, high-frequency 'core' vocabulary of the language is used to the exclusion of items which are more marginal. Conversations are freely laced with 'fillers', such as *enfin*, *quoi*, *tu sais*, *alors*, *voilà*. These are not without meaning in a broad sense; they are part of general conversational strategies, providing thinking time for the speaker as she formulates her next utterance, checking that the interlocutor is paying attention, or signalling that she is or is not ready to relinquish her conversational 'turn'. No such strategies are of course necessary in a written text or a prepared monologue. One can also argue that in face-to-face encounters much information is provided by the context, and by gesture, facial expression, intonation, and so on, all of which are absent in a text, and less significant in a formal one-to-many discourse. Therefore the greater specificity of formal lexis is in a sense redundant in the kinds of situations in which informal registers are used.

Although much high-register vocabulary was originally borrowed from Latin and Greek, it is wrong to assume that all such words remain formal or technical. Many classical borrowings have become workaday terms without any particular stylistic resonance. There is nothing stylistically marked about the adjective *hebdomadaire*, despite the fact that it was borrowed from Greek in the sixteenth century. Conversely, there are many words which are traceable to Vulgar Latin, such as *las* or *trépas*, which most dictionaries label '*litt.*'. Nevertheless, there are numerous cases where a stylistic contrast exists between a Latin borrowing and a French word, as with *expirer* and *mourir*. Similarly, there is frequently a stylistic choice to be made, between a morphologically complex, Latin-based adjective and an adjectival phrase containing an indigenous noun. *Les muscles du bras* and *l'influence des étoiles* are less technical and formal than *les muscles brachiaux* (< Latin *brachia*), and *les influences stellaires* (< Latin *stella*).

The creation and use of complex affixed forms, Latinate or otherwise, can be overdone; Georgin (1973), grammarian and tireless chronicler of contemporary usage, criticised this trend, citing neologisms like *situationnel, conflictuel, élucidateur, désabsolutisation*, as clumsy, pretentious and usually redundant. Huyghe (1991) levels similar accusations at the media, politicians and academics alike, noting a preference for lengthy, obscure and pseudo-scientific expressions – *authentique* for *vrai, commensurable* for *comparable, maïeutique* for *explication, privilégier* for *choisir*, and so on.

Georgin claims that administrative language is particularly prone to pleonasms of the type *formellement interdit, exclusivement réservé*, and *doit obligatoirement*, where the meaning of the adverb is contained in that of the adjective or verb it modifies. He also castigates the use of circumlocutions, where a single word can provide all the necessary information; why say *apporter des modifications* or *mettre en état d'arrestation*, when *modifier* and *arrêter* are available? The longer phrase may be imposing, but it violates the principle of conciseness.

Beauvais (1970) is another wry critic of pretentious language, contrasting the clear lapidary style of genuinely good French with the overwrought and abstract concoctions of some writers, whom he parodies with acid humour:

> Il est indéniable que si, au lieu de: 'L'Etat, c'est moi', Louis XIV avait déclaré: 'Il y a identification fondamentale entre le concept étatique et la fonction présidentielle', son dossier s'en serait trouvé sensiblement allégé au regard de l'histoire.

He points out that circumlocutions lend themselves pefectly to euphemism; *le processus biologique terminal* is less threatening than *la mort*; just as *un pays en voie de développement* is easier on the conscience than *un pays sous-développé* – and certainly than *un pays pauvre*.

REGISTER, SOCIOLECT AND LITERARY STYLE

The manipulation of register and sociolect are only two of many elements which contribute to a writer's style, and a serious attempt to investigate literary style would take us well beyond the scope of this book. However, we have noted the existence of the lexical label *littéraire*, which implies that certain items are more appropriate to literary texts than to, say, administrative documents or conversational style. This compartmentalisation of the lexis was established in the seventeenth century and refined in the eighteenth, when there was much debate over the admissibility of certain items for literary use (see Chapter Eleven).

We find words which were dialectal, *vulgaires* or *bas* in the mouths of servants, thieves or peasants, in literary texts from Villon to Zola, but the narrator's voice was in general subject to strict self-censorship. As social barriers weakened, however, so did the rigid assignment of lexical items to specific modes of communication. Hugo championed the freedom of the writer to use a more varied lexical range, to revive archaic terms, to admit borrowings, and terms hitherto considered too technical or colloquial for inclusion in the work of a serious writer. This desire to free the lexis of literary expression is intimately connected with his political beliefs, and is indeed couched in revolutionary metaphors:

> Je mis un bonnet rouge au vieux dictionnaire...
> J'ai contre le mot noble à la longue rapière
> Insurgé le vocable ignoble, son valet...
>   'Réponse à un acte d'accusation' (1834)

This century, Céline further eroded the barriers between literary and spoken language, to write with a voice that speaks directly to the reader, drawing on many of the structures and idioms of everday speech. He despised academic French – 'un langage figé', and greatly admired both Villon and Rabelais for their use of the spoken language, regretting that this stylistic freedom was subsequently lost. A few lines from *Mort à crédit* (p. 12), in which the narrator reaches a point of total exasperation with the patients who come to his clinic, give an impression of his style:

> J'en ai bien marre des égrotants... En voici trente emmerdeurs que je rafistole depuis tantôt... J'en peux plus... Qu'ils toussent! Qu'ils crachent! Qu'ils se désossent! Qu'ils s'empédèrent! Qu'ils s'envolent avec trente mille gaz dans le croupion!... Je m'en tartine!... Mais la pleureuse elle m'agrafe, elle se pend vachement à mon cou, elle me souffle son désespoir. Il est plein de 'rouquin'... Je suis pas de force à lutter. Elle me quittera plus. Quand on sera dans la rue des Casses qui est longue et sans lampe aucune, peut-être que je vais lui filer un grand coup de pompe dans les miches... Je suis lâche encore... Je me dégonfle... Et ça recommence, la chansonnette. 'Ma petite fille!... Je vous en supplie, Docteur!...'

Analysis of such a passage would show that here we are dealing with just one element in his rich lexical repertoire, the judicious use of words of essentially *familier* register, which would have been well known to his readers; as he states in his *Entretiens avec le Professeur Y*: 'Piment admirable que l'argot! – mais un repas entier de piment vous fait un méchant déjeuner.' The impression of the spoken word emerges just as much from the syntax, with its loosely concatenated sentences and apparently redundant subject pronouns. Subsequently, authors as varied as Alphonse Boudard, Raymond Queneau and Frédéric Dard, creator of the San Antonio books, have felt free to use non-standard syntax, and to draw on the vivid and punchy lexis of the street.

Few writers, however, make more than a very limited use of *argot*, if we mean by this items associated exclusively with a working-class sociolect or, more narrowly, with the occupational style of the criminal fraternity (see next chapter). On the whole writers are concerned to be reasonably easily understood by a wide readership, and their lexis will be drawn from informal registers in general use, reserving more socially restricted items to colour the speech of 'low-life' characters, like Vautrin in Balzac's *Le Père Goriot*. (See Ullmann (1957: 81–93) on the sources of Balzac's and Hugo's knowledge of and fascination with this particular milieu.)

The lexis of some of Villon's *Ballades* can be categorised as *argot* in the traditional sense, and this must have made some of his verses obscure, even for his contemporaries. Boudard, himself familiar with the language of the underworld, is perhaps the contemporary writer nearest to Villon in his use of this kind of lexis.

Writers can play with registers, as composers change key. On some occasions, when the register is apparently inappropriate, the effect may be comic or ironic, as in the exchange between strangers in a bar, at the beginning of Camus's *La Chute*. We hear only one half of the conversation – that of the habitué already installed at the bar, who addresses the newcomer:

'Puis-je, Monsieur, vous proposer mes services, sans risque d'être importun? Je crains que vous ne sachiez vous faire entendre de l'estimable gorille qui préside aux destinées de cet établissement. Il ne parle, en effet, que le hollandais. A moins que vous ne m'autorisiez à plaider votre cause, il ne devinera pas que vous désirez du genièvre'.

'Voilà, j'ose espérer qu'il m'a compris; ce hochement de tête doit signifier qu'il se rend à mes arguments. Il y va, en effet, il se hâte, avec une sage lenteur... Mais je me retire, Monsieur, heureux de vous avoir obligé. Je vous remercie, et j'accepterais si j'étais sûr de ne pas jouer les fâcheux. Vous êtes trop bon. J'installerai donc mon verre auprès du vôtre.'

Soutenu expressions like *importun*, *estimable* (collocating curiously with *gorille*), *se rend à mes arguments*, *se hâte*, *jouer les fâcheux*, set in a framework of polished syntax, are bizarre in this social context, and the reader's curiosity is aroused.

He goes on to comment on his own use of language:

'... Quand je vivais en France, je ne pouvais rencontrer un homme d'esprit sans qu'aussitôt j'en fisse ma société. Ah! je vois que vous bronchez sur cet imparfait du subjonctif. J'avoue ma faiblesse pour ce mode, et pour le beau langage en général... '

The use of the imperfect subjunctive, which is virtually absent from any spontaneous spoken variety, heightens the humorous incongruity. It is soon revealed that the drinker is also a lawyer – a fact that he has already hinted at in a couple of grandiose metaphors.

This mixing of *niveaux de langue*, be it the use of pompous rhetoric (perhaps in the form of malapropisms) in a casual context, or inappropriately earthy and direct language in a formal setting, is one of the devices most favoured by comic writers and performers, from Rabelais to Coluche.

OCCUPATIONAL STYLES

Science and technology

The sort of objections levelled by Beauvais and others at inflated and obscure French in certain sections of the media and government administration are also directed at some technical discourse, which is often criticised as being unnecessarily complex and opaque. (Hence the pejorative overtones of the term 'jargon', in both English and French.) Etiemble (1966) reproached practitioners of the human sciences, in particular, with creating what he considered to be obscure terminologies, largely in order to affirm the scientific validity of their discipline, on a par with the 'exact' sciences like mathematics, physics or chemistry. Medical jargon, too, comes under fire, especially when Greek-based neologisms are preferred to French words that have been in the language for centuries; why invent *lipothimie* 'fainting fit' when *pâmoison* exists? Medicine is certainly a field in which specialists need to communicate with the general public, in whom medical terminology inspires a mixture of awe and mistrust. Doctors who are good communicators are able to adjust their style, and convey information clearly without unnecessary use of technical terms. Even among specialists, it is difficult to see how a term like *céphalée* is any more precise than *migraine*, or *éphélides* than *taches de rousseur* 'freckles'. Etiemble argues that dialectal words, the revival of archaic expressions, and the creation of transparent metaphors are all preferable to Greco-Latin formations as sources of new scientific terminology,.

On this, as on other linguistic issues, Etiemble was waging a rather quixotic battle. Greek and Latin have been the wellspring of scholarly and scientific vocabulary since the Middle Ages, with Greek roots proving particularly productive in the terminologies of modern science and technology. Not only are such terminologies international; the ease with

which the different lexical elements can be combined means that a lot of information can be expressed in a condensed form. Moreover, compounds of Greek origin can be easily suffixed, unlike indigenous compounds (see Chapter Six). So from *polygone* various derived forms – *polygonal*, *polygonacées*, *polygonation* – can be created. The distinctness of Greek roots from the rest of the lexis makes it easier to assign a specific semantic value to such forms, avoiding the heavy polysemy of most everyday lexical items. The meaning of a complex word can thus be 'unpacked', once the meaning of the elements is known: *-ologie* nearly always means 'the study of… ', *hydro-* means 'water', and so on. But even these most consciously unambiguous of lexical fields are not exempt from a degree of polysemy. In some compounds, *-graphe* may have the value 'writer of… ' as in *lexico-graphe*; in others, it indicates a machine which registers or transmits information in visual form, as in *télégraphe* or *spectrographe*. Its meaning is different again in *orthographe* – 'spelling'. Once lexical material is at large, freedom from ambiguity cannot be guaranteed, however important this may be to its users.

Many morphemes, like *poly-* and *-ologie*, recur throughout the different branches of science, while others are characteristic of specific disciplines.[8] The suffix *-acée(s)* marks a word as a botanical term meaning 'member of the family of… ', as in *rosacées*, *graminacées*, while words ending in *-tron*, like *neutron*, *cyclotron*, *électron*, are identifiable as belonging to the field of nuclear physics. Such linguistic elements constitute an indispensable framework for the description of taxonomies which are constantly changing as areas of knowledge are expanded and refined.

Specific lexical items or affixes aside, scientific texts are characterised by a predominance of noun phrases, often very complex in form, with almost every head noun being modified by at least one other noun and/or adjective. The following short passage on the symptoms of asthma, from a textbook on allergic reactions, contains twenty-six nouns, eleven adjectives or past participles and only five verbs:

> L'examen du thorax révèle la mise en jeu des muscles respiratoires accessoires, une distension du thorax, la faible amplitude des mouvements respiratoires, la sonorité augmentée à la percussion (traduisant la rétention thoracique), la diminution du murmure vésiculaire et surtout la présence de sibilants expiratoires (ou aux deux temps de la respiration si la crise est grave) qui signent la crise d'asthme. L'examen cardiovasculaire révèle des bruits du cœur normaux, une tachycardie modérée et une tension artérielle peu modifiée.
>
> From *Allergologie* by J. Bousquet *et al.* (1993)

While most scientific terminology remains obscure to the majority of speakers, a study has shown that once specialised terms are steadily filtering into the lexis of everyday life (see Dubois *et al.* 1960).[9] This may range from the spread of Greek morphemes like *micro-* and *télé-*, now associated with household products and technical gadgets of all kinds, to the metaphorical use of scientific terms, quite detached from their original field, but indicative of the cultural and emotional charge carried by that field (see Chapter Eight).

Computer science, the one true newcomer to the late twentieth-century technological scene, is linguistically speaking a special case, in that its social and commercial applications are such that ease of communication between specialists and non-specialist users is essential; in particular, those responsible for developing the mushrooming terminology associated with the software of microcomputers are highly motivated to keep it as transparent and 'user-friendly' as possible. Large numbers of neo-classical compounds may be acceptable within the scientific fraternity, as an internationally viable tool and symbol of membership of an élite group; but it is likely to be simply off-putting to the average user of the Internet. We are already seeing the development of metaphors like *ascenseur* for 'scroll-box', and neologisms like *surbrillance* for 'highlighting' or *photostyle* for 'light pen'. The monitoring of such a rapidly developing field, international and technical but far from élitist, should prove a rewarding study over the next ten or twenty years.

Law and administration

In the sixteenth century Montaigne asked: 'Pourquoi est-ce que notre langage commun, si aisé à tout autre usage, devient obscur et non intelligible en contrats et testaments?' Many would ask the same question today. The language of the law, above all others, should be unambiguous and clear. Legal terms in French are certainly given very precise definitions, since the system is based on a written legal code (the *Code Napoléon*), unlike the Anglo-Saxon system, based on precedent. Therefore ambiguity is rare, at least for the specialists involved. But to the general public, for whose benefit the legal system exists, much legal language is extremely obscure, both in its syntax and in its lexis. A couple of examples give a flavour of the styles of the Code itself, and of court decisions based upon it. Article 2279 explains the legal position of people involved in the possession of lost or stolen property:

> Article 2279. – En fait de meubles, la possession vaut titre.
> Néanmoins, celui qui a perdu ou auquel il a été volé une chose, peut la revendiquer pendant trois ans, à compter du jour de la perte ou du vol, contre celui dans les mains duquel il la trouve; sauf à celui-ci son recours contre celui duquel il la tient.

The first sentence ('As far as movables are concerned, bona fide possession creates good title', very approximately equivalent to the notion, 'Possession is nine tenths of the law') has syntactic simplicity and elegance. But *meubles* has the older, broader meaning of any movable property, and *titre*, a highly polysemous term in general parlance, has a very precise legal interpretation in this context. The exception to the general rule, explained in the rest of the Article, is more typical of the syntax of the Code, with a number of relative clauses, some of them coordinated, and an impersonal passive ('il a été volé une chose'); the final clause is practically unanalysable, but means in essence that the innocent possessor of such property, on being required to return it to the original owner, can seek redress against the person he acquired it from. (The problem of interpreting the last sentence lies in the absence of a main verb, and in finding a nominal antecedent for *celui-ci*.)

The following extract from a court ruling based on Article 2279 illustrates both the lexical and syntactic obstacles to comprehension, as far as the non-specialist is concerned:

> Attendu que l'arrêt énonce que Tellai soutient que la propriété du fonds de commerce ne présente aucun intérêt, la saisie portant sur des meubles corporels déterminés dont il avait la possession *anno domini* et de bonne foi, conformément aux exigences de l'article 2279 du Code civil, mais que tout d'abord, si l'on se réfère au dispositif de l'assignation introductive d'instance, Tellai demandait à voir dire et juger qu'il était régulièrement propriétaire du fonds de commerce de tissus indigènes sis à Bône, 5 *ter* rue de Jérusalem, et qu'il avait acquis du sieur Attal par acte sous seing privé du 10 janvier 1955, et qu'en outre la saisie a porté sur des lots de marchandises et sur la totalité de l'installation matérielle dudit fonds, que la règle portant qu'en fait de meubles, possession vaut titre, ne s'applique qu'aux meubles corporels susceptibles de tradition manuelle.

The initial phrase *attendu que* precedes any court ruling, but is otherwise semantically empty. The extract constitutes a single sentence and contains about a dozen clauses, beginning with three clauses embedded one within the other. Some expressions, like *assignation introductive d'instance*, *dudit, seing*, and *sieur*, are purely legal terms, while others, like *meubles* and *tradition*, have retained a meaning which has disappeared from general parlance. Latin phrases, like *anno domini*, are not uncommon; but even a good knowledge of Latin is not a great advantage to the non-specialist, as these too have specific meanings in a legal context.

Since such texts are dealing with highly technical matters, within a strictly codified framework, it could be argued that there is no reason why they should be transparent to the average citizen, any more than a text on inorganic chemistry. To render them comprehensible might entail introducing dangerous ambiguities – and would certainly lengthen them considerably. *Sous seing privé*, for example, would have to be glossed as something like 'signé mais non enregistré devant un notaire' – and so on. Most legal terms are a kind of technical shorthand, carrying a highly compressed meaning which is accepted throughout the profession. The syntactic complexity of many texts, however, must be baffling even for specialists.

In recent years, efforts have in fact been made to simplify and modernise legal terminology. A government Circular published in 1977 (*Journal Officiel* 24 September) aimed to 'faciliter la compréhension par les

justiciables du langage employé par les praticiens du droit'. It was proposed that twenty-nine Latin expressions should be rendered in French: for example, *ad nutum* should be replaced by *au gré de*, *de cujus* by *défunt*, *post nuptias* by *après le mariage*; while archaisms like *Le sieur...* should be replaced by *Monsieur...*, and many needlessly lengthy formulae should be shortened, hence 'ordonne l'exécution du jugement' should replace 'dit que le jugement sortira son plein et entier effet pour être exécuté selon ses forme et teneur'.

It would be interesting to discover how many of these recommendations have actually been applied. Such power is invested in the law that those who exercise it may be reluctant to relinquish a part of it by making their language more accessible.

Administrative documents, such as public notices transmitting legal information to the general public, are by comparison models of clarity and simplicity. Nevertheless, they share some of the characteristics of documents used within the legal profession.

Take, for example, the following notice to be found in the Paris metro:

Il est interdit
– d'introduire un animal dans l'enceinte du métropolitain ainsi que dans les voitures. Toutefois, les animaux domestiques de petite taille peuvent être admis lorsqu'ils sont transportés dans des sacs ou des paniers convenablement fermés
– de se livrer à la mendicité
– de troubler la tranquillité des voyageurs de quelque manière que ce soit, et de quêter.
Toute personne est tenue d'obtempérer aux injonctions des agents de la RATP tendant à faire observer les dispositions contenues dans le présent règlement.

Arrêté préfectoral du 9 décembre 1968

The elaborate syntax, with embedded clauses repeated in parallel, and use of the impersonal passive, is reminiscent of the court ruling. At the lexical level, the use of *le présent règlement* rather than *ce règlement*, and of items like *obtempérer à* and *injonctions* are also clear markers of legal/administrative style. One wonders whether the complex verb phrases *se livrer à la mendicité* and *troubler la tranquillité de* would not have been more simply (and clearly) rendered by *mendier* and *déranger*; just as *obtempérer aux injonctions de* essentially means *obéir à*. However, at least part of the function of such notices is to convey the authority and dignity of the law and those who apply it. The style itself is an important part of the message.

Legal–administrative style has influenced that of formal business correspondence; this may after all carry a certain legal weight, committing the writer to some future course of action. Expressions like *susmentionné* 'aforementioned' and *ci-après* 'hereafter' have a legalistic flavour. Others are immediate markers of this type of correspondence, like the opener *Comme suite à votre lettre du...* 'further to your letter of...' or the phrase *dans les meilleurs délais* 'as soon as possible'.

Also specific to this style are elements which may be viewed as redundant from a strictly referential point of view, but which have the function of expressing extreme politeness. Requests are prefaced by expressions like *Veuillez avoir l'obligeance de..., Nous vous serions reconnaissants de bien vouloir...*, and statements by *Nous nous permettons de vous signaler que...* and *Soyez assuré que...* As with administrative and legal language, circumlocutions are often used where simple verbs would be appropriate in *courant* style: *Nous restons dans l'espoir que...*, rather than *Nous espérons que..., Nous sommes au regret de...* rather than *Nous regrettons de...*, and so on.

ADVERTISING – WORDS THAT SELL

It is impossible to characterise the language of advertising as a single variety, either register or occupational style; the range of fields of discourse involved is vast, and copy-writers are masters at manipulating the stylistic resources of the language to suit their purpose. Something as intangible and psychologically complex as the art of persuasion can hardly be reduced to a handful of socio-linguistic variables. If, however, we limit our investigation to the analysis of the slogans or headlines used in display advertising, we find that a number of recurring linguistic features emerge.

Space is expensive, and the reader's attention span short and easily distracted by competing visual stimuli. Advertising slogans are therefore brief, which means that maximum impact must be made with the words used, so that semantically empty grammatical words (pronouns, auxiliary verbs, prepositions and the like) are kept to a minimum. Nouns, adjectives and verbs predominate, particularly nouns.

Brevity also helps to make slogans memorable – another key ingredient. But to be memorable means above all to be innovative; the potential customer must be intrigued and amused. Puns are therefore especially popular with copy-writers, since they have the dual function of compressing a great deal into a small space – two messages for the price of one, so to speak – while inviting the reader to participate in a linguistic game; the solution must be neither too difficult nor too obvious, so that the reader is neither frustrated nor bored; decoding the slogan provides that small thrill that comes with solving a riddle, or seeing the point of a joke. The ambiguity may reside in word boundaries being assignable in two different ways:

Les petits pois sont d'avril [an advertisement for frozen peas]

– or in the polysemy of a single lexical item:

Entre le bricolage et vous, il faut que ça colle [a heavy-duty glue]

The ambiguity inherent in personal pronouns can be cleverly exploited; who or what do *les* and *le* refer to in the *Jil* (men's underwear) headline?

Les discrets de Jil
Pour les voir, il faut le vouloir...

If some familiar phrase – a line from a popular song, a book title, a proverb – is borrowed and then modified, established memorability is combined with the faint shock which comes from the distortion, and the reader must reanalyse the phrase to make sense of it; hence the slogan for a skin product:

A la recherche du teint perdu

or for a brand of cigarettes:

Certains l'aiment Kool

At their most successful, the resonances of the original – in these cases *fin de siècle* elegance, and the brash, sexy dynamism of 1950s America – are in harmony with the product image.

Paradox too makes the reader reflect on how two apparently contradictory statements may in fact apply simultaneously. A Volkswagen car is

La petite géante

– which reassures readers that size is not a measure of a car's performance, while appealing to our sympathy for the tough little guy, the David figure who overcomes Goliath.

Syntax is often used to highlight such antithetical expressions:

La douce violence d'un parfum d'homme

suggests that if *douce* and *violence* are compatible, there is nothing incongruous about a man wearing perfume.

Many stylistic devices to be found in slogans are used in poetry, the most distilled of literary forms. Rhyme, rhythm, alliteration, repetition abound in slogans like

Roquefort: un plaisir fort... un plaisir fou
Crunch, le chocolat qui croustille
Pousse-Mousse: C'est bien plus malin pour se laver les mains

Adjectives may accumulate in climactic fashion:

Femme, de Rochas: Séduisant, sensible, envoûtant, présent, le plus femme des parfums...

This last example shows the freedom with which words can shift from one grammatical category to another. Here, it is the key noun, both the product name and the central concept, strategically placed at the culminating point of the list, that has the shock value of being used as a (masculine) adjective.

An advertisement for *Toastine* rusks uses the brand name as a verb and declines it accordingly, perhaps to suggest it is a product for all the family:

Je toastine, tu toastines, il toastine...

Similar morphological licence is used in

Swatchez-vous?
Swatch. La montre suisse en liberté

while the headline in an advertisement for carpets

Moquettez-vous couture

both turns one noun into a verb, and another (more unusually) into an adverb.

Noun + noun combinations, increasingly popular in many varieties of modern French, lend themselves particularly well to the medium of advertising, because they encapsulate so much information. It is up to the reader to supply the unstated semantic link between the two elements:

Disque Bleu avec filtre pureté
Le film couleur le plus vendu dans le monde
L'avenir automobile, Peugeot l'a déjà rêvé

Blending, which is rare in other varieties of French, comes into its own in advertising slogans:

Le Loto est spormidable!
Croustifondant... Galettes Verkade

A shampoo can be extolled as

Ebloumineux!... Splendifique!...

When it comes to devising brand names, all the devices available to the language are brought into play. Words may be truncated, sometimes with a built-in pun, as in *Permo* (< *eau permanente*) the brand name for a water-filtering system. Self-explanatory compounds like *Tue-tout* (an insect spray) or *Bronzactive* (a suntan lotion) are an easy way to convey the function of the product, while neo-classical forms like *Vérichrome* (a colour film) or *Dermophyl* (a skin lotion) carry an impressively scientific cachet. Both in brand names and in advertising copy the 'hyperbolic' prefixes of Greek and Latin origin, *super-*, *extra-*, *ultra-* and *hyper-* are heavily used – the latter especially in relation to products promoting a 'scientifically researched' image: *fond de teint hyper-matifiant*, and so on.

Possibly the easiest way to create a brand name is simply to change the spelling of a common word or phrase in a kind of orthographic pun. Hence the cheese *Forbon* and *Ferodo* tyres ('du fer au dos'), or *Yaxa* ('il n'y a que ça') for a depilatory cream. Given the popularity of Anglicisms in technical fields, and in youth culture, it is hardly surprising to find them being appropriated as brand names, such as *Wonder* batteries, *Miniwave* setting lotion, or *Dryclean* fabric cleaner, while *Babyliss* (electric hair-curler) is a hybrid compound, in which the French element has been given an anglicised orthography.

Copy-writers are always ready to exploit current slang or catchwords. Hence Joubert (1985) notes a rash of slogans in the early 1980s using the highly popular adjective *branché* 'trendy':

> San Pellegrino, c'est branché

> A table les branchés!
> Nappes et coordonnés Lotus

> Bouquet en branche
> bouquet branché
> bouquet garni Maggi

Although the ingenuity and imagination exercised in the creation of advertising slogans is obviously commercially driven, a delight in wordplay is probably a linguistic universal; it is certainly to be seen in its most spontaneous and unfettered form in the type of lexis which is discussed in the next chapter: that of *argot*, the most remote from the carefully controlled lexis of the written norm.

NOTES

1 Ager (1990) has a useful discussion of the criteria – educational, financial, and so on – according to which the population of France may be classified into socio-economic categories; he also outlines recent major shifts in membership of such groupings.
2 Confusingly, sociolinguists vary in their use of some basic terms. For example Trudgill and others use the term 'style' for what Hudson (and I) calls 'register' – and 'register' to refer to what is here termed 'occupational style'.
3 Class-maintaining suffixes added to verbs, adjectives and nouns often have this expressive function (usually pejorative, occasionally affectionate) in French. One has only to think of *écrivailler* and *écrivasser*, *pâlot* and *pâlichon*, *pleurnicher*, *hommasse* and *femmelette*.
4 Galisson's study of the terminology of football (1978) demonstrates how finer distinctions may be introduced into the notion of occupational style, since he contrasts the highly technical language of professionals – essentially players and

trainers – with that of sports journalists writing for *les amateurs éclairés*, even though this may itself sound relatively obscure to the uninitiated. Occupational style may therefore vary depending on the precise roles of the participants.

5 See, for example, Stourdzé and Collet-Hassan (1969).
6 Batchelor and Offord (1993a: 70–114) provide a brief analysis of the referential and stylistic differences of over 130 groups of near-synonyms.
7 With the availability of massive computer databases, in which concordances for any lexical item can be calculated, habitual collocations can now be established on a truly scientific basis.
8 See Kocourek (1982) for an analysis of the major processes of word formation and semantic change used in technical and scientific French.
9 Dubois *et al.* (1960) demonstrates an increase in the infiltration of scientific and technical terms, in two editions of the *PLI*. Such data must of course be treated with caution. It may not reflect changes in usage so much as changes in the policy of the dictionary makers concerned.

PROJECTS

1 Check in the introductions to three different monolingual dictionaries on the range of lexical labels used in each dictionary. What definitions, if any, are given to these, and to what extent do they vary from one to another? What degree of agreement is there in the labelling of the following?

occulter, agréer, s'éprendre de, infamie, derechef, garce, grabuge, fumiste

2 Using dictionaries of synonyms, thesauri and dictionaries of slang, find as many near-synonyms as possible for *fou, pauvre, beau, ennuyer, avare, sale* and *partir*. Categorise these according to register, and speculate on the reasons for any clustering you find within a specific register.

3 Check on the meanings, contextualised examples and lexical labels of these sets of words, and find out how each word in a set differs from the others, with respect to its habitual collocations, expressivity, or the register to which it is appropriate:

larron, malfrat, scélérat
mâcher, mâchonner, mâchouiller
funérailles, obsèques, enterrement, ensevelissement
doux, douceâtre, doucereux
méticuleux, minutieux, vétilleux
cadavre, dépouille, macchabée

4 Transpose the metro notice on p. 194 into a style more appropriate to informal conversation, as if you were giving a friend the gist of the information it contains.

5 What linguistic devices are used in the following slogans? How successful do you think they are?

Aide-toi et Contrex t'aidera (artificial sweetener)
Vivre de Woolite et d'eau fraîche (fabric softener)
Danessa – une mousse tellement chocolat
Dur avec la saleté, tendre avec les couleurs (soap powder)
Mitsubishi mon amour
Sans parfum la peau est muette

FURTHER READING

Ager, D. 1990 *Sociolinguistics and Contemporary French*, Cambridge, Cambridge University Press; see Chapter 7 for discussion of socio-economic class membership in France, with further bibliography, and Chapters 9 and 10 for some analysis of occupational styles and *niveaux de langue*.

Batchelor, R.E. and Offord, M.H. 1993a *Using French: A Guide to Contemporary Usage*, Cambridge, Cambridge University Press

—— 1993b *Using French Synonyms*, Cambridge, Cambridge University Press

Beauvais, R. 1970 *L'Hexagonal tel qu'on le parle*, Paris, Hachette

Bousquet, J., Godard, P. and Michel, F.-B. 1993 *Allergologie*, Paris, Ellipses

Céline. L.-F. 1952 (4th edition) *Mort à crédit*, Paris, Gallimard

—— 1955 *Entretiens avec le Professeur Y*, Paris, Gallimard

Cellard, J. 1985 *Anthologie de la littérature argotique des origines à nos jours*, Paris, Editions Mazarine; demonstrates the range of themes and genres in which this 'marginal' lexis has been used.

Corbin, P. 1980 ' "Niveaux de langue" ': pèlerinage chez un archétype', *Bulletin du centre d'analyse du discours* 4, Université de Lille III

Corbin, D. and Corbin, P. (1980) 'Le monde étrange des dictionnaires: les marques d'usage dans le Micro-Robert', *Bulletin du centre d'analyse du discours* 4 Université de Lille 3

Dubois, J., Guilbert, L., Mitterand, H. and Pignon, H. 1960 'Le mouvement général du vocabulaire français de 1949 à 1960, d'après un dictionnaire d'usage', *Le Français moderne*, April/July, and in J. Dubois and C. Dubois (eds) 1971 *Introduction à la lexicographie*, Paris, Larousse

Etiemble, R. 1966 *Le Jargon des sciences*, Paris, Hermann

Feyrey, M. 1973 'L'anglomanie dans les marques de fabrique et les raisons sociales françaises', *La Banque des mots* 6

Gadet, F. 1989 *Le Français ordinaire*, Paris, Armand Colin

—— 1992 *Le Français populaire*, Paris, PUF Que Sais-Je?

Galisson, R. 1978 *Recherches de lexicologie descriptive: la banalisation lexicale*, Paris, Nathan

GARS (Groupe aixois de recherches en syntaxe, Université de Provence) have since 1970 been publishing the results of their research into the syntax of spoken French in the journal *Recherches sur le français parlé*.

Georgin, R. 1953 *Pour un meilleur français*, Paris, André Bonne

—— 1963 *L'Inflation du style*, Paris, Editions sociales françaises

—— 1973 *Le Code du bon langage: le langage de l'administration et des affaires*, Paris, Editions sociales françaises

Giles, H. and Powesland, P.F. 1975 *Speech Style and Social Evaluation*, London, Academic Press; includes discussion of studies carried out in Britain, the USA and French-speaking Canada.

Grunig, B. 1990 *Les Mots de la publicité*, Paris, Presses du CNRS; for a detailed linguistic analysis of advertising slogans.

Guiraud, P. 1968a *Le jargon de Villon ou le gai savoir de la Coquille*, Paris, Gallimard

Hudson, R. 1996 (2nd edition) *Introduction to Sociolinguistics*, Cambridge, Cambridge University Press; for a thorough introduction to the key concepts and issues in sociolinguistics.

Hugo, V. 1967 'Réponse à un acte d'accusation', *Les Contemplations I*, 7 in Hugo, *Œuvres poétiques*, Paris, Gallimard

Huyghe, F.-B. 1991 *La Langue de coton*, Paris, Robert Laffont

Joubert, M.-J. 1985 *Slogan mon amour*, Paris, Barrault; a brief, historically oriented account of both political and advertising slogans, from the 1930s to the 1980s, organised by topic.

Journal Officiel de la République française 1985 *Langue française: enrichissement du vocabulaire: textes législatifs et réglementaires*, Brochure no. 1468; see pp. 289-97 for recommendations relating to the modernisation of legal terms.

Judge, A. and Lamothe S. 1995 *Stylistic Developments in Literary and Non-Literary French Prose*, Wales, Mellen Press; for a panoramic view of the changes in the range of styles developed by French writers, from the twelfth century to the present day.

Kocourek, R. 1982 *La langue française de la technique et de la science*, Wiesbaden, Germany, Brandstetter; examines graphic, textual, syntactic and lexical characteristics of technical and scientific texts.

Le Doran, S. 1993 *Le Dictionnaire San-Antonio* Paris, Fleuve noir; gives some idea of the writer's lexical versatility, mixing contemporary slang and idiosyncratic neologisms.

Lefebvre, C. 1983 'Les notions de style', in *La Norme linguistique*, eds. E. Bédard and J. Maurais, Paris, Robert; for an overview of different conceptions of the notion of *niveaux de langue*.

Legrand, E. 1972 *Stylistique française*, Paris, J. de Gigord

Ponthier, F. 1978 *Le grand livre de la correspondance commerciale et d'affaires*, Paris, De Vecchi, Grenoble

Sanders, C. (ed.) 1993 *French Today*, Cambridge, Cambridge University Press, contains a number of chapters relevant to the study of style and register, including: C. Sanders, 'Sociosituational variation', which indicates the kind of phonological and syntactic features which differentiate socially and situationally determined varieties of the language; S. Noreiko, 'New words for new technologies', on the kinds of neologisms favoured in fields such as micro computing; J. Durand, 'Sociolinguistic variation and the linguist', on the analysis of socio-linguistic data in French.

Stourdzé, C. and Collet-Hassan, M. 1969 'Les niveaux de langue', in *Le Français dans le monde* 65: 18–21.

Trudgill, P. 1972 'Sex, covert prestige and linguistic change in the urban British English of Norwich', in *Language and Society* 1: 179–96; for discussion of the covert prestige attached to working-class speech.

—— 1992 *Introducing Language and Society*, Harmondsworth, UK, Penguin (in particular, Chapters 1, 2, 5 and 6); an excellent introduction to socio-linguistic variation and starting-point for further reading.

Ullmann, S. 1957 *Style in the French Novel*, Cambridge, Cambridge University Press

Chapter 10

Argot

From criminal slang to *la langue des jeunes*

One of the most striking characteristics of the French lexis today is the amazing vigour with which new words are being created by certain social groups. This creativity, unrivalled in the languages of European neighbours, has provoked much controversy, as well as providing material for many publications, both popular and scholarly.[1] This type of lexis is given the broad label of *argot*, but as we shall see this is a term which in fact covers quite a heterogeneous collection of phenomena.

DEFINITIONS

Any group with common interests, involved in cooperative activity, be they soldiers, musicians, thieves, sportsmen or radio hams, are likely to develop a distinctive lexis. When the lexis is related to the group's occupation or profession, we can talk about a shared 'occupational style' (see previous chapter), which is likely to be opaque to the outsider. This opacity is an inevitable secondary feature of any specialised terminology. However, the primary function of lexis confined to a specific group may be social: it may be used to enhance solidarity among the members, or to exclude non-members. We may recognise this functional difference by referring to such a lexis as 'slang' or *argot*. Slang expressions are therefore not necessarily technical, but often refer to quite everyday activities.

Dictionary definitions do not always recognise such a distinction, but suggest that the term *argot* applies equally to occupational styles. According to the *PLI*, *argot* is 'Vocabulaire particulier à un groupe social, à une profession; spécialement, langage des malfaiteurs, du milieu'. All dictionaries make reference to the vocabulary of les *malfaiteurs*, *la pègre* or *le milieu*, in other words, of the criminal fraternity, and this is the sense in which the term has traditionally been used in France. We have evidence for this type of slang (first known as *jargon*) going back to the Middle Ages, initially in the account of the trial of the notorious Coquillard gang in the mid-fifteenth century; the poet Villon, who was thought to be implicated in some of their exploits, used *jargon* liberally in some of his *Ballades* (see Guiraud 1968a).

While crime may be considered a profession, it is the consciously cryptic function of much of its lexis which distinguishes it from that of other socio-professional groups. The need for secrecy also helps to explain the vitality of the lexis, in which new expressions are constantly being coined, as the old ones become too widely known.

Some claim (e.g. Calvet 1993) that the classic *argot* of the underworld is on the wane, while others (e.g. Brunet 1990) demonstrate its continuing vigour. Its influence is certainly to be seen in current dictionaries of slang: many of the semantic fields which are teeming with slang terms – those relating to violence, money, jail, the police, alcohol, prostitution – are associated with criminal activity. Colin and Mével (1992) give over thirty words for 'prison' and 140 for 'prostitute'. Many of these are however relics of bygone usage; dictionaries tend to accumulate terms, without necessarily indicating which are current and which obsolete, even when this is known. (The problems of monitoring spoken as opposed to written usage were mentioned in our first chapter.)

Recently, criminal *argot* has been revitalised by a profusion of terms relating to illegal drugs (Cahoreau and Tison 1987). Some expressions, such as *speed* or *crack*, can simply be considered borrowings that have been adopted along with their referent. Others, however, are slang variants of such terms: *hasch*, *shit*, *teush* are synonyms of *haschich*, just as *pompe* and *shooteuse* are equivalents of *seringue*.

FROM *ARGOTIQUE* TO *FAMILIER*

In the last chapter we saw the difficulty experienced by lexicographers in assigning words unequivocally to the category of *argotique*, *populaire* or *familier*. If much small-scale criminal activity is largely the preserve of the dispossessed of urban working-class communities,[2] then there is no problem in classifying the associated lexis as both *argotique* and *populaire*; it is the lexis of a subgroup (defined by activity), of a wider community (defined in socio-economic terms). It is natural that words beginning as criminal slang should be first adopted by the wider working class community – especially if the original users are seen as an élite group. In relation to traditional slang, Céline was convinced that 'C'est la haine qui fait l'argot. L'argot est fait pour exprimer les sentiments vrais de la misère';[3] in other words, he saw slang as an expression of the class struggle. It may even be the case that there is greater lexical creativity in working-class speech generally than in that of other socio-economic groups, if we discount technical domains. The less speakers are exposed to the linguistic norm, the less one might suppose they are fettered by it and by the constraints traditionally placed on lexical innovation.

For the wider public the marginality of the *malfaiteurs* and the taboo nature of much of their activity has made their code a focus of fascination. An additional factor in the social promotion of slang may be the covert prestige of working-class speech, stereotyped in many communities as energetic, masculine and direct (Trudgill 1972), so that its lexis may be used to signal informality, toughness or solidarity by speakers higher up the social scale; that is, it may be adopted as marking *familier* register. In turn, frequent and widespread use makes many originally *familier* terms acceptable as part of the norm, so that they may end up being classifiable as *courant* or even *soutenu. Cambrioleur* 'burglar', *narquois* 'sardonic', *fourbe* 'deceitful', *polisson* 'rascally' and *dupe* are all words which originated in the marginal lexis of criminal slang and climbed the social ladder to respectability. Occasionally, a word remains faithful to its humble origins; the fifteenth-century slang verb *se gourer* 'to boob' is still labelled *argotique* or *populaire* in dictionaries today. The social mobility of slang words is not a recent phenomenon. *Tête* (< *testa* 'tile' or 'broken pot') and *cheval* (< *caballus* 'nag') were probably first used as derogatory or humorous soldiers' slang in the the armies of Imperial Rome, supplanting the Classical Latin *caput* and *equus* in most of the Romance languages. Similarly, *tuer* is derived from the slightly sinister, mock-euphemistic *tutari* 'to

protect', a semantic development echoed in English by the slang expression 'to take care of'.

The difficulties of monitoring a lexis which is essentially cryptic, restricted to the oral mode and confined to small groups may be imagined; one could argue that when items become sufficiently widely known to be admitted to 'slang' dictionaries, most of them have already made the transition to the status of *familier* register. Many of the examples given in this chapter will indeed have extended their function in this way.

The spread of terms from closed milieux to general usage has surely accelerated over the last century, when huge social changes have taken place, blurring formerly rigid class distinctions. People are much more mobile, geographically and socially, than in previous generations, and may belong to any number of different social and professional networks. Above all, universal education and the mass media have exposed people to a much wider range of varieties than ever before. Words coined by a small group can be put into national circulation in a matter of days by media ever hungry for novelty, and eager to show themselves up to date with the latest trend or issue.

ARGOT AND YOUTH CULTURE

Over the last twenty years or so, France has witnessed a veritable explosion of lexical creativity among the young, which has inspired academic research projects, popular media investigations and even 'instruction manuals' for the uninitiated (see for example, Boudard 1990, Bézard 1993, Calvet 1993).

This lexis seems to be very different in function from the classic *argot* of the underworld. If the teenage to young adult group can be thought of as a loosely knit series of social networks, then this *langue des jeunes* can be seen as a kind of broad sociolect marked above all at the lexical level. Recent evidence suggests that there may be a common pool of expressions which are widely used among the young, but also that individual groups, differing according to age, ethnic background, group allegiance or region have distinctive *argots*.[4] Young *Beurs*, or children of immigrants from North Africa, have contributed Arabic expressions, sometimes disguised by the processes of *verlan* (see below), which are apparently being adopted by members of their peer groups of non-Arab origin.

Since youth has such positive connotations in our culture, it is not surprising that older people wish to identify with it, and borrow from this lexical source in their informal use of language. It is even to be found in the headlines of the trendier daily or weekly papers, such as *Libération* or *Le Nouvel Observateur*. This undoubtedly contributes to the rapid turnover of some lexical items, with the young constantly wishing to distance themselves from their elders, and scorning the use of outdated slang.

Moreover, since the standard language symbolises authority, be it of the state, the forces of law and order, or the older generation, lexical creativity beyond the bounds of the norm can be seen as an expression of revolt against or subversion of these powers. As Désirat and Hordé (1988: 56) put it: 'rejeter le lexique estimé "correct" marque souvent le refus des autorités qui le consacrent'. A parallel may be drawn here with Céline's explanation of the origins of traditional slang; but conflict between the generations, like that between the classes, is surely only one of the motivating factors underlying the phenomenon of youth slang. At least as important is the positive sense of belonging to a group sharing tastes in music, dress, food, leisure and sports activities. All types of slang have conflictual and cohesive functions. However, the *argot* of the underworld is more typically professional and cryptic, while *la langue des jeunes* is more an affirmation of group identity, strongly characterised by a purely ludic delight in stretching the lexical resources of the language to the uttermost.

THE SOURCES OF *ARGOT*

Unsurprisingly, for a lexis originating and functioning essentially in the spoken mode, and often restricted to a close-knit social group, quite a high proportion of slang terms have untraceable etymologies. But for those whose origins are known, it is clear that much the same sources, both internal and external, are involved as for the more standard lexis. On the whole, though, internal sources are favoured, and of these, certain morphological and semantic processes have proved especially productive.

Borrowings

Relatively few slang expressions are drawn from foreign sources; those languages that are involved are in close geographical proximity to France, or are spoken within its borders, with the result that prolonged and direct personal contact has fostered linguistic exchange. Occitan, for example, has provided *truc* 'thingummy', *escarper* 'to rob and murder' and *tire* 'car' or 'taxi', and from Italian come *gonze* 'bloke' and *basta* 'enough'.

A few long-established terms, like *berge* 'year' or *chourer* 'to steal', come from Romany, inherited from the time when Romany travellers went from fair to fair and town to town, marginal to settled society and on occasion operating on the margins of the law.

Unusual initial consonant clusters betray the German origins (probably from Alsace-Lorraine) of *schlass* 'drunk', *schlof* 'sleep' and *schnouf*, originally 'tobacco', but recycled to mean 'heroin'. The very fact of containing sounds or sound patterns marginal to the French system may give a word added attraction as an expressive slang term; *tchatcher* 'to sweet-talk' or 'deliver a spiel', with its repeated affricate, is a much-travelled term: it seems to have been borrowed from Spanish into the urban slang of Algiers, and thence into French.

A number of Arabic borrowings reflect the legacy of the French colonial presence in North Africa, some perhaps originating as soldiers' slang. *Toubib* 'doctor' and *bled* 'village' are both widely used, while *maboul* 'crazy', *fissa* 'quickly' and *chouïa* 'a little' have a more limited circulation. More recent still are Arabisms like *zarma!* (meaning something like 'Well, really!') or *gaori* 'Frenchie' introduced by the young *Beurs* of the urban ghettoes.

Given the heavy borrowing from English in many fields, it is perhaps surprising that slang is relatively untouched by it. Of the 960 entries in Calvet's word-list (1993), only 20 come from English, and about half of these are connected with hard drugs, like *shooter*, *sniffer* and *dope*, which might be considered technical borrowings rather than slang alternatives to more standard expressions.

Harder to trace than foreign borrowings, though probably more numerous, according to Guiraud (1968c: 103) are borrowings from French dialects. As we saw in Chapter Four, regional varieties of French have for centuries been a source of lexical enrichment for the standard language, and many such borrowings must have been taken up originally in working-class milieux, sometimes by specific social or professional groups. People migrating to Paris from the provinces, for example, tended to form small local communities, only gradually becoming socially and linguistically assimilated, often contributing a few expressions to the larger speech community in the process. Some loans have remained appropriate to informal speech styles. Northern varieties have given words like *bagnole* 'car', *guibole* 'leg' and *taule* 'jail', while from the west come *cagibi* 'cubby-hole', *barder* 'to deteriorate' and *gouailler* 'to mock', and from the area around Lyon *frangin* 'brother', *gnaf* 'shoe-mender', *pognon* 'cash' and *grolles* 'shoes'. However, further research is needed to test Guiraud's claim (1968c: 105) that 'la majeure partie des mots d'argot – sans doute 80 % à 90 % – sont d'origine dialectale'.

Semantic change

Slang words are more frequently formed by the simple expedient of taking an existing word and giving it a very different meaning. The universal processes of metonymy and metaphor, examined in Chapter Seven, can transform the meaning of a lexical item to such an extent that it takes some effort of the imagination to retrace the connection involved. It is not immediately obvious, for example, why *lourder* should mean *mettre à la porte*, or 'throw out'. *Une lourde* was used to mean 'a door' – originally, it is thought, the heavy door of a prison, from criminal slang; here, one particular aspect of the referent has been taken to stand for the referent as a whole – a typically metonymic shift. (Very similar conceptual connections have been made in the English slang term for jail, 'slammer'.) The noun has then been transformed into a verb by a simple change in word class. A rather more transparent metonymic process has operated in the substitution of *palpitant* or *battant* for *cœur*; in these cases, habitual action stands for the performer of the action.

Slang is also rich in metaphors, or figures of speech involving replacement based on similarity. Hence *une brioche* is a paunch, *une asperge*, a skinny figure, *un ventilateur*, a helicopter. Longer expressions often encapsulate more elaborate or humorous images: *écraser le champignon* is 'to put one's foot down', or 'step on the gas', while *piège à macaronis* is 'a beard'.

Since much of slang is aggressive and contemptuous (remember Céline's assertion 'C'est la haine qui fait l'argot'), and since humans seem to have a traditionally negative view of animals, words for animals, or parts of them, are often used metaphorically of humans. *Pattes* is used to mean both arms and legs, *gueule* and *bec* to mean mouth. Denigratory animal-based words for women include both *chameau* and *cheval*, meaning approximately 'old cow', and *chèvre* and *poule*, meaning 'tart' and 'bit of fluff'.

Police are contemptuously referred to as *les poulets* or *les perdreaux*; the metaphor is probably based on the vulnerable and small-brained nature of these birds, and also perhaps on their habit of pecking hopefully at odds and ends on the ground, much as police may hunt for pieces of evidence. The metaphor of the police as *les condors*, while still in the same broad semantic field, is rather more threatening, as is the metonymic *les cognes* (once again, habitual action stands for the agent of the action).[5]

The commonest slang (now simply *familier*) word for police – *les flics* – comes from a dialectal word for 'fly', based perhaps on the idea of police buzzing around dirty or distasteful events; or indeed, from the villain's point of view, being an irritation and a nuisance.

It is quite common for series of metaphors to accumulate in this way – variations on a semantic theme, so to speak, by what Guiraud (1985) calls 'synonymic substitution'. It is as if one image triggers others on the basis of the same shared features, like the long-established range of images for the head as fruit: *poire, cerise, fraise, pomme, citron...* Some may be both imaginative and humorous, like the elaborate series of metaphors, meaning 'to be a bit crazy' – *avoir un rat dans la contrebasse, un cafard dans la tire-lire, une araignée dans le plafond, une chauve-souris dans le beffroi* – all following the same syntactic pattern and all based on the image of some small desperate creature scuttling around in a confined place. Metonymy of cause and effect is involved in another series of words for 'crazy': *toqué*, *fêlé, tapé, percuté*; the underlying notion here is that of madness being the result of physical damage to the brain.

Complex semantic relationships underly a number of words for money – always a magnetic source of attraction for slang expressions. *Blé* and *fric* (originally *fricot*, a basic stew, or staple food of the poor), rather like 'bread' and 'dough' in English, can be interpreted metaphorically (they are like money in being essential to life), or metonymically (money is the means to buying the essentials of life).

Quantified money tends to be treated metaphorically. *Une brique* (10,000 francs) recalls the shape of a thick wad of notes, while *une balle* (a franc) resembles the shape of a single coin. The expression *pas un radis* 'not a cent' could be either metaphorical or metonymic in origin; either the substitution is based on the shared shape and size of the coin and the vegetable or, like *fric*, *un radis* is taken as a basic and cheap food item; if you can't afford even that, then you really are hard up.

Penury is a notion which has attracted a good many terms – indicating again the popular origins of much slang. *Fauché* and *à sec* are rather like 'cleaned out' in English; while expressions like *être dans la panade* (a soup based on bread) or *dans la purée* (mashed potatoes) both take us back to the connection between money and the staple diet of the poor.

The kind of mental and linguistic short cuts which metonymy often entails make it ideally suited to slang; in informal face-to-face exchanges, shared knowledge and plenty of immediate contextual information make it possible to truncate the message without its becoming impenetrable. A bill can simply be *la douloureuse*, a policeman *un pourri*. A different kind of ellipsis involves reducing nouns in slang expressions to pronouns, or omitting them altogether: *tu me casses les pieds* becomes *tu me les casses* and *il va encaisser* implies *encaisser des coups*. The pronouns *en* and *un* in *je vais m'en jeter un* 'have a drink' can be related to more explicit nouns like *un verre de vin*. On the other hand, *en* in *j'en ai ras le bol* or *je m'en fous* has a very variable meaning, depending on the context in which it is uttered.

The most complete semantic disguise is the use of words to mean their opposite; just as *terrible* has for a long time meant 'terrific' in *familier* register, so now does *méchant*, while *faire un malheur* means to be a huge success. *Pas triste* or *pas gai*, on the other hand, are simply cases of excessive understatement (known as 'litotes'), as they mean 'fabulous' and 'dismal', respectively.

The linguistic taboos normally surrounding subjects like death, sex and madness do not seem to operate where slang is concerned. It is perhaps the very emotional charge of taboo topics which has made them such powerful centres of attraction in the non-standard lexis. Nevertheless, euphemisms are to be detected, sometimes in the form of ironic understatement; *arranger* means 'to fix' or 'sort out' in the sense of 'to beat up', while *buter* (literally 'bump') means 'to kill'.

The plethora of erotic metaphor to be found in any dictionary of slang (over sixty words for the sexual act in Giraud's (1981) work, and even more for the male and female genitals) can be only partially explained by the connection with prostitution, and hence the criminal underworld. Guiraud has a more complex socio-psychological explanation, which is discussed briefly at the end of Chapter Eight.

Word formation

Most of the traditional processes of word formation are used to create slang terms, although some processes seem to be especially favoured. Compounds, of the noun + preposition + noun type, often embody humorous metaphors, like *boîtes à parfum* 'smelly feet' or *jus de chaussettes* 'weak coffee'; while verb + noun compounds tend to be metonymies of habitual behaviour or cause and effect, like *tire-môme* for 'midwife', *pince-cul*, 'a knees-up', *tape-cul* 'an old banger'.

Verbs can easily be created by simply assigning an existing noun, usually itself a slang term, to the regular *-er* conjugation, so that *flingue* 'gun' gives *flinguer* 'to shoot', *pigeon* 'a sucker' gives *pigeonner* 'to fleece' and so on. If *fauché* is 'broke' then *défaucher* is 'to bail someone out', if *rond* is 'drunk', then *se dérondir* is 'to sober up'. (Occasionally verbs can change their precise syntactic function; *assurer* and *craindre* in standard French must have an object; in slang however, *il assure* 'he's cool' or *ça craint* 'it's tough' are used intransitively.)

Rather more unusual is the shift in word class from noun to adjective, as in *être classe* 'classy', or *être galère* 'a drag', or *être canon* 'stunning'. This is not unlike the modish use of nouns in expressions like *être télé*, *être mouvement*, and so on, meaning 'to like, or be in favour of something', which seems to have been taken up by the media.

Many of the suffixes associated with slang, such as *-aille*, *-asse* and *-ard*, have pejorative overtones. The latter is the most productive, as in *soiffard* 'boozer', *chauffard* 'road hog', *motard* 'biker', *chançard* 'lucky bastard'. A generic term for the police is *la flicaille*, a blond can be *une blondasse*, *connasse* means 'silly cow', while *(avoir la) pétasse* means '(to be in) a funk'. Verbs too may be formed with *-asser* or *-ailler*, as in *chiasser* 'to be shit-scared', or *causailler* 'to natter'.

Taboo roots are particularly favoured for whole families of derived forms: *foutre* has given rise to, among others, *foutoir* 'a dump', *foutraque* 'crazy', *foutriquet* 'little twerp' and *foutral* 'amazing', while *merde* has supplied *merdeux* 'arse-hole', *merdique* 'bloody hard', *merdouille* 'crap', *merdier* 'a hell of a mess'.

Occasionally, a 'learned' suffix may be employed in ironic, pseudo-learned fashion: *la punkitude* being derived from *punk* and *la craignitude*, an alternative to *la crainte*. The Latin case-ending *-ibus*, as in *pedibus* (= *à pied*) and *mortibus* (= *mort*), is probably a relic of the Latin-based slang of the Grandes Ecoles of the nineteenth century.

But the most important single process is the use of abbreviation, or 'clipping', a relatively recent development (see George 1980). Either the beginning of a word ('*ricain* from *américain*, '*pitaine* from *capitaine*), but more usually the final syllable or syllables, are lost: *apparte* from *appartement*, *mob* from *mobylette*, *ciné* from *cinéma*.

Clipping started to be used heavily in student slang from the late nineteenth century; hence the long-established forms *rédac* (*rédaction*), *géo* (*géographie* or *géométrie*), *récré* (*récréation*), and so on. It is now so widespread that one might consider it a feature of *français familier*, as well as of *argot*. Recent clipped forms include expressions where the abbreviation has taken place across word boundaries: *tee-shirt* for example being clipped to *teesh'* and *après-midi* to *aprèm'*.

Many clipped forms end in *-o*, like the first element of neo-classical compounds of the *métropolitain*, *thermomètre* type. This ending is extended to clipped words where no '*o*' is present in the full form, as in *alcoolo* for *alcoolique*. The popularity of the ending may also be due in part to the presence of the homophonous diminutive suffix, to be found in a handful of long-established expressive names, nouns and adjectives: *Charlot, Jeannot, angelot, vieillot, pâlot*.

Although it is extremely rare for morphemes to be invented out of thin air, so to speak, a number of suffixes of this kind, with no traceable etymologies, do occur in slang – usually added to clipped forms; hence *Amerloque* for *Américain* and *Chinetoque* for *Chinois*, *fastiche* for *facile*, *cinoche* for *cinéma*, *boutanche* for *bouteille*. (These recall the fanciful suffixes we find in the coded *loucherbem* slang mentioned below.) Sometimes a series of variations on a single root are to be found – not only *Amerloque*, but *Amerlot* and *Amerluche*. Other suffixes have a Spanish flavour: *rapidos* (*rapidement*), *gratos* (*gratis*); or *-aga* as in *pastaga* from *pastis*, *-ida* as in *marida* from *mariage*. Derogatory morphemes may be slipped in, in the guise of innocent 'nonsense' suffixes, *adjutant* becoming *adjupète*, for example, and *sourd* becoming *sourdingue* (*dingue* being slang for 'crazy').[6]

Clipping may also combine with reduplication; hence *jojo* from *joli*, *mimi* from *mignon*, *cracra* from *crasseux*. Very occasionally it is the final syllable that survives to be reduplicated: *zonzon* has been derived from both *maison* and *prison*. These are reminiscent of forms found in child language and lexicalised by adults, such as the established *dodo* for *dormir*, or *pipi* from *pisser*. Sometimes entire words are reduplicated, provided they are monosyllabic, as in *dur-dur* and *gai-gai*.

When several of these processes of affixation and abbreviation are applied, in almost frenzied fashion, the end result bears virtually no resemblance to the original. How can we relate *saucisson*, for example, to *sifflard*? Luckily we have the intermediary form *sauciflard*, which we can see is the result of end-clipping and resuffixation, before its initial syllable is removed.

When semantic change combines with abbreviation, the result is equally impenetrable. Who could guess that *les froms* 'Whites' can be traced back to a metaphor, *les fromages blancs*, which has subsequently been reduced by ellipsis to *fromages*, and then by clipping to *froms*?

SLANG AND WORD GAMES

Children in all cultures play with words as part of the language-learning process (see Plénat 1991). It is perhaps a continuation of this capacity that we see in some of the more unusual transformations used to disguise words in slang.

Some occupational varieties, now vanished or moribund, favoured complex remodelling of ordinary words to establish a kind of secret code. Both **largonji**, first brought to light in an account of nineteenth-century criminal slang (see Vidocq 1973), and **loucherbem**, used by the butchers of La Villette in Paris from the nineteenth century (Robert l'Argenton 1991), involve the same kinds of phonological manipulation of words, in order to disguise them. The names themselves are examples of the encoding processes, operating on the words *jargon* and *boucher*.

Three stages are involved:

1 Remove the initial consonant to the end of the word (*jargon → argon-j*, *boucher → oucher-b*)
2 Put 'l' at the beginning of the word (*largonj-*, *loucherb-*)
3 Add some vowel, or vowel + consonant, as a pseudo-suffix (*largonji*, *loucherbem*).

Although this kind of slang is little used nowadays, a few forms have been lexicalised and entered the general fund of slang lexis – such as *loubé* for *bout* 'a tiny bit', or *loufoque* for *fou*. The latter may even undergo clipping, to *louf*.

Another form of word game, **verlan** (< *l'envers*), which goes back to the sixteenth century, has seen a spectacular renaissance since the second world war. In recent years, it has been taken up with enthusiasm by the young, and is a major feature of *la langue des jeunes* today. Essentially, it consists of inverting the order of syllables or of sounds and seems to operate equally on slang and non-slang expressions. The following set of rules can account for most forms of *verlan*:

1 For words of more than one syllable, the order of the syllables is reversed: *féca* for *café*, *tromé* for *métro*, *guétupor* for *portugais*, *rettegaci* for *cigarette*.[7]

Rider to rule 1: monosyllabic words ending in an orthographic *e* are often treated as if they are bisyllabic (as indeed they are in some varieties of French), so that *grosse* becomes *segro*; in other words, the first vowel is the unstressed central vowel, as in *je* or *le*; alternatively, the very similar *eu* vowel is used, as in *peuclo* from *clope* 'cigarette'.

2 Optionally, after inversion, clipping may take place, to render the word even more unrecognisable: *jobard* 'loony' > *barjo* > *barge*.

3 (a) Monosyllables either undergo simple reversal of the order of the sounds, as in *sub* for *bus* and *auche* for *chaud*, or

(b) more frequently, in monosyllables ending in a consonant, the vowel *eu* is substituted for the vowel of the original, giving for example *keum* for *mec*.

A form like *meuf* for *femme* or *streum* for *monstre* can be regarded as the result of rules 1 and 2; they have been treated like bisyllabic words ending in a central vowel, and clipping has followed.

The apparently anomalous generalisation of the *eu* vowel in rule 3 (b) could be explained as follows: the central or mid front rounded vowel also appears in inverted, unclipped words like *peura* for *rap* and *renoi* for *noir*, despite the absence of any final orthographic *e* in the original, suggesting that there is a general tendency to remodel monosyllabic words as bisyllabic, by adding a central vowel, or *eu*, before inversion take place. Such remodelling, plus clipping, would also account for forms like *keum* for *mec*, or *keuf* for *flic*. In other words we can subsitute a rule adding a final vowel to monosyllables, for rule 3 (b).

Arabe has clearly been transformed, by a combination of *verlan* and clipping, into *beur*, a term which, unlike its denigratory forbears *rat*, *arbicot* and *bique*, has been assumed with pride by the younger generation, and has been used to name the radio station *Radio Beur*. The most recent development of this word has been yet another *verlanisation*, resulting in *reubeu* or *reub*!

Although there are scattered examples of *verlan* as far back as the sixteenth century, it only seems to have been used with any frequency, in school and student circles, from the 1960s. In the last ten years or so it has become associated with the young living in the ghetto-like housing estates of the suburbs, stereotypically members of street gangs, largely unemployed, favouring rap music, and often involved in petty crime and drugs.[8] For these speakers, Bachmann and Basier (1984) suggest, the use of *verlan* is motivated above all by the need for concealment. *Verlan* therefore seems to be the place where traditional slang overlaps with *la langue des jeunes*.

It is impossible to tell whether the phenomenon will continue to flourish, especially since the spotlight of the media has been turned on it. Most *verlan* forms are creations of the moment, but the very widespread use of forms like *keuf*, *keum* and *beur* suggest that it may leave a permanent mark on the lexis of informal French.

ARGOT, *JARGON* OR *JARGOT*?

In the last chapter, occupational style, characterised by a specialised terminology, and often labelled 'jargon' by the outsider, was examined in relation to the language of a number of professional groups. Can a clear distinction be made between this lexis and *argot*? We could perhaps say that the latter has more of a social than a strictly practical function; the exclusion of the outsider and the reinforcing of relationships within the group are the central functions of *argot*, but incidental in the exchange of *jargon*. Close-knit social groups may of course form within a professional context, where working conditions foster camaraderie and interdependence. Two young doctors chatting about a case may well use different lexical items than a junior doctor discussing the same case with a senior colleague, just as an exchange between two privates in the same regiment would differ from one between a private and a senior officer, even on a technical topic. To refer to lexis of this kind, that has the dual functions of *argot* and *jargon*, Sourdot (1991) has coined the useful term *jargot*.

Such lexical items may be considered informal, in-group synonyms of technical terms, resulting from the various formal and semantic processes described above. Typically irreverent metonymies are to be found in the substitution of *gazier* or *pousse-seringue* for 'anaesthetist', and *coupeur de mou* for 'surgeon'. Clipping is predictably the commonest device, giving *réa* for *réanimation*, and *arrêt-car* for *arrêt cardiaque* and *une perf* for *perfusion* 'a drip'. One can imagine that as well as signalling camaraderie among a medical team, such abbreviated expressions can have the often useful function of being obscure to patients or their relatives.

In military slang (Rousselot 1989), clipping is sometimes judiciously combined with re-suffixation, to produce puns such as *juteux* for *adjutant*, *aspirine* for *aspirant féminin* (that is, a female officer cadet).

Doillon (1993) demonstrates the richness of the lexis, both technical and informal, that has developed in the field of sport. In a domain generating so much emotion and enthusiasm, we are not surprised to find slang metaphors substituting for technical terms. In cycling for example, an inner tube is a *boudin*, and the vehicle picking up stragglers in a race is a *balai*.

In Canadian French, an interesting case is the lexis of *cibistes*, or CB radio enthusiasts (see Wolfe 1979); they are atypical of in-groups, in that membership is transitory, the interlocutor is usually unknown, and communication is not face to face; and yet a sense of intimacy is engendered by the one-to-one and often cryptic nature of the exchanges. The feeling of camaraderie is enhanced by the fact that some messages involve warnings about speedtraps and the proximity of traffic police. Metaphors like *ours* and *ours volant* are clearly calqued on North American slang 'bear' and 'bear in the air', meaning 'police' and 'airborne traffic police'. Much of the terminology is both humorous and disparaging of outsiders; mere passengers are *housses* 'seat-covers', and small foreign cars *trottinettes* 'scooters'. In spirit and in function this kind of lexis would seem to be closest to traditional *argot*: the parallel terminology is not specifically technical, but designed primarily for concealment; it is nevertheless characterised by a ludic element which is the hallmark of much in-group linguistic behaviour.

The brief survey of stylistically and socially determined variation outlined in these last two chapters suggests that the language has probably never known such a period of dynamic change and diversification. This is particularly true of lexis associated with the expression of solidarity and with closed or marginal groups. In some quarters, this exuberant lexical creativity is considered corrosive of the standard language, which is

traditionally viewed as the bedrock of French culture and the most powerful symbol of French nationhood. In the next chapter we shall look at the
origins of this highly conservative approach to the language, and examine
some of the arguments on which it is based, in the light of present knowledge about language and linguistic change.

NOTES

1 Of the comprehensive, serious dictionaries that have been produced, Marks and
  Johnson's *Slang Dictionary* (1993) is the most detailed bilingual work; Cellard
  and Rey (1991) and Colin and Mével (1992), the largest and most up-to-date
  monolingual slang dictionaries, both give etymological information, and illustrations of terms in context.
2 Chevalier (1978) explores in depth the relationship between class and crime in
  Paris in the first half of the nineteenth century, both as revealed by available
  statistics and as perceived by contemporary writers. The social divisions were so
  marked by animosity and fear that 'C'est en termes de races que les groupes
  sociaux se considèrent, se jugent et s'affrontent' (p. 670).
3 In *Propos sur Fernand Trignol et l'argot* (1957), republished in *Cahiers Céline*
  (1976) vol. 1: 172. Writing in the 1950s, Céline felt that this kind of slang was
  already less vigorous than before, and in danger of being exploited and trivia-
  lised by writers who were not in touch with the mainstream of working-class
  culture.
4 Bensimon-Choukroun's study (1991) shows how some expressions in use among
  secondary school and university students are both widespread and long-lived,
  while others are much more ephemeral, and may be restricted to specific sub-
  groups in the survey. See also Louis and Prinaz (1990) on the life style and lexis
  of different types of street gangs. While in all cases lexis seems to be the prime
  linguistic marker of group identity, one could also point to the almost obligatory
  tutoiement among coevals, as another generalised feature of youth culture.
5 Guiraud (1985: 61) points out just how complex the etymologies of many slang
  terms can be, as a couple of the examples just given illustrate: *poulet* 'policeman', as well as being a metaphor, is probably influenced by Italian slang *pula*,
  from *polizia*; moreover, *poulet* is also a slang term for horse, which is the basis
  of a whole series of terms for the police: *rouan* 'roan', *roussin* 'warhorse',
  bourrique 'donkey'. Since *cagne* is also a disparaging slang term for a horse,
  it is possible that it triggered *cogne*, a paronym or near-homophone, with a
  conveniently appropriate meaning.
6 In the 1940s and 1950s Céline was inventing neologisms in his novels using
  these very processes of clipping and resuffixation; not only *parloter* and *parlo-
  cher*, from *parler*, but also *bavoucher* and *bavoter* from *bavarder*, and *encu-
  lailler* and *enculguler* from *enculer*. In all, Juilland (1980) found 5,000 such
  neologisms.
7 As Lefkowitz (1989) notes, there is a certain variability in the treatment of three-
  syllable words; for example, *garetteci* and *retteciga* are also possible. This could
  be accommodated by having a rule which moved the first syllable to the end, or
  the last syllable to the beginning.
8 If the recent dictionary of Pierre-Adolphe, Mamoud and Tzanos (1995) is to be
  believed, *verlanisation* is by far the most popular single device used in the slang
  of the *banlieues*.

PROJECTS

1 Suggest which semantic or morphological processes have been used to produce the following slang expressions:

mansarde, plafond, toiture = skull
marteau = crazy
lissépem = to pee
faire le bitume, faire le trottoir, faire le pavé, faire le macadam = to solicit
avoir un cactus dans la poche, avoir un oursin dans la fouille, être constipé du morlingue, tondre les œufs = to be stingy
faire des boutonnières à = to stab
fatma, fatmuche. = woman
mouchodrome = a bald head
flingoter = to kill
beubeu = cannabis
accoucher, cracher, dégueuler = to confess
échanger des politesses, s'expliquer = to fight
en avoir au cul, en avoir dans le ventre = to have guts

2 Check on the morphologically derived forms of the following roots and idioms containing them, in both dictionaries of slang and standard French. Comment on their productivity, their lexical labels (indicating *niveaux de langue*) and their meanings:

chie- pète- con- merde- put- fout- piss-

3 Using Calvet (1993), Cahoreau and Tison (1987) or Marks and Johnson (1993), investigate the lexis associated with illegal drugs, and discuss the problem of differentiating between *argot, jargon* and *jargot* in relation to the terminology found in this field.

FURTHER READING

Bachmann, C. and Basier, L. 1984 'Le verlan: argot d'école ou langue des keums?' *Les Mots* 8: 169–87.
Bensimon-Choukroun, G. 1991 'Les mots de connivence des jeunes en institution scolaire: entre argot ubuesque et argot commun', in D. François-Geiger and J.-P. Goudaillier (eds) *Parlures argotiques, Langue française* 90
Bézard, C. 1993 'Le langage des jeunes', *L'Evénement du jeudi*, 5 August
Boudard, A. 1990 (2nd edition) *Méthode à Mimile*, Paris, Pré aux Clercs
Brunet, J.-P. 1990 *Dictionnaire de la police et de la pègre*, Paris, La Maison du dictionnaire; bilingual dictionary of this semantic field.
Cahoreau, G. and Tison, C. 1987 *La drogue expliquée aux parents*, Paris, Balland
Calvet, L.-J. 1993 *L'argot en 20 leçons*, Paris, Payot
—— 1994 *L'Argot*, Paris, PUF Que Sais-Je?; updates Guiraud's general introduction to the subject in the same series.
Céline, L.-F. 1976 *Cahiers Céline*, Paris, Gallimard
Cellard, J. and Rey, A. 1991 *Dictionnaire du français non-conventionnel*, Paris, Hachette
Chevalier, L. 1978 (2nd edition) *Classes laborieuses et classes dangereuses*, Paris, Librairie générale française
Colin, J.-P. and Mével, J.-P. 1992 *Dictionnaire de l'argot*, Paris, Larousse
Désirat, C. and Hordé, T. 1988 *La Langue française au 20ᵉ siècle*, Paris, Bordas

Doillon, A. 1993 *Argots et néologismes du sport* Paris, Les Amis du lexique français

François-Geiger, D. 1991 'Panorama des argots contemporains', *Langue française* 90

François-Geiger, D. and Goudaillier, J.-P. (eds) 1991 *Parlures argotiques, Langue française* 90; contains a dozen papers by linguists on contemporary slang.

George, K. 1980 'L'apocope et l'aphérèse en français familier, populaire et argotique', *Le Français moderne* 48 (1); traces the origins of clipping to the eighteenth century and shows how it has spread most recently into scientific and technical terminology.

Giraud, R. 1981 *L'Argot tel qu'on le parle*, Paris, Jacques Grancher; a popular, illustrated guide, organised by topic (*corps humain, le vol,* etc.).

Guiraud, P. 1968a *Le jargon de Villon ou le Gai Savoir de la Coquille*, Paris, Gallimard

—— 1968c *Patois et dialectes français*, Paris, PUF Que Sais-Je?

—— 1978b *La Sémiologie de la sexualité*, Paris, Payot

—— 1985 (9th edition) *L'Argot*, Paris, PUF Que Sais-Je?

Juilland, A. 1980 'L'autre français', ou doublets, triplets and quadruplets dans le lexique verbal de Céline', *Le Français moderne*, 48 (1)

Lefkowitz, N.J. 1989 'Verlan: talking backwards in French', *French Review* 63 (2): 312–22.

Louis P. and Prinaz L. 1990 *Skinheads, Taggers, Zulus & Co*, Paris, La Table ronde; an outline of the development of street gangs with distinctive lifestyles, from the 1950s to the present day; based on interviews with gang members, accompanied by a short glossary.

Marks, G.A. and Johnson, C.B. 1993 *Harrap's Slang Dictionary* (English–French/French–English) London, Harrap; the fullest up-to-date bilingual dictionary of slang.

Pétonnet, C. 1989 'Quelques mots d'argot médical', *Documents de travail du Centre d'argotologie* 9, Paris

Pierre-Adolphe, P., Mamoud, M. and Tzanos, G.-O. 1995 *Le Dico de la banlieue*, Paris, La Sirène

Plénat, M. (ed.) 1991 'Les javanais', *Langages* 101, March; the whole issue is devoted to coded languages, in France and elsewhere. Plénat's own article 'Le javanais: concurrence et haplologie', gives an account of the children's word game which consists in inserting the nonsense syllable *av* after each syllable of a word. Unlike *verlan*, it is not used as a socially distinctive code, nor has it resulted in even short-term lexicalisation, except perhaps for the item *pourrav* (= *pourri*).

Robert l'Argenton, F. 1991 'Parlépem largomuche du louchébem. Parler l'argot du boucher' in D. François-Geiger and J.-P. Goudaillier (eds) *Parlures argotiques, Langue française* 90; shows that this code is still surviving among some butchers of the Paris region.

Rousselot, P. 1989 'L'Argot militaire: vers un lexique', *Documents de travail du Centre d'argotologie*, 9

Sandry, G. and Carrère, M. 1976 *Dictionnaire de l'argot moderne*, Paris, Dauphin

Sourdot, M. 1991 'Argot, jargon, jargot', in D. François-Geiger and J.-P. Goudaillier (eds) *Parlures argotiques, Langue française* 90

Trudgill, P. 1972 'Sex, covert prestige and linguistic change in the urban British English of Norwich', *Language and Society* 1: 179–96

Vidocq, F. 1973 [1837] *Les Voleurs, physiologie de leurs mœurs et de leur langage*, Paris, France-expansion, Collection Archives de la linguistique française; an invaluable glossary compiled by a convict-cum-policeman, of over 1,500 terms used in jails in the early nineteenth century. (Both Hugo, in *Les Misérables*, and Balzac, in *Le Père Goriot* and *Splendeurs et misères des courtisanes*, drew on this, and on Vidocq's *Mémoires*. It is clear that Vidocq was in fact the model for Vautrin in Balzac's works.)

Wolfe, D.E. 1979 'A l'écoute de la radio CB', *French Review* (USA) 53 (1), October

Chapter 11

Codification, control and linguistic mythology

In Chapter Three we saw how, by the mid-sixteenth century, the French of Paris and the surrounding region had clearly emerged from the shadow of Latin, as the language of administration and of serious literary creation. Du Bellay, in his *Défense et illustration de la langue française* (1549), made a powerful case for the capacity of French to function in all the domains hitherto dominated by Latin. The question was not an academic one; in a century of increasing national consciousness, a national language was both an essential tool in the exercise of power within the now unified state, and a symbol of the state itself. Although by the end of the sixteenth century there was broad agreement on the role of French, the precise form that the language should take was still to be determined.

ESTABLISHING THE NORM

The basis of any linguistic norm is generally the variety spoken by the ruling élite. In sixteenth-century France this consisted of the Court, based in Paris, with the monarch at its head, an entourage of highly educated bureaucrats, and the upper echelons of the judiciary. The wealthy bourgeois families of the capital also wielded power, albeit of a less overt kind. Linguistically, these groups were far from forming a homogenous speech community, and there was much debate about who commanded the 'best' form of the language. Although the language of the court was an obvious potential model, strong Italian influence on this variety in the latter part of the century, parodied by H. Estienne in his *Deux dialogues du nouveau language français italianisé* (1578), undermined its validity to a certain extent, while under Henri IV court usage was felt to be tainted with provincial *gasconismes*. Until the beginning of the seventeenth century the French used by members of the Palais – that is, the élite of the Paris judiciary, naturally well versed in the art of rhetoric – was thought by many to be the most elegant and correct.

Le bon usage in the seventeenth century

In contrast to the exuberant lexical creativity of the sixteenth century, summed up in Ronsard's much-quoted affirmation, 'Plus nous aurons de mots en notre langue, plus elle sera parfaite', the seventeenth century was marked by a desire to subject the lexis to strict selection and control. Early in the century the court poet Malherbe, in a detailed critique of his predecessor Desportes, set the tone for the prescriptive approach to the language, which was to prevail for three centuries. In relation to the lexis, he condemned neologisms, archaisms, Italianisms, dialectal or technical words, and terms considered *bas*, that is, associated in any way with lower class usage.[1] Malherbe was also concerned with distinguishing clearly between near-synonyms, and many of his remarks involve establishing the semantic and stylistic nuances which differentiate pairs of words like *luire* and *reluire*, *débile* and *faible*, or *neuf* and *nouveau*. In this he foreshadows much of the lexicographic work that was to follow.

Claude Favre de Vaugelas, the most influential figure of the seventeenth century with regard to the codification of the language, was concerned with *le bon usage* in more general terms: where Malherbe's remarks were directed at literary, and even more specifically, poetic usage, Vaugelas commented on the forms appropriate to spoken and written language in polite society. He was first and foremost an acute observer of linguistic usage in Court and salon circles, and it was this that he took as his model. In the best-known quotation from his *Remarques sur la langue française* (1647), he defined *le bon usage* as 'la façon de parler de la plus saine partie de la Cour, conformément à la façon d'écrire de la plus saine partie des auteurs du temps'.

'La plus saine partie de la Cour' is nowhere explicitly defined, and the vagueness of the phrase perhaps allowed Vaugelas some licence in opting for the forms he personally favoured.[2] The central role played by women in the salons, as well as the distaste of the age for the earlier Latinising tendencies of many Renaissance authors, and for pedantry in general, can be detected in his supplementary precept: 'dans les doutes de la langue il vaut mieux pour l'ordinaire consulter les femmes et ceux qui n'ont point étudié, que ceux qui sont bien savants en la langue grecque et en la latine'.

His *Remarques* deal with every aspect of language: pronunciation, orthography, grammar, lexis and style. In matters of grammar, expecially, he was hugely influential, and many of his rulings are still enshrined in contemporary grammars, like *Le Bon Usage* by Grevisse. As far as the lexis is concerned, he is less restrictive than Malherbe, cautiously admitting new words, either borrowings or native neologisms, as long as they serve a clear purpose. He is however resolutely opposed to 'archaic' expressions, even when he appreciates the semantic nuance or stylistic flavour of the word in question. But his approach was above all pragmatic; the *Remarques* can be viewed as a guide to what was socially acceptable in the circles to which many aspired to belong (he himself was dependent on court patronage for most of his life). Together they formed a kind of linguistic manual for the socially ambitious, or for those who wished to polish their image as that of the ideal *honnête homme* of the time. As such the *Remarques* were immensely popular, and formed the basis of many later works written along similar lines.

In lexical matters Vaugelas made rulings not only on which lexical items were acceptable, but also on the precise meanings of words, and on their grammatical function: he said that *auparavant*, for example, should be used only as an adverb, and not as a preposition or a conjunction. In this and many other cases his ruling holds good today, though we cannot know whether this is attributable to the acuity of his intuitions with regard to contemporary linguistic trends, or to the weight his opinions carried over a long period of time – or indeed to chance.[3]

Some of the labels Vaugelas and his contemporaries apply to words refer to the kind of literary texts in which they might be used; an expression which is *sublime*, for example, is suited to the higher forms of poetry, *comique* and *burlesque* to more popular literary genres. Significantly, just as many refer to the social rank of those who might use them, from *noble* through *bourgeois*, to *populaire*, *le menu peuple* and finally, *la lie du peuple*.

Vaugelas's pragmatism is evident in his relative lack of concern with the need to justify linguistic choices on rational grounds, which became a major criterion for later grammarians. He is happy to admit that much of language is arbitrary: 'il n'y a rien de si bizarre que l'Usage, qui est le maître des langues vivantes', and that 'ceux-là se trompent lourdement, et pèchent contre le premier principe des langues, qui veulent raisonner sur la nôtre, et qui condamnent beaucoup de façons de parler généralement reçues, parce qu'elles sont contre la raison'. At the same time he was tireless in his search for the regularities which he perceived to underly much of the morphology and syntax of the language.

Compared to much of the grammatical and lexicographic work of his successors, many of Vaugelas's observations have a remarkably 'modern' ring to them, in that his approach was essentially synchronic and descriptive. His rulings are largely based on observation of contemporary speakers, whom he often used as what today we would term 'informants', and he did not feel that etymology was of paramount importance in resolving linguistic issues. (He holds *erreur*, for example, to be feminine, in line with current usage, against those who claimed it should be masculine, like its Latin etymon.)

Most modern linguists would also concur with Vaugelas's belief that 'la parole qui se prononce est la première en ordre et en dignité, puisque celle qui est écrite n'est que son image'. In matters of literary style, *clarté* and *netteté* were his watchwords; ambiguity and unnecessary complexity should be avoided at all costs.

Later seventeenth-century grammarians, such as Bouhours, took a less empirical and flexible view of language, and felt that the lexis was in need of drastic pruning. The social exclusiveness that underlies this attitude are clear in the following extract from *Les Entretiens d'Ariste et d'Eugène* (1671):

> Ainsi pour polir, pour embellir notre langue, il a fallu nécessairement en retrancher tout ce qu'elle avait de rude et de barbare. Nous devons un si utile retranchement aux soins de l'Académie française, qui se proposa pour but de nettoyer la langue des ordures qu'elle avait contractées dans la bouche du peuple et parmi des courtisans ignorants ou peu exacts.

It followed that it was all the more important to distinguish carefully between the words that were judged acceptable; like Malherbe and Vaugelas, he took pains to differentiate between near-synonyms, such as *audace* and *hardiesse*, or *artisan* and *ouvrier*.

The work of both Vaugelas and Bouhours was closely bound up with the activities of the French Academy, founded by Richelieu in 1635. Among its stated aims were to 'donner des règles certaines à notre langue, et à la rendre pure, éloquente et capable de traiter les arts et les sciences'. It was given the task of producing a grammar and a dictionary, and was the supreme authority in literary matters, on questions of both form and content. Some of the rules laid down concerned the standardisation of pronunciation and orthography, especially the latter. Here, the Academy confirmed the existing bias towards an orthography reflecting the etymology of words (for example ruling in favour of the unpronounced *s* in words like *teste* and *mesme*). Their justification, that 'la Compagnie préfère l'ancienne orthographe, qui distingue les gens de lettres d'avec les ignorants et les simples femmes', is a reminder that, at the time, *les gens de lettres* would naturally be familiar with Latin (see Chapter Three), and that the Academy was in no way concerned with making the written language accessible to a wider public.

In matters of pronunciation, where variants existed, such as *a* and *e* (as in *marquer* and *merquer*), or *ou* and *o* (as in *corbeau* and *courbeau*), arbitrary rulings were often made, sometimes with reference to rather vague aesthetic criteria. However, most of the judgments of the Academy seem to have stood the test of time. Again, we can only speculate whether this was due to the weight of authority their rulings carried with subsequent generations, or if they were simply well attuned to the trends of their time. On the question of which items should be admitted to their dictionary, the first edition of which finally appeared in 1694, the Academy showed a degree of tolerance, admitting numerous archaisms and expressions like *vomir des injures*, which Vaugelas had considered unacceptable.

Eighteenth-century attitudes

In the late seventeenth and early eighteenth century, Vaugelas's broadly empirical attitude gave way to a more theoretical and philosophical approach; now grammar, as the most systematic component of language, became the focus of interest. The *Grammaire générale et raisonnée* by Lancelot and Arnaud (1660), also known as the *Grammaire de Port-Royal*, was less concerned with the detailed practicalities of usage than with seeking to establish the universal principles on which linguistic structures are based. There was a shift of emphasis, too, away from the spoken language and towards the written form. This was in part due to the fact that the absolute power of the monarchy had been weakened, and court usage no longer constituted an unchallengeable model. The linguistic norm was taken to be embodied in the writings of the best authors, and in this respect few felt that the great masterpieces of the seventeenth century had been, or indeed could be, surpassed. Voltaire, with many of his contemporaries, believed that the importance of retaining access to this great canon of literature was in itself sufficient justification for attempting to fix the literary language in an immutable mould:

> Il me semble que lorsqu'on a eu dans un siècle un nombre suffisant de bons écrivains devenus classiques, il n'est plus guère permis d'employer d'autres expressions que les leurs, et qu'il faut leur donner le même sens, ou bien dans peu de temps le siècle présent n'entendrait plus le siècle passé.
>
> (*Dictionnaire philosophique*, 1764)

The belief that the language had reached a peak of perfection in the seventeenth century was not unconnected with the fact that France was then the most powerful, wealthy and populous country in Europe; the language and literature of the time assumed a symbolic significance, recalling the glories of a past Golden Age.

Henceforth, there was to be increasing divergence between the spoken and written forms of the language, with the written language becoming the focus of the codification process. Against this touchstone of correctness could be measured the vagaries of spoken usage, which was less susceptible to control, and of less concern to the literary and academic establishment.

Fixity was maintained above all in the grammatical system. Purism and conservatism applied strictly to the lexis would clearly have made the language non-functional in many fields, within a very short space of time. From the mid-eighteenth century, we find philosophers and scientists arguing that neologisms are essential; even the Academy was persuaded that 'Un traité de néologie bien fait serait un ouvrage excellent et qui nous manque' (1762).

It might be thought that attitudes to the language would have changed dramatically with the Revolution. In fact those who came to power were drawn largely from the educated middle classes, well versed in the existing norm. More importantly, the national language, now thoroughly codified, and enjoying great prestige abroad, was a crucial weapon in the armoury of the new regime, which had to face the threat of invasion from neighbouring countries and reassert centralised control at home. Subsequently, the educational and economic policies of post-Revolutionary governments were to ensure the spread of standard French, and make mastery of the language an essential prerequisite to social and professional advancement (see Lodge 1993, Chapter 7).

THE NORM AND DICTIONARY MAKING

Before the seventeenth century dictionaries were bilingual, used in the learning of another language, or in the interpretation and translation of texts. The first monolingual dictionaries of the seventeenth century were patchy and idiosyncratic; for knowledge of the contemporary lexis, we must rely rather on works of the authors of the day. Not until 1680, with Richelet's *Dictionnaire français*, did a more coherent and comprehensive work make its appearance. Its focus was the accepted literary language of the time, while Furetière's *Dictionnaire universel*, appearing ten years later, is much broader in scope, including archaic, colloquial and dialectal expressions of the kind that would not have been sanctioned by Vaugelas. The dictionary of the Academy (1694) was more in keeping with his precepts; when expressions inappropriate to *le bon usage* were admitted, this was signalled by the use of lexical labels; *d'accord*, for example, was marked *familier*, as opposed to the more acceptable *j'y consens*. To complement this work, with its strong literary bias, the Academy commissioned a scientific and technical dictionary, *Le Dictionnnaire des arts et des sciences*, also published in 1694.

In the eighteenth century several new editions of the dictionaries of Richelet, Furetière and the Academy were published, with that of Furetière maintaining its rather more inclusive policy. Technical dictionaries multiplied, in response to the increased activity in the domains of science, technology, industry and commerce.

Early in the century the first dictionary of synonyms was produced, by l'Abbé Girard (1718); highly praised by Voltaire, among others, it ran to a number of editions.

Diderot's seventeen-volume *Encyclopédie* (completed in 1772) necessarily contained huge numbers of technical terms, which it thereby helped to legitimise. Diderot himself foresaw the inevitable broadening of the lexis of the educated classes, and the spread of the new terminology among the population as a whole:

Les esprits sont emportés d'un autre mouvement général vers l'histoire naturelle, l'anatomie, la chimie et la physique expérimentale. Les expressions propres à ces sciences sont déjà très communes, et le deviendront nécessairement davantage. Qu'arrivera-t-il de là? C'est que la langue, même populaire, changera de face; qu'elle s'étendra à mesure que nos oreilles s'accoutumeront aux mots par les applications heureuses qu'on en fera.[4]

The 1798 edition of the Academy dictionary is an interesting, though isolated, departure from tradition, in that a supplement was added, listing over three hundred new terms relating to the Revolution. Some, like the Revolutionary names for the months, *thermidor* (July–August) and *pluviôse* (January–February) and for the new ten-day week (from *primedi* to *décadi*) proved ephemeral, while others, like the new system of weights and measures, *gramme*, *litre*, *mètre* and so on, remained.

The nineteenth century saw tremendous growth in the demand for both dictionaries and encyclopedias, among a much wider reading public. In the 1835 edition of its Dictionary, the French Academy perpetuated the distinction between the highly selective literary norm, 'la langue française dans toute sa pureté et sa précision, et plutôt dans sa rigueur classique' (see the Preface), and technical and scientific lexis, relegated to a much larger *Complément*, in 1842. Although this and subsequent editions were not widely used by the general reader, the dictionary continued to be influential with writers, and was important as a reference point for other lexicographers, as constituting a kind of core lexis, which they would supplement at their discretion.

The four-volume *Dictionnaire de la langue française* by Littré (1863–73) was to become the prime arbiter of usage and source of lexical information for the educated classes until the mid-twentieth century. Less restrictive than the dictionary of the Academy, though basically normative in approach, *Littré* provided a wealth of examples from literary sources, mostly seventeenth- and eighteenth-century authors. It was as yet too early to admit the works of the contemporary masters of the nineteenth century, like Balzac, Baudelaire and Stendhal, to the established literary canon.

Hatzfeld's *Dictionnaire général*, completed in 1890, was designed as a dictionary of manageable size, which nevertheless provided quite detailed etymological information in its entries, and included an historical overview of the language in its introduction; the presentation of semantic information was also greatly improved, to indicate more clearly the semantic development of words.

From the mid-nineteenth century, the dictionaries of Larousse established a more liberal approach to the lexis, including the colloquialisms of contemporary usage, and admitting many scientific and technical expressions. The fifteen volumes of his *Grand Dictionnaire universel du XIXe siècle*, completed in 1876, combined dictionary, encylopedia and grammar in the most comprehensive work of reference of the period, relating to the language. Unlike *Littré*, it included many quotations from the works of contemporary writers.

Le Dictionnaire alphabétique et analogique de la langue française, by Paul Robert, better known as *Le Grand Robert*, first published in 1953, followed in the more literary and conservative tradition. However, the twentieth century has been notable for a proliferation of shorter, practical *dictionaires d'usage*, designed to reflect contemporary usage, both spoken and written. These include the *Dictionnaire du français contemporain* and *Lexis*, both published by Larousse, and Hachette's *Dictionnaire de la langue française*. The best known, the *Petit Larousse*, has the advantage of appearing in updated editions every few years.

This shift from a prescriptive to a more descriptive perspective is also to be seen in the more recent editions of *Le Petit Robert*, and even of the *Dictionnaire de l'Académie française*. Comparing the Preface in the eighth and ninth editions of the latter (1935 and 1986 respectively), there is a marked evolution in the direction of general usage; now terms like *bagnole* and *baratin* (both labelled *populaire*) are included, and even the occasional twentieth-century English borrowing, such as *bang* (meaning 'supersonic bang') and *blue-jean*. Surprisingly, it is only in the most recent edition that some long-established Anglicisms, such as *boycotter* and *bluff*, make their appearance.

A major lexicographic project has been the production of the *Trésor de la langue française* (*TLF*), or to give it its full title, *Dictionnaire de la langue du XIXe et du XXe siècles – 1789–1960*, of which the sixteenth and final volume was published in 1994. It contains over 100,000 entries drawn from a computerised database of nineteenth- and twentieth-century texts, comprising more than ninety million words. As 80 per cent of the corpus consisted of literary works, and 20 per cent of technical texts, with journalistic texts and data from the spoken language being more or less excluded, the *TLF* is clearly selective, in the tradition of dictionaries of *bon usage*.

By contrast, some lexicographic work in the postwar period has focused on corpora of spontaneous spoken French, with the aim of providing objectively selected material for teaching purposes. From these were derived minimal dictionaries of the most frequently occurring words, like Gougenheim's *Dictionnaire fondamental de la langue française* (about

3,500 words), constituting the core lexis of the language (see Gougenheim *et al.* 1964). Equally distanced from dictionaries based on the literary norm are works devoted to slang and colloquial expressions. The large number of publications, both academic and popular, which have appeared over the last twenty years bear witness to the tremendous growth of interest in this 'marginal' lexis (see Chapter Ten for bibliographical references).

LINGUISTIC MYTHS

Despite enormous advances in our knowledge about language, the ideas that dominated eighteenth-century thought with regard to language have proved remarkably tenacious. We now know, for example, that all living languages are continually changing, and that no amount of effort will halt this change; at the most it will produce an artificial variety that will become increasingly remote from the language of the majority of the speech community. Nor is there any evidence for a distinction between 'primitive' or 'developed' languages, or stages in a language; the grammatical structures of languages used by technologically undeveloped communities are just as rich and complex as those of more 'advanced' societies. As far as the lexis is concerned, at any point in time a language fulfils all the functions required of it by its speakers. If it is required to fulfil new functions (as was the case for example with French, as it gradually came to replace Latin in many domains), its speakers find the resources to do so. To label one state of the language ideal, and to seek to maintain it unchanged, is therefore a questionable exercise. However, once a language assumes symbolic significance, and becomes inseparable from concepts of social prestige, national identity and high culture, it is inevitable that changes in the system should be resisted. It is also natural that the variety of a language selected as the norm should be invested with positive qualities of various kinds – logical, aesthetic, and even moral – which distinguish it from other languages, or varieties of the same language. Usually the precise nature of these supposed qualities is left somewhat vague, but in the present case, the French passion for analysis has meant that they have been spelt out, in so far as this is possible.

La clarté française

Clarity was referred to frequently by Vaugelas and his contemporaries as a key ingredient of *le bon usage*; for them it seems to have been an essentially stylistic notion, involving careful choice of syntax and vocabulary, so that the meaning of a sentence is immediately clear to the reader or hearer, and free of any possible ambiguity. A rather different conception of clarity developed in parallel with this later in the century: clarity was thought to reside principally in the fact that the dominant word order of French is subject–verb–object (SVO), referred to at the time as *l'ordre direct*. That is, clarity was considered to be an inherent property of the language, rather than being characteristic of a specific text or utterance. *L'ordre direct* was held to mirror the order of rational thought. What is more, French was thought to have a monopoly of this word order, and therefore, of inherent clarity. Bouhours was one of the first to formulate the connection: 'La langue française est peut-être la seule qui suive exactement l'ordre naturel, et qui exprime les pensées en la manière qu'elles naissent dans l'esprit'.

Even today we are unable to monitor thought processes in any detail, nor is it clear if it will ever be possible. However, in so far as we do understand it, the relationship between language and thought seems to be far from straightforward and transparent, as was believed in the seventeenth and eighteenth centuries. There is certainly no evidence to suggest that speakers of languages with a dominant word order of subject–object–verb, or verb–subject–object, are any less capable of rational thought than speakers of SVO languages. We must also question the assumption that French does in fact adhere to this 'natural' order. There are numerous counter-examples to the dominant word order, such as inversion of subject and verb in a variety of constructions, and obligatory positioning of the object pronoun before the verb.[5] Are we therefore to suppose that sentences containing these constructions are in some way lacking in clarity, or express less rational thoughts?

Eighteenth-century grammarians also sought rational bases for specific grammatical rules, in the sense of seeking consistent relationships between form and meaning (Vaugelas's earlier insight that 'l'usage fait beaucoup de choses par raison, beaucoup sans raison et beaucoup contre raison', being incompatible with rationalist theory, was lost). Even today, the ingenuity of grammarians is sorely tested, for example, in the attempt to find clear semantic correlates for all uses of the subjunctive (see Grevisse 1969: 684–5); while other irregular features, like words changing gender in the plural, are undeniably arbitrary.[6]

An 'abstract' lexis?

While *clarté* is largely used with reference to the grammar, *abstrait* is an adjective which has often been applied to the lexis of French, usually contrasting it with that of other languages, including English, which are described as *concrets* (see Ullmann 1952: 142–6). The arguments are sometimes based on the preponderance of nouns in French, where English tends to favour verbs, which are considered by some to be more 'concrete'. It is not clear how such a property can be held to be inherent in a particular word class. Since most nouns are 'countable', one could claim that this relates them to a class of objectively verifiable phenomena – i.e. makes them more 'concrete' than verbs. However it is difficult to see how an expression like *faire une promenade* is more 'abstract' than the verb *se promener*.

Abstrait is also used to imply not that there are more abstract expressions (such as *vérité* or *beauté*) in French, but rather to refer to the existence of relatively large numbers of terms in the language which have a somewhat broad meaning. If, as lexicographers agree, there are many more words in English than French, and therefore more cases of one French word being translatable by two or more different English words (like *séduction* corresponding to both 'seduction' and 'seductiveness'), then in a sense we can consider the French word to be the more 'generic' or, if one prefers, 'abstract' item.[7]

It is certainly the case that a series of specific terms sometimes exists in English, corresponding to a single word in French. *Promenade*, for example, might be translated by 'walk', 'ride' or 'drive'; it can of course be further specified as *une promenade à pied, à cheval, à bicyclette, en voiture*, and so on, if the means of locomotion is not clear from the context. The converse situation also holds: one term in English may correspond to more than one in French, such as 'handle' covering the same ground as *anse, manche* and *poignée*. In relation to this question, Ullmann and others have claimed that the relative paucity of specific terms in French can be an advantage: 'L'analyse des notions y gagne, certes, car on dégage ce qui est essentiel et supprime le reste' (Ullmann 1952: 143). This claim seems to imply that if a language contains many specific terms it must be lacking in superordinates; there is however no evidence that this is true of English. Presumably the ideal would be to have a range of both specific terms and superordinates, and to be able to choose the degree of specificity of one's *analyse des notions*.

Any value judgement about the precision of the French lexis has to take into account the highly polysemous nature of many items. While some terms – such as *promenade* – may be considered to have a single broad meaning, many constitute an assemblage of loosely linked meanings. *Combinaison*, for example, refers to different types of all-in-one garment, whose purpose may be further specified, as in *combinaison de plongée* 'wetsuit', but it also means 'combination' in the abstract sense, and has a technical meaning in chemistry. In these cases the reader or hearer must rely on the context – either linguistic or situational – to make the appropriate interpretation.

Discussions involving value judgements about the lexis tend to centre on the written form of the language. Additional potential sources of ambiguity become apparent if we focus on the spoken word. French is known for its large numbers of homophones. This is due mainly to the radical phonological changes that French has undergone, compared to other Romance languages (see Chapter Three, pp. 45–6). These have resulted in many polysyllabic words being reduced to monosyllables, which were further reduced by the widespread loss of final consonants; sets of homophones like *port / porc / pore, cher / chair / chaire, saint / sein / seing / ceint*, are therefore not uncommon. Homophony may also occur because of the phonological process of *enchaînement*, whereby the final consonant in a word or phrase becomes the initial consonant of the next syllable, if the following word begins with a vowel. For example, the syllable division of *d'une autre* will be *d'u + ne͜ autre* – in other words, it will sound just like *du nôtre*. Similarly, *les aulnes* and *les zones*, or *il est ouvert* and *il est tout vert*, will be homophonous. Nor do the rules of stress placement, which in French consist essentially in applying slightly stronger stress to the last syllable of a whole phrase, help to identify word boundaries. For example, the lexicalised compound *tête-de-loup* 'ceiling brush' is homophonous with the phrase *tête de loup* 'wolf's head'. This contrasts with the differentiating function of stress in English, where every full lexical item carries a degree of stress. 'Blackbird', stressed only on the first syllable, is therefore pronounced slightly differently from 'black bird', in which both words carry stress. Hence in the normal flow of an utterance in French, there are few phonological clues to tell the hearer where to locate the beginnings and endings of words.

For both semantic and phonological reasons, then, we can say that the decoding of spoken French in particular is quite heavily reliant on its context. As Ullmann (1952: 317) puts it: 'Arbitraire et abstrait, porteur d'une multiplicité de valeurs objectives et affectives, exposé à des équivoques polysémiques et homonymiques, [le mot français] a, plus que les mots d'autres langues, besoin d'un contexte pour être compris.'

Underlying much of the discussion of these notions of clarity, logic and abstractness is a basic confusion between the language itself and the use made of it. As we have seen, in France there is a long-standing tradition of linguistic awareness. In the educational system there is strong emphasis on clear and accurate use of the language, in both its written and spoken forms (in higher education, oral examinations play a much more important role than in the British system, for example). Philosophy is an obligatory element of the national curriculum at secondary school level, and students are taught how to structure an argument within a formal *dissertation*. Moreover, in philosophical or scientific discourse there is a tradition of focusing on generalities and on overall theory, where the 'Anglo-Saxon' approach has tended to emphasise the empirical bases of a discipline.

It is therefore quite possible that those who have gone through the mill of the French educational system, especially if they are widely read, will be capable of producing texts, or verbal arguments, which have the properties of clarity, precision and abstractness, but this is due to cultural and pedagogical traditions; such qualities cannot be correlated with any inherent characteristics of the language itself.

Ullmann, in the sentence which concludes his discussion of the 'abstract' nature of French, goes so far as to relate the concern for clarity in the use of language to the imprecision of the lexis: 'Ce souci de la clarté lexicale et grammaticale est la réponse du français au danger d'imprécision inhérent à sa structure'.

The above discussion may appear to *enfoncer des portes ouvertes*, or state the obvious, in the light of the mass of research that has been carried out in diachronic and synchronic linguistics since the eighteenth century. And yet it needs to be said, in so far as these beliefs are still widely held, in part because they have become inseparable from concepts of national identity and French culture.

THE LANGUAGE AND NATIONAL IDENTITY

Feelings of group identity are based not only on shared values, interests and beliefs, but also on perceived differences from others, differences which are often translated into feelings of superiority or hostility. This is particularly true when national rivalry on the world stage is involved.

At a time when Italy was a centre of economic power and great cultural prestige, and Italian influence in French politics was deeply resented, it was felt that Italian borrowings were corrupting the language. Moreover, H. Estienne's *Traité de la conformité du langage français avec le grec* (1565) affirmed the superiority of French over Italian, on the grounds that it was more closely related to Greek, while his *De la precellence du langage français* (1566) used vaguer but equally questionable criteria. As Italian economic and political influence waned, so did the linguistic polemics.

The notion of the inherent superiority of French, due to the logical properties of its syntax, which had been first articulated in the seventeenth century, was given new impetus by the publication in 1784 of Rivarol's essay *Discours sur l'universalité de la langue française*.[8] One sentence, 'Ce qui n'est pas clair n'est pas français', has acquired the status of a maxim. However, the following sentence betrays the overtly chauvinistic tenor of much of the essay: 'Ce qui n'est pas clair n'est pas français; ce qui n'est pas clair est encore anglais, italien, grec ou latin.' (It seems that Rivarol was unaware that many other languages, including English and Italian, share the same basic word order as French.)

In the context of the late eighteenth century, when, as the title of Rivarol's essay suggests, French was the language of international diplomacy and was spoken by the educated élite of Europe, the idea that French was inherently superior to other European languages was understandable. What more natural than to assume that inherent properties of the language, rather than political and economic circumstances, were responsible for its success? At any rate, Rivarol had found a theme that both flattered and reassured his public. It buttressed the already firmly entrenched prescriptive and conservative approach to the language; if power and prestige accrued to France by virtue of its language, then it was indeed necessary to preserve this invaluable national asset intact.

During the early, precarious years of the Revolutionary regime, when the majority of the population did not actually speak French, and could be suspected of divided loyalties, the language was used not just to impose government policies, but as the primary symbol of Frenchness. The emotive tone of the *Rapport Barrère* (1794), which advocated the replacement of regional languages by French, gives some idea of the urgency with which the problem was viewed. Just as French was 'l'instrument de la pensée publique, l'agent le plus sûr de la Révolution', other languages, like Breton, Basque or German, were referred to as 'ces instruments de dommage et d'erreur... ces jargons barbares et ces idiomes grossiers qui ne peuvent plus servir que les fanatiques et les contre-révolutionnaires'.

From this time, the language became identified with the nation in a profoundly spiritual sense. Even today it is seen by some as actively promoting not only intellectual but positive social and moral qualities in its speakers:

> Le français exprime des valeurs intellectuelles à l'opposé du sectarisme. Il forme à l'indépendance et à la responsabilité. Il apprend à ne pas subir et à adhérer. Il traduit une double aspiration au progrès moral et à l'affirmation de soi-même, poussée dans les deux cas jusqu'à la grandeur.
>
> (de Broglie 1986: 74)

Such feelings are most strongly articulated at times of crisis and uncertainty. In the aftermath of the second world war, Dauzat (1949) wrote: 'Après nos désastres, nous nous efforçons de nous retremper aux sources de notre vie nationale, de reprendre conscience de nos traditions. La langue est une de ces traditions, un des éléments primordiaux de la patrie.'

Given the immense symbolic significance of the language, it is important to examine government policy with regard to the language in the context of the contemporary political situation, and in particular in the context of France as a contender in the international arena.

THE DEFENCE OF FRENCH

The term 'defence' in relation to the language has been used in two quite distinct ways: to refer both to the maintenance of an acceptable form of the language, and to the promotion of French at home and abroad. The need to establish French firmly within France motivated legislation, from the Edict of Villers-Cotterets in the sixteenth century to a range of revolutionary measures at the end of the eighteenth. From that point onwards, it was the educational system that was the prime means of diffusing the national language. As French remained the undisputed language of diplomacy and of high culture in Europe throughout the eighteenth and nineteenth centuries, measures were not needed to 'defend' it in this role, until it became clear that English, as the language of the British Empire, and of an increasingly powerful United States of America, was beginning to challenge French in the international arena. The creation of the *Alliance française* in 1883, which expanded into a worldwide network of centres devoted to the teaching of French as a second language, and to the propagation of French culture abroad, was one indication that the pre-eminence of that culture and language could no longer be taken for granted.

In relation to the defence of the actual form of the language, although maintenance of the norm had always been a constant preoccupation of writers, linguistic commentators and teachers, and although the Academy continued to produce rulings on points of grammar and lexis, it was not until the twentieth century that the language was felt to be under serious threat – again, principally from English (see Chapter Five). The two defensive imperatives therefore became closely associated, and the institutions that were set up often had the twofold task of promoting French as a world language, and defending it from the depredations of English. The relationship between the two is delicate and complex. Too 'purist' an approach would undermine the viability of French as a modern, international language. In the event, a pragmatic *dirigisme* has informed most of the official measures taken.

Organisations involved in the defence of French

A bewildering variety of bodies concerned with the defence and promotion of the language have emerged this century, mostly during the postwar period. Some were private organisations, like the *Office du vocabulaire français (OVF)*, founded by a group of writers and linguists in 1957. The *OVF* were concerned with neologisms, and above all with formulating a response to the mass of Anglicisms entering the language. They organised referenda on preferred usage among their wide membership, to discover, for example, which Anglicisms were best or least tolerated, and to find the most acceptable French-based alternatives. (*Living-room*, for instance, was voted the most detested borrowing in one survey, with *salle de séjour* the most popular alternative.) Their findings were published regularly in the journal *Vie et langage*, and newspapers like *Le Figaro* often opened up the debate to a wider public.

Rather less pragmatic was the *Défense de la langue française*, an organisation founded in 1959 under the aegis of the French Academy, which sought to maintain the norm, being especially vigilant with regard to the media. Its journal, also called *La Défense de la langue française*, regularly publishes the views of the Academy on grammatical and lexical matters.

From the 1960s, the government became increasingly involved in setting up organisations concerned with promoting, monitoring and controlling the language. Under De Gaulle, the *Haut Comité pour la défense et l'expansion de la langue française* was established, in 1966. This became simply the *Haut Comité de la langue française* (*HCLF*) in 1973, which was responsible for ordering many *commissions ministérielles de terminologie*; their main task was to propose alternatives to Anglicisms in specialised areas, such as telecommunications or the oil industry, for the guidance of civil servants. Once published in the *Journal Officiel* of the Republic, these had the force of law.

The importance of developing new technical terminology which was not reliant on English was a problem that had long been addressed by the state-sponsored *Association française de normalisation en matière de langage technique* (AFNOR), established in 1926. Its main aim, however, was the standardisation and clear definition of terms, with the avoidance of Anglicisms being a secondary issue. The *Comité d'étude des termes techniques français*, set up in 1954, took over from an earlier organisation whose stated task was to 'défendre la langue contre les invasions fâcheuses et désordonnées'; it monitors the borrowing of English terms in many technical fields, in cooperation with numerous scientific and industrial organisations, and recommends French-based alternatives wherever possible.

Canada has taken up the challenge of massive English influence even more energetically than France. An *Office de la langue française* was founded in Quebec in 1961, and various government organisations are involved in both promoting French as the language of administration, education and the workplace, and in keeping Canadian French as free as possible of Anglicisms. Various associations in the French-speaking world, like the *Office du bon langage* in Brussels, and the *Académie mauricienne*, are grouped together in the *Fédération du français universel*.

In 1967 the *HCLF* set up the *Conseil international de la langue française* (*CILF*), a very influential oganisation comprising representatives from nearly twenty countries in which French plays an important role. It is concerned with the promotion of French as an international language and maintaining the unity of the language, in matters of grammar, orthography, and where possible, lexis. *CILF* is responsible for a large number of publications, including specialised dictionaries and authoritative journals such as *La Banque des mots*, *Le français moderne* and *Langues et terminologies*.

In 1984 the *HCLF* was reorganised as a number of Councils and Committees with complementary functions; perhaps the most important today is the *Délégation générale à la langue française*, which has the task of coordinating the activities of the many official bodies involved in the defence of French, in France and abroad, and promoting their recommendations.

Legislation

As we have seen, civil servants are legally bound by the statutory recommendations of the various *Commissions ministérielles de terminologie*, in the writing of official documents. The *Loi Bas-Lauriol* of 1975 went further, in extending legislation into the private sector. Specifically, it forbade the use of English in work contracts, in advertising, and in information supplied with or about products, if an equivalent French expression existed. It can be seen as a measure to protect the employee or the consumer, who might well be misled by being given information in a foreign language. There were problems, however, with its implementation; few prosecutions took place, and firms that were prosecuted usually paid only derisory fines.

The *Loi Toubon* of 1994 was no doubt intended to remedy this situation, in that it threatened much heavier penalties for the use of English in contracts and so on, and also forbade the exclusive use of English in international conferences on French territory. It met with a generally hostile reaction, especially from the media, and certain elements were subsequently judged unconstitutional, and had to be modified. It is not yet clear whether the law will meet with any greater success than its predecessor.

In the early 1960s, when state intervention in linguistic matters was getting under way, there was a good deal of popular rhetoric against English, or rather American influence, with Etiemble as the self-appointed standard-bearer of the campaign. Trescases (1982) relates this upsurge of polemics and governmental activity to a whole series of political crises: the massive redistribution of power after the second world war was followed by the loss of former colonial territories, especially in Indo-China, where America stepped in to play a neo-colonial role. The humiliation of Suez and the deep trauma of the Algerian war of independence added to the loss of confidence, while the military and economic power of the United States fuelled anti-Americanism, one of the constants of postwar politics in France. In other words Trescases claims that American influence on the language aroused so much hostile reaction because it was symbolic of American domination at other levels. That this domination should affect the most cherished aspect of French culture was particularly mortifying.

Over the last twenty years the campaign against Anglicisms has become more muted, and the long period of socialist rule from 1981 created rather more of an internationalist bias in foreign affairs. (We may note that the two pieces of legislation relating to Anglicisms, affecting a wide public, were enacted by right-wing governments.) Recent efforts have been focused rather on forging a central role for France and the French language within Europe. At the same time, the notion of *francophonie* has become increasingly important. This concept involves all nations where French still plays a major role (mainly former colonies), and which may thereby be considered to share certain cultural values, and which have common needs and problems in the fields of economic and social development. The semi-official *Association internationale des parlementaires de langue française* (*AIPELF*) was formed in 1967, with the aim of cooperating on practical measures in these fields. In 1984 the *Haut conseil de la francophonie* was set up, under the aegis of the Ministry of Foreign Affairs, to oversee all policies relating to *francophonie*.

THE ENEMY WITHIN

The threat to French as a linguistic system is perceived as being more profound than that of foreign influence alone. For at least fifty years *la crise du français* has been a recurring theme among grammarians, educators and linguistic commentators. The main symptoms of the malaise have been an 'erosion' of syntax, and the spread of words hitherto categorised as *argotiques* or *populaires* into educated middle-class speech, and even literature. However, it was inevitable that changes in the class structure should lead to a degree of linguistic levelling, with the disappearance of many regional varieties on the one hand, and the wider adoption of working-class forms on the other. The proliferation of scientific 'jargon' (see pp. 189–90), often seen as an undesirable contamination of the standard language, is also inevitable, given the growth of science and technology and their intimate effect on the life of the individual.

Blame for these changes is usually assigned to the educational system, which fails to instil the norm, and to the media, which fail to adhere to it. But experience tells us that it is almost impossible to dictate the usage of the average speaker. If a norm is rigidly maintained it gradually becomes further and further removed from the language of everyday discourse, and eventually a situation of 'diglossia' emerges, with the norm being used only in very formal situations, and possibly being confined to the written mode. That situation has not yet been reached, but one could argue that mastery of the norm is becoming increasingly beyond the reach of many speakers, who are thereby not only socially and economically disadvantaged, but also feel inhibited in their use of the language. Martinet (1969: 29) claimed:

Les Français n'osent plus parler leur langue parce que des générations de grammairiens, professionnels et amateurs, en ont fait un domaine parsemé d'embûches et d'interdits... on les a dressés à obéir, à respecter le précédent, à n'innover en rien; ils n'osent pas forger un mot composé, utiliser librement un suffixe de dérivation, procéder à des combinaisons inattendues.

Since then there has been a certain relaxation in the prescriptive approach to lexis, at least. But a dilemma remains, especially for teachers: how to encourage confident and creative use of language in pupils when the required medium of expression is for many quite distinct from the language they use outside school, or with their classmates? This double-bind is explored with humour by Duneton (1984), himself a teacher of French, writing at a time when research showed an alarming drop in standards of literacy.[9] Paradoxically, even when official bodies do propose minor modifications which bring the standard language more into line with usage, such as the grammatical *tolérances* published by the Academy from the beginning of the century (see Müller 1985: 293), and the more recent attempts to simplify the orthography, there is very widespread resistance to such changes. The language as national monument has become deeply rooted in the national psyche. Or, as Henriette Walter (1988: 252) puts it, in relation to the orthography: 'Nous adorons notre bourreau.'

The media, particularly the press, are in an interesting position, since they must communicate easily with a public wider than the highly educated élite, if they are to flourish. Their mode of communication must therefore be adapted to this end. Rather than being attacked, the media should perhaps be congratulated on building bridges between the spoken language, in all its diversity and potentiality, and the codified norm from which it risks becoming estranged.

Earlier chapters have shown how lexical change has in the past led to enrichment and increased efficacy, and not to 'corruption' or 'debasement'. It is, however, true that the world is changing more rapidly than ever before, and that this presents a special challenge to any language of international standing, with a great literary tradition. The response to this challenge is awaited, in hopeful expectation, by all speakers, students and admirers of the language.

NOTES

1 The pejorative epithets like *rude* and *plébéien* he uses in relation to such expressions are clearly another case of the 'moralisation of status words', mentioned on p. 163.
2 See Ayres-Bennett (1987, Chapter 2) for discussion of Vaugelas's notion of good usage.
3 Occasionally, posterity did not vindicate Vaugelas's views: in his opinion, *longuement* was on the way out, being supplanted by *longtemps*, and *maint* was no longer in use, 'à moins que d'être employé dans un poème héroïque, et encore bien rarement'.
4 From Diderot's entry for the term *encyclopédie*, in the *Encyclopédie*.
5 Harmer (1954, Chapter 2) gives many examples of departures from this word order, and also discusses the notions of clarity and linguistic superiority in broader terms.
6 Harmer (1954, Chapter 5, and 1979) catalogues both apparent anomalies in the grammatical system, and points on which grammarians have been at variance, or where there is intrinsic variability in the system.
7 A somewhat chauvinistic response to the fact of the larger vocabulary of English is often to assert that this represents, not the concise expression of fine semantic distinctions, but simple redundancy: 'Quand plusieurs synonymes recouvrent la même signification le gigantisme du vocabulaire peut se révéler plus une gêne qu'un avantage' Lalanne (1957).
8 Duneton (1984) considers Rivarol's response to be 'l'acte de naissance d'un mythe', although the essay is notable for its opportuneness rather than its originality.
9 In a recent article in *Libération* (7 December 1995), Alain Bentolila, member of the *Observatoire national de la lecture*, deplores the complacency which he claims characterises government attitudes to illiteracy. The article was sparked off by findings of the *Organisation de coopération et de développement*, that as many as 40 per cent of the population have serious reading difficulties. (These findings were rejected by the Ministry of Education, although it had cooperated in the survey.)

PROJECTS

1 What assumptions appear to underly the following statements about the language? Do these assumptions seem to you to be justified?

(a) Les styles sont classés dans notre langue, comme les sujets dans notre monarchie. ... et c'est à travers cette hiérarchie que le bon goût sait marcher. On peut ranger nos grands écrivains en deux classes. Les premiers, tels que

Boileau et Racine doivent tout à un grand goût et un travail obstiné; ils parlent un langage parfait dans ses formes, sans mélange, toujours idéal, toujours étranger au peuple qui les environne; ils deviennent les écrivains de tous les temps et perdent bien peu dans la postérité. Les seconds, nés avec plus d'originalité, tels que Molière ou La Fontaine, revêtent leurs idées avec toutes les formes populaires, mais avec tant de sel, de goût et de vivacité, qu'ils sont à la fois le modèle et le répertoire de leur langue. Cependant leurs couleurs, plus locales, s'effacent à la longue; le charme du style mêlé s'affadit ou se perd et ces auteurs ne sont pour la postérité, qui ne peut les traduire, que les écrivains de leur nation.

(A. de Rivarol, L'Universalité de la langue française, 1784)

(b) La langue française, analytique et d'une richesse syntaxique incomparable, mérite de demeurer langue de référence pour tout ce qui exige, à commencer par les traités internationaux, une impérieuse précision de la pensée...

(Preface to 9th edition (1986–) of the Dictionnaire de l'Académie française)

(c) Le français moderne n'est pas seulement clair, mais tend à l'abstraction et possède de hautes qualités de spiritualisation et de synthèse, au point qu'aujourd'hui encore, on est tenté d'établir une correspondance intime entre la structure du français et l'esprit européen.

Ce caractère si prononcé s'explique par des éléments précis de construction, de syntaxe et de vocabulaire que les grammairiens ont continué d'enseigner. Au premier rang de ceux-ci figure l'ordre direct de la phrase.

(G. de Broglie, Le français pour qu'il vive, 1986)

(d) Je ne reconnais pas à l'usage le pouvoir de se sanctionner lui-même. C'est à l'Académie de sanctionner l'usage, en vertu non d'une doctrine linguistique, mais d'une tradition nationale... Il ne s'agit pas de changer l'usage mais, au contraire, de revenir à l'ancien, à celui de la belle époque de la langue, en annulant un changement fâcheux.

(Défense de la langue française, no. 25, 1964).

(e) Les fautes contre la langue sont graves parce qu'elles portent témoignage d'une décadence des mœurs et de l'esprit public.

(R. Georgin, Pour un meilleur français, 1951)

(f) Nous distinguons donc, dans la force de la langue, deux composantes: la bonne, celle de la raison, qui suit normalement le cours des choses et la mauvaise, celle de l'aveugle nature qui corrompt la grammaire ou qui change le sens des mots.

(Défense de la langue française, no. 19, 1963)

2 In what ways do the following extracts from Vaugelas's *Remarques* reflect seventeenth-century thinking on socially acceptable language? Are his judgements on these items still valid today?

(a) *Foudre*
Ce mot est l'un de ces noms substantifs, que l'on fait masculins ou féminins, comme on veut. On dit donc également bien, *le foudre* et *la foudre*, quoi que la langue française ait une particulière inclination au genre féminin.

(b) *Poitrine*

Poitrine est condamné dans la prose, comme dans les vers, pour une raison aussi injuste que ridicule, parce, disent-ils, que l'on dit *poitrine de veau*; car par cette même raison il s'ensuivrait qu'il faudrait condamner tous les mots des choses, qui sont communes aux hommes et aux bêtes, et que l'on ne pourrait pas dire, *la tête d'un homme*, à cause que l'on dit *une tête de veau*... Néanmoins ces raisons-là très impertinentes, pour supprimer un mot, ne laissent pas d'en empêcher l'usage, et l'usage du mot cessant, le mot vient à s'abolir peu à peu...

(c) *Exact*

Plusieurs disent *exacte*, au masculin, et très mal. *Exacte* ne se dit qu'au féminin.

(d) *Ambitionner*

Il y a longtemps que l'on use de ce mot, mais ce n'est pas dans le bel usage; ceux qui font profession de parler et d'écrire purement l'ont toujours condamné, et quoi que l'on ait fait pour l'introduire, ça a été avec si peu de succès, qu'il y a peu d'apparence qu'il s'établisse à l'avenir. On dit *affectionner, cautionner, proportionner*, et quelques autres semblables, mais ce n'est pas à dire que l'on puisse par analogie former des verbes de tous les noms terminés en *ion*, comme d'*affection* on a fait *affectionner*, et de *caution, cautionner*, etc.

3   Comment on the following remarks, to be found in Dupré's *Encyclopédie du bon français* (1972). To what extent do you think the rulings reflect current usage? Would you agree with the value judgements made?

(a) *Ananas*

l's ne se prononce pas – du moins en principe. En pratique, on le prononce de plus en plus aujourd'hui et il faut avouer que cette 'faute' a deux avantages: elle épargne des fautes d'orthographe à ceux qui la font, et rend la consonance du mot moins ridicule. Mais, dans de pareils cas, linguistes et puristes oublient leurs désaccords habituels pour s'unir contre le bon sens.

(b) *Yacht*

La prononciation [jak] ou [jakt] est certainement préférable, à tous égards, à la prononciation 'à l'anglaise', de caractère affecté, et ne répondant pas aux habitudes phonétiques des Français.

(c) *Août*

Ce mot, réduit à une voyelle: [u] est senti comme trop court, c'est pourquoi on dit souvent le mois d'août, ou au mois d'août.

(d) *Agresser*

Nous partageons pleinement l'opinion de R. Le Bidois; le mot est inutile; il fait double emploi avec *attaquer, assaillir*. C'est un archaïsme qu'il est tout à fait superflu de ressusciter.

(e) *Amour* [Masculine in the singular, feminine in the plural]

Peut-on imaginer la langue française sans la règle: amours, délices et orgues? C'est une stupidité charmante, une des coquetteries absurdes qui mettent en valeur les jolies femmes. Toute une tradition de gentilles plaisanteries est fondée sur elle – et même toute une philosophie: l'amour est mâle, les amours sont femmes...

FURTHER READING

Ayres-Bennett, W. 1987 *Vaugelas and the Development of the French Language*, London, Modern Humanities Research Association

Bédard, E. and Maurais, J. (eds), 1983 *La Norme linguistique*, Paris, Robert; includes a number of papers relating to the French norm.

Bellay, J. du 1549 *Défense et illustration de la langue française*, Paris, Arnoul l'Angelier

Bengtsson, S. 1968 *La Défense organisée de la langue française*, Uppsala, Sweden, Almquist och Wiksells; describes the institutions involved in promoting and controlling the language, from the mid-1930s to the mid-1960s.

Bouhours, D. 1671 *Les Entretiens d'Ariste et d'Eugène*, Paris, S. Mabre-Cramoisy

Broglie, G. de 1986 *Le Français pour qu'il vive*, Paris, Gallimard; interesting both as a late twentieth-century repository of these ideas and for its rhetoric. (De Broglie is former Vice-President of the *Haut Comité de la langue française*).

Brunot, F. 1891: *La Doctrine de Malherbe d'après son commentaire sur Desportes*, Paris, Masson

—— 1905 *La Réforme de l'orthographe*, Paris, Armand Colin

Calvet, L.-J. 1987 *La Guerre des langues et les politiques linguistiques*, Paris, Payot; examines the ideologies behind much of the rhetoric and government policy associated with the French language, from the sixteenth century.

—— 1988 *Linguistique et colonialisme*, Paris, Payot; shows how assumptions about languages and their inherent properties have played a role in the colonial policies of European powers, including France.

Darbelnet, J. 1972 'Le français face à l'anglais comme langue de communication', *Le Français dans le monde*, 89: 6–9; summarises some of the major differences of lexical structure in French and English, taking the traditional view that the French lexis is inherently 'abstract' and 'intellectual'; he sees the polysemy of French as one of its strengths.

Désirat, C. and Hordé, T. 1988 *La Langue française au 20ᵉ siècle*, Paris, Bordas; see Chapter 3 for an overview of twentieth-century attitudes to the norm and official institutions concerned with the language.

Diderot, D. and d'Alembert, J. 1772 *Encyclopédie ou Dictionnaire raisonné des sciences, des arts et des métiers*, Paris, Briasson

Duneton, C. 1984 *A hurler le soir au fond des collèges*, Paris, Seuil

Dupré, P. 1972 *Encyclopédie du bon français dans l'usage contemporain*, Paris, Éditions de Trévise; summarises the views of other contemporary conservative authorities on contentious issues; he also maintains the tradition of explicitly differentiating near-synonyms, such as *fleuve* and *rivière*.

Girard, G. 1718 *Justesse de la langue française*, Paris; this was enlarged in 1736 as *Synonymes français, leurs significations et le choix qu'il faut en faire pour parler avec justesse*.

Gordon, D.C. 1978 *The French Language and National Identity: 1930–1975*, The Hague, Mouton; for the historical–political background to *francophonie* and French as an international language during this period.

Gougenheim, G. 1971 (2nd edition) *Dictionnaire fondamental de la langue française*, Paris, Didier

Gougenheim, G., Michéa, R., Rivenc, P. and Sauvageot, P. 1964 *L'Elaboration du français fondamental*, Paris, Didier

Grevisse, M. 1969 *Le Bon Usage*, Gembloux, Belgium, J. Duculot; Paris, Librairie Hatier

Harmer, L.C. 1954 *The French Language Today*, London, Hutchinson

—— 1979 *Uncertainties in French Grammar*, Cambridge, Cambridge University Press

Haugen, E. 1972 'Dialect, language, nation', in J.B. Pride and J. Holmes (eds) *Sociolinguistics*, Harmondsworth, UK, Pengiun; a seminal work on the processes involved in the standardisation of a language.

Judge, A. 1993 'French: a planned language?' in C. Sanders (ed.), *French Today*, Cambridge, Cambridge University Press; for a clear précis of government policy with regard to the language.

Lalanne, P. 1957 *Mort ou renouveau de la langue française*, Paris, André Bonne

Lodge, R.A. 1993 *French: From Dialect to Standard*, London, Routledge; see Chapters 6–8, on the codification, acceptance and maintenance of the norm.

Malherbe, F. 1630 *Les Œuvres de Mre François de Malherbe*, Paris

Martinet, A. 1969 *Le Français sans fard*, Paris, PUF; the chapter 'Les puristes contre la langue' points to some undesirable effects of the prescriptive tradition.

Matoré, G. 1968 *Histoire des dictionnaires*, Paris, Larousse; a concise historical survey, with a brief analysis of the various elements which constitute dictionary entries.

Müller, B. 1985 *Le Français d'aujourd'hui*, Paris, Klincksieck; see Chapter 9 for discussion of the rift between general spoken usage and the traditional norm.

Poirier, C. 1978 'L'Anglicisation au Québec et l'héritage français', *Travaux de linguistique québecoise* 2

Pride, J.B. and Holmes, J. (eds) 1972 *Sociolinguistics*, Harmondsworth, UK, Penguin

Quémada, B. 1968 *Les Dictionnaires du français moderne, 1539–1863*, Paris, Didier; provides a typological classification of lexicographic works during this period, together with a detailed bibliography.

Rey, A. 1983 'Norme et dictionnaires', in E. Bédard and J. Maurais (eds) *La Norme linguistique*, Paris, Robert; on the effect of the norm on contemporary dictionary-makers.

Rivarol, A. 1991 *L'Universalité de la langue française*, Paris, Arléa

Trescases, P. 1982 *Le Franglais vingt ans après*, Montreal/Toronto, Guerin, *Langue et société* series

Vaugelas, C.F. de 1975 [1647]: *Remarques sur la langue française*, Paris, Larousse

Bibliography

Ager, D. 1990 *Sociolinguistics and Contemporary French*, Cambridge, Cambridge University Press

Aimard, P. 1974 *L'Enfant et son langage*, Villeurbanne, Editions Samép

—— 1975 *Les Jeux de mots des enfants*, Villeurbanne, Editions Samép

Aitchison, J. 1987 *Words in the Mind*, Oxford, Blackwell

Allan, K. and Burridge, K. 1991 *Euphemism and Dysphemism: Language Used as Shield and Weapon*, New York, Oxford University Press

Ayres-Bennett, W. 1987 *Vaugelas and the Development of the French Language*, London, Modern Humanities Research Association

—— 1996 *A History of the French Language through Texts*, London, Routledge

Bachmann, C. and Basier, L. 1984 'Le verlan: argot d'école ou langue des keums?' *Les Mots* 8: 169–87

Bailly, R. 1968 *Dictionnaire des synonymes de la langue française*, Paris, Larousse

Batchelor, R.E. and Offord, M.H. 1993a *Using French: A Guide to Contemporary Usage*, Cambridge, Cambridge University Press

—— 1993b *Using French Synonyms*, Cambridge, Cambridge University Press

Battye, A. and Hintze, M.-A. 1992 *The French Language Today*, London, Routledge

Baudot, J. 1992 *Fréquence d'utilisation des mots en français écrit contemporain*, Montreal, Presses de l'Université de Montréal

Baugh, A.C. 1951 *A History of the English Language*, London, Routledge and Kegan Paul

Beaujot, J.-P. 1978 'Idéologie de la langue et idéologie du dictionnaire', *Bulletin du centre d'analyse du discours* 3, Université de Lille III

Beauvais, R. 1970 *L'Hexagonal tel qu'on le parle*, Paris, Hachette

Bécherel, D. 1981 'A propos des solutions de remplacement des anglicismes', *La Linguistique* 17 (2): 119–31

Bédard, E. and Maurais, J. (eds) 1983 *La Norme linguistique*, Paris, Robert

Bellay. J. du 1549 *Défense et illustration de la langue française*, Paris, Arnoul l'Angelier

Bengtsson, S. 1968 *La Défense organisée de la langue française*, Uppsala, Sweden, Almquist och Wiksells

Bensimon-Choukroun, G. 1991 'Les mots de connivence des jeunes en institution scolaire: entre argot ubuesque et argot commun', in D. François-Geiger and J.-P. Goudaillier (eds) *Parlures argotiques, Langue française* 90

Bézard, C. 1993 'Le langage des jeunes', *L'Evénement du jeudi*, 5 August.

Black, M. 1969 'Some troubles with Whorfianism', in *Language and Philosophy: A Symposium*, ed. S. Hook, New York, New York University Press

Bloch, O. and von Wartburg, W. 1950 *Dictionnaire étymologique de la langue française*, Paris, PUF

Boudard, A. 1990 (2nd edition) *Méthode à Mimile*, Paris, Pré aux Clercs

Bouhours, D. 1671 *Les Entretiens d'Ariste et d'Eugène*, Paris, S. Mabre-Cramoisy

Broglie, G. de 1986 *Le Français pour qu'il vive*, Paris, Gallimard

Brooke-Rose, C. 1970 *A Grammar of Metaphor*, London, Martin Secker and Warburg

Brunet, E. 1981 *Le Vocabulaire français de 1789 à nos jours* (3 vols), Paris, Slatkine-Champion

Brunet, J.-P. 1990 *Dictionnaire de la police et de la pègre*, Paris, Maison du dictionnaire

Brunot, F. 1905–53 *Histoire de la langue française des origines à nos jours* (13 vols), Paris, Colin

Bynon, T. 1977 *Historical Linguistics*, Cambridge, Cambridge University Press

Cahoreau, G. and Tison, C. 1987 *La Drogue expliquée aux parents*, Paris, Balland

Calvet, L.-J. 1980 *Les Sigles*, Paris, PUF Que Sais-Je?

—— 1987 *La Guerre des langues et les politiques linguistiques*, Paris, Payot

—— 1988 *Linguistique et colonialisme*, Paris, Payot

—— 1993 *L'Argot en 20 leçons*, Paris, Payot

—— 1994 *L'Argot*, Paris, PUF Que Sais-Je?

Catach, N. 1995 (6th edition) *L'Orthographe*, Paris, PUF Que Sais-Je?

Catach, N., Golfond, J. and Denux, R. 1971 *Orthographe et lexicographie*, Paris, Didier

Céline, L.-F. 1952 (4th edition) *Mort à crédit*, Paris, Gallimard

—— 1955 *Entretiens avec le Professeur Y*, Paris, Gallimard

—— 1976 *Cahiers Céline*, Paris, Gallimard

Cellard, J. 1985 *Anthologie de la littérature argotique des origines à nos jours*, Paris, Editions Mazarine

Cellard, J. and Rey, A. 1991 *Dictionnaire du français non-conventionnel*, Paris, Hachette

Charest, G. 1974 *Le Livre des sacres et blasphèmes québecois*, Montreal, L'Aurore

Chaurand, J. 1977 *Introduction à l'histoire du vocabulaire français*, Paris, Bordas

Chevalier, L. 1978 (2nd edition) *Classes laborieuses et classes dangereuses*, Paris, Librairie générale française

Chomsky, N. 1970 'Remarks on nominalization', in R. Jacobs and P. Rosenbaum (eds) *Readings in English Transformational Grammar*, Waltham, Mass., Blaisdell

Clarke, E. 1993 *The Acquisition of the Lexicon*, Cambridge, Cambridge University Press

Colin, J.-P. and Mével, J.-P. 1992 *Dictionnaire de l'argot*, Paris, Larousse

Corbin, D. 1987 *Morphologie dérivationnelle et structurale du lexique* (2 vols) Tübingen, Germany, Max Niemeyer Verlag

Corbin, D. and Corbin, P. (1980) 'Le monde étrange des dictionnaires: les marques d'usage dans le Micro-Robert', *Bulletin du centre d'analyse du discours* 4, Université de Lille III

—— 1982 *La Part de l'autonomie dans la construction de la compétence lexicale*, Lille, Actes du 54e congrès de l'AGIEM

Corbin, P. 1980, ' "Niveaux de langue": pèlerinage chez un archétype', *Bulletin du centre d'analyse du discours* 4, Université de Lille III

Cottez, H. 1988 (4th edition) *Dictionnaire des structures du vocabulaire savant*, Paris, Usuels du Robert

Darbelnet, J. 1972 'Le français face à l'anglais comme langue de communication', *Le Français dans le monde* 89: 6–9

—— 1976 *Le Français en contact avec l'anglais en Amérique du nord*, Québec, Presses de l'Université Laval

Dauzat, A. 1937 'L'appauvrissement de la dérivation en français', *Le Français moderne* 5

—— 1949 *Le Génie de la langue française*, Paris, Payot

Dauzat, A. and Rostaing, C. 1963 *Dictionnaire étymologique des noms de lieux en France*, Paris, Librairie Guénegaud

Dauzat, A., Delandes, G. and Rostaing, C. 1978 *Dictionnaire étymologique des noms de rivières et des montagnes en France*, Paris, Klincksieck

Dell, F. 1973 *Les Règles et les sons: introduction à la phonologie générative*, Paris, Hermann

—— 1979 'La morphologie dérivationnelle du français, et l'organisation de la composante lexicale en grammaire générative', *Revue Romane* 14

Deroy, L. 1956 *L'Emprunt linguistique*, Paris, Belles Lettres

Désirat, C. and Hordé, T. 1988 *La Langue française au 20e siècle*, Paris, Bordas

Diderot, D. and d'Alembert, J. 1772 *Encyclopédie ou Dictionnaire raisonné des sciences, des arts et des métiers*, Paris, Briasson

Di Sciullo, A.M. and Williams, E. 1987 *On the Definition of Word*, Cambridge, Mass., MIT Press

Doillon, A. 1993 *Argots et néologismes du sport*, Paris, Amis du lexique français

Dubois, J. 1962 *Etude sur la dérivation suffixale en français moderne et contemporain*, Paris, Larousse

—— 1963 *Le Vocabulaire politique et social en France de 1869 à 1872*, Paris, Larousse

Dubois, J. and Dubois, C. (eds) 1971 *Introduction à la lexicographie*, Paris, Larousse

Dubois, J. and Guilbert, L. 1961 'Formation du système préfixal intensif en français moderne et contemporain', *Le Français moderne*, April

Dubois, J., Guilbert, L., Mitterand, H. and Pignon, H. 1960 'Le mouvement général du vocabulaire français de 1949 à 1960, d'après un dictionnaire d'usage', *Le Français moderne*, April/July, and in J. Dubois and C. Dubois (eds) 1971 *Introduction à la lexicographie*, Paris, Larousse

Duchesne, A. and Leguay, T. 1988 *L'obsolète: dictionnaire des mots perdus*, Paris, Larousse

Duneton, C. 1984 *A hurler le soir au fond des collèges*, Paris, Seuil

Dupré, P. 1972 *Encyclopédie du bon français dans l'usage contemporain*, Paris, Editions de Trévise

Durand, J. 1993 'Sociolinguistic variation and the linguist', in C. Sanders (ed.) 1993 *French Today*, Cambridge, Cambridge University Press

Elcock, W.D. 1960, *The Romance Languages*, London, Faber and Faber

Estienne, H. 1885 [1578] *Deux dialogues du nouveau langage français, italianisé et autrement déguisé*, Paris, Ristelhüber

Etiemble, R. 1964 *Parlez-vous franglais?* Paris, Flammarion

—— 1966 *Le Jargon des sciences*, Paris, Hermann

Ewert, A, 1954 *The French Language*, London, Faber and Faber

Failliot, P. 1995 *Dicosport 95*, Suresnes, DPS

Ferguson, C.A. 1959, 'Diglossia', *Word* 15: 325–40. Reprinted in P.P. Giglioli (ed.) 1972 *Language and Social Context*, Harmondsworth, UK, Penguin

Feyrey, M. 1973 'L'anglomanie dans les marques de fabrique et les raisons sociales françaises', *La Banque des mots* 6

Fierro-Domenech, A. 1986 *Le Pré carré*, Paris, Robert Laffont

Finkielkraut, A. 1979 *Fictionnaire*, Paris, Seuil

François-Geiger, D. 1991 'Panorama des argots contemporains', *Langue française* 90.

François-Geiger, D. and Goudaillier, J.-P. (eds) 1991 *Parlures argotiques, Langue française* 90

FRANTEXT, a computerised database used for the *TLF*, available to the public, consisting of the works of 500 authors; produced and administered by the Institut national de la langue française

Frey, M. 1925 *Les Transformations du vocabulaire français à l'époque de la révolution*, Paris, PUF

Gadet, F. 1989 *Le Français ordinaire*, Paris, Armand Colin

—— 1992 *Le Français populaire*, Paris, PUF Que Sais-Je?

Galisson, R. 1978 *Recherches de lexicologie descriptive: la banalisation lexicale* Paris, Nathan

Gebhardt, K. 1975 'Gallizismen im Englischen, Anglizismen im Französischen: ein statistischer Vergleich', *Zeitschrift für Romanische Philologie* 91

Genette, G. 1972 *Figures III*, Paris, Seuil

George, K. 1980 'L'apocope et l'aphérèse en français familier, populaire et argo- tique', *Le Français moderne* 48 (1)

Georgin, R. 1951 *Pour un meilleur français*, Paris, André Bonne

—— 1963 *L'Inflation du style*, Paris, Editions sociales françaises

—— 1973 *Le Code du bon langage: le langage de l'administration et des affaires*, Paris, Editions sociales françaises

Gertner, M.H. 1973 *The Morphology of the Modern French Verb*, The Hague, Mouton

Giglioli, P.P. (ed.) 1972 *Language and Social Context*, Harmondsworth, UK, Penguin

Gilbert, P. 1971 *Dictionnaire des mots nouveaux*, Paris, Hachette

—— 1973 'Remarques sur la diffusion des mots scientifiques et techniques dans le lexique commun', *Langue française* 17

—— 1987 *Dictionnaire des mots contemporains*, Paris, Usuels du Robert; an extended and updated version of the *Dictionnaire des mots nouveaux*

Giles, H. and Powesland, P.P. 1975 *Speech Style and Social Evaluation*, London, Academic Press

Girard, G. 1718 *Justesse de la langue française*, Paris; this was enlarged in 1736 as *Synonymes français, leurs significations et le choix qu'il faut en faire pour parler avec justesse*

Giraud, R. 1981 *L'Argot tel qu'on le parle*, Paris, Jacques Grancher

Godefroy, F. 1961 (reprinted from 1880) *Dictionnaire de l'ancienne langue fran- çaise*, New York, Kraus Reprint Corporation

Goosse, A. 1975 *La Néologie française aujourd'hui: observations et réflexions*, Paris, Conseil international de la langue française

Gorcy, G. 1989 'Le TLF: un grand chêne isolé', in *Lexiques* – special issue of *Le Français dans le monde*, August–September

Gordon, D.C. 1978 *The French Language and National Identity: 1930–1975*, The Hague, Mouton

Gougenheim, G., Michéa, R., Rivenc, P. and Sauvageot, A. *L'Elaboration du français fondamental*, Paris, Didier

—— 1970 *Etudes de grammaire et de vocabulaire français*, Paris, A.J. Picard

—— 1971 (2nd edition) *Dictionnaire fondamental de la langue française*, Paris, Didier

Graddol, D. and Swann, J. 1989 *Gender Voices*, Oxford, Blackwell
Grevisse, M. 1969 *Le Bon Usage*, Gembloux, Belgium, J. Duculot; Paris, Librairie Hatier
Grunig, B. 1990 *Les Mots de la publicité*, Paris, Presses du CNRS
Guilbert, L. 1965 *La Formation du vocabulaire de l'aviation*, Paris, Larousse
—— 1975 *La Créativité lexicale*, Paris, Larousse
Guinet, L. 1982 *Les Emprunts gallo-romans au germanique*, Paris, Klincksieck
Guiraud, P. 1962 *Les Locutions françaises*, Paris, PUF Que Sais-Je?
—— 1966 *Le Moyen français*, Paris, PUF Que Sais-Je?
—— 1967 *Structures étymologiques du lexique français*, Paris, Larousse
—— 1968a *Le Jargon de Villon ou le Gai Savoir de la Coquille*, Paris, Gallimard
—— 1968b *Les Mots savants*, Paris, PUF Que Sais-Je?
—— 1968c *Patois et dialectes français*, Paris, PUF Que Sais-Je?
—— 1975 *Les Gros Mots*, Paris, PUF Que Sais-Je?
—— 1978a *Dictionnaire érotique*, Paris, Payot
—— 1978b *La Sémiologie de la sexualité*, Paris, Payot
—— 1985 (9th edition) *L'Argot*, Paris, PUF Que Sais-Je?
Hagège, C. 1987 *Le Français et les siècles*, Paris, Odile Jacob
Harris, M. and Vincent, N. (eds) 1988 *The Romance Languages*, London, Croom Helm
Harmer, L.C. 1954 *The French Language Today*, London, Hutchinson
—— 1979 *Uncertainties in French Grammar*, Cambridge, Cambridge University Press
Hasselrot, B. 1972 *Etude sur la vitalité de la formation diminutive française au XXe siècle*, Uppsala, Sweden, Almqvist och Wiksells
Haugen, E. 1972 'Dialect, language, nation', in J.B. Pride and J. Holmes (eds) *Sociolinguistics*, Harmondsworth, UK, Penguin
Henry, A. 1971 *Métonymie et métaphore*, Paris, Klincksieck
Herman, J. 1975 *Le Latin vulgaire*, Paris, PUF Que Sais-Je?
Hope, T. E. 1962/3 'Loan words as cultural and lexical symbols', *Archivum Linguisticum* 14 (2) and 15 (1) .
—— 1971 *Lexical Borrowing in the Romance Languages*, Oxford, Blackwell
Houdebine-Gravaud, A.-M. 1987 'Le français au féminin', *La Linguistique* 23 (1)
Hudson, R. 1996 (2nd edition) *Introduction to Sociolinguistics*, Cambridge, Cambridge University Press
Hugo, V. 1967 'Réponse à un acte d'accusation', *Les Contemplations* I, 7 in Hugo, *Œuvres poétiques*, Paris, Gallimard
Huyghe, F.-B. 1991 *La Langue de coton*, Paris, Robert Laffont
Ifrah, G. 1985 *Les chiffres: histoire d'une grande invention*, Paris, Robert Laffont
Jakobson, R. and Halle, M. 1956 *Fundamentals of Language*, The Hague, Mouton
Jespersen, O. 1905 (10th edition 1982) *Growth and Structure of the English Language*, Oxford, Blackwell
Johnson, J. 1946 *Etude sur les noms de lieu dans lesquels entrent les éléments -court, -ville et -villiers*, Paris, Droz
Joubert, M.-J. 1985 *Slogan mon amour*, Paris, Barrault
Journal Officiel de la République française 1985 *Langue française: enrichissement du vocabulaire: textes législatifs et règlementaires*, Brochure no. 1468
—— 1986 'Féminisation des noms de métier, fonction, grade ou titre (16 March), reprinted in *Dictionnaire des néologismes officiels*, 1988, Paris, Direction des journaux officiels
Judge, A. 1993 'French: a planned language?' in C. Sanders (ed.), *French Today*, Cambridge, Cambridge University Press

Judge, A. and Lamothe, S. 1995 *Stylistic Developments in Literary and Non-Literary French Prose*, Wales, Mellen Press

Juilland, A. 1980 ' "L'autre français" ', ou doublets, triplets, and quadruplets dans le lexique verbal de Céline', *Le Français moderne*, 40 (1)

Juilland, A. Brodin, D. and Davidovitch, C. 1970 *A Frequency Dictionary of French Words*, The Hague/Paris, Mouton

Kempson, R. 1977 *Semantic Theory*, Cambridge, Cambridge University Press

Kesselring, W. 1981 *Dictionnaire chronologique du vocabulaire français au seizième siècle*, Heidelberg, Winter

Kittay, E.F. 1987 *Metaphor: Its Cognitive Force and Linguistic Structure*, Oxford, Clarendon Press

Kocourek, R. 1982 *La Langue française de la technique et de la science*, Wiesbaden, Brandstetter

Koessler, M. 1975 *Faux-amis des vocabulaires anglais et américain*, Paris, Vuibert

Koestler, A. 1964 *The Act of Creation*, London, Hutchinson

Lakoff, G. 1987 *Women, Fire and Dangerous Things*, Chicago, University of Chicago Press

Lakoff, G. and Johnson, M. 1980 *Metaphors We Live By*, Chicago, University of Chicago Press

Lalanne, P. 1957 *Mort ou renouveau de la langue française*, Paris, André Bonne

Le Doran, S. 1993 *Le Dictionnaire San-Antonio*, Paris, Fleuve noir

Lefebvre, C. 1983 'Les Notions de style', in E. Bédard and J. Maurais (eds) *La Norme linguistique*, Paris, Robert

Lefkowitz, N.J. 1989 'Verlan: talking backwards in French', *French Review* 63 (2)

Legrand, E. 1972 *Stylistique française*, Paris, J. de Gigord

Le Guern, M. 1972 *Sémantique de la métaphore et de la métonymie*, Paris, Larousse

Lehrer, A. 1974 *Semantic Fields and Lexical Structure*, Amsterdam/London, North Holland Publishing

Lenoble-Pinson, M. 1977 *Le langage de la chasse: gibiers et prédateurs*, Brussels, Facultés universitaires Saint-Louis

—— 1991 *Anglicismes et substituts français*, Paris, Duculot

Lewis, C.S. 1960 (2nd edition, reprinted in 1991) *Studies in Words*, Cambridge, Cambridge University Press

Lodge, A. 1993 *French: From Dialect to Standard*, London, Routledge

Louis, P. and Prinaz, L. 1990 *Skinheads, Taggers, Zulus & Co*, Paris, La Table ronde

Lucy, J.A. 1992 *Language Diversity and Thought*, Cambridge, Cambridge University Press

Lyons, J. 1977 *Semantics* (2 vols), Cambridge, Cambridge University Press

Mackenzie, F. 1939 *Les Relations de l'Angleterre et de la France d'après le vocabulaire*, Paris, Droz

Malherbe, F. 1630 *Les Œuvres de Mre François de Malherbe*, Paris

Maquet, C. 1979 *Dictionnaire analogique: répertoire moderne des mots par les idées*, Paris, Larousse

Marcellesi, C. 1973 'Le langage des techniciens de l'informatique: quelques aspects de leur vocabulaire écrit et oral', *Langue française* 17

Marchand, H. 1951 *Esquisse d'une description des principales alternances dérivatives dans le français d'aujourd'hui*, Lund, Studia Linguistica vol. 5: 95–112

Marks, G.A. and Johnson, C.B. 1993 *Harrap's Slang Dictionary* (English–French/French–English), London, Harrap

Martin, R. (ed.) 1971 *Dictionnaire des fréquences, vocabulaire littéraire des XIXe et XXe siècles*, Paris, Didier

Martinet, A. 1967 *Eléments de linguistique générale*, Paris, Armand Colin

―― 1969 *Le Français sans fard*, Paris, PUF

Martinet, A. and Walter, H. 1973 *Dictionnaire de la prononciation de la langue française, dans son usage réel*, Paris, France-Expansion

Matoré, G. 1951 *Le Vocabulaire et la société sous Louis-Philippe*, Paris, Droz

―― 1953 *La Méthode en lexicologie*, Paris, Didier

―― 1968 *Histoire des dictionnaires*, Paris, Larousse

―― 1985 *Le Vocabulaire et la société médiévale*, Paris, PUF

―― 1988 *Le vocabulaire et la société du XVIe siècle*, Paris, PUF

Mel'cuk, I.A. 1984 *Dictionnaire explicatif et combinatoire du français contemporain*, Montreal, Presses de l'Université de Montréal

Melka, F.J. and Zwanenburg, W. 1993 'Femme et féminin en ancien français', *Cahiers de lexicologie* 62

Messner, D. 1975 *Essai de lexicochronologie française*, Salzburg, University of Salzburg

Miller, G.A. 1991 *The Science of Words*, New York, Scientific American Library

Mitterand, H. 1968 *Les Mots français*, Paris, PUF Que Sais-Je?

Mossé, F. 1943 'On the chronology of French loan words', *English Studies* 25 (1)

Muller, C. 1973 *Initiation aux méthodes de la statistique linguistique*, Paris, Larousse

―― 1993 *Langue française: débats et bilans*, Paris, Champion-Slatkine

Müller, B. 1985 *Le Français d'aujourd'hui*, Paris, Klincksieck

Nègre, E. 1963 *Les Noms de lieux en France*, Paris, Armand Colin

Noreiko, S. 1993 'New words for new technologies', in C. Sanders (ed.) *French Today*, Cambridge, Cambridge University Press

Oliviéri, C. 1988 'Vers une langue non-sexiste', *Diagonales* 8, supplement 220 of *Le Français dans le monde*

Pergnier, M. 1989 *Les Anglicismes*, Paris, PUF

Pergnier, M. (ed.) 1988 *Le Français en contact avec l'anglais (en hommage à Jean Darbelnet)*, Paris, Didier-Erudition

Pétiot, G. 1982 *Le Robert des sports*, Paris, Robert

Pichon, E. 1942 *Les Principes de la suffixation en français*, Paris, D'Artrey

Picoche, J. 1977 *Précis de lexicologie française*, Paris, Nathan

―― 1994 *Dictionnaire étymologique*, Paris, Robert

Pierre-Adolphe, P., Mamoud, M. and Tzanos, G.-O. 1995 *Le Dico de la banlieue*, Paris, La Sirène

Plénat, M. (ed.) 1991 'Les Javanais', *Langages* 101, March

Poirier, C. 1978 'L'anglicisation au Québec et l'héritage français', *Travaux de linguistique québecoise* 2

Ponthier, F. 1978 *Le grand livre de la correspondance commerciale et d'affaires*, Paris, De Vecchi

Pope, M.K. 1961 *From Latin to Modern French*, London, Butler and Tanner

Posner, R. and Green, J.N. (eds) 1993 *Trends in Romance Linguistics and Philology* (5 vols), Berlin/New York, Mouton de Gruyter

Price, G. 1971 *The French Language: Present and Past*, London, Edward Arnold

Pride, J.B. and Holmes, J. (eds) 1972 *Sociolinguistics*, Harmondsworth, UK, Penguin

Quémada, B. 1968 *Les Dictionnaires du français moderne, 1539–1863*, Paris, Didier

―― 1993 *Mots nouveaux contemporains*, Paris, Klincksieck

—— (ed.) 1983 *Dictionnaire de termes nouveaux des sciences et des techniques*, Conseil international de la langue française, Paris, Agence de coopération culturelle et technique

Reboul, S. 1994 'Le vocabulaire de la télématique du discours au lexique', doctoral thesis, Université de Paris X

Retman, R. 1978 'L'adaptation phonétique des emprunts à l'anglais en français', *La Linguistique* 14 (1): 111–24

—— 1980 'Un inventaire des suffixes adjectivaux du français contemporain', *Le Français moderne* 48 (1): 6–14

Rey, A. 1983 'Norme et dictionnaires', in E. Bédard and J. Maurais (eds) *La Norme linguistique*, Paris, Robert

—— 1990 *Dictionnaire de proverbes et expressions*, Paris, Robert

—— 1993 *Dictionnaire historique de la langue française*, Paris, Robert

Rey-Debove, J. (ed.) 1990 *Le Robert méthodique*, Paris, Robert

Rey-Debove, J. and Gagnon, G. 1980 *Dictionnaire des anglicismes*, Paris, Robert

Richards, I.A. 1936 *The Philosophy of Rhetoric*, Oxford, Oxford University Press

Rickard, P. 1989 *A History of the French Language*, London, Hutchinson

Rivarol, A. de 1991 *L'Universalité de la langue française*, Paris, Arléa

Robert l'Argenton, F. 1991 'Parlépem largomuche du louchébem. Parler l'argot du boucher', in D. François-Geiger and J.-P. Goudaillier (eds) *Parlures argotiques*, *Langue française* 90: 113–125

Robins, R.H. 1967 *A Short History of Linguistics*, Harlow, UK, Longman

Rolland, J.-C. and Laffitte, J.-D., 1995 *Dicofle* (on diskette), Sèvres, Centre international d'etudes pédagogiques

Rousselot, P. 1989 'L'argot militaire: vers un lexique', *Documents de travail du Centre d'Argotologie* 9

Saint Robert, P. de 1985 *Guide des mots nouveaux*, Paris, Nathan

Sanders, C. 'Sociosituational variation', in C. Sanders (ed.) *French Today*, Cambridge, Cambridge University Press

Sanders, C. (ed.) 1993 *French Today*, Cambridge, Cambridge University Press

Sandry, G. and Carrère, M. 1976 *Dictionnaire de l'argot moderne*, Paris, Dauphin

Saussure, F. de 1915 *Cours de linguistique générale*, Paris, Payot

Schane, S.A. 1968 *French Phonology and Morphology*, Cambridge, Mass., MIT Press

—— 1973 'Sur le degré d'abstraction de la phonologie du français', *Langages* 32, December

Schlieben-Lange, B. 1993 'Occitan: French' in *Bilingualism and Linguistic Conflict in Romance*, vol. 5 of *Trends in Romance Linguistics and Phonology*, eds J. Green and R. Posner, The Hague, Mouton de Gruyter

Sourdot, M. 1991 'Argot, jargon, jargot', in D. François-Geiger and J.-P. Goudaillier (eds) *Parlures argotiques*, *Langue française* 90

Spence, N.C.W. 1976 *Le Français contemporain*, Munich, Wilhelm Fink Verlag

—— 1987 '*Faux amis et faux anglicismes*: problems of classification and definition', Forum for Modern Language Studies 23 (2), April

Spencer, A. 1991 *Morphological Theory: An Introduction to Word Structure in Generative Grammar*, Oxford, Blackwell

Stourdzé, C. and Collet-Hassan, M. 1969 'Les Niveaux de langue', *Le Français dans le monde* 65: 18–21.

Thévenot, E. 1972 *Les Gallo-Romains*, Paris, PUF Que Sais-Je?

Tournier, M. 1967 *Vendredi, ou les limbes du Pacifique*, Paris, Gallimard

Trescases, P. 1979 'Les anglo-américanismes du Petit Larousse Illustré de 1979', *French Review* 53 (1)

—— 1982 *Le Franglais vingt ans après*, Montreal/Toronto, Guérin, *Langue et société* series.

—— 1983 'Aspects du mouvement d'emprunt à l'anglais reflétés par trois diction-naires de néologismes', *Cahiers de lexicologie* 42 (1)

Trudgill, P. 1972 'Sex, covert prestige and linguistic change in the urban British English of Norwich', *Language in Society* 1: 179–96

—— 1983 *Sociolinguistics*, Harmondsworth, UK, Penguin

—— 1992 *Introducing Language and Society*, Harmondsworth, UK, Penguin

Ullmann, S. 1952 *Précis de sémantique française*, Berne, Francke

—— 1957 *Style in the French Novel*, Cambridge, Cambridge University Press

—— 1962 *Semantics: An Introduction to the Science of Meaning*, Oxford, Blackwell

—— 1977 *The Image in the Modern French Novel*, Cambridge, Greenwood Press

Väänänen, V. 1963 *Introduction au latin vulgaire*, Paris, Klincksieck

Vaugelas, C.F. de 1975 *Remarques sur la langue française*, Paris, Larousse

Vidocq, F. 1973 [1837] *Les Voleurs, physiologie de leurs mœurs et de leur langage*, Paris France-expansion, Collection Archives de la linguistique fran-çaise

Voirol, M. 1993 *Anglicismes et anglomanie*, Paris, Centre de formation et de perfectionnement des journalistes

Walker, D.C. 1982 *Dictionnaire inverse de l'ancien français*, Ottawa, Editions de l'Université d'Ottawa

Walter, H. 1988 *Le Français dans tous les sens*, Paris, Robert Laffont

—— 1989 *Des Mots sans-culottes*, Paris, Robert Laffont

Warnant, L. 1968 *Dictionnaire de la prononciation française*, Gembloux, Belgium, Duculot

Wexler, P. 1955 *La formation du vocabulaire des chemins de fer en France (1778–1862)* Geneva, Droz

Whorf, B.L. 1956 *Language, Thought and Reality*, Cambridge, Mass., MIT Press

Williams, J.M. 1976 'Synaesthetic adjectives: a possible law of semantic change', *Language* 52 (2)

Wind, B.H. 1928 'Les mots italiens introduits en français au XVIe siècle', doctoral thesis of the University of Amsterdam, Deventer

Wolfe, D.E. 1979 'A l'écoute de la radio CB', *French Review* (USA) 53 (1), October

Wright, R. (ed.) 1982 *Late Latin and Early Romance in Spain and Carolingian France*, Liverpool, UK, Francis Cairns

—— 1991 *Latin and the Romance Languages in the Early Middle Ages*, London, Routledge

Yaguello, M. 1987 *Les Mots et les femmes*, Paris, Payot

Zeldin, T. 1988 *The French*, London, Collins Harvill

Zink, G. 1990 *Le Moyen français*, Paris, PUF Que Sais-Je?

Zipf, G.K. 1945 'The meaning–frequency relationship of words', *Journal of Gen-eral Psychology* 33: 251–66.

Zwanenburg, W. 1983 'Productivité morphologique et emprunt', in *Studies in French and General Linguistics*, supplement to *Linguisticae Investigationes* 10

Index

Pages where a term is defined, or discussed in detail, are indicated in **bold** type.

Académie Française 223, 224, 225, 234, 238; dictionary of the Académie 18, 225–7, 240
acronyms 18, 86, 97, **125**–7, 129
administrative language 186, 194–5
advertising, language of 195–8
affixes, affixation 2, 19, **103**ff, 127n, 161–2; in Latin 29–31; combinations of root and affix 115–17; the form of affixed words 112–15
allomorph, allomorphic variation 77n, **105**, 112–15, 119, 127n
ambiguity 90, 96, 111, 230
American English, influence of 85, 86, 99, 237; American slang 215
Anglicisms 14, 50; the assimilation of 81, 90–5; in brand names 198; false 88; legislation relating to 95, 236; opposition to 79, 234–7; in slang 207, 227; in sport 98
Anglo-Saxon loan-words 37, 81
antonym **19**, 21
Arabic: early borrowings 14, 63, 67, 72–5; arabised forms 74, 77n; recent borrowings in slang 205, 207
argot 38, 62, 69, 148, 169, 171, 183, 199, **202**–19; criminal *argot* 202–5; dictionaries of *argot* 228; writers' use of *argot* 187–8
argotique (as a lexical label) 182, 237
'aspirate' h 38, 43
associative field 6, 20, 22
aural borrowings 91ff, 100

back formation 30, 54, **108**
Balzac 188, 226

Baudelaire 144, 150, 226
Beauvais, R. 186, 189
Bellay, J. du 48, 220
Beur 205, 207, 213
blends **125**, 197
Boudard, Alphonse 188
Bouhours 223, 229
Brazil, borrowings from the languages of 76
Breton loan-words 34; Breton French 60

calques 82ff, **89–90,** 94, 96, 97, 215
Camus 188–9
Canadian French 90, 165, 171, 215; Canadian language policies 235
Caribbean, borrowings from the languages of 75–6
Catalan loan-words 71
Céline 179, 187, 203, 206, 216
Celtic: influence 32–4, 36; place-names 39–40
Chinese loan words 75
clarté as an inherent property of French 228ff
clipped forms, clipping 122, **124**–5, 126; in slang 211–13, 215
co-hyponyms 8, 19, 20
collocations 12, 19ff, 163, 168, 184, 199n
commedia dell'arte 68
comparison 138
componential analysis *see* semantic components
compound words 94, **103**, 105, 120–3, 125, 130, 190; in Latin 30–1;

suffixation of compounds 128n; verb + noun compounds 110, 124, 148, 210
conceptual fields 5–6ff
connotation **4**, 25n
conversion *see* zero affixation
core vocabulary 17, 38, 80, 185, 228
Corneille 48, 152–3

Dard, Frédéric 188
denotation **4**
Desportes 221
dictionaries 17–20, 22n; the development of French dictionaries 225–8; *dictionnaires analogiques* 20; electronic 21; of slang 98, 203, 216n; of synonyms 20–1, 184, 225
Diderot, his *encyclopédie* 225–6
diglossia 41, **43n**, 47, 51, 56, 238
doublets 33, 46, 51, 60, 67
Dutch loan-words 37
dysphemism **170**–2

ellipsis 30, 88, **108**, 111, 124, 149, 209, 212
enchaînement 231
encyclopedias 17–18, 21, 225–6
English borrowings in French *see* Anglicisms
Estienne, Henri 220, 232
Etiemble, René 79, 88, 99, 189, 237
etymology **12**ff; of slang terms 206, 211, 216n; and orthography 223
etymon **12**, 136, 222
euphemism 147, **169**–70, 171, 186; in slang 209–10
expressive function of words 178; of suffixes 198n

faux amis 89–90
Flaubert 150
français courant **181**, 195, 204
français familier 171, **181**, 183, 187, 203–5, 209, 211, 225
français populaire **181**–2, 183, 200, 203–4, 222, 227, 237
français soutenu **181**, 182, 183–6, 204
francien 35, 47, 59
francophonie 237, 242
Franco-Provençal loan-words 62
franglais 79, 85, 125
Frankish *see* Germanic

franricain 85
frequency of lexical items 16ff, 23n

Gallicisms in English 80–1, 83, 95
Gallo-Romance 38, 40
Gaulish 34, 39, 40; *see also* Celtic
Georgin, René 184
German loan-words in slang 206
Germanic influence 34–8, 42n; place-names 40; suffixes 38
grammatical words 3, 16–17
Greek 13ff; affixes in French 161–2, 175n, 198; elements in scientific terminology 19, 50–1, 189–90; loan-words in French 63, 146, 185; loan-words in Latin 31–2, 49; the orthography of Greek loan-words in French 55; place-names of Greek origin 40; *see also* neo-classical compounds

Hindi loan-words 14, 75
homonymic clash 29, 53–4
homonymy **11**, 22n, 92, 111–12, 128–9
homophone **22n**, 29, 53, 54, 125, 216, 230–1
Hugo, Victor 187–8
hypallage 152
hyperbole 178, 185, 197; hyperbolic prefixes 198
hyponym, hyponymy **8**, 9, 22, 146; as the result of borrowing 87

idiom 19, 137, 157, 160, 217
inflectional morphemes **103**, 108, 110, 113, 119, 129
Italian influence: condemnation of 220–1; early period 62–5; French rivalry with Italian 232; later period 68–9; Renaissance period 65–8; in slang 206, 218

jargon 178, 189, 214, 237
jargon (early slang) 202
jargot 214–5

Langue d'Oc see Occitan
Langue d'Oïl 35, 42n, 47, 59ff
largonji **212**
Latin 13ff; differences between Classical and Vulgar Latin 26–31; the different functions of Latin and

French 41–2, 47–9; the form of Latin loan-words 52–3; influence on the orthography 43n, 54–6, 223; loan-words in the Middle French period 49–50; in scientific and technical terminology 19, 51; suffixes in slang 211; *see also* neo-classical compounds
Lavoisier 50
'learned' elements (as opposed to 'popular') **45**–6, 53, 117–19, 130, 131; *see also* Latin, Greek
legal terminology 191–4
lexeme (lexical item) **2**
lexical competence 15, 16–17, 127n
lexical fields 5–6
lexical gaps 9–10, 115–16, 129
lexical labels **180**–3, 217; in the seventeenth century 222, 225
lexical paradigms **9**–10, 77, 91, 94, 104, 115, 117, 129, 171
lexicon 15, **22**, 118, 120, 134
litotes 209
loan translations *see* calques
loucherbem 211, **212**

Malay loan-words 75
Malherbe, F. de 221, 223
marques d'usage see lexical labels
Matoré 7, 37, 76, 158, 159, 172
metaphor(s) **133–5**, 138; fossilised 136, 137, 142, 155; lexicalised 136, 138, 139, 155, 160; literary 133–4, 149–52; in slang 207–10, 212, 215; as a source of technical terminology 98
metonymy 111, **133–5**; fossilised 137; lexicalised 137–8; literary 149–50, 152–4; in slang 207–10; types of metonymic connection 146–8
Mexico, borrowings from the languages of 75
Molière 48, 153
moralisation of status words 163, 239n
morpheme(s) **2–3**, 19, 103, 119; bound **105**, 119; free 105

neo-classical compounds 50, **122**–3, 130, 190–1, 197
niveaux de langue see register
non-recurring morphemes 119–20
Norman French: in England 80–1; loan-words 59, 60; place-names 40

Occitan 35, 42n; loan-words from 61–2, 70, 206
occupational style **178**–80, 189–95, 198n, 199n, 202, 214–15
Old Norse loan-words 37, 40
opacity, opaque forms 115, 119, 121, 131, 148, 157
orthography, orthographic 43, 54–6, 71, 197–8; orthographic 'h' 43n; reform of 238; standardisation of 223

parasynthesis 109–10
paronym 216n
pérégénismes **69**, 95, 100
Persian loan-words 14, 63, 72
Peru, loan words from 75
phonological conditioning 113, 115, 122–3, 127n
Picard loan-words 59, 60
polysemy **11**, 18, 53, 87, 90, 96, 128–9, 132, 164, 190, 192, 196; of affixes 111–12, 129; due to English influence 59–60; of neo-classical elements 128n
popular (v. 'learned') 53, **117**–18, 119, 129, 130
Portuguese influence 71, 72, 75
pre-Celtic elements in French 39
prefixes, function of 109–11; of Greek origin 128n, 198
Proust 151
Provençal 61; *see also* Occitan
proverbs 137, 161, 168
puns 195, 215

Queneau, Reymond 188

Rabelais 49, 187, 189
Racine 48, 152, 240
recomposés see neo-classical compounds
reduplication 211
reference 19-20, 177; referent 17, 136, 145, 147, 203; referential 73, 182, 198
register 62, 148, 169, 170, 171, **177**–89, 198n; mixing registers 118
re-suffixation 212, 215, 216
Rivarol 232–3, 240
Romany loan-words 206
Ronsard 221

root morpheme 106, 113, 117, 119, 122,
   123

Saussure F. de 5, 11, 16
savant see 'learned'
selectional restrictions 12
semantic borrowing 52, 70, 83, 89–90
semantic components 7–9, 23
semantic fields **5–6**, 10, 20, 136, 157,
   160ff
sigles, siglaison see acronyms
simile 138–9
slang *see argot*
sociolect **177**–9, 180, 186, 188, 205
Spanish influence 70ff, 75, 77n; in slang
   207, 211
stem 114
Stendhal 229
suffixes 29–30, **103**; diminutive 109,
   130, 211; the functions of
   106–9, 111–12; pejorative 109, 198n,
   210, 213
superordinate term **8**, 18, 22n, 23n; *see
   also* hyponymy
suppletion **115**, 127n
synaesthesia **143**–5, 150, 151
synecdoche **146**, 150, 151, 152
synonyms, synonymy 51, 112, 116,
   118, 119, 164, 171, 172, 180, 182,
   183; distinguishing between near-
   synonyms 21, 199n, 221, 223, 242; in
   slang 203, 215

syntactic category *see* word class

taboo 147, **169**–72, 182, 204, 209, 210
Tamil loan-words 75
thesaurus 20ff
transformational rules 118
transparent terms 30–1, 45, 91, 121,
   136, 148; transparent suffixes 107,
   191
truncation *see* clipping
Turkish loan-words 63, 67, 72, 75

Ullmann 154, 160, 188, 229ff

Vaugelas 221–4, 225, 229, 240–1
verlan 205, **212–14**, 218
Verlaine 133
Villon 187, 188, 200, 202
visual borrowings 91ff, 100
Voltaire 81, 224
vulgaire (as a lexical label) 181, 182,
   187
Vulgate 27

Walloon loan-words 60
word, definition of the term **2**–3
word class 11, **106**, 109, 115, 119, 149
word formation rules 118–19, 120, 129

zero affixation 107–**8**, 127
Zola 150–1, 187